HAGIT LAVSKY

BEFORE CATASTROPHE
THE DISTINCTIVE PATH OF GERMAN ZIONISM

WAYNE STATE UNIVERSITY PRESS, DETROIT
THE MAGNES PRESS, THE HEBREW UNIVERSITY, JERUSALEM
LEO BAECK INSTITUTE, JERUSALEM

Published with the assistance of

The Memorial Foundation for Jewish Culture

Keren Kayemeth Leisrael, Research Institute for the History of the Land and Settlement

Ben-Eli Hebrew University Fund in Memory of Dr. Nahum Ben-Eli (Honig), 1891–1971

Federman Fund, The Hebrew University of Jerusalem, The Institute of Jewish Studies

The Hebrew University Internal Fund

Library of Congress Catalog Card Number 96–60988.

ISBN 0–8143–2673–0

Printed in Israel
Typesetting: Philippa Bacal, Jerusalem

CONTENTS

Preface   9

Introduction: Setting the Stage 11

Chapter One: German Zionism – The First Phase 18
   The Emergence of the Zionist Movement in Germany 18
   German Zionism as a Focal Point in the WZO 23
   The Seeds of National Radicalism 25

Chapter Two: The Impact of the War on German Zionism 32
   Transition in the World Zionist Movement 32
   The Impact of War on German Zionism 35
   The Weimar Republic 39
   The Victory of Palestinocentric Radicalism 42

Chapter Three: Plans for the Development of Palestine 46
   The Jewish National Home 46
   Between Socialism and *Étatisme* 49
   Shaping a Socioeconomic Program 52
   The Establishment of *Keren Hayesod* 57

Chapter Four: The Basis for Cooperation with Chaim Weizmann 61
   The Zionist Movement, the Jewish World and Palestine 61
   The Challenge: *Palästinaarbeit* or *Gegenwartsarbeit* 66
   Confronting the *Binyan Haaretz* Faction 73
   The Radical Victory in Germany and World Zionism 84

Chapter Five: For the Sake of the Land of Israel 88
Keren Hayesod and the Tithe 88
Cooperation with the Non-Zionists 90
The Contribution to Palestine 94
Keren Hayesod as the Bone of Contention 96
Pioneer Training and Immigration 102

Chapter Six: Zionist Responsibility 106
The Rise of General Zionism 106
Unity at the 13th Zionist Congress 109
The Right-Wing Challenge 113
Pro-Left Consolidation 117
The 14th Zionist Congress and the Failure of Pro-Left Neutrality . . 122

Chapter Seven: The Leftist Center 126
Establishment of the *Linkes Zentrum* 126
The Economic Reform Program 129
The Crucible of "Leftist" Orientation 131
The *Linkes Zentrum* at the 15th Zionist Congress 135
The End of the Path 139

Chapter Eight: First Encounter with The Arab Question 141
The Roots of Moderation 141
In the Wake of the May 1921 Disturbances 142
The Response: Binationalism 147
Resolution of Compromise 151

Chapter Nine: *Brith Shalom* 162
Confronting the Revisionist Challenge: The Binational Plan 162
The 14th Zionist Congress and the Establishment of *Brith Shalom* . . 167
Brith Shalom in Germany: The Test 170
The Binational Plan and the Zionist Executive 176

Chapter Ten: In the Wake of the 1929 Riots: A Breakdown of Unity . 181
Turning Inward 181
The 1929 Riots and the Public Response 185
The German Zionists versus Weizmann 189
Crisis in the ZVfD 195

Chapter Eleven: Weizmannism on Trial 207
  The Confrontation 207
  The Jena Convention and the Restored Pact 219

Chapter Twelve: Confronting the Nazi Threat 227
  The Transition: 1929–1932 227
  On the Brink: 1933–1938 233
  The Challenge of Expansion 235
  Cooperation in a Time of Crisis 239
  The Zionist Movement and the Nazis 245
  From Germany to Palestine 249

Chapter 13: German Zionism in Retrospect 254
  Centrality and Changing Roles 254
  Between East and West 255
  National Radicalization 256
  Palestinocentrism 258
  Socioeconomic Policy and Political Moderation 259
  The Political Role 261
  Palestinocentrism at the Service of German Jewry 263
  Epilogue 264

Abbreviations 266

Bibliography 267

Index 279

Tables
  Table I: German Zionism – Statistics for 1921–1932 34
  Table II: *Keren Hayesod* Income 97
  Table III: Jewish Emigration from Germany to Palestine and the U.S. 104
  Table IV: Jewish Emigration from Germany in 1933–1938 252
Plates follow pages 32, 144, 224

PREFACE

Just as the Jews were scattered worldwide so was the Zionist movement. Its various branches were integral parts of the Jewish communities in which they functioned. Local conditions dictated different patterns of development, the particular role of the movement in Jewish communal life and status in the world movement.

The present book is an attempt to analyze German Zionism within the context of world Zionism, and to throw light on Zionism as a force in the German Jewish community until its liquidation by the Nazis.

This book is a revised and expanded version of *Beterem Pur'anut* (Before Catastrophe) published in Hebrew (The Magnes Press, The Hebrew University, Jerusalem 1990, 292 pp.). While the Hebrew edition dealt almost exclusively with the Weimar period (1918–1932) the current volume presents a more comprehensive history of German Zionism.

My interest in this field is embedded in a long family legacy. Both my maternal and paternal grandfathers, Karl Jeremias and Isaac Plessner, were among the first German Zionists. Jeremias was the founder of the Posen Zionist *Ortsgruppe*; his untimely death in 1914 cut short an intensive Zionist life that was to have a lasting impact on his offspring. My parents, Martin Meir Plessner and Eva Esther née Jeremias, were active Zionists. Thanks to their strong Zionist beliefs both families immigrated to Palestine on time, in 1933, and were spared the horrors of Nazi Germany.

At the outset of my research and through the various stages prior to the publication of this book, I have benefitted from the advice and cooperation of many people. I am indebted to my teachers and colleagues at the Avraham Harman Institute of Contemporary Jewry, the Institute of Jewish Studies and the Department for Jewish History all at the Hebrew University of Jerusalem. These institutions, as well as the Leo Baeck Institute in Jerusalem and New York and the Memorial Foundation for Jewish Culture have assisted me along the way through various grants and scholarships. Prof. Israel Kolatt was my supervisor at the doctoral stage. Prof. Shulamit Volkov's advice was invaluable in the early stages of transforming my doctoral thesis into a book. In revising it for the English edition, I was assisted by my translator, Dr. David Strassler, and especially by my editor, Gila Brand, who turned a complicated discussion into a fluent story, and helped me present my ideas more clearly than I was ever able to, even in my native Hebrew. My friend Dan Benovici, director of the Magnes Press, was always there to lend a hand, with great efficiency. Daniela Ashur, who indexed the Hebrew book, also took charge of the English edition. Dr. Moshe Goodman and Ms. Philippa Bacal deserve thanks for their great help in preparing the computerized final manuscript.

I would also like to express my gratitude to all directors and workers of the archives and libraries in which I spent so much time over the years: The Central Zionist Archives in Jerusalem, the National and University Library in Jerusalem, and especially its archival department; the Schocken Archives in Jerusalem; the Weizmann Archives in Rehovot; the Leo Baeck Institute Archives in New York and the Oral History Division at the Institute of Contemporary Jewry of the Hebrew University of Jerusalem. I would also like to thank the Central Zionist Archives of Jerusalem for permission to publish the illustrations in this book. I thank them all deeply.

The publication of this book would not have been possible without the financial support of the Memorial Foundation for Jewish Culture, the Keren Kayemeth Leisrael Research Institute for the History of the Land and Settlement, Ben-Eli Hebrew University Fund, the Federman Fund of the Hebrew University – Institute of Jewish Studies, and the Hebrew University Internal Fund. I thank them all, and I wish also to express my gratitude to Wayne State University Press, the Magnes Press and the Leo Baeck Institute Jerusalem for taking upon themselves the co-publication of this book.

However, my first and foremost debt is to my family. I was fortunate to enjoy the aid of my dear late mother, who was able to decipher many illegible handwritten papers in German and thanks to her clear memory, relay fascinating "behind the scenes" stories of the *Zionistische Vereinigung für Deutschland*. The encouraging atmosphere at home, and especially the support of my husband, Nathan, created the framework which enabled me to complete the long and difficult process of research and writing.

In one of the discussions I was privileged to conduct with the late Robert Weltsch, he expressed his belief that only through the combination of personal involvement and historical discipline could the history of German Zionism be reconstructed and understood. If this study even begins to approach his expectations, I will see that as my reward.

Hagit Lavsky

Jerusalem, April 1996

INTRODUCTION

SETTING THE STAGE

During the final decades of the nineteenth century, Germany became the cultural and intellectual center of Europe. It was here that the major contemporary schools of thought originated and confronted one another, and it was German that served as the *lingua franca* shared by Eastern and Western Europe. The controversial issues of the time were debated on the pages of German periodicals and students throughout Europe flocked to German universities. Germany also became the epicenter of Jewish scholarship and culture. With a Jewish population of about 600,000, Germany of the late nineteenth and early twentieth century was far from claiming a large segment of the world's Jews. Nevertheless, this community stood at the forefront of various trends in modern Jewish history. German Jewry instigated the great debates over emancipation, and played an important role in spreading enlightenment eastward during the *Haskala* period. Major religious schisms found fertile ground in Germany, and it served as a transit point for multitudes of Russian and Polish Jews moving to the West. German Jews were targeted by critics of assimilation, yet they experienced antisemitism and the failure of emancipation.

The Jews of Germany became fully emancipated with the unification of the German Reich in 1871. By 1869, the North German Reichstag had removed most of the professional and political restrictions on the Jews, and further progress was made toward the end of the century, when industrialization was in full swing. Jews took an active part in German affairs. They played a central role in setting up the capitalist economy, and were behind much of the modernization introduced in German society. Toward the end of the nineteenth century, Jews underwent an accelerated process of urbanization, which also involved a shift of population from eastern to central and western Germany. Berlin, Breslau, Cologne, Frankfurt, and Hamburg were transformed into centers of Jewish life. This transition was accompanied by a growing social

Germany. Berlin, Breslau, Cologne, Frankfurt, and Hamburg were transformed into centers of Jewish life. This transition was accompanied by a growing social and economic mobility that brought the German Jews into the upper middle class. It was then that they entered the world of large-scale commerce and banking, and began to send their sons to university. The number of academics and other white-collar professions also multiplied steadily. There were some Jews involved in politics and the civil service, but not many, and their progress up the ladder was slow. Against this backdrop, there emerged a growing tendency toward social and cultural assimilation fostered by the hope that the emancipation would succeed and Jews would be fully accepted into German society.[1]

It was at this very moment that a new wave of antisemitism began to emerge in Germany, sparked by a sense of dissatisfaction and mistrust of both modernization and emancipation. An anti-Jewish, anti-emancipation mindset was already evident in the mid-nineteenth century among those Germans who opposed liberalism and capitalism. However, only in the wake of the 1873 depression and the prolonged recession from 1875 to 1896 did a new brand of German nationalism, featuring antisemitism as major component, begin to take shape. Latent social problems created by the transition to disintegrative capitalism now came to the fore. The response was a growing anti-capitalist *völkisch*-nationalist reaction. Every minority group perceived as upsetting the socio-national fabric was in danger, all the more so the Jews. The emancipation process was far from complete and people still clung to traditional negative stereotyping. In the eyes of the vulnerable lower middle class, it was the Jew who represented the banking and commercial interests of capitalism triumphant. Indeed, the new antisemitism gave vent to the anger of many people at the modernization process. The Jew was depicted as the archetypal despised capitalist bent on exploiting the hard-working masses, and as the embodiment of alienated modern society that was undermining the time-honored loyalties of traditional German life. Thus antisemitism became an essential part of an emerging political culture around whose flag the conservative forces rallied.[2]

---

1 Avraham Barkai, "Die Juden als sozio-ökonomische Minderheitsgruppe in der Weimarer Republik," in *Juden in der Weimarer Republik*, ed. Walter Grab and Joachim Schoeps (Stuttgart and Bonn, 1986), 330–46.

2 For different approaches to the development of modern antisemitism in Germany, see: Hans J. Bieber, "Anti-Semitism as a Reflection of Social, Economic and Political Tension in Germany, 1880–1933," in *Jews and Germans from 1860 to 1933 – The Problematic Symbiosis*, ed. David Bronsen (Heidelberg, 1979), 33–77; Hermann Greive, *Geschichte des modernen Antisemitismus in Deutschland* (Darmstadt, 1983); Sanford Ragins, *Jewish Responses to Antisemitism in Germany, 1870–1914*

In the political consolidation of modern antisemitism in Germany, 1879 was a turning point. The beginning of that year saw the publication of Wilhelm Marr's *Der Sieg des Judenthums über das Germanenthum* [The Victory of Judaism over Germanism], which became a best seller. Encouraged by his success, Marr established the *Antisemiten-Liga* (The League of Antisemites) in September. This was the premier appearance of the term "antisemitism", a neologism expressing a hatred of the Jews that went beyond traditional Christian antipathy. It was an enmity no longer religious in nature, but directed against the Jews as an ethnic or national group. Around this time, the imperial court chaplain Adolf Stöcker delivered a speech which was openly antisemitic and made no effort to disguise the antisemitic platform of the anti-socialist Christian-Social Workers Party which he had formed a year earlier. As a result, the *Berliner Bewegung* ("Berlin Movement") was born. Antisemitism in politics was further advanced by the coalition between Chancellor Bismarck and the conservative camp, and the relatively large number of Jews who joined the liberal and social-democratic parties of the opposition.

The new antisemitism was not confined to the lower classes. In November 1879, the noted historian and statesman Heinrich von Treitschke published an antisemitic article in the respected journal *Preußische Jahrbücher*. Although it did draw some angry response, similar pieces followed, penned by von Treitschke and others. Antisemitism thus became legitimized in academic circles. In 1880, a German student society in Berlin constitutionally barred Jewish membership, and the trend caught on in other cities. Antisemitic activity reached such a pitch that the *Berliner Bewegung* presented Bismarck with a petition in April 1881 calling for the exclusion of Jews from public office and restricting their participation in the legal system, education, and the academic world. The petition was signed by a quarter of a million persons, including some four thousand students throughout Germany. Berlin saw violent riots that year, and it was not long before the antisemite Adolf Stöcker was elected to the Reichstag.[3]

(Cincinnati, 1980), 1–22; Reinhard Rürup, "Emancipation and Crisis – The 'Jewish Question' in Germany, 1850–1890," *LBIYB*, 20 (1975): 13–25; Shulamit Volkov, "Antisemitism as a Cultural Code – Reflections on the History and Historiography of Antisemitism in Imperial Germany," *LBIYB*, 23 (1978): 25–46. For a detailed discussion of the economic background of German antisemitism, see: Arthur Prinz, *Juden im deutschen Wirtschaftsleben – Soziale und Wirtschaftliche Struktur im Wandel, 1850–1914*, ed. Avraham Barkai (Tübingen, 1984).

3   Jacob Katz, *From Prejudice to Destruction – Anti-Semitism, 1700–1933* (Cambridge, Mass., 1980), 245–72; Moshe Zimmermann, *Wilhelm Marr, "The Patriarch of Anti-Semitism"* (New York, 1986); Gordon A. Craig, *Germany, 1866–1945* (New York and Oxford, 1980), 150–57; Ismar Schorsch,

Along with the growing antisemitism in Germany there were certain disturbing events in Eastern Europe which also affected the German Jews profoundly. The murder of Czar Alexander II, the reactionary regime of Czar Alexander III, the violent pogroms of 1881, the daily exposure to persecution and discrimination – all these led the Jews of Russia to flee *en masse*.

Emigration had been brisk since the 1870s, due to demographic and economic pressures, but after the pogroms in 1881, the expulsions from Moscow and St. Petersburg in 1891, and especially the failed *Coup* in 1905, it assumed major proportions. An estimated 100,000 Jews left Russia every year between 1905–1914, bringing the total number of *emigrés* since the 1870s to two and a half million. During this period, another 400,000 Jews left the Polish provinces of the Austro-Hungarian Empire and Rumania for political and economic reasons. In other words, about three million Jews had moved west-ward by World War I. Germany was the natural land bridge out of Eastern Europe for those heading toward America, but many of them opted to stay in Germany. Population figures for 1910 show that there were 615,000 Jews in the country, 80,000 of whom were immigrants, i.e., 13 percent. However, the immigrants tended to congregate in certain areas, especially Berlin, where they accounted for 20 percent of the city's 90,000 Jews. On the eve of World War I, 57 percent of the immigrants were from Galicia and 10 percent from Hungary. Many of them were German-speaking and at home in German culture.

One noticeable outcome was that large numbers of Russian Jewish students, long barred from higher education, streamed to the celebrated German universities. Whereas only 60 Jewish students of Russian origin were registered at these institutions in 1888, the figure had swelled to 2,500–3,000 by the beginning of the twentieth century. Of this number, three-fourths were distributed between five universities: Berlin and Leipzig, with about 500 and 350 students respectively, as well as Breslau, Königsberg, and Munich.

The visibility of these students was all the greater because they were concentrated in certain faculties which offered career opportunities – mainly medicine, chemistry and mathematics, with a smaller number in engineering. These students maintained an independent social and cultural life, and unlike other immigrant groups, they did not assimilate quickly into their surroundings. As we shall see, their presence made a crucial contribution

Jewish Reactions to German Antisemitism, 1870–1914 (New York and London, 1972), 54–5; Richard S. Levy, *The Downfall of the Antisemitic Political Parties in Imperial Germany* (New Haven and London, 1975), Chapter One.

toward the development of a renewed sense of Jewish awareness among the Jews of Germany.[4]

The arrival of the East European Jews fanned the flames of German antisemitism. That these two phenomena were connected was obvious to the Jewish community, but at first it was too shocked to react. This was especially true of the older community leaders. Born during the early years of the nineteenth century, they had taken part in the 1848–1849 Revolution and fought in the Prussian army in the wars of the 1860s and 1870–1871. In consequence, they did well financially, many had built successful careers, gained prominence in their respective fields, and attained a large measure of prosperity. The path to full social and cultural assimilation seemed short. Recalling the fleeting reactionary phase following the 1848–1849 Revolution that, at the time, seemed to jeopardize all their achievements, the Jewish leaders perceived the events of the 1870s and 1880s as no more than ripples that would do little to disrupt the prevailing current. They avoided taking action against these manifestations of antisemitism in the belief that any response would threaten the attainments wrought by emancipation and harm their chances for complete integration into German society.[5]

The Jewish community's response to immigration from Eastern Europe was more complex. On the one hand, this immigration added fuel to antisemitic allegations regarding the foreignness of the Jews. Many German Jews, especially in liberal circles, were thus antagonistic toward the East Europeans. They were convinced that these Jews from the backward East would hinder their progress in becoming full-fledged members of German society. They frowned upon accepting them as part of the Jewish community, and fought against giving them the vote in organizational affairs. At the same time, German Jewish organizations were willing to extend philanthropic assistance to their "brethren from the East." This aid was granted not only to those who sought to continue on their westward journey, but also to those who stayed.[6]

Whatever their own inclinations, the community leaders could not stop the younger generation from reacting in a totally different manner to the historical coincidence of mass immigration and rising German antisemitism. The younger generation, born into emancipation, had reaped the fruits of their parents' sacrifices and achievements. They had received an education unrestricted by

---

4   Jack Wertheimer, *Unwelcome Strangers – East European Jews in Imperial Germany* (New York and Oxford, 1987).

5   Ragins, *Jewish Responses*, Chapter Two; Schorsch, *Jewish Reactions*, 65–71.

6   Wertheimer, *Unwelcome Strangers*, 123–75.

their Jewish origins, and internalized the German spiritual and cultural heritage. Now they fully expected to take their place under the sun. The rub was
that they found themselves looked upon as a distinct social group, their Jewishness constituting an insurmountable wall that prevented them from joining the
German professional and political elite. As a result, this generation embarked
on a slow process of retreat from assimilation, a kind of "dissimilation."
Willingly or not, they were tagged by a Jewish group identity. With the outbreak of antisemitism, they felt impelled to examine the limits of assimilation
and the positive aspects of being Jewish. The arrival of the East European Jews
served them as a source of encouragement and inspiration, for here they found
authentic Jewish culture and tradition worthy of emulation that was deemed
capable of reviving and nourishing Jewish life in Germany.[7]

  This frame of mind was particularly widespread among Jewish students.
Toward the end of the nineteenth century, the German universities became the
hothouse for a new Jewish response to the events of the time. As German Jews
flocked to the universities in growing numbers, these institutions became
important forces in molding the country's Jewish elite. It was during their
student years that they prepared to take their places in the world in general,
and as Jews, in particular. It was also at the universities that they encountered
the evils of antisemitism. As young intellectuals, they felt constrained to
respond, and shaped their world views accordingly. In addition, they were
brought face-to-face with young Jews from East Europe – a meeting which,
occurring at a crucial juncture of their lives, further strengthened their deter-
mination to take a stand on Jewish issues.

  Born during the 1860s or the early 1870s, these Jewish students had no personal experience of the momentous legislation of 1869 that removed so many
barriers. Their parents had infused in them the belief in progress and emancipation, and like their parents, they saw themselves as rooted in German
culture. But as they matured, they became increasingly disillusioned and pessimistic. It began at the gymnasium and continued into the university years.
Expecting to participate in the social and cultural life on which they had been
reared, they were sorely disappointed. Those with any trace of Jewish self-
respect withdrew and formed student associations of their own. These were
first conceived as purely academic, but before long, the *Viadrina* society in

7   Shulamit Volkov, "The Dynamics of Dissimilation – Ostjuden and German Jews," in *The Jewish
    Response to German Culture*, ed. Jehuda Reinharz and Walter Schatzberg (Hanover and London,
    1985), 195–211; Steven E. Aschheim, *Brothers and Strangers – The East European Jew in German and
    German Jewish Consciousness, 1800–1923* (Madison, 1982).

Breslau, organized in 1886, became the first group with the explicit goal of strengthening Jewish pride. During the 1890s, similar groups emerged in other university towns, and in 1896, they came together under the aegis of the Kartell Convent der Verbindungen deutscher Studenten jüdischen Glaubens (United Order of Associations of German Students of the Jewish Faith; hereafter, Kartell Convent).

These Jewish societies preached courage and self-esteem, urging their members to develop their Jewishness and at the same time to fight for their rights as German citizens. Thus an entire segment of the younger generation adopted a new stance vis-à-vis antisemitism – one which would completely transform their identities as both Jews and Germans, and dictate their future patterns of behavior. It was the leaders of these student associations who became the driving force behind the Centralverein deutscher Staatsbürger jüdischen Glaubens (Central Association of German Citizens of the Jewish Faith; hereafter, the Centralverein), which was formed in 1893 and grew to be the largest Jewish organization. The Centralverein advocated the fight against antisemitism, and insisted upon the Jews' full right to integrate into German society without relinquishing their Jewishness.

However, despite their declarations on the subject of Jewish pride, the Jewish student societies were largely modelled after those of Germans. They were basically a protest against antisemitism, but the codes of behavior were the same and they were not notable for any positive Jewish content. The students did not differ from the Jewish community as a whole in their desire for complete integration into German culture and society.[8] Yet from the same stratum of Jewish university students came another, quite different response to the events of the day – one which led to the creation of the Zionist movement.

8   Moshe Zimmermann, "The Impact of German Nationalism on Jewish Nationalism – The German Jewish Students' Organizations in Germany at the Beginning of the Twentieth Century," *Zion*, 45 (1980) (Hebrew): 299–326; Jehuda Reinharz, *Fatherland or Promised Land – The Dilemma of the German Jew, 1893–1914* (Ann Arbor, 1975), 30–6; Ragins, *Jewish Responses*, Chapter Two.

CHAPTER ONE

GERMAN ZIONISM – THE FIRST PHASE

The Emergence of the Zionist Movement in Germany

The German Zionist movement was the response of one particular sector of the German Jewish community – a small group of Jewish university students – to the major trends that touched the lives of the Jews of Germany in the 1870s and 1880s: emancipation, political antisemitism, and the mass emigration from Eastern Europe.

It is difficult to say why these events affected members of the same generation so differently. Most of the Jewish students were from secular middle-class homes steeped in German culture, who fought antisemitism because it posed an obstacle to full integration into German society. It was mainly the promise of emancipation that lured them on. They rebelled against their parents' policy of waiting quietly until the storm blew over, firm in their belief that emanci-pation and assimilation were worth the battle. Why, then, did one small group veer off in another direction and immerse itself in Jewish nationalism? A possible answer lies in certain subtle but significant variations in social background. The members of the upper middle-class, prosperous factory owners, merchants and prominent public figures had no doubt that they would achieve full integration. The early Zionists, on the other hand, belonged to the less comfortable lower middle-class, an "academic and commercial proletariat" of doctors, lawyers and small businessmen who were less entranced by the possibilities offered by merging with German society. They were also far more exposed to the hardships of the prolonged economic recession in the 1870s and 1880s, which led to social discontent and the rise of antisemitism. As a result, they viewed both German society and the Jewish

they viewed both German society and the Jewish community with a critical eye, and looked toward Zionism as a conceivable alternative.[1]

Clearly, these young people were alarmed not only by the antisemitism in their own country, but by the fate of their brethren in Eastern Europe. They saw the relationship between the two, and realized the time had come to take stock of their existential situation as Jews. The ground was thus ripe for absorbing the direct and indirect influences of East-European Jewry and the birth of a new movement.

The wave of immigration to Palestine in the 1880s and 1890s, known as the First *Aliya*, accounted for only a small fraction of the Jews who fled Eastern Europe. Nevertheless, the First *Aliya* signalled a turning point in the Jews' approach to settlement in Palestine. The effects of this *aliya* reverberated in Germany as well, especially among those who were aware of the growing proportions of antisemitism and those who had been brought up on the traditional love of *Eretz Israel*, among them Rabbi Isaak Rülf of Memel, who advocated Colonization in Palestine. The first German *Hovevei Zion* (Lovers of Zion) groups arose in the 1880s and quickly formed a close alliance with *Hovevei Zion* in Russia. Notable among them were the *Zion* group, which conducted its activities in Heidelberg under the leadership of mathematics professor Hermann Schapira; the *Esra* association, promoting Jewish agricultural settlement in Palestine, which was founded in Berlin in 1884 and headed from 1886 by Willy Bambus; and *Ahavat Zion* (Love of Zion), established in Hamburg in 1885.

The primary goal of these societies was to solve the problem of Russian Jewry through settlement in Palestine. The *Esra* association was the most active, with about 3,000 members, many of them Orthodox, in 80 cities. In 1886, *Esra* began fund-raising on behalf of the agricultural settlements and put out the first issue of its monthly, *Serubabel*, which served as the organ of *Hovevei Zion* in Eastern and Western Europe for the next two years.[2]

Although *Hovevei Zion* was active in Germany until World War I, there were other, more direct sources of influence on the Jewish students. Many of

---

1   Moshe Zimmermann, "Social Structure and Social Expectations in German Zionism before World War One," in *Nation and History – Studies in the History of the Jewish People*, vol. II, ed. Shmuel Ettinger (Jerusalem, 1984) (Hebrew), 177–99. Most illustrative are the biographies and memoirs of some of the early German Zionists, for example: Jehuda L. Weinberg, *Aus der Frühzeit des Zionismus – Heinrich Loewe* (Jerusalem, 1946); Max I. Bodenheimer, *Prelude to Israel – The Memoirs of M. I. Bodenheimer* (New York, 1963).

2   Yehuda Eloni, *Zionismus in Deutschland von den Anfängen bis 1914* (Gerlingen, 1987), 2–72; Jehuda Reinharz, "The *Esra Verein* and Jewish Colonisation in Palestine," *LBIYB*, 24 (1979): 261–89.

the East-European students who came to Germany brought with them Zionist ideas that struck a responsive chord in the face of the rampant antisemitism on the university campuses. The first genuinely nationalistic Jewish society was the *Russischer-Jüdischer wissenschaftlicher Verein* (the Russian-Jewish Scientific Society), formed in December 1888 at the initiative of a dozen Russian Jewish students (among them Shmaryahu Levin, Leo Motzkin, and later, Chaim Weizmann) and one German Jew, Heinrich Loewe, who studied at the *Hochschule für die Wissenschaft des Judentums* (Institute for Jewish Studies) in Berlin. In 1892, Loewe established the *Jung Israel* (Young Israel) association, that was joined mostly by young Russian Jews, although Willy Bambus, a German member of *Hovevei Zion*, was also affiliated. On the whole, the number of Germans was very small, and those who did belong, such as medical students Theodor Zlocisti and Max Jungmann, were born of East-European parents. The first society in which native German Jews figured prominently was the *Jüdische Humanitätsgesellschaft* (the Jewish Humanities Society), established in Berlin in 1893. Among the founders were the law students Adolf Friedemann and Arthur Hantke. Thus we see that many of the activists were young academics about to enter the free professions. Their involvement with Zionism was very much a product of their encounter with Jews from Russia, with whom they felt a sense of national solidarity and whose ideas they respected.[3]

In 1895, a decade after the founding of the *Viadrina* student association, *Jung Israel* and the Jüdische Humanitätsgesellschaft merged and became the *Vereinigung jüdischer Studierender an der Universität Berlin* (Jewish Student Association of the University of Berlin). Unlike the assimilationist *Kartell Convent*, the *Vereinigung jüdischer Studierender* sought contact with other Jewish groups, and in 1901, established the *Bund Jüdischer Corporationen* (Alliance of Jewish Associations). It was the leaders of the *Bund Jüdischer Corporationen* who went on to become the moving forces behind German Zionism. In addition to Arthur Hantke, Theodor Zlocisti, Max Jungmann, Heinrich Loewe and Adolf Friedemann, the list included a new generation of younger students born in the 1880s: Richard Lichtheim, Isaak Zwirn, and Felix Rosenblüth. The first student society that was explicitly Zionist appeared in

---

3   Eloni, Zionismus in Deutschland, 36–100; Reinharz, *Fatherland or Promised Land*, 90–107; Richard Lichtheim, *The History of Zionism in Germany* (Jerusalem [1951]) (Hebrew), 61–120; Bodenheimer, *Prelude to Israel*; Weinberg, *Aus der Frühzeit*; Max Jungmann, *Erinnerungen eines Zionisten* (Jerusalem, 1959); Zimmermann, "The Impact"; Hagit Lavsky, "German Zionist Leadership," in *Zionist Leadership*, ed. Jehuda Reinharz and Anita Shapira (forthcoming); *Dokumente zur Geschichte des deutschen Zionismus, 1882–1933*, ed. Jehuda Reinharz (Tübingen, 1981), Introduction.

1906: the Kartell Zionistischer Verbindungen (United Zionist Association). In 1914, this group and the *Bund Jüdischer Corporationen* came together to form a Zionist student union known as the *Kartell Jüdischer Verbindungen* (United Jewish Associations – KJV).

One of the central figures in the creation of a Zionist establishment in Germany was Max Isidor Bodenheimer, the son of a well-to-do assimilated family from Stuttgart who studied law and opened a practice in Cologne. His encounter with antisemitism as a student prompted him to found a Jewish scientific society in that city, in 1890. The following year, he published a pamphlet calling for the settlement of the East-European Jews in Syria and Palestine, and urged the German *Hovevei Zion* groups to unite. In 1894, after qualifying as a lawyer, Bodenheimer collaborated with David Wolffsohn, an immigrant from Eastern Europe who was now a businessman in Cologne, to found the *Verein zur Förderung der jüdischen Ackerbaukolonien in Syrien und Palästina* (Association for the Furtherance of Jewish Agricultural Settlement in Syria and Palestine).

When Herzl published *Der Judenstaat* in 1896, it was warmly received among the German Zionists, and he found immediate and almost unanimous support for his idea of establishing the Zionist Organization as an international political movement. The German Zionists convened in Bingen on the Rhine in July 1897, even before the First Zionist Congress (which was supposed to have been held in Munich but was blocked by the anti-Zionist protests of the Association of Rabbis in Germany). That same year they met on two more occasions, in Basel during the Zionist Congress, and in Frankfurt, at which time the ground-work was laid for the *Zionistische Vereinigung für Deutschland* (Zionist Federation of Germany – ZVfD). Bodenheimer and Wolffsohn were thus instrumental in channelling the Zionist ideology that was gaining momentum in Germany, into an organization that stood firmly behind Herzl. They also helped to transform Zionism from a philanthropic cause to an organized political movement that was to become part of the World Zionist Organization (WZO). Since both Bodenheimer and Wolffsohn resided in Cologne, the operational headquarters of the ZVfD were located there. While Berlin was the center of Jewish life in Germany, the Zionist institutions had not yet moved there because of a struggle between the Herzlian Zionists, led by Heinrich Loewe, and their opponents under Willy Bambus.

In 1904, the struggle came to an end. A united Berlin Zionist association had been established, and it was decided to move the main office to this city. Appointed to head its activities were two longstanding student leaders – Arthur Hantke and Eduard Leszynsky, along with Emil Simonsohn.

Max Bodenheimer, who remained in Cologne, served as chairman of the ZVfD until 1910, and was replaced by Hantke, who held the post until 1920.

As in the other bodies belonging to the WZO, membership in the ZVfD was based on payment of the *Shekel*, a symbolic fee recalling the tax paid to the Temple in ancient times. All *Shekel* contributors were entitled to a membership card. The ZVfD was composed of *Ortsgruppen* (local chapters) and *Landesverbände* (regional organizations). Each local chapter sent a delegate to the *Delegiertentag* (delegates convention) which generally met once every two years. Those with over fifty members were entitled to larger delegations. At this forum the program and budget of the *Zentralkomitee,* the chief executive body, were reviewed, and elections were held. The ZVfD also had district information offices and *Vertrauensmänner* (trustees) in places that had very small groups or were remote from the regional bureaus.

The ZVfD could not effectively spread its message without an official publication. This function was first filled by the *Jung Israel* journal, *Zion*, under the editorship of Heinrich Loewe. When the debate between the supporters and opponents of Herzl, headed by Willy Bambus, led to the closure of this publication, the ZVfD reached an agreement with the *Israelitische Rundschau* in 1896, and turned it into the official organ of Zionism in Germany. In 1902 the ZVfD took over the paper, nominated Heinrich Loewe as Chief Editor and changed its name to *Jüdische Rundschau* (Jewish Review). Until 1914, the Rundschau competed not only with the anti-Zionist press, but also with the WZO's German-language *Die Welt*. When this paper folded in 1914, the importance of the Rundschau rose considerably, even more so after the war. In addition to the official paper, a large number of journals and periodicals were published in Germany by other Zionist groups and even by private individuals. Between 1897 and 1938, close to forty such publications appeared in Germany at one time or another.

Despite this flurry of activity, the German Zionist movement, from its inception until World War I, remained a small and much-maligned minority. During these years, most of its energy was directed toward warding off attacks from the liberal leadership of the German Jewish community, and strengthening Jewish national awareness in a bid to lend power and dignity to the Zionist alternative. Yet by 1910, after years of effort, the German Zionists had no more than 6,200 *Shekel*-paying members, and represented with their families about two or three percent of the country's 615,000 Jews.[4]

German Zionism as a Focal Point in the WZO

A tiny minority in its own country, the German Zionist movement never represented more than five percent of the World Zionist Organization in all the years of its existence. Yet the importance of this small group far exceeded its size. The German Zionists were notable for their education, their intellectual interests and their organizational ability. Virtually all the leaders were university graduates, most of them in "white collar" professions. Even the handful of merchants, bankers and industrialists had academic degrees. A collective profile shows that more than a quarter were lawyers, with only a slightly smaller number of physicians. Many were trained in the social sciences, especially political economy. Other fields were technical sciences such as geology and agronomy, architecture, education, and, of course, the liberal arts. In short, they were not very different from the general run of Jewish university students. Coming from the Jewish middle-class, they had absorbed German culture and mannerisms, along with the characteristic order and discipline. As young intellectuals, their outlook was built along philosophical lines, using reason and logic. Moreover, from the circles they travelled in, they had imbibed a sense of openness and receptivity to new ideas and progress. All of these qualities came together to place the German Zionists on a special footing in the WZO.[5]

Further prestige came from the important ideological role played by German Jewry in the burning issues of the time, one of which was the emergence of Herzlian Zionism. Even before Herzl appeared as a rallying force, Berlin took the place of Vienna as the center of Jewish nationalism in the West.

As noted, Herzl found a well-organized group of supporters in Germany, and it was here that the first steps were taken toward the establishment of the WZO, although Herzl himself was based in Vienna. Indeed, a unique relationship was forged between the German Zionist leadership and the central institutions of the WZO. Max Bodenheimer and David Wolffsohn, the founders of

---

4   *Dokumente*, xxiii, 55–6; Stephen M. Poppel, *Zionism in Germany, 1897–1933 – The Shaping of a Jewish Identity* (Philadelphia, 1977), Table Three, Appendix; Eloni, *Zionismus in Deutschland*, 258–9. See also note 3 above.

5   Lavsky, "German Zionist Leadership"; Lichtheim, *The History of Zionism*, 101–3.

the movement in Germany, were Herzl's right-hand men. Even though they resided in Cologne and were not members of the Vienna-based Inner Actions Committee, they were influential in the establishment of the earliest Zionist institutions, the Jewish Colonial Trust, in 1899, and the Jewish National Fund (JNF), in 1901.

Language was also a factor. As the official language of the Zionist movement, the meetings of the Zionist Congress, the Greater Actions Committee, and other bodies, were conducted in German, and the movement's chief publications, *Die Welt,* and the *Jüdische Rundschau,* catered to the German-speaking public. Most of the contributors to these newspapers were German Zionists, and it was the leaders of German Zionism who became Herzl's spokesmen and collaborators.

The centrality of the German Zionists in the WZO was fully apparent after Herzl's death, when it became clear that those who assumed the mantle of leadership were not members of Herzl's circle in Vienna, but rather his supporters and colleagues in Germany. From 1905 until World War I, Germany was the seat of the WZO, with its organizational center – the Central Zionist Office (CZO) in Cologne. In 1911, when the botanist, professor Otto Warburg was elected as head of the movement, the focus of activity shifted to Berlin.

This move further strengthened the ties between the WZO and the German Zionist movement, whose center was already in Berlin. There was overlapping on both the personnel and organizational levels. Max Bodenheimer was chairman of the ZVfD until 1910 and the chairman of the JNF from 1907 to 1914. His successor in the ZVfD, Arthur Hantke, was also a member of the Inner Actions Committee from 1911. The offices of the ZVfD were in the same building. Thus it was only natural for most of the administrative jobs to be placed in the hands of German Zionists. Many of the future leaders of the German Zionist movement began their careers with the WZO in Berlin: Kurt Blumenfeld, who served as secretary-general of the WZO from 1911; Julius Berger, who was secretary of the CZO under Wolffsohn; *Die Welt* editor Richard Lichtheim, another CZO secretary who was sent to the Zionist delegation in Constantinople in 1912; and Martin Rosenblüth, who was secretary of the CZO in both Cologne and Berlin for various periods of time. All were "second generation" German Zionists – academics born in the 1880s who had gone on to found or play an active role in Zionist student associations.[6]

6   Lavsky,"German Zionist Leadership."

Germany was not only the administrative center of the WZO, but also its political headquarters, especially after the policy shift from "political Zionism," whose goal was diplomatic recognition of the Jewish right to a homeland as the precondition for settlement, to a "practical Zionism," where political status was a later goal, to be preceded by settlement and the laying of infrastructure for a solid Jewish community. The initiative for the institutionalized Zionist activity in Palestine emanated from Berlin, with Otto Warburg as the chairman of the Palestine Department. The Palestine Office, the Zionist Organization's first official settlement agency in Palestine, was founded in 1908 by the German Zionist Arthur Ruppin. The activities in Palestine intensified after the CZO was moved to Berlin, when Warburg assumed the presidency. The German orientation of Zionist foreign policy, which was notable even in Herzl's time, became more pronounced under Wolffsohn and Warburg.[7]

The Seeds of National Radicalism

From its inception, German Zionism was distinct from both Western and East-European Zionism; in ideology, as in geography, it could be termed "Central European." Like Western Zionism, it was not a product of physical distress or deep religious feelings. Rather, it was a response to emancipation, political and social liberation, and growing secularization; it was a "post-assimilatory" Zionism, offering an answer to those who sought to retain their Jewish identity and self-respect, and forging a link with the Jewish issue of the day – the plight of East-European Jewry. Western Zionists were characterized by a philanthropic approach on the one hand, and a "platonic" love of Palestine, on the other. What distinguished the Western Zionists from other Jewish philanthropists was an attempt to correlate between the problem in Eastern Europe and their own identity crisis. They perceived their relationship with the Jews of Eastern Europe as one of shared nationhood that could be brought to fruition in Palestine. While such an attitude might have cast doubt upon their rootedness in their countries of residence, it was largely theoretical; socially and spiritually, the Zionists in Germany were no exception. They remained very much anchored in their land of birth.

German Zionism was, however, shaped by other factors that distinguished it from the West: antisemitism and the powerful encounter with East-European

7   Isaiah Friedman, *Germany, Turkey and Zionism, 1897–1918* (Oxford, 1977).

immigrants. In this respect, it was closer to the kind of Zionism that emerged
in Eastern Europe in response to persecution and the Jewish experience. While
antisemitism in Germany during the late nineteenth century had no parallel in
the West, this was not true of westward emigration, which affected other
countries, too. Yet emigration was to have a particularly strong impact in
Germany because it fanned the flames of antisemitism, on the one hand, and
generated an inspiring meeting between immigrant and German Jewish
students, on the other.

This combination of forces, unique to Germany, produced a Zionist movement that differed from Zionism in the West in its skepticism regarding the
future of the Jews in the Diaspora. Hence its opposition to the battle against
antisemitism waged by the *Centralverein,* an organization which arose at the
same time in response to the same phenomena, but was founded on the belief
that the Jews did have a future in Germany. This bleak outlook also led the
Zionists to reject organized participation in German politics.[8]

On the other hand, the German Zionists displayed a special interest in
Palestine. The early leaders had been nourished by the Central European
national movements of the late nineteenth century, and had absorbed many of
their ideas about nationalism and the need for social and economic change.
While the social issue was uppermost in European nationalism, the first step
for the Jews was to secure a territorial basis and lay foundations capable of
supporting a new social entity. The notion of amelioration through productive
labor and farming thus predated the establishment of the Zionist movement,
and was later incorporated in Jewish national ideology as a major component
bound up with the return to Palestine.

Especially important was the influence of ideas that were circulating
concerning social betterment and the avoidance of the negative aspects of
capitalist and industrial societies. The first generation of German Zionists thus
formulated their nationalist theories along moderate socialist lines, and from
the start envisaged farm-based settlements. Among the planners were Professor
Franz Oppenheimer, who drew up plans for cooperative settlement, and
Professor Otto Warburg, who dealt with the practical aspects of agricultural
settlement in Palestine. The idea of national land ownership was proposed

8   Jehuda Reinharz, "The Zionist Response to Antisemitism in Germany," *LBIYB,* 30 (1985): 105–40.

by two other German Zionists, Professor Hermann Schapira and Max Bodenheimer.[9]

German Zionism was closely linked with Palestine even in the days of *Hovevei Zion* and Herzl, but the connection was strengthened all the more when practical Zionism won the upper hand after the 8th Zionist Congress in 1907, and Berlin, the stronghold of this orientation, became the headquarters of the WZO in 1911.

Yet these high hopes for Palestine and the skepticism with which the first generation of German Zionists viewed Jewish existence in the Diaspora, did not cause the Jews of Germany to change their course. For the first two decades, German Zionism was primarily a "platonic" philanthropic movement. Palestine and the plans for settlement there were viewed as a solution to the problems of East-European Jewry, and the concerns vis-à-vis the Diaspora remained theoretical, and only marginally touched their own lives. The early German Zionists perceived themselves, after all, as loyal citizens, devoted to the German culture upon which they had been brought up.[10] However, the seeds of another type of thinking lay below the surface and began to sprout later, when the time was right.

The German Zionists' centrality in the WZO exposed them to East-European Zionism and the practical side of settlement in Palestine. The fact that the students and university graduates continued to play a dominant role also perpetuated ideological debate and furthered the on-going adoption of new variants of Zionist thought. This trend intensified after the death of Herzl, when the political and administrative headquarters of the WZO moved to Germany.

All the while, circumstances in Germany were changing. A new generation joined the circle of Zionist activists in the decade preceding World War I, and it was these newcomers who effected a true radicalization in national outlook and orientation toward Palestine. The "second generation" of German Zionists, born toward the end of the nineteenth century, embraced Zionism during their

---

9 Joachim Doron, "Social Concepts Prevailing in German Zionism, 1883–1914," *Studies in Zionism*, 5 (Spring 1982): 1–31; Derek J. Penslar, *Zionism and Technology – The Engineering of Jewish Settlement in Palestine, 1870–1914* (Bloomington and Indianapolis, 1991), 41–102; Michael Berkowitz, *Zionist Culture and West European Jewry before the First World War* (Cambridge, 1993).

10 Jehuda Reinharz, "Three Generations of German Zionism, *The Jerusalem Quarterly*, 9 (Fall 1978): 95–110; Ragins, *Jewish Responses*, Chapter Four. Both authors use the term "political-philanthropic." I prefer "platonic," which implies an impersonal attitude to Palestine, rather than "political," which overlooks the social and economic connotations bound up with the solution of the Jewish problem since the emergence of Zionism in Germany.

university years and assumed political and ideological leadership of the German Zionist movement in the decade after World War I. Like their predecessors, Kurt Blumenfeld, Felix Rosenblüth, Richard Lichtheim, and Julius Berger experienced social prejudice and antisemitism on the university campus. They did the same soul-searching and reached the same conclusions as had the founders of German Zionism. But from the start, the second generation did not find emancipation as promising and intoxicating as those before them, and they were less hopeful of integrating into German society.

Unlike the first generation, many members of the second generation responded in a radical manner to the antisemitism they confronted and took a pessimistic view of their own personal destiny in Germany. Moreover, this generation was largely estranged from Jewish tradition, and had no spiritual life to fall back upon. Two of the most prominent figures, Blumenfeld and Lichtheim, came from totally assimilated homes suffused with German culture. Uncertain of their future in Germany, they chose another path which brought them closer to their people and their heritage. Not only was Zionism a means of preserving self-respect in the face of antisemitism, as it had been for their predecessors, but it was also a fulfillment of their deep need for Jewish identity. It thus presented an alternative to both assimilation and traditional Judaism.[11]

These second-generation German Zionists were not satisfied with "platonic," philanthropic Zionism, which condoned integration, at least for the time being. They sought a more personal, embracing, and demanding type of Zionism that would uproot the Jews from German society *(Entwurzelung)*, re-root them in the soil of Jewish nationhood *(Verwurzelung)*, and eventually bring them to Palestine.[12] Hence they were drawn to a whole host of ideological schools that challenged Herzlian Zionism. These included the "cultural" Zionism of Ahad Ha'am and the Democratic Faction organized by Ahad Ha'am's followers, Weizmann, Motzkin, and Buber; the "practical" and "synthetic" Zionism that advocated settlement activity combined with political and cultural endeavors, and the socialist Zionism of the workers' groups of the Second *Aliya*.

These were all offshoots of East-European Zionism that found a warm reception among the young Zionists of Central Europe. Common to each of them was the demand for radicalization on two levels: ideology and implementation. On the ideological plane, Zionism was called upon to define its goals in a more

---

11   Kurt Blumenfeld, *Erlebte Judenfrage* (Stuttgart, 1962); Richard Lichtheim, *Rückkehr* (Stuttgart, 1970); Reinharz, "Three Generations"; Ragins, *Jewish Responses*, Chapter Five.

12   Kurt Blumenfeld, "Ursprünge und Art einer Zionistischen Bewegung", *BLBI*, 4 (1958): 129–40.

prehensive and binding manner that would go beyond the attainment of a political framework in Palestine and provide for the building of a new social, cultural and economic entity. On the implementation level, it was called upon to broaden its diplomatic and organizational activity to include programs in both Palestine and the Diaspora that enhanced Jewish awareness and furthered the process of national revival.

In their search for a definitive Zionism, the young German Zionists of the early twentieth century absorbed and developed a variety of radical Zionist doctrines that were articulated at ideological and political forums of the WZO. In consequence, the East-European influence that had impressed itself upon German Zionism from the start became greater still, and radicalism gained a solid foothold in Germany. The publication society of the Democratic Faction, the *Jüdischer Verlag*, was established in Berlin in 1902, and the writings of Ahad Ha' am found a large audience in German translation. The teachings of Ahad Ha' am were further disseminated by the young philosopher, Martin Buber, who was active in the *Jüdischer Verlag,* and who spoke and wrote extensively about seeking the roots of national identity in Jewish cultural heritage.[13]

As the younger generation became more involved in the day to day organizational affairs of Zionism, radicalization spread. The *Bund Jüdischer Corporationen* students organization headed by Hantke, Lichtheim, Blumenfeld and Rosenblüth, became openly Zionist in 1908–1910. Beginning in 1910, Hantke took over the chairmanship of the ZVfD and former student activists were appointed to key posts in the WZO and CZO. The *Blau-Weiss* (Blue-White) youth movement, established in 1912, also contributed to the radicalization process through the ongoing contact between the youth leaders and their charges. No less notable was the fact that thousands of new members joined the ZVfD between 1910 and 1914. Nearly 9,000 people paid the *Shekel* in 1912–1913, compared with 6,200 in 1910, representing now about four percent of German Jewry.[14]

The feeling among certain groups of German Zionists, and especially Kurt Blumenfeld, was that the time had come for greater emphasis on Jewish culture. Blumenfeld maintained that preparation on a personal, spiritual, and

13 Jehuda Reinharz, "Ahad Ha'am und der deutsche Zionismus," *BLBI*, 61 (1982): 3–73; Jehuda Reinharz, "Martin Buber's Impact on German Zionism Before World War I," *Studies in Zionism*, 6 (Autumn 1982): 171–83; Ernst A. Simon, "Martin Buber and German Jewry," *LBIYB*, 3 (1958): 3–39.

14 Eloni, *Zionismus in Deutschland*, 250–312; Poppel, *Zionism in Germany*, 45–67 and Table Three; Lavsky, "German Zionist Leadership."

practical level, along with a deliberate detachment from German society and culture, were prerequisites for a national life in Palestine. The young people were thus asked to put aside their professional aspirations and give priority to a vocation that would be useful in Palestine. They were also expected to abstain from participation in German public and political life, and to relinquish the fight against antisemitism as futile. Life in the Diaspora was considered the root of all the evils that had befallen the Jews, and hence unworthy of effort in either the public or the private domain.

Pressured by Blumenfeld and his supporters, the German Zionist conventions held in Posen (1912) and Leipzig (1914) adopted radical, Palestinocentric resolutions such as placing the accent in Zionist education on personal fulfillment in Palestine, negating the value of Jewish life in the Diaspora, and obligating all Zionists to make immigration to Palestine part of their life plan. These resolutions caused some of the older, veteran "Herzlian" Zionists, among them Adolf Friedemann and Franz Oppenheimer, to retire either temporarily or permanently from Zionist activism.[15]

German Zionism was thus characterized from its inception by certain tendencies that distinguished it from Western Zionism in general, and led it to adopt a radical Palestine-oriented approach in the years before World War I. At that point a significant break took place in the relations between the German Zionist leadership and the major Jewish organization in Germany – the *Centralverein*. Until then, the two had maintained a certain *modus vivendi*, however uneasy. As the Zionists became more outspoken, the *Centralverein* turned its back on the movement altogether and joined forces with the anti-Zionist Jewish liberals. The antagonism reached a peak in 1913, when the *Centralverein* banned its members from any affiliation with the Zionist movement.[16]

This development was virtually unavoidable, a consequence of the rise of the younger radical generation, the establishment of the WZO Central Office in

---

15 *Dokumente*, 106, 132–42; Lavsky, "German Zionist Leadership." The term "Palestinocentrism" is used to denote an exclusive Palestine-oriented approach.

16 Reinharz, *Fatherland or Promised Land*, 171–245; Jehuda Reinharz, *The German Zionist Challenge to the Faith in Emancipation, 1897–1914*, (Spiegel Lectures in European Jewish History, no. 2, ed. Lloyd P. Gartner, Tel Aviv, 1982); Ragins, *Jewish Responses*, Chapter Five; Marjorie Lamberti, "From Coexistence to Conflict – Zionism and the Jewish Community in Germany, 1897–1914," *LBIYB*, 27 (1982): 53–82; Evyatar Friesel, "The Political and Ideological Development of the Centralverein before 1914," *LBIYB*, 31 (1986): 121–46; see also: Jehuda Reinharz, "Advocacy and History: The Case of the *Centralverein* and the Zionists," *LBIYB*, 33 (1988): 113–22; Marjorie Lamberti, "The Centralverein and the Anti-Zionists – Setting the Historical Record Straight," *LBIYB*, 33 (1988): 123–8.

the heart of the German Jewish community in Berlin and the growing displeasure of the non-Zionists who constituted the anti-Zionist front. By the outbreak of World War I, the German Zionists were still a small minority, but a militant and vociferous one whose ideas had to be reckoned with.

World War I prevented German Zionism from putting its new radicalism to the test. However, the course of the war and its aftermath presented the Zionists with fresh opportunities and posed a serious challenge to the Palestinocentric approach.

CHAPTER TWO

THE IMPACT OF THE WAR ON GERMAN ZIONISM

Transition in the World Zionist Movement

World War I, which erupted in August 1914, had a profound impact on the WZO and German Zionism, in particular. Most crucial for German Zionism was the break in communications between the Berlin-based Central Zionist Office and the Zionist centers in Russia, Britain and France, which required a reorganization of the political and administrative apparatus of the WZO and a relocation in neutral countries. The Zionist Bureau was set up in Copenhagen, the JNF Board and the Political Committee in The Hague, and the Provisional executive committee for General Zionist Affairs in New York. Formally, the Central Zionist Office remained open until its transfer to London in 1919, but it no longer played an influential role. Its work was confined to liaison with the *Yishuv* (The Jewish community in Palestine) via the Zionist Office in Constantinople, a connection which was possible because Turkey and Germany were allies. However, this was not sufficient to perpetuate a position of leadership in the WZO.

During the war, when Britain's importance in any post-war world order became apparent, London emerged as the new hub of political Zionist activity, drawing upon the illustrious Zionist leader, Chaim Weizmann, and other activists. The Balfour Declaration in November 1917 marked a resounding success for the Zionist movement, with Britain pledging its support for the establishment of a Jewish national home in Palestine. The Zionist movement was now on the eve of a new era. As British forces led by General Allenby conquered Palestine and the Zionist Commission was formed with the recognition of the British Government, there was no longer any doubt that London was the political nexus of the WZO.

This shift from Berlin to London was also part of a far-reaching change that was to affect the whole constellation of the Zionist movement. The political developments that jolted Central, and particularly Eastern Europe, during and after the war, further accelerated the wave of westward migration that was already in full swing, especially to the United States. With Jewish public life in Russia at a virtual standstill in the wake of the 1917 Bolshevik Revolution, the former leaders of Russian Zionism found a niche in the Zionist organizations in Paris, London, Berlin, New York and Jerusalem.

During this period, the American Jewish community rapidly gathered strength not only because of its economic and numerical superiority, but because of the special political status of the United States during and after the war. American Jews began to take an increasingly active role in defending and speaking out on behalf of European Jewry and the *Yishuv* in Palestine, and as they shouldered these new responsibilities, the Federation of American Zionists (FAZ) grew in influence, too. Some of its members assumed key positions in the WZO, and by World War I, the American Jewish community was the financial mainstay of the Zionist movement.[1]

Nonetheless, Europe remained the great wellspring of human resources, with the major Zionist strongholds now situated in Poland and Germany. The Polish Jewish community, numbering three and a half million, was the largest and most vibrant entity in the Jewish world, and the Polish Zionists counted more members than any other national grouping in the WZO. The German Jewish community was much smaller in size, with only 568,000 souls, and the percentage of Zionists was lower, too, although the figures doubled after the war to 20,000, as they did elsewhere, due to the greater international prestige enjoyed by the Zionist movement. Even so, the German Zionists comprised average 4.5 percent of the WZO (see Table I). Size, however, was not all. The German Jewish community continued to stand out on account of its economic fortitude, political stability, and cultural and intellectual prowess – none of which was subdued by the war.

---

1   Melvin I. Urofsky, *American Zionism from Herzl to the Holocaust* (New York, 1975), 195–245; Yonathan Shapiro, *Leadership of the American Zionist Organization, 1897–1930* (Urbana, Chicago and London, 1971), Chapters Four–Six.

Table I: German Zionism – Statistics for 1921–1932

Year	Total WZO membership	German Zionists	% of German Zionists in WZO	German Jewish Population	%[**] of Zionists among German Jewry
1921[*]	778,487	20,000	2.6		
1922	373,217	18,185	4.9		
1923[*]	584,765	33,339	5.7		
1924	300,267	20,847	6.9		
1925[*]	638,017	21,910	3.4	568,000	7.7
1926	214,384	13,826	6.4		
1927[*]	416,767	20,686	5.0		
1928	217,550	10,816	5.0		
1929[*]	387,106	15,559	4.0		
1930	201,250	9,539	4.7		
1931[*]	425,987	17,584	4.1		
1932	152,214	7,546	5.0	503,000	3.0
Average: 1921–1932	390,834	17,480	4.5	536,000	7.0
Congress years	538,521	21,300	4.0		

*   Zionist Congress convened that year
**   This percentage refers to the total population (including children) represented by adult members.

Source: Poppel, *Zionism in Germany*, Appendix, tables 1–3.

The Impact of War on German Zionism

World War I changed German Zionism in many ways and reinforced trends that had caught up with the younger generation even before the war. As German forces marched into Eastern Europe, the Jewish soldiers among them were deeply affected by the vibrant Jewish life they saw there, unleashing longings for a heritage they had never known. At the same time, they were confronted by the antisemitism of many of their comrades in arms. Even more distressing was the infamous *Judenzählung* or "Jew count" conducted by the War Ministry in 1916 in response to rumors that Jews were shirking the front. Consequently, the younger generation of German Jews began to doubt that integration in German society was possible, even if they demonstrated absolute loyalty to Germany and shouldered the burden equally on the battlefield. As a young soldier on the eastern front, Ernst Simon described himself as a person devoid of all Jewishness who suddenly became a Zionist without any personal desire to be one and without even being aware of it. A growing number of German Jews began to subscribe to the radical argument that the only solution to antisemitism was the eradication of Jewish life in the Diaspora. Henceforth, the young Zionists under Kurt Blumenfeld would maintain that antisemitism was an integral part of existence in a non-Jewish world, and as such, the battle against it was futile. For young Jews such as Ernst Simon and Alfred Landsberg, whose war experiences had led them to Zionism, the radical approach was the only one which seemed valid.[2]

The aggressive ultranationalism that was spreading throughout Central Europe and especially Germany, added another dimension to the radicalization process among the Zionists. Germany's defeat, with its subsequent economic and political consequences, added coal to the fire of the ultranationalists who threatened the fragile foundations of the new republic and posed a clear danger to democracy and liberalism. It was understandable for the German Jews to react strongly, because their integration into German society was dependent on these values. For the German Zionists, however, it was important to disassociate Jewish nationalism from German nationalism. Zionism was defined as an enlightened form of nationalism, seeking to liberate the oppressed and restore

---

2   Ernst A. Simon, "Unser Kriegserlebnis (1919)," in *Brücken – Gesammelte Aufsätze* (Heidelberg, 1965), 17–23; Interview with Eva Pelz about her father Alfred Landsberg, November 6, 1981, OHD; Kurt Blumenfeld, "Innere Politik," *Der Jude*, 1 (1916/1917): 713–7; *Dokumente*, xxxv–xxxvi. On the outbreak of antisemitism during the war, see: Werner Jochmann, "Die Ausbreitung des Antisemitismus," in *Deutsches Judentum in Krieg und Revolution, 1916–1923*, ed. Werner E. Mosse and Arnold Paucker (Tübingen, 1971), 409–510.

the dignity of the Jewish people through universal values and respect for basic human rights. This was a far cry from the selfishness and belligerence of German nationalism.

At the end of the war, Europe also witnessed the fall of old regimes and a pivotal change in the course of history. The Socialist revolutions in Russia and Germany, and the rise of democratic or multinational governments in Central and Eastern Europe presented new vistas and inspired hope. Many young German Jews joined the revolutionary camp, dreaming of an end to social injustice and especially chauvinism. The Zionists, however, took a different path. Their Zionism was born of despair at solving the Jewish problem in the Diaspora, and although they yearned for a new society founded on equity and equality, they did not perceive Marxist, cosmopolitan socialism as the answer. The socialist awakening around them inspired them to flesh out their Zionist radicalism with a synthesis of national and social ideals that had a special appeal for those who had been drawn to Zionism by their war-time experiences. These inclinations were further enhanced by the influence of the encounter with East-European immigrants who had already embraced a blend of socialism and nationalism.[3] While this socialist-Zionist amalgam was of course not new, the war and its aftermath rekindled interest in it, although the special circumstances prevailing in Germany produced a variant that was rather moderate from both the socialist and nationalist perspectives.

World War I thus gave a clear shape to the Palestine-oriented radicalism of the second generation of German Zionists, and strengthened their bond with the Jews of Eastern Europe whom they perceived as the embodiment of authentic Judaism. It was the war that completed their break with Europe and Germany, and it supplied radical Zionism with a new socialist and national-humanist dimension. World War I was crucial for the development of Zionism in another sense, as well: It laid the political groundwork for the Balfour Declaration and the British Mandate which enabled the Zionists to move ahead with the plan for a Jewish national home. Faced with the challenge of building a new society in Palestine, the German Zionists had a further incentive to cut

---

3   Robert Weltsch, "Deutscher Zionismus in der Rückschau" (1962), in *An der Wende des modernen Judentums* (Tübingen, 1972), 51–64; Simon, "Martin Buber"; Gershom Scholem, *From Berlin to Jerusalem – Memories of My Youth* (New York, 1980), 83–94; interviews with Robert Weltsch, February 21, 1980, Jacob (Jole) Tahler, March 22, 1982, Ernst Simon, March 16 and 23, 1982, Meir and Meta Flanter, May 9, 1982, OHD. On the Jews in the socialist and communist movements, see: Hans H. Knütter, *Die Juden und die Deutsche Linke in der Weimarer Republik* (Düsseldorf, 1971); Robert S. Wistrich, *Socialism and the Jews – The Dilemma of Assimilation in Germany and Austria-Hungary* (London and Toronto, 1982), 72–89.

themselves off from their German surroundings and concentrate on their new goals.

In the same way that World War I brought Palestinocentric concerns to the fore, it also had implications for Zionist activity in the Diaspora. However, it was mainly the older generation of Zionists that was pulled in this direction. The young had turned to radicalism even before the war, and their doubts about the future of the Jews in Germany were solidified at the front. There they met East-European Jews and also felt the sting of antisemitism on their own flesh. The older Zionists were not unaffected by such experiences, but the confrontation was not as direct.

Caught up in the patriotic enthusiasm that swept Germany when the war broke out, the veteran German Zionists rejoiced in the new-found opportunity to cooperate with other sections of the Jewish establishment, even anti-Zionists such as the *Centralverein*. Moreover, since Germany was allied with the Turks, Palestine and the *Yishuv* suddenly came under their wing. Efforts to assist the Jews of Palestine were politically in line with German interests and thus perfectly legitimate. Manifestations of antisemitism during the war were another cause for common concern. The *Centralverein*'s confidence that anti-semitism would disappear was badly shaken, and the Zionists had serious mis-givings about the efficacy of the struggle. This was the basis for the hope that the two could eventually work together.

In fact, the pendulum swung back and forth on this collaboration due to changes in German policy deriving from the military situation on the one hand, and the diminishing political status of the Zionist movement, on the other.[4] Be that as it may, the fact that Zionists and non-Zionists were able to communicate to the point of cooperating on certain common Jewish goals, seemed to constitute a major breakthrough.

The war was still in its early stages when senior Zionist leaders, among them Franz Oppenheimer and Adolf Friedemann, worked with representatives of *B'nai B'rith* and the *Centralverein* to organize the *Komitee für den Osten* (Committee for the East). This committee, which operated under the auspices of the German Army, extended assistance to Jews residing in German-occupied

---

4   On the relations between the Zionists and Jewish organizations that were non-Zionist and anti-Zionist, see: David Engel, "The Relations between Liberals and Zionists in Germany During the First World War," *Zion*, 47 (1982) (Hebrew): 435–62; Isaiah Friedman, "The *Hilfsverein der deutschen Juden*, the German Foreign Ministry and the Controversy with the Zionists, 1901-1918," *LBIYB*, 24 (1979): 291–320; Jürgen Matthäus, "*Deutschtum und Judentum* Under Fire – The Impact of the First World War on the Strategies of the *Centralverein* and the *Zionistische Vereinigung*," *LBIYB*, 33 (1988): 129–48.

sectors of Eastern Europe, thereby cultivating sympathy for the German authorities. Since Jewish solidarity and German patriotism served the same interests, the government took a favorable view of German-Jewish cooperation and encouraged activities on behalf of the "*Ostjuden.*" In the wake of the mass immigration during, and especially after the war, these activities continued to receive support and branched out in new directions. The infrastructure for collaboration between the Jewish organizations already existed, and the Zionists cooperated actively in the welfare enterprises coordinated by the *Zentralwohlfahrtsstelle der deutschen Juden* (Central Welfare Bureau of German Jews) which was established at the end of 1917 to help the immigrants. The feeling was that both they and the immigrants stood to benefit. On the one hand, their own Jewish ties would be enhanced, and on the other, the immigrants would develop a Zionist awareness.[5]

Developments toward the end of the war increased the will for cooperation among the Jewish organizations. In the early part of 1917, as Germany's diplomatic standing deteriorated, especially vis-à-vis the United States, Foreign Ministry officials stepped up their collaboration with the Zionists. Zionism thus became "politically correct" and even the non-Zionists recognized that supporting the *Yishuv* was an act of German patriotism. On the battleground, however, the tables turned in favor of the *Entente*. With the Ottoman Empire on the verge of collapse, Britain became the power with the greatest interest in Palestine. Under the leadership of Chaim Weizmann, British sympathy was gained for the Zionist cause, culminating in the issuance on November 2, 1917 of the Balfour Declaration.

This turn of events had a tremendous impact on the German Jewish leadership and the German government. Jews and non-Jews alike understood that Zionism had captured the hearts of the Western world. In consequence, the German government issued a pro-Zionist statement, in light of which even the non-Zionists felt challenged to reconsider their stand. Now that the Zionist movement had achieved international recognition, it was necessary to unify the Jewish position for presentation at the peace conference. Hence, toward the end of 1917, the initiation of contacts between the Zionists and associations such as the *Centralverein* and the *Hilfsverein der Deutschen Juden*, a move which

---

5   Jacob Toury, "Organizational Problems of German Jewry – Steps Towards the Establishment of a Central Organization (1893–1920)," *LBIYB*, 13 (1968): 57–90; Trude Maurer, *Ostjuden in Deutschland, 1918–1933* (Hamburg, 1986). On the *Komitee für den Osten*, see also Egmont Zechlin (with the collaboration of Hans J. Bieber), *Die deutsche Politik und die Juden im ersten Weltkrieg* (Göttingen, 1969), 126–54.

effectively ended the boycott of Zionism by the German Jewish organizations.[6]

The results of the war also set the stage for unhampered development of Jewish communal and cultural life. The Zionists were no longer restricted in their educational and public pursuits, and their enhanced status enabled them to win over large segments of the German Jewish community.[7]

These were exciting times for German Zionism. The struggle on two fronts was over. Jewish nationalism was now a legitimate and dignified alternative, that could make its voice heard in international forums and freely proclaim its aspirations concerning Palestine. Moreover, a basis had been created for cooperation with the non-Zionists and the way was clear for installing Jewish nationalism as a major component of public life in the Diaspora.

The Weimar Republic

After World War I, Germany was in a state of upheaval. On the eve of the German surrender a sailors' mutiny at Kiel set off an armed insurrection that spread throughout the country. Bavaria was proclaimed a republic, the Kaiser abdicated and fled to Holland and the leader of the Social Democrats, Friedrich Ebert, formed a provisional government.

With its economic infrastructure badly damaged by the war, the infant republic faced a complete breakdown of law and order. The country was flooded by demoralized former soldiers who could not find employment. Communist and nationalist uprisings broke out and the government was powerless to restrain them. National elections were held in January 1919, but the newly-elected national assembly which convened in Weimar to draft a new republican constitution did not return to Berlin until September. The vacuum created by the nonassertive Social-Democratic government was filled by the *Freikorps*, self-styled vigilante groups who took violent action to suppress the rioting while the government turned a blind eye. Early in 1919, the heads of an extreme left-wing group known as *Spartacus*, Rosa Luxemburg and Karl Liebknecht, were arrested and brutally murdered. This was followed by the

6 "Das deutsche Judentum und die Balfour Deklaration," *JR*, November 23, 1917: 377–8; Hantke's circular to the *Zentralkomitee*, December 16, 1917, CZA, A15/VII/29; Friedmann, *Germany, Turkey and Zionism*; Zechlin, *Die deutsche Politik*. See also note 4 above.

7 Max P. Birnbaum, *Staat und Synagoge – Eine Geschichte des Preußischen Landes-Verbandes Jüdischer Gemeinden (1918–1938) (Tübingen, 1981)*, 15–35; Maurer, *Ostjuden in Deutschland*, 508–86.

assassination of the Bavarian prime minister, Kurt Eisner, and then of other
members of his government, among them, Gustav Landauer. Terror continued
to rule the streets until the failed "Kapp *Putsch*," a *coup* attempted by
conservative politician Wolfgang Kapp in March 1920.

Even after the disbanding of the *Freikorps*, life in Germany did not return to
normal. The bitter defeat and humiliating terms of the Treaty of Versailles,
sparked an aggressive nationalism which laid the blame for Germany's disgrace
on the shoulders of the republic. Furthermore, the war debt and reparations
led to runaway inflation which completely spun out of control by 1922. As the
monetary system broke down in 1923, the economy teetered on the verge of
total collapse. Unemployment was rampant, millions lost their livelihood, and
the crime rate rose dramatically. Acts of terrorism were carried out by
paramilitary underground organizations, and the foreign minister, Walther
Rathenau, was assassinated. In November 1923, the Nazi Party, established in
1919, attempted a *coup* in Munich (the Beer Hall *Putsch*). Only toward the end
of 1923 and the beginning of 1924, when the Stresemann government managed
to bring inflation under control, did German life slowly resume some
semblance of normalcy for the first time since the war.

On the surface, 1924–1929 were peaceful years. However, the foundations of
the republic were none too solid and governments based on shaky coalitions
came and went. At the same time, the conservative and reactionary elements
in German society were perpetuated through the administration, the courts, the
military and the educational system. These tendencies were strengthened by the
1925 election of Von Hindenburg, a representative of monarchism and Prussian
militarism to the presidency. The rebuilding of the economy was slow and
plagued by setbacks. The Nazi Party, reorganized in 1925, launched a massive
propaganda campaign and became increasingly influential. Its militia, the SS
(*Schutzstaffel*) and SA (*Sturmabteilung*), instigated violence in the streets.

Nonetheless, it seemed that the democratic system was becoming entrenched
and the economy was on the road to recovery. Germany, and Berlin in particular, was regaining its former eminence as a center of European culture, and
the arts, literature and sciences flourished. In the eyes of its citizens and others
around the world, the Weimar Republic was a bastion of modern culture, an
intellectual trendsetter endowed with a healthy political system and a thriving
economy. The signing of the Locarno treaties and the evacuation of the Ruhr
Valley in 1925, followed by the acceptance of Germany by the League of
Nations in 1926, seemed to signify that old animosities had been laid aside.

German Jewry, which had prospered and attained a large measure of political
and civic equality before the war, flourished even more under the Weimar

Republic. All remaining discrimination was abolished and there were no restrictions on participation in German public life. Jews figured prominently in the leadership of the ruling Social-Democratic and Democratic parties. Two members of the provisional government set up by Friedrich Ebert were Jews, as was Kurt Eisner, the Bavarian prime minister. After Eisner's assassination, Jewish intellectuals such as Gustav Landauer and Ernst Toller were part of the new revolutionary government. The Social-Democrat and Reichstag delegate Oskar Cohn (who later joined the Zionist Socialist Party, *Poalei Zion*) was appointed to the parliamentary committee that investigated the role of the military in Germany's defeat. Jews sat on the workers' and soldiers' councils which were formed during the socialist revolution, and were among the authors of the Weimar constitution (Hugo Preuss). Walther Rathenau, the Minister of Finance and later the Foreign Minister, was Jewish. Other Jews held senior positions in the civil service. Hans Goslar, head of the Government Press Office, and Herrmann Badt, a Social-Democrat and the first Jew to serve in the Prussian government after the war, were supporters of Zionism.

The Jews of the Weimar Republic suffered from the same economic hardships as other Germans, but their recovery was rapid. As the last professional restrictions of the monarchist period fell away, they established themselves in the universities, civil service, law, business, banking and the free professions. Certain spheres were virtually monopolized by the Jews and their contribution to journalism, literature, theater, music, the plastic arts and entertainment was considerable. The Jews were prominent in intellectual circles and scientific research, and some scholars contend that they were ultimately the wellspring of "Weimar culture," the bustling creative activity that built Germany's reputation as a major cosmopolitan center.[8]

The Weimar Republic offered such a wealth of opportunity that the terrors of the early post-war years were all but forgotten. So heady and enticing was German life that many Jews lunged ahead prepared to sacrifice their Jewishness for the sake of total integration. Intermarriage soared to 45 percent, and many Jews converted or severed their ties with the Jewish community.

Alongside civil rights fully enjoyed by the Jews as individuals, the Weimar Republic placed no limits on the development of Jewish communal and cultural life. The Jewish community was redefined as a *Korporation des öffentlichen Rechts*, i.e. a corporation by public law. This afforded recognition on a

---

8 Craig, *Germany*, 396–553; Donald L. Niewyk, *The Jews in Weimar Germany* (Louisiana and London, 1980); Barkai, "Die Juden als sozio-ökonomische Minderheitsgruppe"; Peter Gay, *Weimar Culture – The Outsider as Insider* (New York, 1968).

democratic secular basis, and allowed elected committees to work freely in the spheres of religion, education, health and welfare. The community thus developed a broad array of Jewish welfare services and organizations that were especially important in view of the increasing number of immigrants from Eastern Europe both during the war and afterwards, as new borders were delineated in the east. The *Zentralwohlfahrtsstelle* coordinated between these different organizations and the community employment bureaus that were set up to help the immigrants find jobs.[9]

Nonetheless, antisemitism was far from dead. There were ultranationalist outbreaks throughout the 1920s, and some were violent indeed. The *Central-verein*, the largest German Jewish organization, channelled much of its energy into fighting antisemitism, but underneath was the belief that the forces of progress, which had never been stronger, would eventually win. Most of the Jews of the Weimar Republic, both those who were totally assimilated and those who kept up their Jewish affiliation, were united in the belief that full political, social and cultural integration in the German homeland was only a matter of time.

The Victory of Palestinocentric Radicalism

As German Zionism geared up for its new mission after World War I, it was torn by internecine rivalry between the Palestine-oriented radicals and the conservatives of the Diaspora school. It was basically a conflict of generations. Although the radicals won an important advantage during the war, three other alternatives were weighed before Palestinocentrism proved victorious. One of these alternatives was the organization of a German Jewish Congress. The Zionists had been in contact with the *Hilfsverein* and the *Centralverein* since 1917 with the aim of forming a delegation to deal with Jewish affairs at the peace talks. At the end of 1918, the ZVfD proposed the convening of a German Jewish body that would be affiliated with the World Jewish Congress, an initiative of the American Zionists, and serve as the official representative of German Jewry. The driving force behind this plan was ZVfD chairman

---

9   Birnbaum, *Staat und Synagoge*, 15–35; Maurer, *Ostjuden in Deutschland*, 508–716; Michael Brenner, "The *Jüdische Volkspartei* – National Jewish Communal Politics during the Weimar Republic," *LBIYB*, 35 (1990): 219–43; Walter Breslauer, "Vergleichende Bemerkungen zur Gestaltung des jüdischen Organisationslebens in Deutschland und England," in *In zwei Welten – Siegfried Moses zum fünfundsiebzigsten Geburtstag*, ed. Hans Tramer (Tel Aviv, 1962), 87–96.

Arthur Hantke. Among his supporters were older Zionists such as the lawyers Alfred Klee and Gustav Witkowski, who had long been Jewish community activists, and young radicals, such as Kurt Blumenfeld and Nahum Goldmann. The plan was presented at the 15th ZVfD convention and a committee was appointed to work out the details.[10] However, the approach was so overwhelmingly Zionist and fixated on Palestine that it was doomed to failure. It managed to engage the interest of only a few members of the *Centralverein*, which was clearly the most important potential partner, and those who responded favorably were already inclined toward Zionism.

The second alternative was to transform Jewish communities in the Diaspora into democratic national entities. This idea had been a favorite among older Zionists since the time of Herzl, but it enjoyed little support in the ZVfD. World War I, however, had made the prospect of Jewish national enclaves considerably more attractive and likely to succeed. Furthermore, a precedent had been set by the cooperation between Zionists and non-Zionists in aid of East-European Jewry. This made it easier to rally the community around the notion of local Jewish nationalism without the Palestinian emphasis, and to sign up thousands of new members for the Zionist movement. In 1919, these circumstances warranted the establishment of the *Jüdische Volkspartei* (Jewish People's Party) under the leadership of Alfred Klee, Max Kollenscher, Gustav Witkowski, Georg Kareski and others who had long been active in this regard. The party sought to disseminate Zionist ideology and gain control of the Jewish leadership, but it also purported to represent the East-European immigrants who were often denied the vote in community elections.[11]

While this turn towards community activism was the fulfillment of an old dream, the party itself was a compromise of sorts. For the older Zionist leaders, it afforded a welcome opportunity to engage in Diaspora politics, but in a framework that was separate from the ZVfD. This guaranteed that its work was not relegated to the sidelines, which might have been the case if it were part of the ZVfD. For the younger leaders, the party freed the ZVfD agenda from local concerns and allowed them to concentrate their energies on a platform that was entirely Palestine-oriented.

The third and final alternative was the most problematic and also the closest to Palestinocentric Zionism: cooperation between Zionists and non-Zionists to

---

10 Toury, "Organizational Problems"; Donald L. Niewyk, "The German Jews in Revolution and Revolt, 1918–1919," *Studies in Contemporary Jewry*, 4 (1988), 41–66, and especially 50–9; minutes of *Zentralkomittee* meeting, November 24, 1918, CZA, A15/VII/29.

11 Brenner, "The *Jüdische Volkspartei*"; Maurer, *Ostjuden in Deutschland*, 508–86.

improve the lot of the *Yishuv*. This issue was raised in 1920, upon the establishment of *Keren Hayesod* (created by the WZO to finance immigration and settlement in Palestine). Here is where the older German Zionists launched and lost their last battle. The 1921 German Zionist convention in Hanover made it clear that German Zionism had undergone a change of guard. Henceforth older Zionists worked mainly in the context of the *Jüdische Volkspartei*, allowing the radicals free run of the ZVfD.[12]

The Palestinocentric approach dominated the ZVfD until the early 1930s. Despite the opportunities offered by the Weimar Republic, the radicals went about their affairs as if the Zionist movement existed in a vacuum. When prospects for integration into German society beckoned, Zionist leaders responded with a campaign to convince the Jews that the lure of assimilation was chimerical. Antisemitic incidents further bolstered their view and were cited as proof that Zionism was the correct path. True to its convictions, the ZVfD stubbornly refused to join the *Centralverein* in fighting antisemitism. It also took no part in communal politics. That arena was left to the *Jüdische Volkspartei* which made significant inroads in the 1920s, especially in Berlin, where it gained the upper hand in Jewish community elections from 1926–1930. These achievements were proof of the scope of influence enjoyed by Zionism. Nonetheless, political activity remained the prerogative of the *Jüdische Volkspartei*, while the ZVfD continued to frown upon such involvement until the late 1920s.[13]

There was only one sphere of activity in the Diaspora in which the ZVfD's involvement was above and beyond that of the *Jüdische Volkspartei* – assisting the Jewish immigrants from Eastern Europe. This show of national solidarity had been a significant factor in the emergence and development of German Zionism and continued to play an important role after World War I. Among the ZVfD activists in immigrant absorption were the brothers Alfred and Julius Berger. A significant portion of the Zionist youth activities sponsored by the ZVfD took place in neighborhoods with large immigrant populations. The *Jüdisches Volksheim* (The Jewish Community Center), for example, which opened in Berlin in 1916 and became the headquarters of pioneer youth movements after the war, served mainly immigrant families. In effect, through its affiliation with young immigrants, the ZVfD created the infrastructure for

---

12 See Chapter Four.

13 In "The Zionist Response," 110–26, Reinharz maintains that there was a change in attitude toward antisemitism during the 1923 outbreak, but it was slight and short-lived. See also *Dokumente*, xx–xxviii, 470–2.

a larger German Zionist movement. When these youngsters grew up and joined the organization as adults, they helped to bring about the momentous political and social changes that ensued in the 1920s. It must, however, be emphasized that most of the work with immigrants was accomplished through the youth movements, political parties and committed individuals rather than direct ZVfD programming.[14]

The bulk of the ZVfD's activities continued to revolve around Zionist propaganda, fighting assimilation, and countering the anti-Zionist polemic, all of which were increasingly important in view of the challenges posed by the Weimar Republic. Assimilation and the belief in emancipation were greater than ever, and Zionism was perceived as a threat to these goals. Nonetheless, the Zionist movement, despite its small size, enjoyed a heightened respectability, and given the international legitimacy bestowed upon it by the Balfour Declaration, could no longer be dismissed as a transient, marginal phenomenon. The outcome was a rise in both supporters and bitter opponents. Moreover, the nature of the Zionist cause had changed dramatically and was bound up with Palestine in a way that it had not been before.

In summary, despite the new horizons that presented themselves during the Weimar period, the Zionist leaders in Germany cast their lot with the national home in Palestine.

---

14 Maurer, *Ostjuden in Deutschland*, 653–78. The relationship between the Zionist parties and East-European Jewry merits further study. Maurer's contention that *Hapoel Hatzair* was a party of immigrants is questionable. On the *Jüdisches Volksheim* and the youth movements, see interview with Jole Tahler, March 22, 1982, OHD; Scholem, *From Berlin to Jerusalem* 83–94; Richard Markel, "Brith Haolim – Der Weg der Alija des Jung-Jüdischen Wanderbundes (JJWB)," *BLBI*, 9 (1966): 119–88.

CHAPTER THREE

PLANS FOR THE DEVELOPMENT OF PALESTINE

The Jewish National Home

After the Balfour Declaration and the end of World War I, a new page was opened in the history of the Zionist movement. Before the war, Zionism was more of an idea than anything else, with goals that were bound up in some misty, uncertain, future. Thus Zionist activity in Germany revolved mainly around internal politics, education, ideological debates and propaganda aimed at the wider Jewish public. Now the movement was called upon to translate its aspirations into tangible economic and social programs, and to fashion the tools to carry them out. As a result, the building of Palestine took center stage in all WZO forums, and in the ZVfD as well.

Soon after Germany's defeat, at the very moment that revolutions began to wrack the country, the ZVfD held its 15th convention in Berlin. Despite the turbulent political situation and the restrictions on travel, 140 delegates gathered there on December 25–27, 1918, some of them hailing from the French-occupied territories in west Germany. The convention was also attended by 1,500 guests, and proceeded in remarkable tranquility considering the chaos that was going on around it. It was devoted exclusively to the future of Zionism in Palestine, and the ZVfD chairman, Arthur Hantke, called for Diaspora Zionists to dedicate all their energies to this cause.[1] Six months later, another Zionist convention was held in Berlin. The *Palästina Delegiertentag* (Palestine Convention), which met on May 26–29, 1919, brought together some 200 delegates of local Zionist groups, representing a cross-section of the

---

1   For a general description of the convention see *JR*, December 31, 1918, editorial; partial minutes, *JR*, December 31, 1918 and January 7, 1919; see also: *Protokoll des XV. Delegiertentages der Zionistischen Vereinigung für Deutschland* (Berlin, 1919).

entire political spectrum. This forum focused on social and economic planning.[2]

It was the economic and social advancement of Palestine that captured the interest of the German Zionists, while issues such as cultural and political development were pushed aside. Richard Lichtheim's lecture on economics at the 15th ZVfD convention was published in the form of a pamphlet,[3] and this subject was dealt with extensively in the *Jüdische Rundschau* and other German Zionist journals, among them *Die Arbeit* of *Hapoel Hatzair* and *Volk und Land*, whose editor, veteran Zionist Davis Trietsch, had long been interested in the economics of the Jewish homeland. German Zionist leaders also expressed their opinions and outlined development proposals in the JNF's annual German-language publication, *Erez Israel*, printed in The Hague.[4]

The German Zionists were not alone in their preoccupation with economics. This issue had been the subject of public debate in Palestine and elsewhere prior to and during the war, and had become all the more pertinent afterward as the notion of Jewish nationhood received political sanction.[5] Moreover, while the Zionist leadership and its diplomatic arm were immersed in political and international affairs, it was felt that questions of economic policy should be settled within the movement. Nonetheless, no other national organization of Zionists was involved so early, and with such intensity and attention to detail, as the ZVfD.

One possible explanation for this overwhelming absorption with economic planning was a highly developed sense of responsibility. The German Zionist leadership had enjoyed a senior position in the WZO before the war, and although this was no longer the case due to far-reaching political changes, the deep commitment remained. The majority of post-war Zionist leaders in Germany – Kurt Blumenfeld, Richard Lichtheim, Felix and Martin Rosenblüth, Julius and Alfred Berger, and of course the older leaders Arthur Hantke, Otto

2   See report of convention and list of delegates in: *JR*, June 6, 1919: 315, 323; convention minutes, *JR*, May 27, 1919, June 3, 1919, and June 6, 1919.

3   Richard Lichtheim, *Der Aufbau des Jüdischen Palästinas* (Berlin, 1919).

4   The bi-weekly *Jüdische Rundschau*, the official organ of the ZVfD from 1902, was edited by Weltsch from 1919 until the Nazis closed it down in 1938. *Die Arbeit, Organ der zionistischen volkssozialist-ischen Partei Hapoël Hazaïr* was published in Berlin from 1919. At first it was a fortnightly, but it later became a monthly and appeared regularly until 1924. *Volk und Land, Jüdische Wochenschrift für Politik, Wirtschaft und Palästina-Arbeit* was put out in Berlin in 1919, for about a year. *Erez Israel, Mitteilungen des Hauptbüreaus des jüdischen Nationalfonds* was published annually between 1916 and 1923.

5   See Jacob Metzer, *National Capital for a National Home, 1919–1921* (Jerusalem, 1979) (Hebrew).

Warburg and Max Bodenheimer, were trained in the institutions of the WZO. In consequence, it was their obligation towards the main Zionist issue of the day that was uppermost, whereas *Gegenwartsarbeit* (here-and-now activity in the Diaspora) was belittled. In the pre-war period, the German Zionists were inclined to ignore what was going on around them and scoffed at investing their energy in a country where they felt they had no future. In this respect, German Zionism differed from Zionism in other countries such as Poland. Hence the focus on the major concerns of economic and social development in Palestine. Moreover, the radical views of the young German Zionists that emerged before the war imbued the socioeconomic process with ideological significance without connection to the circumstances that furthered the Zionist cause after the war.

The human dimension was another factor. A large number of German Zionists were academicians and free professionals. Even the businessmen usually had university degrees. This background enabled them to discuss theoretical and scientific issues on a high level, and ultimately attracted them to the economic and social questions that required such an approach. In Germany the social sciences enjoyed enormous prestige, advances in this sphere being deemed crucial for the consolidation of the German nation. At the time, Germany was the cradle of major social and economic theories, and the German Zionists who were nurtured in this atmosphere developed similar inclinations.

The leaders of the German Zionist movement were not new to economic theory and planning. Otto Warburg and Arthur Ruppin had directed economic policy in Palestine before the war. Warburg was still official Chairman of the WZO's Inner Actions Committee in Berlin, and Ruppin was considered the foremost expert on the subject in the WZO. His book, *Der Aufbau des Landes Israel* (The Upbuilding of the Land of Israel), published in Berlin in 1919, became an indispensible reference in all future deliberations on the economy of Palestine.[6] There were others who could offer input from their practical experience in Palestine. The agronomist Solomon Dyk had managed Merhavya, the agricultural cooperative in the Jezreel Valley initiated by Franz Oppenheimer, and opened a training farm for pioneers upon his return to Germany. The physician and citrus grower, Wilhelm Brünn, had served as the director of Nathan Straus's Health Center in Jerusalem before serving in the German army. Elias Auerbach had worked as a physician in Haifa in 1909, and architect Alexander Baerwald had prepared the designs for the Haifa Technion

6   Arthur Ruppin, *Der Aufbau des Landes Israel* (Berlin, 1919); also see Metzer, *National Capital*, 69.

and other public buildings in Palestine. The experience of these men, all of whom were now in Germany, played an important role in riveting the attention of the German Zionist leadership on the building of Palestine and the economic issues involved.

Between Socialism and *Étatisme*

The economic debate among the German Zionists took place at a time when socialism was on the rise. We have already seen that the political and social changes in Europe after World War I created fertile ground for socialist and anti-chauvinist thinking among young Jews in general, and the Zionists in particular. Such views were especially prominent among German Jews both because of the nationalist violence they so abhorred and their encounter with East-European Jewish immigrants. The blend of socialism and Zionist nationalism, which was new in Germany, was given an added impetus by the prospect of building a new society in Palestine.

This combination was first articulated in Germany through the Zionist labor organization *Hapoel Hatzair*, which became active at the end of 1917 under the leadership of Chaim Arlosoroff, whose family had immigrated from East Europe when he was a child, and Israel Reichert, who had joined the movement in Palestine and came to study in Germany during the war. Interest in *Hapoel Hatzair* spread rapidly, and its membership soon included members of the Zionist student societies, young intellectuals and even older Zionists such as Martin Buber, Kurt Blumenfeld and Robert Weltsch, a recent arrival from Prague who went on to become editor of the *Jüdische Rundschau*.

The attraction of *Hapoel Hatzair*, which maintained ties with the *Hapoel Hatzair* party in Palestine and the *Tzeirei Zion* groups in Russia, lay in a platform that offered a synthesis of the moderate socialist and nationalist beliefs upheld by German Zionists, and opposed the concept of class struggle. The socialism of *Hapoel Hatzair* was of the humanist-ethical variety rather than revolutionary and class-conscious. Its main goal was a new society founded on justice, cooperation and equality in which the Jewish individual and the Jewish community were placed above political rebirth and supremacy. *Hapoel Hatzair* thus emphasized the importance of embracing physical labor, especially agriculture, and called for a return to the Jewish sources as a wellspring of culture and social equity.

From 1919, *Hapoel Hatzair* published a bi-weekly newspaper in German, *Die Arbeit*, that swiftly gained respect among the German Zionists and served as a sounding board for ideas on the socioeconomic future of Palestine. That year, *Hapoel Hatzair* held its first convention in Germany. Shortly afterwards, the *Palästina Delegiertentag* convened, and 39 of its 200 delegates were from *Hapoel Hatzair*.[7]

However, not all the socialists in the German Zionist organization were affiliated with *Hapoel Hatzair*. In the heady, hopeful days after the war, the Zionist movement was joined by many young socialists, among them Fritz Sternberg, who was to become an outspoken critic of Marxism, and David Baumgardt, who later made a name for himself in the United States as a writer and philosopher. At the *Palästina Delegiertentag* in May 1919, there were 14 socialist delegates with no party affiliation. Together with the socialists of *Hapoel Hatzair*, they comprised a bloc representing about a quarter of all the delegates. The socialists thus exercised considerable influence on the decision-making of the German Zionist movement.[8]

While the penetration of moderate socialism was exceedingly important for the Zionist movement, no mistake should be made about the social and political orientation of most German Zionists, many of whom belonged to the enlightened middle-class. Their social ideas had been acquired in their student days through exposure to the *Verein für Sozialpolitik* (Association for Social Policy), an updated version of the Historical School which had been the predominant school of thought in the social sciences, political science and economics since the mid–19th century. The Historical School was a response to the political discord and economic backwardness of Germany at that time. In an effort to achieve national unity and break into the industrialized world, a socioeconomic theory based on *Étatisme* was developed, according to which the state would take the lead in regulating the economy and stimulating economic growth. The Historical School maintained that the concerns of the community were not necessarily reconcilable with those of the individual, and that the individual had an obligation toward the community. Above all, however, it accentuated state intervention in the economy.

This approach also harbored social implications which were molded into a theory of social policy by the *Verein für Sozialpolitik* both prior to and following World War I. Support for *Étatisme* continued to grow after the unification of Germany and especially during the Great Depression. Later

---

7 Statistics taken from *JR*, June 13, 1919: 333–4. On *Hapoel Hatzair* see Baruch Ben-Avram, "The German '*Hapoel Hatzair*' – The History of an Intellectual Group (1917–1920)," *Zionism*, 6 (1981) (Hebrew): 49–95.

8 The statements of the socialists appear in the above-mentioned ZVfD convention reports.

experience further convinced the *Verein für Sozialpolitik* that state supervision of the national economy was imperative both to close the gap between Germany and the West and to promote domestic stability. It was argued that free enterprise caused social distortions that in the long run retarded economic development. The solution was a synthesis between liberal capitalism, which alone had failed to solve the problems of state and society, and socialism, which rejected private initiative. The proposed synthesis borrowed the belief in private enterprise from the liberals and the desire for social justice from the socialists, yet turned away from the liberal *laissez faire* approach that gave free reign to private individuals and the unbridled forces of the marketplace. It was the state that would step in to temper this activity and insure, through a network of laws and economic regulations, that the country moved ahead financially without generating social injustice.

These were the views of the *Kathedersozialisten* – the "academic socialists" who expounded their theories from the university podium. Among them were Max Weber, a professor of sociology and political economy at the universities of Freiburg, Heidelberg and Munich; and Werner Sombart, an economic historian at the universities of Breslau and Berlin, who was revered as a teacher despite the antisemitic overtones of his nationalist approach and economic beliefs (in his old age, he became a Nazi). Many of the German Zionist leaders were exposed to these teachings during their university years.[9]

It is not difficult to imagine the impact of these *Étatist*-nationalist views on Zionism. After all, the Zionist idea was predicated from the outset on the creation of a new, more equitable society. To attain the goal of an independent entity in the Land of Israel, the Zionists required a plan for rehabilitation, that among other things, would encourage productivity and vocational diversity. This was perceived as a *sine qua non* for the building of a cohesive, vital and autonomous Jewish community. When political circumstances created the possibility of bringing the Zionist vision to fruition, the process of national rehabilitation became linked with the Jewish homecoming and with the campaign for the systematic development of Palestine, adding a new urgency to the need for a combined social and economic program.[10]

---

9   On the *Kathedersozialisten* see Joseph Schumpeter, *History of Economic Analysis* (Oxford, 1954), Chapter Four; Jacob Oser and William C. Blanchfield, *The Evolution of Economic Thought* (New York, 1975), Chapter Eleven. For the influence on Jewish students, see Blumenfeld, *Erlebte Judenfrage*, 146–7.

10   This was emphasized by Hantke and Lichtheim at the 15th convention. See also Metzer, *National Capital*, Chapter One.

The *Étatist* approach also had another common denominator with German Zionism: its affinity with socialism, especially the moderate version embraced by German Zionists, which emphasized the nationalist dimension rather than class. Hence the great interest of the German Zionist movement and the eventual consensus that was reached on the issue of socioeconomic planning.

Shaping a Socioeconomic Program

The socioeconomic future of Palestine was the subject of debate at the 15th ZVfD convention in Berlin at the end of December 1918, and continued to stir up passions the following year at the *Palästina Delegiertentag* and on the pages of the German Zionist press. The main thesis, that the Zionist objective in Palestine was the building of a new kind of society and not just the transfer of Jews, was not even contested. However, when it came down to strategy, there were two different approaches, each with its own order of priorities.

One approach was to give center stage to public initiative and the higher institutions of the WZO. The major proponents of this view were the socialists Chaim Arlosoroff, Rudolf Samuel and Albert Baer of *Hapoel Hatzair*, Fritz Sternberg, and the Social-Democrats Hans Goslar and Hermann Badt, who were also active Zionists. This group advocated nationalizing most or all of the production network. Even non-socialists such as Arthur Hantke and Richard Lichtheim, and the old-school Zionists Heinrich Loewe and Elias Auerbach, concurred on this point. They, too, believed in the investment of public capital, not only as a means of greasing the wheels of immigration and settlement, but as a tool for creating communal holdings and a more just society.

Supporters of this approach all agreed that if the object was to build a new society, the work must begin at the foundations, which meant laying the physical infrastructure, step by step. Thus it was imperative for immigration to Palestine to be selective and well-planned, under the supervision of the national institutions and preceded by proper training. A public effort to promote agricultural settlement was deemed the best way to alter the employment structure of Jewish society and set it on a new and better path. It was the return to the soil that promised to change the ingrained tendencies of the Jewish people and restore the Jewishness of Palestine. For this reason agriculture was placed on a high pedestal and, in light of the physical obstacles, the proponents of public initiative called for a concerted Zionist effort in this sphere.[11]

Another approach was taken by those who believed that private capital held the key to development. The main champions of this view were the agronomist Wilhelm Brünn, public activist and economist Davis Trietsch, and Otto Warburg, who functioned as chairman of the WZO since 1911. These persons had been involved in the colonization of Palestine when opportunities were still limited, and they could see the potential that was now opening up. They argued that practical and political factors were no less important than the final goal, and that the first priority of the Zionist movement should be amassing a large Jewish population, if not the majority, in Palestine. They feared that time was of the essence, and that if the bull was not taken by the horns, the chance for a Jewish national home might be lost. It could not be expected that the momentum would last forever or that the powers, and especially Britain, would always be willing to help. In their eyes, it was wrong to assume that "judaizing" Palestine could be simultaneous with the creation of a new social and economic entity – by nature, a prolonged process. Only after a substantial Jewish community had struck roots there would the time be ripe for social, economic and cultural amelioration.

Brünn, Trietsch and Warburg based their arguments on the supposition that immigration and settlement were more accessible goals than those of their opponents. Hence their demand that the gates be opened to massive non-selective immigration. They also favored industry over agriculture on the grounds that industry was better suited to Jewish inclinations and economic conditions in Palestine. To succeed in agriculture, large sums were required for farmer training and soil enrichment. Industry, on the other hand, provided more jobs and offered a much quicker return on investments. The greater absorptive capacity of industry was also perceived as an advantage in light of the anticipated wave of immigrants. According to this approach, private investment held more promise for economic growth than public funding because the capital was readily available and could be utilized more efficiently. Most of the Jews belonged to the middle or lower middle-class, and would probably be prepared to take part in the upbuilding of Palestine if the financial opportunities were sufficiently enticing. It was also felt that private entrepreneurs would act swiftly and mobilize investment capital more successfully than public bodies.

---

11 The following discussion is based on the reports of the two conventions (see notes 1 and 2 above) unless other sources are cited.

Warburg and his colleagues were no less interested in an equitable society, but they preferred to put this off until some later date. Meanwhile, they warned against pseudo-socialist policies that might deter private investors and subsequently impede the development of the national home.[12]

These two approaches were not as divergent as they appeared. None of those who favored the gradual unfolding of a new order was against private capital. On the contrary, the majority were liberal or moderate in their socialist views which were along the lines of *Hapoel Hatzair*. With the exception of Arlosoroff, who advocated public funding only, no one demanded that a socialist society be built from the outset. They all recognized the benefits of private investment and expected entrepreneurs to participate in building the country. However, for this very reason they wanted the infrastructure to be built by the public sector, which would set the tone. While the socialists called for a massive injection of national capital to lay the basis for a regulated economy, they were also looking one step further, towards nationalizing the means of production. Nevertheless, this was seen as a process that would evolve over time. They well understood the prevailing attitudes among Jews and were willing to compromise and make use of private capital to reach their aim. Furthermore, they assumed that the other side, namely the entrepreneurs, would be equally flexible. The supposition was that the Jews who invested in Palestine would not be purely motivated by profit; surely some Zionist feeling would be involved. In consequence, they would be amenable to certain dictates imposed by the national institutions for the sake of national-social betterment. Thus to one extent or another, the vast majority of German Zionists recognized the potential inherent in private initiative and very few insisted that the country be developed without it.

On the other hand, not even the leading advocates of capitalist enterprise envisaged the private sector as standing alone. It was universally understood that such investment was unfeasible unless a national effort was made to lay the infrastructure. Warburg, for one, believed in nationalizing the land reserves and chief natural resources, building public utilities and acquiring ownership of monopolistic enterprises such as energy plants, public transportation and vocational training facilities. There was also the social factor. Even those who supported private initiative and rapid advancement accepted the Zionist notion of a just society and recognized that public infrastructure would allow such a society to develop at a later stage. Infrastructure in this sense was a guiding

12 See also articles of Warburg, Brünn and Trietsch in *JR*, January 1, 1919, February 18, 1919, and August 3, 1920, respectively.

public hand that would prevent distortions of the kind that might frustrate the emergence of a new social order. Hence the virtual consensus among the German Zionists that national assets and a public sector operating alongside the private one were vital for the wellbeing of the Jewish national home.[13]

Wisely, neither side demanded exclusivity for any one sector. Therefore, it was possible to reach an agreement on the strategies of developing the national home. The consensus was especially strong on the land issue which was central to all discussions of Zionist settlement policy.

The idea of transforming all the land in Palestine into the national property of the Jewish people had been an integral part of Zionism since the establishment of the JNF at the turn of century.[14] After World War I, it took on new significance. The fact that the land was not free for the taking but owned by individuals and governments turned acquisition of land ownership into the key determinant of the future of the *Yishuv*. From the onset, the Zionists were thus united on the need to bolster the JNF and amass large blocs of nationally-owned land. This was perceived as a substitute for political sovereignty and a means of keeping the land from falling into non-Jewish hands. It also guaranteed equal settlement opportunity, and prevented the land from being monopolized by a small number of profit-seeking individuals. The implication was concern for the public welfare on both the national and the social levels. Thus even the proponents of private initiative, who felt that public capital should be resorted to on a very limited basis, advocated the nationalization of land. In fact, in their eyes, this was the chief purpose of public capital.

Differences of opinion on the land issue were merely a question of degree. The proponents of step-by-step development were particularly enamored with the moral aspect of nationalization and the fact that it would hinder speculation and control of the land by a selected few. They looked down on private ownership and sought to nationalize as much land as possible. There was little contest in this matter between socialists such as Fritz Sternberg and Chaim Arlosoroff, and non-socialists such as Richard Lichtheim and Elias Auerbach.

On the other hand, the champions of rapid development held that national funding of land should also be kept within bounds. They doubted that the public sector could raise sufficient capital for all the land on such short notice,

---

13   Davis Trietsch was the only delegate who wanted national capital earmarked exclusively for mass immigration.

14   As for the idea of agrarian reform and its origins in Central European thought, see Chapter One, note 9.

and therefore advocated a combination of nationalization and private land purchase. Instead of immediately nationalizing the entire corpus of land, which was unrealistic in their view, they proposed gradual nationalization in accordance with the availability of public resources.

It was in this sphere that the common ground shared by most German Zionists was displayed. The vast majority believed that nationalized land ownership was justified for national and social reasons, but that private purchase could not be ruled out for the sake of economic efficiency. The partial nationalization approach subscribed to by many German Zionists was articulated by Albert Baer of *Hapoel Hatzair*. He explained that while the German Zionists were not willing to relinquish the right to private property, they were prepared to accept certain limitations, especially in the area of real-estate. As for the socialists, land was the only issue on which they insisted that the public sector be given full control.[15]

The support for a combination of capitalist entrepreneurship and nationalization had its roots in two ideologies prevalent among the German Zionists: bourgeoisie *Étatisme* and moderate socialism. What distinguished the *Étatists* from other liberal capitalists, and moderate socialists from those of the Marxist camp, was their acute vision of the national objective. Towards this end, the *Étatists* were prepared to accept restrictions on their right to private property, and the socialists, to modify their dream of a universal revolution. Both sides acknowledged the importance of the public sector for economic and social advancement without denying the role of private investment, but the emphasis was different. For the *Étatists*, the national objective was paramount and social reform secondary. Consequently, they sought limitations on public funding. For the socialists, the creation of an equitable society took pride of place, which entailed greater control over private enterprise.

This broad consensus enabled the ZVfD, as a national federation, to formulate a social and economic program for the building of Palestine that was submitted to the WZO. Behind this initiative was *Hapoel Hatzair*, whose large delegation at the *Palästina Delegiertentag* in May 1919 undertook to draft the resolutions. Due to the national justification for many of the socialist demands presented at the forum, the non-socialists put their differences aside, even in the case of outright conflict, such as on the land issue.

The opening sentence of the ZVfD platform was characteristic of the spirit of unity in which it had been drafted: "The convention demands that the

---

15 See article by Albert Baer in *Die Arbeit*, May 25, 1919; and articles by Emil Simonsohn and Klara Boschwitz in *JR*, March 11, 1919 and March 25, 1919.

efforts of the WZO to build a Jewish community in the Land of Israel be guided by the social legislation of ancient Judaism." The resolutions themselves dealt with the nationalization of land, transportation, ports, electricity, gas and water works, forests and natural resources and called for public initiative in the realms of agriculture and industry. They also spoke of support for regulated commercial, agricultural, and industrial ventures in the private sector; free health and educational services; and general supervision of all economic activity.

In the wider Zionist context, the German consensus was notable for two reasons. First of all, the German Zionists had succeeded in putting together a platform at a time when the higher institutions of the WZO had only begun to broach the subject. Members of the Actions Committee had met informally in London in February 1919, just months before the *Palästina Delegiertentag* for preliminary clarifications. Secondly, the German Zionists were able to overcome differences between the center and the left. No radical positions were articulated at the meeting of the Actions Committee (from which the German Zionists were barred because the British considered them citizens of an enemy country) as well, and even the leading supporter of private investment, Meir Dizengoff, acknowledged the need for public supervision. However, the atmosphere in London was permeated by criticism of the "socialist experiments" of the workers parties in Palestine and strong reservations regarding overall nationalization of the land.

It was these two features – early agreement and a moderate slightly left-wing approach – that allowed the German Zionists to assume a chief role from this point on in molding future Zionist settlement policy.

The Establishment of *Keren Hayesod*

In the summer of 1919, the leaders of the Zionist movement, including representatives of the American and German branches, met in London to discuss the financing of the Zionist undertaking in Palestine and reached an agreement on the need for public funding of infrastructure. At this stage, the debate centered on how the money would be raised and the institutional channels through which it would be transmitted. At the Annual Conference of the WZO in London a year later, *Keren Hayesod* (Palestine Foundation Fund) was established for this purpose, with a budget based on a self-imposed annual tax or "tithe."[16]

The German Zionist movement helped to shape *Keren Hayesod* in two ways. First, it was in Germany that the idea of a Zionist tax was put into practice, and second, among the major architects of the institution were ZVfD leaders Otto Warburg and Arthur Hantke. None of this would have been possible without the broad consensus among the German Zionists on the urgency of developing Palestine through national channels.

Hantke was among the first exponents of a national funding body, and had already established a framework quite similar to *Keren Hayesod* in Germany. The *Palästina Delegiertentag* accepted his plan to replace all Zionist fundraising aside from that done by the JNF, with an annual tax known as the *Zionistensteuer*. This was not really a tax in the sense that it could not be enforced and was dependent on the good will of each member of the Zionist movement. Nonetheless, a taxation index was drawn up based on earnings and a schedule of four annual payments.[17]

The new fund set a precedent for *Keren Hayesod* in putting an end to the friction between different fundraising organizations and eliminating the competition for donors which was liable to decrease overall contributions. Moreover, a united appeal was crucial if the allocation of money was to be carried out by a centralized authority. The voluntary tax was another innovative idea that was designed to create a sense of public duty in the sphere of Zionist philanthropy. Hantke explained this as follows:

> With the declaration of the *Zionistensteuer*, the *Zionistische Vereinigung für Deutschland* is firmly paving the way for the building of a Jewish commonwealth in Palestine. The development of Palestine and the strength of the Zionist organization will no longer be dependent on contributions and gifts. As the *Zionistensteuer* goes into effect, we declare it incumbent on each and every one to share in the needs of the community of which he is part. This is the payment he owes for the protection and general cultural heritage bestowed upon him by that community. The fact that we are now defining the relationship between the individual and the community in material terms shows more than

---

16 Metzer, *National Capital*, 69–101.

17 *JR*, June 17, 1919 main headline devoted to the decision of the *Zentralkomittee*.

anything else that the Zionist movement has made great strides.... Every German mark we contribute today will serve the Land of Israel, which is being given to us as an entity in the making. Without difficulty we shall see how our tax payments become the building blocks of the enterprise in Palestine.... The imposition of this tax is both a privilege and an obligation. No more shall we seek donations for the Zionist organization; we shall now tax ourselves, for the sake of our people. Whomsoever sees himself as belonging, let him prove it....[18]

Since the meeting in London in 1919, the Zionist leadership had been grappling with the question of how to organize national-public funding. Among the possibilities was the mobilization of capital through contributions and expanding the scope of the JNF to include immigration and settlement in addition to land purchase. Another idea was to create a businesslike framework in the form of a colonization company, national loans or a credit system under the auspices of the Jewish Colonial Trust. Personalities in the WZO responsible for economic planning, among them Arthur Ruppin and Julius Simon, argued in favor of a commercial or quasi-commercial set-up. Most of the German Zionists, led by Hantke, remained faithful to the type of framework they had devised in Germany: a large-scale fund perpetuated by a self-imposed tax rather than outright philanthropy or a business-type venture. They objected to a commercial body on the premise that investments in Palestine could not be expected to reap profits in the foreseeable future, and would not attract investors. The German Zionist approach proved victorious at the Actions Committee meeting in February 1920, and unsurprisingly, it was Hantke who drafted a resolution calling for the financing of basic infrastructure by means of a large national contribution totalling 25 million pounds sterling. At the same time, private investment would be directed toward commercial profit-seeking ventures. The resolution won a majority vote and laid the foundations for the decision to establish *Keren Hayesod* at the Annual Conference of the WZO in July 1920.[19]

At this forum, *Keren Hayesod* was designated as the sole fundraising institution for immigration and settlement, and its resources, along with those of the JNF, were declared national capital. All monies raised were to be

---

18 *JR*, June 17, 1919: 339. (All quotations translated by the author unless otherwise stated.)

19 Metzer, *National Capital*, 69–101; Protocol of Actions Committee Meeting in February 1920, CZA, Z4/252/2. See also articles by Lichtheim in *JR*, February 10, 1920 and March 9, 1920.

transferred to a central Zionist authority empowered to determine economic policy and channel funds accordingly. *Keren Hayesod* was thus an instrument that would allow the Zionist movement to direct the settlement enterprise in Palestine in accordance with national and social objectives.[20]

The point being made here is not that the German Zionists were the chief actors in the establishment of *Keren Hayesod*. The emergence of the fund was the outcome of a whole range of factors, and German Zionism was but one. Nonetheless, the German Zionist movement had taken an influential stand on the national capital issue and certain Zionist principles that had not been sufficiently worked out by the end of the war were presented coherently by the ZVfD and subsequently accepted as world Zionist policy. The development of the Jewish national home enjoyed top priority among the German Zionists, who also accentuated spiritual, economic and social renewal before these aspects were embraced by the movement as a whole. Early on, German Zionism recognized that the building of Palestine demanded a combination of private and public initiative, carefully supervised to insure the attainment of national and social goals. Finally, the conceptual basis for a unified fundraising body to generate national capital had its roots in Germany. The public debate of these issues in German Zionist forums and the broad consensus that was achieved within a short span of time set the stage for further activism on the part of German Zionists and an attempt to reach out to those who thought likewise in the world movement. In this way, German Zionism became a force to contend with in the carving out of a national settlement policy.

---

20 See Metzer, *National Capital*, 97–101.

CHAPTER FOUR

THE BASIS FOR COOPERATION WITH CHAIM WEIZMANN

The Zionist Movement, the Jewish World and Palestine

The Balfour Declaration and the post-World War I peace negotiations presented the Zionist movement with the double challenge of creating a Jewish national home in Palestine and lending substance to the new respect for Zionism and Palestine among the Jewish people. Through the establishment of *Keren Hayesod* it hoped to meet both challenges. On the one hand, *Keren Hayesod* would help define the Zionist goals behind the Jews' national aspirations, on the premise that physical development was merely the means toward an end. It was felt that national rebirth, a renaissance of Jewish culture and the Hebrew language, and socioeconomic rehabilitation, could be achieved through productive labor, a return to the soil and a social system based on justice and morality. Along with the JNF, *Keren Hayesod* would raise the national capital needed to carry out these ideas and shape the national home into more than just another economic or political entity.

On the other hand, *Keren Hayesod* would be an instrument for global Jewish cooperation. International political developments after the war had elevated the Zionist movement and made it the spokesman of the Jewish people on all matters concerning Palestine. Even more important, there was a growing perception of the Jews, however scattered, as a national-political body whose interests were represented by the Zionist Organization. This affirmation by outside elements and the reshuffling within the movement sparked by the upcoming Peace Conference, produced in the Zionist leadership a sense of responsibility toward the Jewish community at large. A burning issue during the early post-war years was the political status of the Jews in the emerging Central and East European states. This problem had been exacerbated by the war, and was especially acute in Poland and the Ukraine, where the Jews were suffering from terrible persecution and pogroms. The leaders of the Zionist organization thus realized that their role did not end with Palestine, but they were far from united on how to proceed.

The "Palestinocentrists" led by Chaim Weizmann and Menahem Ussishkin relegated Diaspora Jewish affairs to a lower rung on the Zionist agenda, whereas Leo Motzkin, who headed the Committee of Jewish Delegations at the Versailles Peace Conference, held that the Zionist leadership should spearhead the fight for Jewish rights in the Diaspora. After the war, prominent Zionist leaders such as Yitzhak Gruenbaum in Poland and Max Soloveichik in Lithuania devoted themselves to winning national minority status for the Jews and strengthening their representation in the democratic governments that were being formed. This approach was paralleled in Germany by Alfred Klee and Max Kollenscher, who were among those who wished to see the Zionists at the helm of the local Jewish communities.

The change in status of the Zionist movement was also nourished by the greatly altered approach of the non-Zionists. Many of those who had previously taken a skeptical or negative view of Zionism were now ready to acknowledge that development of the national home in Palestine was the mission of all Jews. Some joined the Zionist movement, increasing membership considerably in various countries. Others simply expressed their support and were willing to help from the sidelines. There seemed to be a consensus that success in Palestine was a test of the entire Jewish people. At the same time, international recognition of the Zionist goal mitigated fears that this might conflict with efforts to move ahead politically in the Diaspora.

In its bid for global Jewish cooperation, the Zionist movement was also guided by practical considerations. It was presumed that many non-Zionists would wish to participate in the building of Palestine, and that a wealth of financial and executive potential lay outside the movement, waiting to be harnessed for the Zionist cause.

This growing affinity between Zionists and non-Zionists was notable in Germany, too. Attempts to cooperate had begun during World War I, and intensified after the Balfour Declaration and Germany's statement of support in early 1918. Thanks to this statement, the political prestige of the Zionists was enhanced and the non-Zionists were freed from concern that favoring a Jewish national home might be misconstrued as disloyalty to Germany. Efforts to create a framework for pan-Jewish collaboration in anticipation of the Peace Conference did not bear fruit.[1] However, the moment economic aid to

1   See Chapter Two, and notes 9, 10 and 11 there.

Palestine rose to the top of the Zionist agenda, a basis for an alliance was created. For both Zionists and non-Zionists, economic cooperation was a solution that was politically and ideologically safe. In May 1918, *Pro Palästina – Deutsches Komitee zur Förderung der jüdischen Palästinasiedlung* (German Committee for Promoting Jewish Settlement in Palestine) was established with the backing of the German government. Its role was to draw public attention to the political significance of Zionist settlement in Palestine, but it also gave a special boost to the joint endeavors of Zionists and non-Zionists.[2]

However, it soon became clear – and not in Germany alone – that any organ-izational attempt to cooperate necessitated certain decisions on the ideological plane. The two sides were forced to reach some agreement on the political definition of the Jewish people, the role of the Zionist movement, the meaning of a Jewish national home, and its priority on the list of Jewish and Zionist concerns. The participation of non-Zionists thus became a pivotal issue in the reorganization of the Zionist camp as it prepared for its new mission in Palestine.

This possibility was thoroughly explored at the August 1919 meeting in London of the Zionist Actions Committee, which was devoted to the subject of a Jewish Council. Britain had expressed an interest in a body representing the Jewish people as a whole with which it could consult on all matters pertaining to the Jewish national home. On the committee agenda were questions such as how to go about setting up a council of this type, who would belong to it, how it would operate, and what kind of effect its existence would have on the Zionist Organization. The American Zionist leader and Supreme Court Justice Louis D. Brandeis, proposed that the Zionists open their door to all Jews prepared to take part in the development of Palestine, thereby turning the Zionist Organization itself into a Jewish Council. Brandeis's suggestion was based on the view that the Zionist movement had already fulfilled the political function that distinguished it from other Zion-oriented Jewish groups, and the one goal that remained was the actual building of the national home. Supporters of this approach felt that articulating the desire to participate in this enterprise was sufficient to qualify for membership in the movement. Moreover, as this was the only goal shared by all nationally-committed Jews, there would be no difference between the Zionist Organization and the proposed Jewish Council.

---

2 *JR*, May 3, 1918: 133–4; Hantke's letter to Warburg, May 24, 1918, Schocken Archives, 531/241.

Brandeis was opposed by most of the European Zionist leadership, and especially Chaim Weizmann, the rising star of the WZO. The European leaders also aspired to involve as many Jews as possible in the building of Palestine, but they were not willing to pay the price of reducing the scope of the Zionist movement and limiting its purpose to the settlement enterprise. Nor did they agree that a Jewish homeland, with all its centrality in Jewish national consciousness, was the single common goal. In contrast to Brandeis they demanded that the Zionist Organization remain a separate entity. The Jewish Council would speak for the Jewish people on matters pertaining to the national home, but it would be headed by the Zionist Organization. This would achieve three goals: preserving the special identity of the Zionist Organization as a national movement, allowing a wide spectrum of Jews to share in the development of Palestine, and insuring that the Jewish Council acted in the spirit of the national-social aspirations of the Zionist establishment. The European leaders believed that in time, such an approach would pave the way for yet another goal, namely the birth of a Jewish nation under Zionist leadership. The Jewish Council, led by the Zionist Organization, would thus become the mouthpiece and guide of the greater Jewish community in all spheres of national activity.

Although the conflict between the Weizmann and Brandeis camps reached its full proportions in the summer of 1919, it remained unresolved in light of the British Government's recognition of the Zionist Organization as the "Jewish Agency for Palestine." This temporary arrangement filled in for the lack of a global Jewish authority to handle liaison with Britain and the League of Nations, and was written into the British Mandate. As a result, non-Zionist participation, in which both camps were interested, also remained an open question. It was clear to all that the non-Zionists would not join the movement in its radical nationalist form and that alternative frameworks were needed. As time passed and the magnitude of the economic need in Palestine became apparent, the Zionist leadership realized the importance of attracting Jewish capital from every possible source, Zionist or not.

The idea of amassing a sizeable body of national capital only increased their interest in the non-Zionists. The national financial instrument they envisaged would wield considerable power and be able to steer the country in the desired direction, socially as well as economically. This was more than the Zionist Organization could manage on its own, and there was a growing sense that the non-Zionists could fill the void. This approach was already embodied in the first financial programs drawn up by the economists of the Zionist movement. Arthur Ruppin's Colonization Company, Julius Simon's bank credit proposal and the national loan schemes discussed by the Greater Actions Committee in

February 1920 were all based on a mobilization of national capital from non-Zionist sources. When it was decided to replace these business-oriented programs with the establishment of *Keren Hayesod*, the Zionist movement was not retreating from the idea of economic cooperation under its aegis. Its intention was to harness Jewish financial power without relinquishing the Zionist goals that transcended the settlement enterprise.

Keren Hayesod had a two-fold aim: public financing and pushing Palestine to the top of the Zionist agenda, and on the other hand, establishing a framework that could absorb non-Zionist capital and encourage entrepreneurship under Zionist auspices. However, the Annual Conference in London in July 1920 reached its decisions without working through all the problems involved. Thus *Keren Hayesod* became a bone of contention that seriously rocked the Zionist movement and delayed the beginning of Zionist activity in Palestine.

One question was whether the development of the Jewish national home was a *raison d'être* or merely a stage, however vital, in the attainment of a higher goal – the political, social, and cultural revival of the Jewish people. The founders of *Keren Hayesod* supported the latter view. For them, *Keren Hayesod* was a framework for economic cooperation without making this aspect the "be all and end all" of the Zionist program. Hence the reawakened debate with the Brandeis faction which maintained that the building of Palestine was the sole purpose of the Zionist Organization and that a separate apparatus was superfluous. This issue lay at the heart of the "Brandeis-Weizmann controversy" that erupted in full force after the formal establishment of *Keren Hayesod* in July 1920.[3]

A second question was the priority of *Palästinaarbeit* (Palestine-oriented work) as opposed to *Gegenwartsarbeit* ("here-and-now" activity in the Diaspora). The climate in the Weizmann group was such that the question did not come up for deliberation and no theoretical position was formulated, although in practice, Palestine was indeed afforded top priority. As far as Brandeis was concerned, there was no need to even ask. In his view, all affairs not directly connected to Palestine simply had no place on the Zionist agenda. However, for the veteran leaders of the German Zionist movement, the concepts of *Palästinaarbeit* and *Gegenwartsarbeit* had been highly pertinent long before the creation of the *Keren Hayesod*.

---

3   Metzer, *National Capital*, 102–27. There is a wealth of literature dealing with this controversy, but it is still far from complete. See Ben Halpern, *A Clash of Heroes – Brandeis, Weizmann and American Zionism* (New York and Oxford, 1987) and the bibliography there.

The Challenge: *Palästinaarbeit* or *Gegenwartsarbeit*

In Germany, the radical Palestine-oriented school was solidly entrenched by the end of the war, but the legitimacy of Diaspora-oriented activity was still under debate. Until *Keren Hayesod* was founded, this matter was overshadowed by the excitement generated by the newly-opened possibilities in Palestine.

In principle, *Keren Hayesod* was a means of mobilizing all Jews on behalf of the Jewish national home, but it was inevitable that cooperation in other areas would be considered. Predicated on the idea that the Jewish people had common objectives beyond the creation of the national home, the Zionist movement was now confronted with the task of defining these objectives and drawing up a plan of action. However, the implicit assumption behind the establishment of *Keren Hayesod* was that anything beyond the settlement enterprise was outside the framework of Zionist-Jewish cooperation. This was unacceptable to those who attached importance to the Zionist role in the Diaspora. They saw in the Balfour Declaration a tremendous achievement in that it invested the Zionist movement with much-sought legitimacy and lay the groundwork for collaboration between Zionists and non-Zionists. By limiting this partnership to a single sphere, *Keren Hayesod* would be diminishing the vast potential of the new situation and the likelihood of friction between different Jewish groups.

These concerns were first voiced in the spring of 1920 resulting in the idea of *Keren Hayesod* and the Palestinocentrists being branded "radical" for their support of *Entwurzelung* – uprooting the Jews from their Diaspora environment. In the eyes of the older Zionist leaders, *Entwurzelung* posed a threat to Jewish existence in Germany and undermined efforts to disseminate Jewish education and Zionism.[4]

This opposition to Palestinocentrism led to an upheaval in the German Zionist movement. On the agenda of the 16th convention held in Berlin in June 1920 was the completion of an economic program for the building of Palestine to be submitted at the Annual Zionist Conference in London, and the formulation of a plan of action to be followed by the German Zionists. Instead, preconvention activities and the convention itself became a battleground for the dispute over Zionist activity in the Diaspora, pushing all matters pertaining to Palestine aside. Personal forces were also involved. Arthur

4   See articles by Gotthold Weil and Arno Wagner in *JR*, February 27, 1920: 107–8, and March 3, 1920: 146–7; and responses of Walter Preuss and Moritz Bileski in *JR*, February 31, 1920: 156–7, and May 18, 1920: 243.

Hantke, the chairman of the ZVfD and a leader of the Palestine-oriented radical trend, had been called to London early that year to help draw up the plans for *Keren Hayesod*. His place was filled by Alfred Klee, a proponent of Herzlian Zionism and *Gegenwartsarbeit*, and one of the founders of the *Jüdische Volkspartei*, who saw Jewish communal politics as a primary concern of the Zionist movement.[5]

The result was a division of the German Zionist movement into political factions. In preparation for the 16th convention, factional lists were put together and the Berlin delegates were chosen by political affiliation and platforms rather than on a personal basis as in other German cities. As the hub of the German Zionist movement, these developments in Berlin could not fail to radiate outwards. Eventually the entire German Zionist movement became factionalized. The chief groups, in addition to the longstanding *Hapoel Hatzair*, were the *Freie Zionistische Gruppe* (Free Zionist Group) and *Zionei Zion* (Zionists of Zion).[6]

The strongest challenge to the radical front was presented by the *Freie Zionistische Gruppe* headed by Professor Gotthold Weil, who had not achieved prominence until that time. His list for the Berlin elections comprised 15 candidates, none of them leading personalities, but it was common knowledge that this faction enjoyed the backing of Alfred Klee.[7]

The *Freie Zionistische Gruppe* constituted the first step toward the formation of a strong opposition in Germany, and therein lay its importance. This faction held that Palestine was merely one component of a national historical-cultural endeavor to unite the Jewish people. Alongside its work on behalf of the Jewish national home, it was felt that the Zionist movement had an obligation to consider the needs of Diaspora Jews and to shape its Zionist activity accordingly, especially in the field of education. Rather than concentrating exclusively on Palestine and the training of pioneers, this faction called upon the movement to work toward greater self-awareness in the Jewish community and the dissemination of Jewish culture and history. Special emphasis was also placed on gaining the upper hand in Jewish communal politics and conducting community affairs in the spirit of Jewish nationalism. In theory, the *Freie Zionistische Gruppe* gave equal weight to *Palästinaarbeit* and *Gegenwartsarbeit*. In practice, however, activity in the Diaspora was accentuated, and Palestine

5   See Chapter Two. On Hantke's transfer to London and his replacement by Klee, see *JR*, January 16, 1920: 21.

6   Full details in *JR*, June 1, 1920, June 11, 1920, June 17, 1920, July 13, 1920.

7   Founding conference, list of candidates and platform in *JR*, June 1, 1920: 276, June 4, 1920: 283.

was relegated to the sidelines. Its educational platform, for example, made no mention of pioneer training, stressing instead pan-Jewish cooperation, particularly in the cultivation of Jewish self-esteem and the fight against antisemitism.

The *Freie Zionistische Gruppe* challenged another aspect of Palestine-oriented radicalism – the idea that the enterprise in Palestine should be guided by national and social principles beyond the political program adopted at the First Zionist Congress, in Basel, in 1897. As a proponent of political Zionism, this faction maintained that the essence of the Zionist revolution lay in the recognition of a Jewish national entity and the political end this entailed.

The criticism of the *Freie Zionistische Gruppe* was thus directed against all facets of radical Zionism, setting it apart from the majority view and placing it at the farthest end of the opposition camp despite the open support of Alfred Klee. As the most salient expression of traditional German Zionism versus the new radical school, it roused the German Zionists from their silence on the question of Diaspora activity, and forced the Palestinocentrists to formulate a clearer position.

The chief spokesmen of the radicals was *Hapoel Hatzair*. As we have seen, *Hapoel Hatzair* enjoyed great prestige among the German Zionists at the time, and its leadership submitted the radical program for the development of Palestine adopted by the ZVfD.

Indeed, *Hapoel Hatzair*'s approach to Diaspora activity was a logical outgrowth of Palestine-oriented radicalism. If the Zionist goal in Palestine was the creation of a just society based on cooperative enterprise and the centrality of the worker, especially farmers, then Zionist endeavors in the Diaspora should revolve around preparation for pioneering settlement and Hebrew language instruction. This was the spirit in which work was carried out among the East-European immigrants in Germany. Even the non-Zionists were called upon to support the establishment of a new society in Palestine. Any Diaspora activity that was not directly related to Palestine was frowned upon.[8]

However, despite the logic of its approach and its prestigiousness, *Hapoel Hatzair* failed to provide a satisfactory answer to the *Freie Zionistische Gruppe* because its position was an extreme one, implying a total break between German Zionists of the old and new schools. The traditional Diaspora orientation remained deeply-rooted in Germany even among those groups that willingly supported the radicalization process. One of them was the *Jung-zionistische Gruppe* (Young Zionists Group), headed by two former *Blau-Weiss*

---

8   List of candidates and platform in *JR*, June 1, 1920: 276, June 4, 1920: 283; interview with Robert Weltsch, February 21, 1980, OHD. See also Chapter Two.

leaders, Walter Moses and Georg Strauss. Moses and Strauss had been highly successful in motivating and training young people for *aliya*, and later established factories in Palestine (in the 1920s Strauss organized the *Blau-Weiss* workshops and Moses was a founding partner of the Dubek cigarette factory). Nevertheless, the faction they created, which joined forces with *Hapoel Hatzair* prior to the 16th convention elections, was not as forthright as *Hapoel Hatzair* in rejecting Diaspora pursuits unrelated to *aliya*. The *Jungzionistische Gruppe* platform stated:

> The central idea of this faction is the national revival of the Jewish people and the upholding of radical nationalism as the nerve center of Zionism.... At the same time, it also regards Zionism as the renewal of each human being...and sees the focal point of Zionist activity in Germany in the education of young people, who must be recruited as early as possible for the Zionist cause. The ultimate purpose of education is to create a person who synthesizes ideology and life, and devotes himself to the service of his people. To implement this educational work we must...cultivate Hebrew culture and provide vocational training for youth in accordance with the needs of both Palestine and the Diaspora. The faction advocates the development of cultural institutions, settlements that support themselves through crafts and agriculture, and institutions that foster social life – all of them national endeavors that will strengthen independent Jewish existence in the Diaspora....[9]

The emphasis, then, was on educating individual Zionists without necessarily directing them toward Palestine.

But the ZVfD still sought to formulate its goals in a way that would accord with the Palestine-oriented approach without running counter to the traditions of German Zionism. At the same time the leaders of the growing radical trend had to take heed lest the Zionist movement become a narrow sect and block the avenues for Jewish cooperation on behalf of Palestine.

The attempt to mediate between the two extremes was undertaken by a group called *Zionei Zion*. Heading this faction were Heinrich Loewe, a veteran Zionist and member of *Hovevei Zion*, and his brother-in-law Elias Auerbach, who had served as a physician in Haifa before the war, and returned to

---

9   *JR*, June 8, 1920: 291.

Germany to serve in the army. Also espousing the *Zionei Zion* position was Julius Berger, one of the early advocates of *Keren Hayesod* who became the director of its Department for Central Europe in Berlin and emigrated to Palestine in 1924 as an executive of the JNF. *Zionei Zion* perceived *Keren Hayesod* as a bridge between *Palästinaarbeit* and *Gegenwartsarbeit* on the grounds that it had the potential to rally Diaspora Jewry around a common aim. It was felt that the propaganda and fundraising activities sponsored by this fund would foster ties between Diaspora Jews and Palestine, and consequently strengthen Jewish life in the Diaspora. Paradoxically, to gain greater Jewish participation in the building of Palestine, it was imperative that Jewish life in the Diaspora enjoy the legitimacy that the Palestinocentric goals threatened to negate. This was the point made by Julius Berger in his speech at the 16th German Zionist convention. He maintained that Diaspora Jews should not be looked down upon as inferiors even if they did not emigrate to Palestine, and that assisting the development of the Jewish national home was a worthy cause for Jews wherever their place of residence. The scope of *Palästinaarbeit* would thus be broadened to embrace all Zionist work in the Diaspora:

> We must grasp concretely that what we do for Palestine is for the sake of the Jewish people, and that it is the people as a whole to whom we turn. In consequence, the entire nation will be strengthened...and the great ideal of national unity with Palestine at the center, will approach realization. The importance of this lies in the fact that it encompasses all of world Jewry. The moment this is understood, the people will see that we are speaking of a matter vital to their very existence.... We are completely convinced that wherever Jews live, they will be satisfied as Jews only under a national flag....[10]

The roots of this view lay deep in the heart of German Zionism. In Germany, Zionism was first and foremost an expression of national awareness; the role of the Zionist movement was to foster this awareness and cultivate the kind of Jewish life that would win respect in the eyes of both Jews and those around them. *Zionei Zion* shared the *Freie Zionistische Gruppe* view of Jewish national life in the Diaspora as totally legitimate. Zionist activism outside Palestine was not a temporary preoccupation that would end with the establishment of a

---

10 *JR*, June 29, 1920: 333. Platform presented in *JR*, June 4, 1920: 283.

Jewish homeland. On the contrary, it was part and parcel of the national ideal itself. *Zionei Zion* and the *Freie Zionistische Gruppe* further concurred on the practical side of *Gegenwartsarbeit*. Both groups believed it should extend to all sectors of Jewish life, including education, culture and local politics.

Despite this common ground, the two factions differed in their points of departure and ultimate goals. The *Freie Zionistische Gruppe* was entrenched in the pre-war German Zionist tradition that sought to preserve Zionism as a form of Jewish identity. Its members had no intention of allowing the new possibilities in Palestine to detract from the serenity and self-confidence they had built up as proud Jews in the Diaspora. They were pleased with the turn of events after the Balfour Declaration because it brought them closer to their longstanding desire for the acceptance of Jewish nationalism by Jews and non-Jews alike. Here was an unprecedented opportunity to unify all the groups that had hitherto fought vehemently against Zionism, and even gain control of the leadership. It was feared that this could be sabotaged by growing radicalism. They were particularly apprehensive about *Keren Hayesod* restricting the co-operation between Zionists and non-Zionists to the Palestine issue, and the possible jeopardy to the political achievements of the Jews in their countries of residence as well as the Zionists' standing within the Jewish community. The platform of the *Freie Zionistische Gruppe* thus emphasized the loyalty to one's country of origin and dispelled any doubt as to the Zionist movement's right to lead the Jewish people in its dispersion.[11]

For *Zionei Zion*, the point of departure was the radicalization of German Zionism as Palestine became the pivot of the Zionist program. *Zionei Zion* sought to integrate this new emphasis with the traditional approach. Palestine would give Diaspora activity the justification and direction it needed, and confirm the status of the Zionist movement as the rightful leader of the Jewish people. In consequence, the Jews of the Diaspora would be stimulated to take part in the building of Palestine using *Keren Hayesod* as their channel. *Zionei Zion* recognized that Palestine would not put an end to Jewish life elsewhere and that delegitimizing the Diaspora would only antagonize the non-Zionists, obviating any joint endeavor. Thus *Zionei Zion*'s point of departure was closely related to its objective, with *Keren Hayesod* as the connecting link. The idea was to direct attention toward Palestine and achieve momentum through comprehensive Jewish cooperation. The *Zionei Zion* platform, then, was built

---

11   See articles by Weil, Wagner, and Holdheim in *JR*, February 27, 1920, March 26, 1920, and June 4, 1920 respectively; Weltsch's letter to Bergman, February 25, 1921, NULA, 1502/1334/2.

on mutuality: Zionist activism on behalf of the Diaspora Jews with the ultimate aim of involving them in the realization of the national home.

It was this approach that resolved the German Zionist dilemma. *Zionei Zion* had found a formula that retained traditional tendencies while greatly narrowing the gap between the extremes represented by *Hapoel Hatzair* and the *Freie Zionistische Gruppe*. This formula enabled the Zionists to take full advantage of the dramatic opportunities created by the Balfour Declaration, on the one hand enhancing their standing in the Diaspora, and on the other, establishing global Jewish cooperation in the development of Palestine.

The *Zionei Zion* platform even won the approval of Richard Lichtheim, one of the fathers of Palestinocentrism in the Zionist movement. At the 16th German Zionist convention, he spoke at length on this issue, and openly endorsed the views of this faction over those of *Hapoel Hatzair*:

> Transcending the apparent conflict, there is a force which unites Palestine and the Diaspora and is represented by Zionism. This unifying force is embodied in the national desire...to create a Jewish Palestine.... To continue harboring this desire despite the opposition in the Diaspora, as a bulwark against natural or intentional assimilation and a response to antisemitism and persecution, in the face of all obstacles posed by the world around us, is only possible for the Jew who perceives the Jewish national goal as more important than all other worldly ties and associations. This is what has been called radical Zionism. It is the genuine antithesis to assimilation and to all those who are uncomfortable with the emphasis on national feeling, who can never be brought over entirely to the cause of a Jewish Palestine. Everyone accepts that this cause is naturally espoused by those who plan to live in Jewish Palestine. But we Zionists also carry this banner in the Diaspora. Otherwise, Zionism would not be a true movement engaging one's entire being, but only a kind of "philo- Zionism".... The presumption behind all Zionist activity in the Diaspora is that Jewishness takes precedence over all other spiritual and moral ties between the Jew and his environment. Here, as in Palestine, the Zionist lives for the rebirth of the Jewish people....[12]

---

12 *JR*, June 29, 1920: 329–32.

The resolutions adopted by the Berlin convention were in three different areas. First, there were a number of decisions on administrative matters, culture, pioneer training, and education, thereby illustrating the importance attributed to *Gegenwartsarbeit*, albeit on a limited scale, exclusive of communal politics. Secondly, a new, two-man executive was chosen. The previous chairman, Alfred Klee, stayed on as the representative of the traditional approach, and Felix Rosenblüth was elected as a proponent of the new radical line. This was an acknowledgement of the differences in the German Zionist movement, but it also reflected a certain lack of confidence in Klee. Indeed, not long afterward Klee resigned from the chairmanship of the ZVfD to devote himself fully to what he saw as the essence of Zionist activity, namely amassing political support in the Jewish communities and organizations. Thirdly, delegates were nominated for the Annual Zionist Conference in London where the Zionists planned to discuss ways and means of developing Palestine. Most of the delegates belonged to the new, Palestine-oriented camp, among them Richard Lichtheim, Kurt Blumenfeld, Chaim Arlosoroff, and Walter Moses.[13]

The Berlin convention thus marked the end of efforts to return the German Zionist movement back to the old, Diaspora-oriented mode. However, the struggle of the radical Zionists was far from over.

Confronting the *Binyan Haaretz* Faction

The radical Zionists' fight against the traditional school did not end with the Diaspora issue. The Annual Zionist Conference in July 1920 adopted a series of resolutions on settlement in Palestine that revolved mainly around the JNF's land-acquisition policy and the establishment of *Keren Hayesod*. The building of the national home was declared paramount and it was hoped that non-Zionists would also help to shoulder the burden under the auspices and leadership of the Zionist movement. In other words, these resolutions embodied the tenets of radical Zionism, to which the opposition in Germany objected with all its strength.

Nevertheless, for the next six months the German opposition refrained from speaking out against either radical Zionism or *Keren Hayesod*. The *Freie Zionistische Gruppe* continued to exist and let its voice be heard on certain issues, but the main topic was pointedly skirted. During this same interval, the

---

13 Various resolutions in *JR*, June 23, 1920, June 26, 1920, and August 3, 1920.

founders of *Keren Hayesod*, headed by Weizmann, were locked in a fierce draw with the American opposition led by Brandeis. The reverberations of this dispute reached Germany, but the matter was treated as a general Zionist problem rather than one which directly concerned the Jews of Germany.[14] Meanwhile, the German Zionists of the radical camp were intensively preparing to activate the *Keren Hayesod*.

This silence on the part of the German opposition was the calm before the storm. The first signs of the approaching gale were Alfred Klee's resignation from the chairmanship of the ZVfD and his affiliation with the *Freie Zionistische Gruppe*.[15] However, two more months passed before the actual cloudburst. It is unclear whether this pause was due to a last minute vacillation of the opposition or a sudden notion that it was best to allow the radicals to pursue their goal of Jewish cooperation as they saw fit. In any event, the opposition leaders finally declared their intention of forming a new party, citing their disillusionment with being able to exert influence from within and their dissatisfaction with the path taken by *Keren Hayesod* since its inception. Despite the points of agreement between them, they did not coordinate the breakaway with Brandeis and the American opposition, but rather saw themselves as a direct continuation of the *Freie Zionistische Gruppe* in Germany.

On March 23, 1921, members of the *Freie Zionistische Gruppe* and other long-standing Zionists met in Berlin to organize the establishment of a new Zionist federation. A few weeks later, *Binyan Haaretz* ("Building the Land") was born.[16]

Unlike the *Freie Zionistische Gruppe*, *Binyan Haaretz* attracted a long line of prominent figures in the Zionist movement. Professor Karl Lewin, Professor Gotthold Weil and Arno Wagner of the *Freie Zionistische Gruppe* were joined by Max Bodenheimer, Adolph Friedemann, Alfred Klee, Eduard Leszynsky, Izaak Zwirn, and Max Kollenscher. Before the war, Kollenscher, a lawyer by profession, had been a Jewish community leader and an active Zionist in Posen. When this city was placed under Polish sovereignty, he moved to Berlin and resumed his Zionist activities, becoming the moving spirit behind *Binyan*

---

14 Many editorials and articles on this issue appeared in the *JR* between August 1920 and January 1921, and especially in October and November 1920. It was also discussed at length in the *Landesvorstand* (National Leadership consisting of the *Zentralkomitee* and the *Geschäftsführender Ausschuß* (executive Committee). See minutes of January 9-10, 1921, CZA, KH2/3/1.

15 *Landesvorstand* minutes, January 5, 1921, CZA, KH2/3/1.

16 Circular issued by the preparatory committee, February 22, 1921, CZA, KH2/27/1; *JR*, March 15, 1921: 146, and April 8, 1921: 193.

Haaretz and later an outspoken member of the right-wing general Zionist camp. On the founding committee of *Binyan Haaretz* there were also veteran Jewish community leaders such as Professor Julius Zitron and Gustav Witkowski of Berlin, whose involvement in this faction marked the end of a long Zionist career. Another member was Georg Kareski, also from Posen, a staunch supporter of the *Jüdische Volkspartei* who later became the head of the Berlin Jewish community and an active Revisionist.

While *Binyan Haaretz* presented itself as the heir of the *Freie Zionistische Gruppe* negating radical Zionism and claiming a place among the Herzlian Zionists, its positions were also shaped by disappointment with *Keren Hayesod* and the controversy sparked by the Brandeis group in America. Unlike its predecessor, *Binyan Haaretz* also constituted a serious threat to the unity and integrity of the ZVfD.

Binyan Haaretz differed from the *Freie Zionistische Gruppe* in attaching more weight to the essence of the Zionist objective in Palestine than to Jewish nationalism in the Diaspora. Zionism was perceived as a political movement geared to creating a Jewish political entity in Palestine – a goal achieved by the Balfour Declaration, the San Remo Conference in April 1920 at which Great Britain received the Palestine Mandate, and the inauguration in Palestine of a British civil administration. With these developments, the Zionist movement had completed its first phase and entered the second, namely large-scale settlement based on solid international recognition. It was this recognition that made the building of the national home the legitimate concern of the entire Jewish people, thus setting the stage for pan-Jewish cooperation. Once the Zionist movement's exclusive political mission was accomplished and its practical work in Palestine became the affair of all Jews, there would no longer be a barrier between Zionists and non-Zionists. Jewish nationalism was no less than a political fact, turning the dream of a Jewish Palestine into a valid pursuit rooted in a new reality. *Binyan Haaretz* maintained that the time had come to tear down whatever fences remained so that all Jews could collaborate on the development of Palestine and the Zionist Organization could become a world Jewish institution able to devote itself to this undertaking without jeopardizing Jewish interests elsewhere.

This approach was the absolute antithesis of radical Zionism. *Binyan Haaretz* accused the radicals of sowing diversity among Jews through their insistence that every member of the Zionist movement participate in the building of Palestine as a personal obligation. In its original, political form, the Zionist movement sanctioned Jewish nationalism in the Diaspora and granted it equal status to Palestine-oriented activity. Another counter-productive demand was that the national home be shaped according to social and political theories that did not emanate directly from the Zionist idea and were not prerequisites for its realization. Nothing in the Basel Program stipulated that Zionism was a movement for social and cultural revival, and the national home merely a framework. Zionism was not the purveyor of a social ideology, socialist or otherwise, nor did it bear a unique cultural message. It was felt that Jewish tradition could amply provide cultural distinctiveness and assure social justice. All the radical demands were appendages to the original Zionist idea, and their sole effect was to replace the former political divisions with others that could continue to provoke and create rifts at the very moment when it was most critical to work together. Political and practical Zionism enabled the Jews to participate en masse in the task of the hour, whereas the radical approach blocked cooperation and posed a threat to the successful building of the national home.

Binyan Haaretz held that eliminating all extraneous demands would facilitate concentration on the development of Palestine itself. Most Jews would be quite willing to share in the burden if there were no ideological strings attached. It was up to the Zionist movement to organize the economic dimension and to employ efficiency as its only guide. Abortive socialist experiments would thus be discouraged, and private enterprise would be promoted instead, through the help of *Keren Hayesod. Binyan Haaretz* insisted that this institution lay the foundations for economic initiative in such a way that it would appeal to all Jews and none would be turned away on the ground that they did not conform to a certain social ideology.[17]

Binyan Haaretz was thus the direct heir of the *Freie Zionistische Gruppe*. Both groups held that the Zionist movement had completed its task in the realm of internal politics and should utilize external political achievements to promote a unified Jewish action. They also maintained that Palestine should not be the sole focus of such action. However, the emphasis in *Binyan Haaretz* leaned very strongly towards *Palästinaarbeit*.

In its publicity, *Binyan Haaretz* stressed its support of private enterprise and opposition to the socialist or quasi-socialist elements of radical Zionism. To some members of *Binyan Haaretz* this was the very cornerstone of the group's philosophy, which was not surprising in view of the fact that most of its affiliates were bourgeois Zionists of the older generation, whereas the radical

---

17 Circular in note 16 above; programmatic articles by Kollenscher and Freundlich in *JR*, March 30, 1921, and May 13, 1921; "Was will Binjan Haarez," *Mitteilungsblatt des Binjan Haarez* 1, no. 1 (May 1921); Gustav Witkowski, *Die Krise im Zionismus* (Bonn, 1921).

position appealed chiefly to young people who espoused socialism and belonged to the Zionist labor movement. Furthermore, the WZO's post-war economic involvement in Palestine was bound up with the cooperative program of the labor movement. Economic failures could thus be blamed on "socialist experiments," and the radical Zionist objective of creating a new social order. As a result, criticism of *Keren Hayesod* and the economic endeavors of the WZO was closely intertwined with opposition to socialism.[18]

Insofar as practical conclusions were concerned, *Binyan Haaretz* joined the Brandeis group in calling for an alternative economic structure to replace the centralized format of *Keren Hayesod*. Instead, *Binyan Haaretz* proposed individual investment companies that would operate according to business principles and receive only general guidelines from a higher Zionist authority.[19]

Binyan Haaretz presented radical Zionism with a political and ideological challenge of the first order. Aside from its prestigious membership, the platform of this faction was very attractive to veteran German Zionists and created a viable alternative to the existing leadership. All the more strength was gained by coordinating positions with the American opposition, whose battle against Weizmann and *Keren Hayesod* reached a climax in the spring of 1921. *Binyan Haaretz* also demanded recognition as a party independent of the ZVfD, and from its earliest days embarked on a series of informative and political activities that specifically addressed the non-Zionists and aspired to create a substitute for *Keren Hayesod*. This took place just as the *Keren Hayesod* began to operate in Germany and negotiations to gain the cooperation of the non-Zionists were underway. The competition posed by *Binyan Haaretz* thus threatened to halt the progress made by existing leadership.[20]

The radical Zionists' response to *Binyan Haaretz* was the *Nationaler Einheitsblock* (National Unity Bloc), which brought together the organizations behind the radical trend, *Hapoel Hatzair* and the *Kartell Jüdischer Verbindungen*. Among its leaders were Kurt Blumenfeld, Arthur Hantke, Richard Lichtheim, and Felix Rosenblüth, and other central figures such as the lawyer Fritz Loewenstein, a Zionist student leader who immigrated to Palestine in 1924; the

---

18 Max Bodenheimer, "Eine Fraktion des zionistischen Bürgertums," *JR*, April 15, 1921: 207.

19 Max Kollenscher, *Ein Wort an den 12. Zionisten-Kongress* (Berlin, 1921).

20 The subject of negotiations with the non-Zionists was extensively discussed in internal correspondence, CZA, KH2/24, and in the *Landesvorstand*, May 29, 1921 and June 9, 1921, Schocken Archives, 531/32. See also *Binyan Haaretz* circular of June 10, 1921, Schocken Archives, 538/4; and Chapter Five.

lawyer Salli Hirsch, a staunch supporter of Kurt Blumenfeld; Egon Rosenberg, a founder of the *Hasmonaea* student society established in Berlin in 1903; and the lawyer Siegfried Moses, who began his career in the *Nationaler Einheits-block* and went on later to head the ZVfD until he moved to Palestine in 1937, and became the first State Comptroller.[21]

On the theoretical plane, the establishment of the *Nationaler Einheitsblock* led to a clear formulation of the radical Zionist ideology and its implications for the Jews of the Diaspora. Confronted with the questions of Zionism's special mission once the building of Palestine became a reality and within reach of every Jew, the *Nationaler Einheitsblock* focused the spotlight on Jewish national spirit:

> We are fighting for the rebirth of the Jewish nation, a mission in which most non-Zionists are unable to participate. Without our distinctive national spirit, we might as well commit suicide. The Zionist Organization is an institutionalized expression of the national desire to solve the Jewish question in Palestine.... National policy is something which never ends.[22]

The radicals maintained that it was the power of nationalism borne aloft by the Zionist movement that would lead to victory in Palestine in the realms of politics, education and settlement. All the movement's political achievements to date could be attributed to this power. Even if the external battle was over, Zionism was not defunct. On the contrary, to put the Basel Program into effect, it was necessary to find persons who were personally committed to the national endeavor. The new Zionist mission thus lay in education. Only a movement fired by national, political and social ideals could make demands on people and inspire the younger generation to seek fulfillment through settlement in Palestine. The Zionist movement would supply the link between the traditional love of *Eretz Israel* and the urge to leave the Diaspora by devoting itself to education, which was the preparation for *aliya*. The *Nationaler Einheitsblock* charged that *Binyan Haaretz*, with its concern for efficient economic organization and neutral "platonic" approach which shied away from

---

21 Announcement, *JR*, March 15, 1921: 146; official letter of Fritz Loewenstein, March 3, 1921, Schocken Archives, 538/5; circular of preparatory committee, March 1921, LBIA, 7185/4/1.

22 Lichtheim's speech at the 17th ZVfD convention, *JR*, May 17, 1921: 273-5.

personal demands on the Diaspora Jews, would never bring people to uproot themselves and immigrate.[23]

To be sure, the national home could not materialize without global Jewish cooperation of major proportions. But it was self-deceptive to imagine that such cooperation could be won by giving up the national ardor – the best weapon in the Zionist arsenal. It was undiluted authentic Zionism that would motivate non-Zionist Jews to lend a hand. The Zionist passion would have a positive influence on Jewish life that would be impossible to ignore. The first step to engaging the partnership of others was one's own resolve. By making ideological compromises, it was felt that *Binyan Haaretz* was liable to achieve the very opposite effect and drive the non-Zionists away. As Kurt Blumenfeld put it, "If we chase them, they will run away. If we walk ahead, they will run after us."[24]

How would the self-strengthening of the national movement generate the desired cooperation? The answer of the radical Zionists lay in the idea of the *Bündnis* (covenant), which would serve as a bridge that linked Zionists and non-Zionists, but did not compromise their separate identities. If Zionist aspirations in Palestine were national-political and the time-honored Jewish bond was religious, the possibilities opening up in Palestine established a convergence between the political and the traditional. In practical terms, this meant that numerous areas of cooperation were conceivable between the Zionist movement and other Jewish elements interested in building the land. It was here that the *Bündnis* concept would be integrated, but in such a way that the Zionist movement would be distinct from the cooperative mechanism. The idea was that *Keren Hayesod* would operate as a separate body and bring together sectors of the Jewish public without impinging on the political character of the Zionist movement. This *Bündnispolitik* was the brainchild of Kurt Blumenfeld, who had outlined the main points in 1917 when the idea of a joint organizational framework for German Jewry was under discussion. Blumenfeld's program was now perfected and incorporated as an integral part of radical Zionism. *Bündnispolitik* allowed the Zionist movement to pursue educational activities, foster a partnership with non-Zionists and steer development in Palestine as it saw fit. The Zionist Organization, as distinct from the *Bündnis* apparatus, would assume responsibility for the Jewish national home.

---

23 Circular of March 1921 and the program of the *Nationaler Einheitsblock*, LBIA, 7185/4/1; speeches of Blumenfeld and F. Rosenblüth at the 17th convention, *JR*, May 17, 1921; and article by Landauer, *JR*, April 27, 1921: 233–4.

24 *JR*, May 17, 1921: 280.

As Blumenfeld pointed out: "The corollary of *Bündnispolitik* is the true radicalization of Zionism."[25]

The *Nationaler Einheitsblock* claimed that *Binyan Haaretz* threatened the existence of the Zionist movement. It reasoned that the loss of the movement's national political character would spell the end of the Jewish national home. However, virtually nothing was said about the nature of the national home or the strategies for building it. The ideological debate revolved entirely around the significance of radical Zionism in the Diaspora, the movement's educational role, and the desired relationship with the non-Zionists.

Paradoxically, then, the challenge of *Binyan Haaretz* helped to hone radical Zionist policy and shape *Keren Hayesod* as an instrument for work not only in Palestine, as originally envisaged, but also in the Diaspora. By incorporating *Keren Hayesod* in the fabric of radical Zionism, the *Nationaler Einheitsblock* became the standard-bearer of *Keren Hayesod* in the world Zionist arena.

The political confrontation was particularly fierce in light of the *Binyan Haaretz* attempt to free itself from the shackles of the ZVfD and against the actions already undertaken in rivalry with the elected ZVfD leadership. It was feared that as an independent faction, *Binyan Haaretz* would join the American Brandeis group and create together an opposition within the WZO powerful enough to unseat Weizmann. Immediately upon establishment, the *Nationaler Einheitsblock* defined its primary goal as upholding the unity of ZVfD and the authority of its elected bodies. The objective was to establish a united front of all German Zionist bodies to work in concert with the students' *Kartell Jüdischer Verbindungen*, the *Blau-Weiss* youth movement, and *Hapoel Hatzair*.[26]

Nationaler Einheitsblock spokesmen Felix Rosenblüth, Fritz Loewenstein, and Salli Hirsch, along with Georg Landauer of *Hapoel Hatzair*, tried to keep *Binyan Haaretz* from being recognized as a faction.[27] They denied that it was the bearer of a distinctive Zionist message, and argued that it offered tactical solutions only. Moreover, these solutions threatened to impoverish the concept of Zionism and drain it of content. As Georg Landauer stated:

---

25 Blumenfeld, "Innere Politik," *Der Jude*, 1 (1916/1917): 713-7, and his speech, *JR*, May 17, 1921.

26 Official letter of Loewenstein, March 4, 1921, Schocken Archives, 538/5; Weltsch's letter to Bergman, March 3, 1921, NULA, 1502/1334/2.

27 The WZO consisted of: (a) National federations whose members were General Zionists and eligible to vote following the purchase of the general *shekel*; and (b) worldwide factions. According to WZO statutes any group with at least 20,000 signatories was recognized as a separate faction and empowered to distribute its own *shekels*.

The sole task of the Zionist Organization, its *raison d'être*, is the national building of Palestine. The justification for factions is that they offer different perspectives on this upbuilding.... The significance of a *Zionist faction* [emphasis in original] is that it views affairs which are typically Zionist in a distinctive manner. For example, it is not the *Mizrahi*'s approach to Torah that differentiates it from non-Zionist Jewish groups.[28] Its right to exist as a Zionist faction lies not in Orthodoxy per se, but in its outlook on the role of Judaism in the development of Palestine.... *Binyan Haaretz* has no building plan. It advocates private enterprise for the sole purpose of economic prosperity. That does not constitute a program, and there is nothing singular about it. Moreover [*Binyan Haaretz*] has explicitly declared that it is not interested in singularity and has no distinctive view of Zionism.... *Its desire is to be a special faction for all those who seek nothing special* [my emphasis, H.L.].... It dismisses all the unique national demands upon Diaspora Jews as well, and seeks to abolish all the national commitments required for membership in the Zionist Organization. In other words, *Binyan Haaretz* represents the exceptional case of a Jewish Diaspora movement.... Its Diaspora program has nothing to do with Zionism and its Palestine program touches upon nothing extra-Zionist.

The bid for organizational unity was thus turned into a struggle for ideological purity, with the radical group presenting itself as the only legitimate brand of Zionism. The *Nationaler Einheitsblock* maintained that it was not a Zionist party but an aggregate of members from different parties, and as such, it embodied the true national Zionism.[29]

Binyan Haaretz countered these efforts to deny it party status by accusing the radicals of creating an alliance with the left and claiming a monopoly over Zionism. It contended that the radicals were bent on debilitating anyone who

28 The religious Zionist *Mizrahi* Party, founded in 1901, was the oldest of the WZO factions. It sought to combine Zionist realization and Jewish religious law.

29 Landauer's article in *JR*, April 27, 1921: 233–4; circular of May 1921, LBIA, 7185/4/1; Rosenblüth's article in *JR*, March 23, 1921: 159; Loewenstein's letter to Salman Schocken, March 23, 1921, Schocken Archives, 538/5; various announcements by the *Nationaler Einheitsblock*, *JR*, March 15, 1921; March 20, 1921.

did not share their social theories, including faithful Zionists who had stood by the movement from the start.[30]

Yet the chief battleground between the *Nationaler Einheitsblock* and *Binyan Haaretz* was in the political sphere. As the German Zionist leaders conducted negotiations with the non-Zionists to involve them in *Keren Hayesod*, *Binyan Haaretz* initiated parallel discussions and tried to win the non-Zionists over to their side. These simultaneous efforts endangered the success of *Keren Hayesod* and triggered an allout war against *Binyan Haaretz*. The *Nationaler Einheitsblock* called upon its members to organize local chapters, recruit new supporters, pass resolutions denouncing *Binyan Haaretz* at local and regional conventions, and participate in the *Landesvorstand* meeting in order to tip the scales against *Binyan Haaretz*. The *Nationaler Einheitsblock* also approached the non-Zionists who had been in contact with *Binyan Haaretz* and made them aware of the problem in the hope of persuading them to break off negotiations with *Binyan Haaretz*.[31]

The persistence of the *Nationaler Einheitsblock* bore fruit. Despite the prestigious leadership of *Binyan Haaretz*, it was not long before the radical Zionists won a total victory. This was borne out at the 17th ZVfD convention in Hanover held on May 13–17, 1921. At the numerous local and regional meetings which preceded the convention, *Binyan Haaretz* had been endlessly censured for its rebellion against mainstream Zionism. As a result, *Binyan Haaretz* boycotted the ZVfD convention. Of the five factions competing in the elections, the largest was the *Nationaler Einheitsblock*, headed by Arthur Hantke, followed by its ally, *Hapoel Hatzair* led by Robert Weltsch. The deliberations and resolutions of this convention all revolved around Palestine and demonstrated complete identification with the policies formulated by the World Zionist Executive in preparation for the 12th Zionist Congress scheduled for September of that year. The major speeches, delivered by Richard Lichtheim, Felix Rosenblüth, and Kurt Blumenfeld, expressed the consolidation and victory of the radical Zionist view. Rosenblüth was re-elected as chairman, this time alone, and *Binyan Haaretz* was conspicuously absent from the admin-

---

30 Article by Bertram Stein in *JR*, April 4, 1921: 206.

31 Loewenstein's letter to Schocken, March 3, 1921, and Siegfried Moses's letter to the *Nationaler Einheitsblock*, April 11, 1921, Schocken Archives, 538/5; *Landesvorstand* minutes, April 4, 1921, Schocken Archives, 538/32. See also note 20 above.

istrative coalition. By the end of the Hanover convention, there could be no dispute about the changing of the guard in German Zionism.[32]

However, *Binyan Haaretz* had not yet breathed its last. The group continued to operate independently, publishing its own bulletin, *Mitteilungsblatt des Binjan Haarez*, and preparing for the 12th Zionist Congress elections in which it planned to contend as a separate faction under Max Kollenscher. Running opposite *Binyan Haaretz* was a united list, headed by Arthur Hantke, of all the factions represented at the Hanover conference. Apart from the slightly different emphasis of each faction, this list presented a solid consensus on all issues then on the world Zionist agenda. Only the German *Mizrahi* faction excluded itself from this union and had its candidates run under the aegis of the world *Mizrahi* movement. In the pre-Congress elections, *Binyan Haaretz* received only 11 percent of the vote which gave it one delegate to the Zionist Congress – Max Kollenscher; the united list won nine delegates. However, German representation at the Congress also included members of the Zionist Actions Committee – Hantke, Rosenblüth, Loewe, and Blumenfeld, as well as Richard Lichtheim, who already had a seat in the World Zionist Executive.

The German Zionist delegation to the Twelfth Congress was thus quite heterogeneous. Aside from the well-known radicals and *Nationaler Einheitsblock* founders – Arthur Hantke, Felix Rosenblüth, Kurt Blumenfeld, Siegfried Moses, and Egon Rosenberg, there was also a distinguished group of *Hapoel Hatzair* representation which included Martin Buber, who was then at the height of his Zionist political activity, and Georg Landauer, who was just beginning to gain prominence and would become a leader of *Brith Shalom*. Also attending the Congress were *Zionei Zion* leaders Heinrich Loewe and Julius Berger, and several older Zionists of the Herzlian school: Hugo Schachtel, who had headed the Breslau Zionist Association from its inception; Ernst Kalmus, chairman of the Hamburg association since Herzl's time; and the writer and attorney Sammy Gronemann. Other delegates were relatively new to Zionist activism, among them Salman Schocken, a businessman who had been involved in cultural affairs until that time but would play an influential role in Zionist economic policy. With the exception of Max Kollenscher, the

---

32 Reports on regional meetings, *JR*, April 8, 1921, April 20, 1921; report by the ZVfD executive committee, *JR*, May 13, 1921: 267–70; information on meetings and convention minutes, *JR*, May 3, 13, 17, and 24, 1921; *Binyan Haaretz* circular, June 10, 1921, Schocken Archives, 538/4; protocol of *Zentralkomitee* (Ussishkin and Ruppin also attended as representatives of the World Zionist Executive).

German Zionists at the Congress stood as one behind the policies of the Weizmann leadership, particularly with regard to *Keren Hayesod*.[33]

The support of radical Zionism in Germany thus cut across all ages and ideological sectors. Despite the initial fanfare accompanying the establishment of *Binyan Haaretz*, its influence was very marginal. For a while, it continued to exist as an independent faction, but at the Kassel convention in 1922, it rejoined the ZVfD.[34] The German Zionist Federation, united once more and dominated by the radical Zionists, went on to lay the foundation for Zionist activity in close alliance with the World Zionist Organization and Chaim Weizmann.

The Radical Victory in Germany and World Zionism

Zionist literature deals extensively with the so-called "Brandeis-Weizmann controversy" in the years following the Balfour Declaration, which reached a peak after the *Keren Hayesod* was founded. This controversy is usually described as a dispute between the old-time European Zionism headed by Weizmann and a new brand of American Zionism that had not caught on in Europe. However, Brandeis's ideas did enjoy support in other countries, and, conversely, the Weizmann group had quite a few American supporters, who were instrumental in defeating the Brandeis camp.[35]

As noted, *Binyan Haaretz* was one of the best-known advocates of the Brandeis position. In the few works which address the Zionist movement in Germany, this faction is portrayed as the German parallel of the Brandeis group, and the infighting in the ZVfD as a pale reflection of the battle between giants that was waged in the United States.[36] To be sure, both campaigns were part of the same struggle. In Germany, as in the general Zionist arena, the consolidation and ascendancy of radical Zionism was not passively accepted. The leadership saw radicalization as a matter of life or death for Zionism, and in both arenas, its victory dictated the course of events for many

---

33 Seven issues of the *Mitteilungsblatt des Binjan Haarez* were published in 1921–1922. See information there and in *JR*, July 26, and 29, 1921, August 9, and 16, 1921. Also see Kollenscher, *Ein Wort*; *Protokoll des XII. Zionisten-Kongresses 1921*.

34 Correspondence in Schocken Archives, 531/32, 538/4; Rosenblüth's circular, October 27, 1921, CZA, Z4/2141/II.

35 See note 3 above.

36 Reinharz, in his introduction, *Dokumente*, xliii–xliii; Lichtheim, *The History of Zionism*, 148–50.

years to come. Due to the very nature of the opposition and the political aspirations involved, it is tempting indeed to draw a parallel between the two groups. However, by no means was the German episode a mirror image of what was happening in the general Zionist sphere. The roots of German opposition lay in the unique Jewish and Zionist history of that country, creating a focal point and manner of confronting the problem that were not comparable to any other community.

The impetus for the emergence of both groups was basically the same, namely the establishment of *Keren Hayesod*, envisaged as a vehicle for involving non-Zionists in the building of the national home. Underlying the *Keren Hayesod* idea was the view that the Zionist movement had been entrusted with a special mission, and should remain insulated from broad-based cooperation mobilized for the specific purpose of settling and developing Palestine. Opposition to *Keren Hayesod* in both Germany and the United States, was a rejection of this separatist approach and an articulation of the desire for full collaboration that would blur the distinction between Zionists and non-Zionists, or at least those who displayed an interest in Palestine.

Yet just as American Zionist traditions and political reality differed from those in Germany, the format for pan-Jewish cooperation differed, too. Brandeis advocated a Zionist council that would replace the existing movement and deal exclusively with the building of Palestine – the only area in which he believed it was possible to rally general, worldwide Jewish cooperation. This approach had nothing in common with any previous Zionist tradition; its springboard was the new political opportunity created by the Balfour Declaration and the San Remo conference. It reflected the notion that American Jews were American in all their being and in their commitment to the American system. As members of the Jewish people, nothing changed except their willingness to take part in the Palestine enterprise.

In contrast, the alternative proposed by the German opposition was a Zionist organization that did not create barriers between Palestine-directed activity and other areas of common concern in the Diaspora. This approach was based on political Zionist traditions that emphasized nationalism, Jewish communal politics and active participation as Jews in the political systems of countries where Jews resided.

In other words, American opposition was directed against the breadth of the radical approach whereas German opposition targeted its Palestinocentrism. The Brandeis group was unhappy with the radical attempt to spread the Zionist movement's aegis over Jewish concerns in the Diaspora; *Binyan Haaretz* protested its disparaging attitude toward Diaspora activity that was not directly related to the building of the national home. Brandeis was out to narrow and limit, while Kollenscher and his supporters sought greater inclusiveness. From the radical point of view, Brandeis was a threat in that he was interested in transforming the Zionist Organization into an agency focused on Palestine and devoid of Jewish national content. Kollenscher posed a similar danger by seeking to denude communal politics in the Diaspora of the centrality and guiding influence of Palestine.

Despite these differences in Jewish and Zionist outlook, there was a marked resemblance in the conclusions drawn by the two groups and their mode of action. Both were reluctant to disturb the political and civil tranquility enjoyed by their respective communities, or to allow the building of Palestine to interfere in any way. At the same time, they were loathe to miss out on the opportunities created by the Balfour Declaration for broad Jewish participation in this sphere. They thus arrived at the same conclusion, namely that the Zionist Organization should open its doors to as many Jews as possible. Both groups saw the economic enterprise as the essence of Zionism at that point in time, and objected to the radical Zionist attempt to impose far-reaching national and social goals. Hence their opposition to the centralized and rigidly-directed *Keren Hayesod* and their call for a more business-like development policy. Private enterprise was especially advocated by Kollenscher and his supporters, who, unlike Brandeis, were patently anti-socialist in their thinking.

The leadership was responding to various threats to radical Zionism from both its Palestine and Diaspora angles. Having said that, the objective of the world leadership and the German Zionists was much the same. They dreamt of a distinctive Zionist movement that would be able to preserve its special character, direct the economic enterprise in Palestine without compromising its principles, and continue its nationalist work outside Palestine.

A by-product of the confrontation with *Binyan Haaretz* was the conception of *Keren Hayesod* as a tool for implementing the radical approach in the Diaspora. At the meeting of the Zionist Actions Committee in Prague in July 1921 and the Twelfth Zionist Congress in Carlsbad that September, German Zionists Hantke and Blumenfeld spoke out on behalf of *Keren Hayesod* and effectively charted its course. They encouraged its transformation from the *ad hoc* fund envisioned by its founders to a permanent financing body, and maintained that activities connected with *Keren Hayesod*, such as publicity, educational work and fundraising, should constitute the bulk of Zionist activity in the Diaspora. Through efforts in this sphere Zionism would emerge strengthened and its message would be brought to all sectors of the Jewish people.

This was a further justification for keeping *Keren Hayesod* separate from the Zionist movement. On the one hand, the Zionist mission of the movement would remain unsullied by economic considerations, and on the other, a reciprocal relationship could exist wherein the two bodies would reinforce each other. Promoting *Keren Hayesod* would bolster the Zionist movement and vice versa. It was felt that cross-fertilization of this type would elevate the Zionist movement to the status of a sovereign leader in the development of Palestine.[37]

The struggle of the radical Zionists in Germany thus won a new footing for German Zionism in the WZO. From the outset, the Germans shared in the forging of the radical approach and Weizmann's socioeconomic model for the Jewish national home. In their rejection of *Binyan Haaretz*, they helped develop yet another element – Diaspora Zionism. In consequence, the German Zionists again joined the vanguard, waving the flag of *Keren Hayesod* as an institution that would allow for the implementation of the radical approach in both Palestine and the Diaspora.

The confrontation between the German Zionist leadership and *Binyan Haaretz* was also a preview of the battle for survival of the general Zionist camp in the WZO. Beginning in the early 1920s, the general Zionists lost much of their strength to Zionist parties that leaned right or left. Eventually, the pro-leftists gained the upper hand, a victory which created greater unity among the German Zionists and prevented splintering into factions. Moreover, it lay the foundations for an alliance between the Germans and the leftist-leaning Weizmann leadership. The fate of this alliance was less dependent on the partners themselves than on party politics in the Zionist movement. However, at the time, it was an alliance between victors.

---

37 Remarks of Hantke and Blumenfeld to Actions Committee, July 14–15, 1921, CZA, Z4/255/2, and at the congress, *Protokoll des XII. Zionisten-Kongresses,* 1921, 201–6, 548–52.

CHAPTER FIVE

FOR THE SAKE OF THE LAND OF ISRAEL

Keren Hayesod and the Tithe

Keren Hayesod was the uncontested leader of *Palästinaarbeit* in Germany. It was also instrumental in attracting the support of non-Zionists and enhancing the repute of the Zionist movement among them. The fact that the German Zionist leadership had been involved in shaping the fund was an important factor in its success in Germany. This involvement was both personal and institutional. Arthur Hantke, ZVfD chairman until 1920, was a member of the committee that had laid the ideological foundations, and immediately after the establishment of the fund at the Annual Conference, Berlin was chosen as its Central European headquarters (Department of the Keren Hayesod for Central Europe). Hantke, Kurt Blumenfeld, and Julius Berger were the directors. The *Keren Hajessod – Palästina Grundfonds Zentrale für Deutschland* (*Keren Hayesod – Palestine Foundation Fund Center for Germany*) was also established at this time, with the new ZVfD chairman Felix Rosenblüth as chairman and lawyer Moritz Bileski, an up and coming Zionist activist who settled in Palestine in 1924, as director-general. Shortly afterward, it was registered as a German company – the *Verein Palästina Grundfonds, Keren Hajessod E.V.* (*Keren Hayesod* Inc.).[1]

From the outset, the German branch of *Keren Hayesod* was notable for the seriousness with which it approached the self-imposed tithe that was a major component of *Keren Hayesod*. This tithe was meant to turn fundraising for *Keren Hayesod* into an obligation, rather that a voluntary contribution as in the case of the JNF. It was defined as a Jewish national tax, and although one could not be forced to pay, it was expected that Jews would do so as a civic,

---

1 Report of *Keren Hajessod Zentrale für Deutschland*, January 3, 1921, LBIA, 7185/4/1; *Informationen der Zionistischen Vereinigung für Deutschland*, 2 (March 1921); *Keren Hayesod, Report 1921*, 27, 55–7.

national duty. The monies raised would be earmarked by the Zionist Executive for projects decided upon by the Zionist Congress and the Zionist Actions Committee. The term, "tithe", from the Hebrew *ma'aser,* a tenth of one's property set aside for the priests in biblical times, was chosen with this association in mind. However, the amount was not necessarily one-tenth. Rather, it was a progressive tax determined by the conditions prevailing in each country. Also, it was not meant to be collected annually, but was to be paid in installments over a period of a few years.[2]

The German Zionists were apparently the only ones who took the tithe idea literally. Such taxes were not new in Germany. The German Zionists were already accustomed to the *Zionistensteuer* being used for Zionist activities in Germany. In September 1920, the ZVfD announced the *Keren Hayesod* tithe according to which every Zionist would contribute the equivalent of ten percent of his property in payments spread over five years. Local trustee committees appointed to appraise the financial worth of each member set the minimum at 1,000 German Marks, and those who paid were awarded a *Keren Hayesod* certificate (which was a kind of a share). Collection of the tithe was methodic and well-organized.[3]

When necessary, however, the approach could also be pragmatic and down-to-earth. During the spiralling inflation of 1922–1923, in which the white-collar workers (the class to which most German Zionists belonged) were particularly hard hit, *Keren Hayesod* issued a special exemption from the tax. At the end of 1923, when the country plunged into depression following the stabilization of the Mark, the tax for all was lowered from ten to five percent.[4]

Germany was the only country where fundraising for *Keren Hayesod* operated like clockwork. All the regulations governing the tithe were worked out and executed as if they had been issued by a sovereign state with the power to enforce payment and punish offenders. It was this stubborn adherence to principle, tempered by pragmatism and flexibility when the occasion arose, that

2   Metzer, *National Capital,* 91–101; see also Chapter Three.

3   *Landesvorstand* minutes, September 5, 1920, Schocken Archives, 531/52; report of *Keren Hayesod,* January 3, 1921, LBIA, 7185/4/1; minutes of ZVfD financial committee, November 21–2, 1920, December 23, 1920, February 2, 1921, CZA, KH2/3/1; Berger's letter to Reich, May 26, 1921, CZA, KH2/27/II.

4   See *Maaser Ordnung für das Jahr 1923,* CZA, KH2/37/II; letters of Hantke and Berger to the heads of the local chapters and *Keren Hayesod* activists, February 3, 1925, CZA, KH2/178/I.

insured the efficiency of the tithe mechanism in Germany and led most German Zionists to honor their commitment to *Keren Hayesod*.[5]

Cooperation with the Non-Zionists

Keren Hayesod's achievement in Germany was its ability to involve the non-Zionists in the development of Palestine. The London Conference which had set *Keren Hayesod* on its feet did not provide any program for cooperation between Zionists and non-Zionists, and many of the obstacles to such joint action were posed by the two conflicting aims of the institution. On the one hand, it was to be an instrument for supervising the development of the national home according to Zionist principles, and on the other, a framework that would attract economists and financiers who did not perceive themselves as Zionists.

This double aim was a problem for the many Jews who sought to participate in the building of Palestine, but without being bound by the priorities of the Zionist movement. *Keren Hayesod*, as a separate body, seemed ideal for this purpose. It would allow them to join an economic corporation and maintain control over their money. True, *Keren Hayesod* was not a profit-seeking institution; it was designed for investment in basic infrastructure that was not usually attractive to entrepreneurs, in order to ready the ground for private investment in the future. Both Zionists and non-Zionists were aware of this. Nevertheless, potential investors from the non-Zionist sector insisted upon a decentralized and businesslike format that would enable a direct connection between the investor and his project. They stipulated that their contributions be earmarked in advance and not be subject to the dictates of the WZO, although they did not object to WZO coordination. The only way to achieve this, they believed, was by creating a fund that was jointly managed by Zionists and non-Zionists, and capable of operating independently of the Zionist Executive. The intention to involve non-Zionists thus contradicted the aim to develop *Keren Hayesod* as a Zionist Executive instrument.

Throughout 1921, the advocates of each view battled with one another over the essence of the Zionist movement and its mission in Palestine and the Diaspora. The balance eventually tipped in favor of WZO control, and in the

5   *Keren Hayesod, Report 1923, 1925, 1927; Keren Hajessod Zentrale für Deutschland* circular to *Zentral Komitee*, May 21, 1925, CZA, KH2/180/I; account of *Keren Hayesod* conference at Erfurt, *JR*, August 31, 1926: 490.

process the chance to use *Keren Hayesod* as a tool for economic cooperation with non-Zionists was basically lost. In the summer of 1921, the Zionist Actions Committee and the 12th Zionist Congress voted to establish a *Keren Hayesod* Board of Directors with delegates of Zionist institutions only, and the proposal to set up a council in which the non-Zionists would be represented as shareholders, was deferred.

Before the conflict reached a head, the founders of *Keren Hayesod* envisaged an institution that would both raise funds and allocate them along the lines of a public shareholders corporation. In this way, the non-Zionists would have had some control over their contributions. Once it was decided against a council the idea of sharing responsibility for the allocation of funds was dropped, too. World *Keren Hayesod* thus became an instrument for financing immigration and settlement in Palestine whereas all the decision-making was in the hands of the Zionist Executive. In this respect, *Keren Hayesod* was the Zionist "treasury" and its Board of Directors in London insisted that all monies raised in the Diaspora be transferred to the Zionist Executive via its offices.[6]

In Germany, however, events took a different turn. Here, the Zionist community attributed tremendous importance to the assistance of non-Zionists and were not readily willing to forgo it. In the spring of 1921, Hantke and Blumenfeld began negotiating with prominent personalities in public life and economic affairs in Germany such as Professor Moritz Sobernheim of the Foreign Office; Oskar Wassermann, a director of the *Deutsche Bank* and a supervisory council member of the *Reichsbank*, the central bank of Germany; and Hamburg banker Max Warburg. Jewish community leaders such as Rabbi Leo Baeck, head of the *Allgemeiner Rabbiner-Verband in Deutschland* (Association of Rabbis in Germany), also participated in the discussion, and even members of the *Centralverein*, an organization that was openly hostile toward Zionism and the notion of cooperation, declared their support.[7]

6 Metzer, *National Capital*, 85–137; *Keren Hayesod, Report 1921, 1922;* minutes of the Zionist Actions Committee meeting in Prague, July 1921, CZA, Z4/255/2; Hantke's remarks at the congress, *Protokoll des XII. Zionisten-Kongresses 1921*, 548–52; *The World Zionist Organization and the Keren Hayesod Controversy in America* (London, 1921).

7 *Informationen der Zionistischen Vereinigung für Deutschland*, 2; Hantke's report at *Landesvorstand*, May 29, 1921, Schocken Archives, 531/32; Hantke's letter to Eugen Landau, Paul Nathan, Leo Baeck, Moritz Sobernheim and Siegmund Hirsch, May 30, 1921, CZA, KH2/24; Blumenfeld's letter to Schocken, June 7, 1921, in Kurt Blumenfeld, *Im Kampf um den Zionismus – Briefe aus fünf Jahrzehnten*, ed. Miriam Sambursky and Jochanan Ginat (Stuttgart, 1976), 70–2; on the opposition in the *Centralverein* led by Alfred Apfel, see *JR*, April 4, 1921: 213. Also see Birnbaum, *Staat und Synagoge*, 17.

In Germany, too, the non-Zionists insisted on exercising control over investments made with their money. Their participation was conditional on the German *Keren Hayesod*'s separating itself from the world organization in the spheres of funding, project initiation, business investment and the encouragement of private enterprise. The German Zionist leaders, unlike their London-based counterparts, were ready to compromise largely due to the internal pressures they faced. The *Binyan Haaretz* faction had been negotiating with non-Zionist Jewish leaders such as Paul Nathan of the *Hilfsverein*, industrialist Siegmund Hirsch, and banker and philanthropist Eugen Landau. By so doing, this faction threatened the exclusivity of the ZVfD as the sole representative of the Zionist camp. To complicate matters, it offered the non-Zionists an attractive alternative to the Zionist movement in the form of a jointly-run body that would combine Palestine and Diaspora activities without bias. Faced with two options, the non-Zionists could afford to be even more skeptical about *Keren Hayesod* as a fledgling institution whose policies were still in the making.

It should be borne in mind that the Reorganization Commission sent to Palestine by the Zionist Executive in the autumn of 1920 had recently lashed out at the financial policy of the Zionist Commission. Its report, published in the spring of 1921, laid the blame for most of the failures in Palestine on centralized economic control. The heads of the Reorganization Commission, Julius Simon and Nehemia De-Lieme, resigned from all their Zionist posts after their return from Palestine and their criticism was used by the Brandeis group in the United States and *Binyan Haaretz* in Germany to fight against the centralization of *Keren Hayesod*. This no doubt strengthened non-Zionist antagonism towards *Keren Hayesod* and made it even more likely that they would choose the alternate plan of cooperation offered by *Binyan Haaretz*.[8]

The readiness of German Zionist leaders to compromise with non-Zionists was of no avail; the WZO leadership insisted on subordination to the Zionist Executive even at the expense of such a partnership. As a result, the German efforts were nipped in the bud and the centralization of *Keren Hayesod* was institutionalized at the 12th Zionist Congress.

8 *Landesvorstand* meeting, May 29, 1921, and June 9, 1921, and draft of agreement with the non-Zionists, Schocken Archives, 531/32; *Binyan Haaretz* circular of June 10, 1921, Schocken Archives, 538/4; on the Reorganization Commission see Hagit Lavsky, *The Foundations of Zionist Financial Policy - The Zionist Commission, 1918–1921* (Jerusalem, 1980) (Hebrew), 28-30, 99–114, 174–89; on the repercussions of the proposal in Germany, see Felix Rosenblüth's circular of July 28, 1921, Schocken Archives 538/4; *JR*, April 27, 1921 (lectures of Julius Simon): 227–8.

However, support for the position of the German Zionists came from an unlikely corner: the long period of inflation after the war and the accelerated devaluation of the German Mark from the autumn of 1921 until the summer of 1922. In light of the fact that domestic price rises lagged behind the foreign exchange rate, the Zionists allowed the German *Keren Hayesod* to use funds independently. Spending German Marks to buy equipment for Palestine was clearly preferable to exchanging them into Pounds Sterling for transfer to London, which meant taking a considerable loss. In this way, German *Keren Hayesod* achieved the freedom to allocate funds as it saw fit.[9]

Negotiations between Zionists and non-Zionists thus resumed, and in early 1922, a unique solution was devised whereby two *Keren Hayesod* funds would operate in Germany. One was a "Zionist" fund – *Verein Palästina Grundfonds, Keren Hajessod E.V.*, which had been set up in 1920 to collect the tithe and whose income would be sent to London. The other was a neutral institution whose purpose was canvassing non-Zionists only and carrying out projects under the joint management of Zionists and non-Zionists.

The new body, *Keren Hajessod (Jüdisches Palästinawerk) E.V. (Keren Hayesod* – Jewish Palestine Work, hereafter: neutral *Keren Hayesod*), was registered as a German company on January 1, 1922. According to its articles of association, it would engage in independent fundraising and allocation of monies. The non-Zionists thus gained a certain measure of control over their investments, although the Zionists were also involved and the work of the fund was co-ordinated with the central Zionist institutions in London. The non-Zionist banker Oskar Wassermann was named chairman and his deputies were Eugen Landau (also a non-Zionist) and Hantke, head of the Department of the *Keren Hayesod* for Central Europe. Among the non-Zionists who belonged to the neutral *Keren Hayesod* were Solomon Kalischer, grandson of the proto-Zionist Rabbi Zvi Hirsch Kalischer, who was a professor at the Berlin Polytechnikum and head of the *Deutscher-Israelitischer Gemeindebund* (German-Jewish Communities Association); Rabbi Leo Baeck; and lawyer Alfred Apfel of the *Centralverein*, who was already sympathetic to the Zionist cause and would later join the Zionist movement. The Zionists included ZVfD chairman Felix Rosenblüth; Kurt Blumenfeld who was on the Board of Directors of the Department of the *Keren Hayesod* for Central Europe; and Arnold Aron Barth, a Board member of World *Keren Hayesod*. There were also delegates from the

---

9 *Keren Hayesod, Report 1922*, 31–3; Felix Rosenblüth's letter to Lichtheim, June 22, 1922, CZA, Z4/2141/II; on the price fluctuations, see William A. Lewis, *Economic Survey, 1919–1939* (London, 1949), 24–9.

Jewish communities of Hamburg, Frankfurt a.M. Cologne, Munich, and Breslau. Non-Zionist banker Alfred Lisser represented Hamburg, and Frankfurt a.M. sent the head of its local Zionist association, Fritz Sondheimer. The secretary of neutral *Keren Hayesod* was a Zionist, Walter Turnowsky, who managed the fund for all intents and purposes until 1923 when he was succeeded by *Poalei Zion* leader Alfred Berger.[10] Thus the dual institutional system was a way of solving the dilemma between local independence and operation under a framework of Zionist guidance.

Neutral *Keren Hayesod* offices also opened in other countries, such as Holland, Argentina, Czechoslovakia, Bulgaria and Yugoslavia, but because the Zionist federations in these countries were relatively small, their neutral committees did not pose a challenge to *Keren Hayesod* in London. Of the important Zionist centers, which included Poland, Germany, Britain, the United States and South Africa, Germany was the only one with a neutral fund and a true partnership between Zionists and non-Zionists.[11]

Owing to two indisputable achievements – implementation of the tithe and collaboration with the non-Zionists, *Keren Hayesod* was able to make a substantial contribution to the development of Palestine, and to capture the attention of German Jewry to such an extent that the work of *Keren Hayesod* came to be considered the zenith of Zionist activism in that country.

The Contribution to Palestine

In the same way that the rampant inflation in Germany was largely responsible for the establishment of the German *Keren Hayesod*, it also dictated the manner in which it operated, and paved the way for financial success. *Keren Hayesod*'s first project was to help three pioneering groups, one hailing from Germany, who were unable to establish agricultural settlements in Palestine because of a critical shortage in settlement funds. Leo Kaufmann, an emissary for these groups, was sent to Germany in June 1922 in search of a backer, and neutral *Keren Hayesod* took up their cause. Kaufmann travelled all over Germany campaigning on the fund's behalf, and in return, *Keren Hayesod* undertook to buy the equipment necessary for settlement. The shipment arrived in Palestine in September 1922, and by November, the groups had settled in the eastern

---

10 Regulations of neutral *Keren Hayesod,* CZA, KH2/37/I; *Keren Hayesod, Report 1922,* 31–3; *1923,* 31–3.

11 *Keren Hayesod, Report 1922,* 31–3.

Jezreel Valley, where they established the *kibbutzim* of Beit Alpha and Heftziba. Henceforth, *Keren Hayesod* could point to tangible property – cows and tractors – purchased with German contributions.[12]

The successfulness of this project was good both for fundraising and the continuation of settlement. In 1922, the Jewish youth associations in the Rhine region set up an office expressly for the purpose of outfitting the pioneers before their immigration. The Markenhof group, which took its name from the training farm in Germany, went to Palestine in early 1923 fully equipped, although its actual settlement was postponed until 1927, when it established *Kibbutz* Beit Zera in the Jordan Valley. In 1925, the German *Keren Hayesod* granted a special loan to the *Solel Boneh* construction company. It also funded the *Hehalutz* (Pioneer – Zionist organization) agricultural training projects, and sponsored the settlement of *Blau-Weiss* youth movement members.[13]

All enterprises of *Keren Hayesod* in Germany were characterized by a combination of adherence to principles and flexibility demonstrated in the collection of the tithe, and carried out under the aegis and approval of World *Keren Hayesod* and the Zionist Executive. At the same time, they followed proper business practices and operated under the watchful eye of the non-Zionist partners. In order to attract private initiative, German *Keren Hayesod* published financial data and information on investment opportunities in *Palästina Wirtschaft* (Palestine Economy), a quarterly journal that appeared until 1925. Later, the German Jewish National Fund monthly, *Aufbau* (building), served this purpose. Today it is difficult to gauge the effectiveness of these measures.[14]

Because of its unique activities, German *Keren Hayesod*'s share in total *Keren Hayesod* income was very large compared with the percentage of German Zionists in the world movement. Throughout most of the 1920s, Germany was

---

12 A detailed memorandum (undated and unsigned) on the events from July to November, CZA, KH2/37/I.

13 Letter of Palestine Executive treasurer to the *Finanz- und Wirtschaftsrat* (Financial and Economic Council) in London, July 26, 1923, CZA, KH2/37/III; Walter Turnowsky, *Die Arbeit des Keren Hajessod in Deutschland* (Berlin, 1924); exchange of letters between the Markenhoff group and *Keren Hayesod* in Germany, CZA, KH2/37/I; interview with Meta Flanter on May 9, 1982, OHD; exchange of letters between *Solel Boneh*, German *Keren Hayesod* and the central office in London, March 1925, CZA, KH1/121/d1, KH1/121/e2; *Landesvorstand* minutes, February 8, 1925, and the letter of ZVfD presidency to the *Keren Hayesod* Board of Directors, February 13, 1925, CZA, KH2/178/I. Also see *Keren Hayesod, Report 1923,* 31-3, *1925,* 144 and *1931,* 36-7, 62.

14 *Keren Hajessod Zentrale für Deutschland, Palästina Wirtschaft – Berichte über Handel, Industrie und Aufbau in Pälastina* (Berlin, 1922–1925); *Aufbau – Blätter des Keren Kajemeth Lejisrael (Jüdischer Nationalfonds)* (Berlin, 1924–1928).

the leading donor in Europe, and ranked third in the world after the United States and South Africa – although the sums brought in by the United States were, of course, much greater. Between April 1921 and March 1929, German *Keren Hayesod* raised close to 172,000 pounds sterling (see Table II). This did not include the purchases and the special projects mentioned above. German *Keren Hayesod* was able to keep up this standard until the Great Depression in 1929. In consequence, the German fund was held aloft as an example for the entire Zionist movement. In a letter from New York in February 1924, Chaim Weizmann wrote:

> I have just received the returns of the German *Keren Hayesod*. In the ten weeks I have been here nothing has given us all more encouragement and joy than this report, which is a shining example of what can be achieved by devoted work. I think I am not giving away a secret if I mention the fact that the American *Keren Hayesod* was so impressed by Weltsch's telegram that I decided to pass a resolution of congratulation to our German colleagues. I have no doubt that this effort, apart from its immediate utility for Palestine, will assist greatly in the work here. May I express my own hearty congratulations to our German friends.[15]

Keren Hayesod as the Bone of Contention

Neutral *Keren Hayesod* gained the support of various German Jewish organizations, among them the *Verband jüdischer Jugendvereine Deutschlands* (Union of Jewish Youth Associations in Germany), *Allgemeiner Rabbiner-Verband in Deutschland* and the Grand Lodge of *B'nai B'rith*. The chairman of the Berlin Jewish community was also active on the fund's behalf. There were some, however, who had their reservations, among them the *Vereinigung für das liberale Judentum in Deutschland* (Union for Liberal Jewry in Germany). The ultra–orthodox *Agudat Israel* and the largest German Jewish organization, the *Centralverein*, actually fought the fund tooth and nail.[16]

---

15 Weizmann's letter to Actions Committee president, February 14, 1924, in *Weizmann Letters*, vol. 12, 135.

16 Report of German *Keren Hayesod* to 18th ZVfD convention in Kassel, *JR*, September 8, 1922: 474.

Table II: *Keren Hayesod* Income
(Pounds Sterling, current prices[*])

Year	Total Income	German-Jewish £	%
1921/2	427,857	14,723	3.4
1922/3	381,710	4,382	1.1
1923/4	466,991	15,301	3.3
1924/5	495,769	30,212	6.1
1925/6			
1926/7	1,143,850[**]	48,723	4.3
1927/8	440,624	27,718	6.3
1928/9	417,454	31,273	7.5
1929/30	389,148	29,828	7.7
1930/31	258,029	20,989	8.1
Total:	4,421,432	223,149	5.0

Notes:
[*] Rounded numbers, fiscal year from April to March.
[**] Inclusive data for 1925/6 and 1926/7.

The *Centralverein* had no more than 60,000 members at the end of the Weimar period, but because other Jewish organizations were affiliated with it, it encompassed, at least indirectly, a weighty segment of German Jewry. The rivalry between the Zionist movement and the *Centralverein* had gone through ups and downs, but there was no real fight between them as long as Zionism remained a marginal phenomenon and posed no immediate challenge to the integrationist aspirations of German Jewry.[17] This changed dramatically during Weimar, when Zionism gained legitimacy and became a real alternative for German Jews. Moreover, the radical Palestine orientation took center stage, making practical demands upon members and preaching against any kind of assimilation into German society. For the *Centralverein*, this was a clear and present threat. The ascendancy of Zionism appeared to strengthen the antisemitic argument that Jews could not be loyal citizens just when

17 See Chapters One and Two.

antisemitism was seen as the last obstacle to full integration. By propagating the belief that any effort to fight antisemitism was futile in principle, Zionist radicalism threatened the *raison d'être* of the *Centralverein*. The more Zionism grew in strength, the greater the damage and the weaker the prospects for eradicating antisemitism. Previously theoretical arguments about the status and future of the Jews in Germany thus developed into a genuine political struggle.[18]

In the Zionist camp the confrontation remained below the surface. The new ZVfD leadership preferred to expend its energies in a positive direction, educating the Jewish public and participating in the building of the national home. It had no desire to enter an open political contest with hostile organizations or lobby for control of Jewish communities which, according to its views, were temporary by nature and destined to disappear. German Zionists who thought otherwise had joined the *Jüdische Volkspartei*. But the *Centralverein* saw things differently, and its leaders girded themselves for a full-blown war against an element that was jeopardizing its policies and standing in the Jewish community. Thus they refused to cooperate with efforts to establish a German Jewish Congress at the end of World War I, and it goes without saying, any *Keren Hayesod* program on behalf of Palestine. They did not rest here, but embarked upon a vicious campaign to discredit the Zionist movement.[19]

Keren Hayesod's incessant activity and high visibility resulted in greater support for the Palestine enterprise, but it further antagonized its opponents. Their fury climaxed in early 1925, when neutral *Keren Hayesod* invited WZO president Chaim Weizmann to Berlin. It was Weizmann's first visit to the German capital after the war, and on his agenda were meetings with the Chancellor, prominent statesmen, Jewish personalities such as Albert Einstein, and neutral *Keren Hayesod* leaders Oskar Wassermann and Eugen Landau. He also attended a reception at the German Foreign Office, participated in a press conference and newspaper interviews, and appeared at gatherings organized by non-Zionist organizations such as neutral *Keren Hayesod* and *B'nai B'rith*. This visit created much excitement in the Jewish community and general public, and the events in Weizmann's honor turned into impressive rallies for the Zionist cause. Articles in support of Palestine and Zionism appeared in highly regarded

---

18 Evyatar Friesel, "Jewish-Zionist Relations in Germany During the Weimar Republic," in *Proceedings of the Seventh World Congress of Jewish Studies – The History of the Jews in Europe* (Jerusalem, 1981) (Hebrew), 179–84.

19 See Chapters Two and Four.

German newspapers such as *Frankfurter Zeitung, Berliner Tageblatt, Kölnische Zeitung,* and *Vossische Zeitung,* who sent special correspondents to Palestine. The impressive economic growth in Palestine at the time, along with the stablilization of the German economy, enabled *Keren Hayesod,* as the organizer of the visit, to shine the spotlight in the direction of the Jewish national home.[20]

The anti-Zionist counterattack came swiftly on the heels of Weizmann's visit. The leaders of the *Centralverein* saw that German *Keren Hayesod,* thanks to its neutrality, had increased the interest in Zionism and Palestine, and they feared for their own status in the Jewish community and Germany at large. Now their struggle took on a new focus, with *Keren Hayesod,* rather than Zionism as a whole, as the main target. They called for people to stop contributing to *Keren Hayesod,* and tried to tarnish its trustworthy image by claiming there was nothing neutral about it and that it was none other than a nationalist political party.[21]

The recession that plagued the German economy from the summer of 1925 until the fall of 1926 soon turned the campaign against *Keren Hayesod* into an economic issue. The crisis struck mainly at the commercial sector, especially the grain and clothing industries, as well as small businesses, in which many Jews were employed, among them a large number of *Centralverein* supporters who were also neutral *Keren Hayesod* contributors. The election for the *Preußischer Landesverband jüdischer Gemeinden* (Prussian Land Association of Jewish Communities) in the summer of 1925 highlighted the aspect of financial rivalry and made it clear to all that *Keren Hayesod* was the *Centralverein's* foremost enemy and competitor.

At the end of 1925, when rumors began to spread about the onset of an economic crisis in Palestine that the WZO was powerless to alleviate, the *Centralverein* intensified its attack. The major American Jewish welfare organizations had now become interested in the possibility of Jewish settlement in the Crimea, and the *Centralverein* seized upon this idea as a positive opportunity for Jewish economic solidarity rather than "wasting" money, as they saw it, on the ailing enterprise in Palestine. As the economic situation in Germany and Palestine deteriorated, the *Centralverein's* rage against *Keren Hayesod* grew, reaching a peak at its annual conference in March 1926 when its

20 For the accounts of Weizmann's visit, see *JR* of January 9, January 13, January 16, and January 28, 1925; undated report by neutral *Keren Hayesod,* CZA, KH2/178/I; *Keren Hayesod, Report 1925,* 47.

21 Circular of Rabbi Hugo Fuchs, January 1, 1926, LBIA, Fuchs Collection, file 3; Alfred Berger's letters to Rabbi Fuchs, March 2, 1926, CZA, KH1/121/e1.

members were forbidden to participate in any project sponsored by *Keren Hayesod*.[22]

The straited circumstances of most German Jews, compounded by the continuous denunciations of the *Centralverein*, took their toll on the income of *Keren Hayesod*. However, the setback proved to be only temporary. In response to the attacks of the *Centralverein*, many of *Keren Hayesod*'s leaders picked up the cudgels in defense of the Zionist cause. Rabbi Leo Baeck, Rabbi Fuchs of Chemnitz, Rabbi Lazarus of Wiesbaden and others, held meetings and issued statements that accentuated the neutrality of *Keren Hayesod* and the importance of the Palestine enterprise for all Jews. The climax was a public rally in Berlin on March 4, 1926, just after the *Centralverein* declared *Keren Hayesod* off limits to its members. Among the speakers were Albert Einstein, neutral *Keren Hayesod* president Oskar Wassermann, Rabbi Leo Baeck, banker Alfred Lisser, industrialist Sigmund Hirsch, and *Berliner Tageblatt* journalist Felix Pinner.

The fact that many respected non-Zionist personalities had linked their name to Zionism enhanced its prestige and generated new interest in Palestine among Jews and non-Jews alike. One of the indications was the stationing of permanent correspondents in Palestine by the *Frankfurter Zeitung, Berliner Tageblatt*, and *Vossische Zeitung*, and visits by German government officials and academicians, for example Count von Schoenaich and Professor Edward Mayer, a well-known historian. A number of travelogues were soon published that described Palestine favorably and even enthusiastically. Around this time, German tourism to Palestine began to increase.

The high point of this positive interest in Palestine was the establishment of the *Deutsches Komitee Pro Palästina* (German Pro-Palestine Committee) of 1926. It was open to Jews and non-Jews, and its members included Wassermann and Baeck, economics professor Auhagen, the Prussian minister of culture Professor Becker, writer Thomas Mann and many others. The committee emerged in the midst of the recession, when anti-Zionist propaganda abounded, and despite the threats that politicians who joined would lose the Jewish vote.[23]

---

22   A. Berger's letter to Blumenfeld, September 26, 1925, CZA, KH1/121/e1; *JR*, March 9, 1926: 140. See also Berger's letters to Leo Herrmann, June 15, 1925 and September 3, 1925, CZA, KH2/121/d2, letters of November 23, 1925 and January 11, 1926, CZA, KH1/121/e1; Berger's letter to Blumenfeld, September 26, 1925, CZA, KH1/121/d2.

23   Rosenblüth's letter to Keren Hayesod Board of Directors, September 11, 1921, CZA, KH1/121/d1; Rabbi Fuchs' circular of January 28, 1926 and responses of rabbis Paul Lazarus, Emil Levy and Leo Baeck, LBIA, Fuchs Collection, File 3; Hantke's letter to Rabbi Baeck, March 1, 1926, and Berger's letter to Rabbi Fuchs, March 2, 1926, CZA, KH1/121/e1; *JR*, March 5, 1926; pamphlet published

This encouraging response served to counteract the damage done by the economic crisis in Germany, and the income of *Keren Hayesod* actually doubled. There was also a dramatic rise in the number of contributors, from 9,505 at the end of March 1925 to 11,274 two years later.[24] Thus the popularity of the Palestine enterprise among the non-Zionists did not decline, but increased all the more, the anti–Zionist propaganda and problems in Palestine notwithstanding.

As a result of the strong bond forged between the Zionists and non-Zionists who worked together in *Keren Hayesod*, there was a growing demand to include non-Zionists on a broader scale, and to involve them in executive positions. This joint activity in Germany also allowed many of the problems of an institutionalized relationship between the two camps to be elucidated and resolved prior to the enlargement of the Jewish Agency in 1929.[25]

However, the conflict between the Zionists and anti-Zionists had implications for the ZVfD itself. As long as this conflict pushed the Jewish public into taking a greater part in the development of Palestine, the ZVfD concentrated on its work in this sphere. But toward the end of 1925, the focus shifted towards power and influence in the German Jewish community, as was apparent by the ZVfD resolution to increase its support for the *Jüdische Volkspartei*. Kurt Blumenfeld, who became ZVfD chairman in 1924, was not prepared for

in the wake of the rally on March 4, *Keren Hajessod, Das Palästinawerk*, CZA, Z4/2758; *Bericht über die Tätigkeit der Zionistischen Vereinigung für Deutschland an den XXI. Delegierentag in Erfurt* (Berlin, 1926), 2–4; Berger's letter to *Keren Hayesod* Board of Directors, February 16, 1927, CZA, Z4/3567/I; *Keren Hayesod, Report 1927*, 53–8. Among the travelogues published were: Alfred Wiener, *Kritische Reise durch Palästina* (Berlin, 1927); Felix Pinner, *Das Neue Palästina* (Berlin, 1928); Freiherr von Schoenaich, *Palästina – Eine Fahrt ins gelobtes Land* (Halberstadt, 1926). See also: Joseph Walk, "Das 'Deutsche Komitee Pro Palästina', 1926–1933," *BLBI*, 52 (1976): 162–93.

24 Martin Rosenblüth's report to *Landesvorstand*, April 4, 1927, Schocken Archives, 531/31; *Keren Hayesod, Report 1927*, 53–9. See also report of the German *Keren Hayesod* conference in *JR*, August 31, 1926: 490.

25 German Keren Hayesod meeting of April 18, 1925, CZA, KH1/121/d1; *Landesvorstand* meeting of April 19, 1925, CZA, KH2/178/II, and May 20, 1925, CZA, KH2/180/I; memorandum of Siegfried Moses to *Landesvorstand* members, May 3, 1925, and other memoranda, Schocken Archives, 531/241. Berger's letters to *Keren Hayesod* Board of Directors, January 21, 1925 and to Leo Herrmann, September 30, 1925, CZA, KH1/121/d1; Blumenfeld's letter to Berthold Feiwel, March 10, 1926, CZA, KH1/121/e1.

concessions and maintained that the fight against the anti-Zionists was a matter of life or death.[26]

In the long run, this struggle, compounded by other factors that emerged in the late 1920s, turned the attention of German Zionists toward Jewish community politics at the expense of Palestine.

Pioneer Training and Immigration

The German Zionist orientation toward Palestine led the ZVfD into yet another area of activity: pre-settlement training. Responsibility for this sphere was mostly in the hands of the youth movements, the *Hehalutz* organization, the Zionist student associations and the *Brith Halutzim Datiim* (*Bahad*-Association of Religious Pioneers), but the ZVfD sponsored and funded many of these programs. The training they offered was very intensive and had clearly defined goals. The youngsters were encouraged to sever ties with their surroundings, abstain from local politics and shy away from the German political and economic establishment. Instead, they were immersed in Hebrew and Jewish culture. They socialized on a daily basis with other young Zionists and chose professional careers in medicine, agronomy, geology, engineering, and so forth, in keeping with opportunities in Palestine. They attended courses in the Hebrew language, the most noted of which were offered by the *Hebräische Sprachschule* (Hebrew Language School) organized by the student association, *Kartell Jüdischer Verbindungen*, and directed by Moshe Smoira, later Chief Justice and first president of the Israeli Supreme Court. The enthusiasm of these youngsters was also fired by youth leaders from Palestine, many of whom came to Germany as students, who taught Hebrew songs and folklore. Many young Zionists underwent agricultural training at the Markenhof and other Jewish training farms. Some worked privately for German farmers or tradesmen, signed up for university studies in agronomy, or enrolled at the

---

26 Communal affairs committee meeting, March 20, 1925, CZA, KH2/178/II; Kurt Blumenfeld's confidential circular of October 18, 1925, CZA, KH2/180/I, and Weltsch's letter to Hans Kohn, October 20, 1925, NULA, 1502/1334/3; Berger's letter to *Keren Hayesod* Board of Directors, February 16, 1925, and minutes of ZVfD executive committee meeting, April 26, 1927, CZA, Z4/3567/I.

gardening school in Ahlem, near Hanover. The religious pioneers were trained at the *Bahad* farm Rodges.[27]

All this training and academic study was geared toward immigration to Palestine.

Groups of pioneers had already settled in Palestine in the 1920s, among them the *"Avoda", "Zvi"* and "Markenhof" groups who joined the *kibbutzim* of Heftziba, Ein Harod, and Beit Zera. In the early 1920s, many immigrants had come on their own at the invitation of various institutions. Among them were Richard Kaufmann and Lotte Cohn, architects for the Palestine Land Development Company; Fritz Kornberg, one of the designers of the Hebrew University of Jerusalem on Mount Scopus; carpenters, some of them employed at the *Blau-Weiss* cooperative workshops; Stefan Löwengart, a geologist; and a large number of physicians. The number of German Jews leaving for Palestine rose sharply in 1924: 500 – compared with 150 in 1923. The turnabout boosted *aliya* to the top of the ZVfD agenda, especially in view of the fact that major German Zionists such as former ZVfD chairman Felix Rosenblüth and Moritz Bileski of *Keren Hayesod* were among those who left. Neither one remained in Palestine for long: Rosenblüth was soon appointed head of the Zionist Executive's Organization Department in London, and Bileski returned to Germany in the wake of the economic crisis in Palestine in 1926–1927. In any event, much of the German Zionist convention at Wiesbaden at the end of 1924 was dedicated to the problems of German Jews in Palestine, and a liaison office was opened there to facilitate contact between the immigrants and the ZVfD. The *Jüdische Rundschau* also strengthened its connection with Palestine by appointing Gerda Arlosoroff as its resident correspondent. *Aliya* from Germany peaked in 1925 with the departure of 963 immigrants.

Germany of the 1920s was not a country of distress as far as the Jews were concerned, and emigration was a limited phenomenon. Only about 40,000 Jews emigrated during the Weimar period, many to the United States which had been the chief destination for Jews leaving Germany since the 19th century. Now Palestine became a new destination, although the proportions were much lower. Until the beginning of 1933, only 3,300 German Jews immigrated to Palestine, which was less that half the number leaving for the United States or about 8 percent of the total Jewish emigration (see Table III).

---

27 Based on my questionnaire distributed to 40 persons who settled in Palestine in the 1920s. See also *Meilensteine – Vom Wege des Kartell Jüdischer Verbindungen (KJV) in der Zionistischen Bewegung (eine Sammelschrift)*, ed. Eli Rothschild (Tel Aviv, 1972), Chapter Three. Joseph Walk, "The Torah Va-Avodah Movement", *LBIYB*, 6 (1961): 236-56.

Table III: Jewish Emigration from Germany to Palestine and the U.S.

Year*	To United States	To Palestine
1920–1921	1,396	360
1922	600	44
1923	864	149
1924	1,986	480
1925	521	963
1926	652	325
1927	546	84
1928	361	87
1929	235	201
1930	167	138
1931	98	122
1932	45	353
Total:**	7,371	3,306

Notes:

*   Figures for Jewish immigration to Palestine follow calendar years. Those for immigrants to the U.S. are according to statistical years (1921/1922 = 1922).

** Estimates for Jewish emigration from Germany, 1920–1932: out of a total of 40,000, 18.4% to the U.S.; 8.3% to Palestine.

Source: Figures cited by Doron Niederland, *Emigration Patterns of German Jews 1918–1938*, (Ph.D. Dissertation, The Hebrew University of Jerusalem, 1988) (Hebrew), 21–23.

The data shows that immigration to Palestine was not dictated by the situation in Germany alone. Jewish emigration was highest in 1923, when inflation was at its peak, and continued into 1924, with the onset of the stabilization crisis. From 1925, the number of emigrants began to drop. Figures for *aliya*, on the other hand, rose in 1924, and doubled in 1925. Out of a total of 3,300 German Jews who immigrated to Palestine in the 1920s approximately 1,400 arrived during 1924–1925. By this time, the worst was over in Germany, and there was no special emigration impetus. It thus seems that Zionist propaganda in Germany and the positive reports from Palestine were the major influence. This is also borne out by the profile of these emigrants, who were mostly young and unmarried, and had undergone vocational training in Germany in agriculture, landscaping gardening, and various trades, often in accordance with the employment opportunities in Palestine. Only a few were university graduates or free professionals. These facts demonstrate that the state of the Palestine economy was an important consideration in planning *aliya*. However, it should also be borne in mind that the runaway inflation in Germany led to a significant reduction in the number of Jewish university students and a change in their career choices.

Aliya dropped almost to nil in the second half of the decade, when the German Jewish community received word of the depressed economy in Palestine and heard reports of immigrants who returned to Germany in despair. This coincided with the general trend in the late 1920s, when German Zionism turned inward and concentrated more on local affairs than on Palestine. In the 1930s, however, political developments in Germany changed all this and triggered yet another surge of immigration to Palestine.[28]

---

28 *Bericht über die Tätigkeit, Wiesbaden* (1924); minutes of the Wiesbaden convention, *JR*, January 2, 1925, especially Felix Rosenblüth's letter from Palestine, 3–4; reports of the Palestine Office in Berlin, in *Bericht über die Tätigeit, Erfurt (1926)* and *Breslau (1928)*. On the emigration of Jews from Germany see Niederland, *Emigration Patterns*, 22–5.

CHAPTER SIX

ZIONIST RESPONSIBILITY

The Rise of General Zionism

The leaders of the Zionist movement had been preoccupied with the issue of pan-Jewish cooperation in the development of the national home since 1919. However, their insistence on maintaining the uniqueness of the movement stood in the way of the establishment of a general representative body. The Mandate charter, ratified in 1922, thus recognized the WZO as the "Jewish Agency for Palestine" until such a body was formed. Contrary to expectations, *Keren Hayesod* failed to fulfil this task and the slot for a council representing common Jewish interests remained open and irksome to the Zionist leaders, upon whom this heavy burden had been thrust.

In 1922, Weizmann began to push for the expansion of the Jewish Agency beyond the narrow confines of the Zionist Organization. He fought for this on two fronts: on the outside, among the non-Zionists and especially the American-Jewish establishment; on the inside, among his colleagues in the Zionist movement, who were his most intractable opponents. Weizmann's policies sparked disagreements within the WZO that rocked the organization throughout the 1920s. It was not the expansion of the Jewish Agency that was the issue, but the nature, function and authority of the expanded framework. Was the rapid mobilization of Jewish financial resources and expertise of the essence, or rather the formation of a Jewish democratic party that would concentrate on the development of Palestine? Weizmann, who was most pressured by the material burden, sought immediate negotiations with financially powerful individuals and organizations with an interest in Palestine. To gain their cooperation, he promised that their status in the Jewish Agency would be no less than that of the WZO. Weizmann found his main supporters among General Zionists in Western European and America. The American Zionists were also his intermediaries in contacts with the American Jewish establishment. Of like mind were General Zionists in Poland who had formed the *Et Livnot* (Time to Build) group under Leon Levite and Jehoshua Gottlieb.

Opposition to Weizmann came from two sectors. The "political" Zionists, such as Vladimir Jabotinsky who resigned from the Zionist Executive in 1923 and later established the Revisionist party, objected to the expansion of the Jewish Agency in the belief that the Zionist movement should not compromise its political objectives or deflect attention from their attainment. The other sector opposed to Weizmann's plans was composed of the religious *Mizrahi* party, the left-wing parties, and many left-leaning East European General Zionists, prominent among them members of the *Al-Hamishmar* faction in Poland led by Yizhak Gruenbaum. As their main concern was the formation of a broad democratic partnership under the leadership of the Zionist movement, they demanded that the WZO organize an international Jewish Congress to elect a representative agency for Palestine headed by the Zionists. In this way they sought to ensure that the responsibility for the national home would be in the hands of the Jewish people itself and not some group of "notables," that Palestine's development would not be transformed from a national enterprise into an economic colonization project, and that the Zionist movement would maintain its uppermost status. As the harsh reality in Palestine became apparent to all, Weizmann's detractors realized that a Jewish Congress was still far off, and their opposition weakened. But the road to consensus was long, and an agreement with the non-Zionists was reached only in 1929 when the enlarged Jewish Agency came into being.[1]

The German Zionists were among Weizmann's most enthusiastic supporters. As those who had been instrumental in the establishment of *Keren Hayesod* and long sought a partnership with non-Zionists, they had already incorporated the idea of an expanded Jewish Agency in their Zionist platform. The German *Keren Hayesod* had demonstrated the advantage of a *Bündnis* (pact) with the non-Zionists. Experience had shown that such cooperation was a means of strengthening the Zionist Organization on the one hand, and expanding the circle of friends and supporters of Palestine, on the other. *Keren Hayesod* modus in Germany was thus defined as Zionist responsibility.

The concept of Zionist responsibility was developed by Kurt Blumenfeld, Felix Rosenblüth and Robert Weltsch as an outgrowth of the sociological theories of Max Weber. They argued that the policies adopted by a public body could not be guided solely by some lofty ideal; it was also imperative to

---

1   Yigal Elam, *The Jewish Agency – Formative Years, 1919–1931* (Jerusalem, 1990) (Hebrew).

consider the realities of time and place. Those who clung to ideals alone were liable to get nothing done, whereas those who charged ahead without them were sure to lose their way. "Policy" meant building a bridge between ideals and actions. Thus a statesman had to be a person who operated responsibly and was ready to compromise and organize his priorities in a way that enabled the ideals to become an attainable reality. Responsibility was therefore of the essence in political work. In the Zionist context, it meant concentrating on the building of a strong economy as the prerequisite for a Jewish national entity. In light of the obstacles and financial constraints which presented themselves and made this task even more difficult, the Zionist leaders had a responsibility to share the burden with non-Zionists, even if the price was relinquishing the democratic principle that required the convening of a Jewish Congress. *Keren Hayesod* was perceived as a more realistic way of expanding the Jewish Agency, by moving from a limited economic partnership, to a shared responsibility in which all contributors took part.[2]

There were, of course, German Zionists who opposed the expansion of the Jewish Agency, in particular Richard Lichtheim, who had aligned himself with Jabotinsky and thereby taken his first step toward Revisionism. There was also a small General Zionist group in Germany, along the lines of *Al Hamishmar* in Poland, which favored the Congress idea. Most of its members were recent East European immigrants, among them Moses Waldman, a journalist and head of the Association of East European Jews, *Verband der Ostjuden*; Max Soloveichik, who had been minister of Jewish affairs in the Lithuanian government until 1922 and a member of the Zionist Executive since the 12th Zionist Congress; and Nahum Goldmann, who came to Germany as a youngster and became involved in Zionist activities after World War I. Other opponents of an expanded Jewish Agency were veteran Zionists Rudolf Samuel of *Hapoel Hatzair*, and Aron and Lazarus Barth of *Mizrahi*.[3]

2 Weltsch's article, "Von Karlsbad nach Kassel," in *JR*, September 8, 1922, and his editorial in *JR*, May 4, 1923; Rosenblüth's remarks at the Kassel convention, in *JR*, September 15, 1922, and the Berlin Zionist assembly, May 30, 1923, in *JR*, June 1, 1923: 260; Blumenfeld's remarks at the Dresden convention, in *JR*, June 29, 1923: 324, the General Zionist assembly preceding the Carlsbad congress, in *Haolam* (London), August 17, 1923: 593–4, and at the 13th Zionist Congress, *Protokoll des XIII. Zionisten-Kongresses 1923*, 248–52. Weber's influence on Blumenfeld's political beliefs can be seen in his article in *JR*, July 7, 1925: 465, and his letters to Schocken, November 9, 1931 and Ben-Gurion, February 6, 1949, in Blumenfeld, *Im Kampf um den Zionismus*, 114, 231.

3 Lichtheim's article in two parts, in *JR*, May 11 and May 23, 1923. As for the attitudes of other opponents, see: minutes of the Dresden Convention, *JR*, June 29, 1923 and July 3, 1923.

Nonetheless, the opponents were in the minority. The 19th annual convention of the ZVfD at Dresden on June 25–27, 1923, showed as much. All the delegates were in agreement that the economic development of Palestine was the foremost objective and that this work should be carried out under the banner of national revival and the guidance of the Zionist movement.

The platform for the soon-to-be-convened 13th Zionist Congress was prepared by the "central bloc" led by Rosenblüth, the outgoing ZVfD chairman, who was about to settle in Palestine. This platform was supportive of the expansion of the Jewish Agency, but left open the manner in which it would be achieved. Even those who objected to Weizmann's policy of negotiating with "notables" found it acceptable, since it emphasized the need for reorganization and the establishment of financial institutions without reference to the enlargement issue. Thanks to the consensus on the centrality of the economic objective, the platform was approved by a vote of 61 to 28, although there were 27 abstentions. The ZVfD also elected a new chairman, Alfred Landsberg, a lawyer from Wiesbaden. Landsberg was a relatively recent convert to Zionism as one of the many Jewish soldiers jarred by the *Judenzählung* and antisemitism encountered at the front during World War I. However, with his election, he rose to become a highly dedicated and active German Zionist leader. Blumenfeld, the chief ideologue and formulator of the "Zionist responsibility" concept, was then experiencing a lull in his career. In late 1922, he had been sent to the United States as an emissary of the Zionist Executive and *Keren Hayesod*, but apparently was not very successful. On returning to Germany the following summer, he considered retiring from Zionist activity and devoting himself to business. Meanwhile, it was Rosenblüth who led the ZVfD delegation at the 13th Congress.[4]

Unity at the 13th Zionist Congress

The 13th Zionist Congress at Carlsbad in August 1923 gave the ZVfD its first opportunity to present a unified front and further strengthened the will of the ZVfD leaders to continue in their chosen path. Of the 292 Congress delegates,

---

4   *Landesvorstand* meetings of April 4, 1923, June 6, 1923, CZA, KH2/3/I; and June 7, 1923 and July 21, 1923, CZA, F4/32; minutes of the Dresden convention, *JR*, June 29, 1923, July 3, 1923. On Landsberg, see my interview with his daughter, Eva Pelz, on November 6, 1982, OHD. See also Jochanan Ginat's introduction to Blumenfeld, *Im Kampf um den Zionismus*, 9–21.

168, or 57.5 percent, represented national *Landsmannschaften* organizations. The Polish federation was the largest contingent, with 39 delegates, followed by the German and Austrian delegations, with 13 each. The remaining 42.5 percent were party delegates: *Mizrahi* was first in line with 70 representatives, and the *Hitahdut* (*Hapoel Hatzair* and *Tzeirei Zion*) was second with 33.

This complicated structure was a reflection of serious political differences which came to the fore in the Jewish Agency issue and produced an ambivalence towards Chaim Weizmann. It became clear during the proceedings that expanding the Jewish Agency was opposed not only by *Mizrahi* and the left-wingers, but also by the many General Zionists. During the Congress, the *Al Hamishmar* group from Poland met likeminded Zionists from other countries and set up the Radical Faction which was joined by nearly 40 delegates. Opposition also came from Jabotinsky and his supporters, who eventually formed the Revisionist party.

In the other camp were the 11-member American delegation, the Polish *Et Livnot* faction and the German Zionists, who established the pro-Weizmann *Vereinigte Landsmannschaften* (United Federations). This bloc included only General Zionists and was smaller than the opposition, to which all the political parties belonged. Also, its basis for cooperation – support of an expanded Jewish Agency, was confined to this one issue. Unlike the German Zionists, the *Et Livnot* and American delegates were against the idea of national capital and the alliance with the Left in the sphere of settlement. Their interest in a broader Jewish Agency derived largely from their desire to see a change in Weizmann's economic approach. However, the political disagreement in the opposition was far greater. Even the Jewish Congress question was in dispute, let alone leadership policy. The *Hitahdut* and Radical Faction rejected Weizmann's notables policy but supported his pro-labor socioeconomic program; *Mizrahi* was against Weizmann altogether. Furthermore, none of the large factions could present an alternative candidate to Weizmann.

Despite the size of the opposition, these deep rifts kept it from deposing Weizmann or forcing him to change his policy. The Congress approved both his continued leadership and his plans for the Jewish Agency. Nonetheless, the opposition did have some influence: expansion plans were linked to the continuation of efforts to convene a Jewish Congress. The lack of full support for Weizmann was expressed in the makeup of the new Zionist Executive. True, the reelection of Menahem Ussishkin was blocked by the elimination of the post of chairman in the Zionist Executive in Palestine, and Richard Lichtheim was also voted out – both of them Weizmann opponents, whereas Weizmann stalwart Louis Lipsky was elected. On the other hand, Weizmann still had to contend with members of the *Hitahdut* and *Mizrahi* who were on the Executive, as well as Radical Faction leader Max Soloveichik.[5]

The conclusion reached by German Zionists such as Rosenblüth, Weltsch, and Bileski was that the WZO was in need of reorganization if it was to function as a democratic political body. As a group that had undertaken to back Weizmann in full, the ZVfD delegation decided to set itself up as the core of a majority bloc with political clout that would attract other Weizmann supporters. As soon as the Congress was over, the German Zionists and colleagues from the *Landsmannschaften* opened the *Informationsstelle für die gemeinsamen Interessen der zionistischen Landsmannschaften* (Information Bureau for the Common Interests of the Zionist Federations) in Berlin. Three of the five members were German Zionists – Bileski, Hantke and Isaak Feuerring, one of the heads of the *Herzl Bund*, an association of Zionist businessmen. The two others were *Et Livnot* representative Mathias Hindes and Zionist statesman Victor Jacobson, who was appointed office director.

However, this political initiative soon lost its momentum. The stumbling block was adherence to General Zionism and a disdain for party politics. The German Zionist leadership was guided by the concept of Zionist responsibility, and argued that it was General Zionism that had undertaken to further the Zionist cause in the spheres of politics, finance, outreach and cultural activity. The General Zionists had laid the foundations for the development of Palestine and the dissemination of Jewish culture and fostered the unity required for external political activity. In contrast, the political parties emphasized divisiveness and narrow interests that outweighed their sense of Zionist duty. This left General Zionism to shoulder the day to day responsibility for Zionism, and virtually paralyzed the WZO as a political organization. The baleful influence of party politics had been borne out at the Zionist Congress, where the political bloc had almost succeeded in ousting Weizmann although it could offer no viable alternative. According to Rosenblüth and his colleagues, the political parties had allowed themselves to act irresponsibly because they were used to depending on the General Zionists for a solution. In this case, however, the shift in the balance of power had led to serious consequences. The electoral power amassed through selfishness had weakened the General Zionists and their capacity for decisionmaking and homogeneous leadership. In Rosenblüth's eyes, it was imperative that General Zionism become the

---

5   *Protokoll des XIII. Zionisten-Kongresses, 1923;* Böhm, *Die Zionistische Bewegung,* vol. II, (Tel Aviv, 1937), 342–53; Weltsch's article in *JR,* August 22, 1923, no. 71/2 (unpaginated); F. Rosenblüth, *JR,* September 7, 1923: 473–4. Soloveichick resigned from the Executive shortly after.

nucleus of the WZO so that aside from day-to-day affairs, it could assume responsibility for major political decisions. By unifying the national Zionist organizations, it was hoped that General Zionism would be restored to its former status and the parties relegated to the sidelines as before.[6]

In consequence, the German Zionists refrained from reorganizing along political lines and remained loyal to General Zionism. The *Informationsstelle* in Berlin soon closed and the plans for organizational reform, unification and greater support for Weizmann came to nought.

Weizmann was partly responsible for this failure. Toward the end of 1923, *Jüdische Rundschau* editor Robert Weltsch was sent to London as Weizmann's secretary for public relations and internal Zionist affairs. Weltsch had attempted to reestablish communication between the political center in London and the national Zionist organizations, and to consolidate a General Zionist framework in favor of Weizmann. However, Weizmann ignored Weltsch's pleas to campaign amongst his supporters. He refused to admit that he was no longer the undisputed leader and was dependent on the backing of an organized public, although he did agree to appear at the ZVfD convention in 1924. Indeed, Weizmann's participation opened a new era in his relations with the German Zionists, and he was soon invited to Berlin as a guest of the German *Keren Hayesod*.[7]

The German Zionists were thus undergoing a transition from "*Stam Zionismus*" ("ordinary" Zionism) with a radical Palestine orientation to a politicized General Zionism in support of Weizmann. However, they stopped short of establishing a political party. There is no doubt that Weizmann's passive, even derisory attitude worked against this, but it was probably not the major factor since Weizmann did make an appearance before his supporters in Germany. Another excuse for avoiding political organization was the argument

6   Articles of Weltsch and Rosenblüth, see note 5 above; Bileski's circular of November 23, 1923, Schocken Archives, 538/62; Rosenblüth's memorandum prior to *Zentralkomitee* meeting, October 7, 1923, Schocken Archives, 531/241; *Zentralkomitee* decisions, October 7, 1923, Schocken Archives, 531/51; Bileski's remarks to the *Landesvorstand*, December 20, 1923, CZA, KH2/3/II; Information Bureau circulars of early 1924, Schocken Archives, 538/62.

7   On Weltsch's mission see decisions of *Zentralkomitee*, note 6, above; *Landesvorstand* meeting, November 11, 1923, CZA, KH2/3/I; Weltsch's letters to Weizmann, November 2, 1923, November 23, 1923, January 1, 1924, January 15, 1924, January 28, 1924, February 12, 1924 and December 1, 1924, WA; Weizmann's letters to Weltsch, January 15, 1924 and February 29, 1924, and to Feiwel, Jacobson and Weltsch, February 15, 1924, in *Weizmann Letters*, Vol. XII, 91–7, 136–9, 151–5. Landsberg's circular, distributed before the convention to all the Zionist associations, December 5, 1924, Schocken Archives, 431/241; Weltsch's editorial in *JR*, December 16, 1924. On Weizmann's Berlin visit, see Chapter Five.

that Zionist work on behalf of Palestine required a unified General Zionist approach. General Zionism was touted as a channel for practical achievement whereas political parties supposedly spent all their time propagandizing. Yet even according to the German Zionist outlook, which drew upon the concepts of a democracy in a sovereign state, there was room for a Zionist Organization made up of parties with different views. The Zionist Executive would then be in the hands of the majority party, and the development of Palestine would follow this party's principles. In consequence, the Organization's operations in the political, settlement, financial and educational spheres would be up for constant review, and periodic changes would be made as determined by the majority party in power.

The adherence of the German Zionists to non-partisan General Zionism was probably due to the key importance they attributed to economic development and the participation of non-Zionists. Their success in promoting the economic advancement of Palestine and engendering such cooperation was highly reliant on stressing common interests rather than elements which sowed discord. Thus they embraced neutrality, shunned political splintering, and even though they recognized the need for reforms in the Zionist Organization, they chose a middle path.

The Right-Wing Challenge

The onset of the Fourth *Aliya* in summer 1924 raised questions about the Zionist settlement policy at the beginning of the decade that called for the creation of a powerful public sector in Palestine which could direct private investment in accordance with social and national objectives.

During the years of the Third *Aliya* (1919–1923), the Zionist Executive had determined guidelines for the use of the national capital. In the realm of infrastructure, the acquisition and reclamation of land was declared top priority, and in the area of social services, the development of a Hebrew educational system. Most of the public resources, however, found their way into the agricultural settlement enterprise, both because of its crucial national importance and the enormity of the task. As a result, the public sector went beyond laying infrastructure and guiding and aiding private initiative to become an entrepreneur in its own right. Moreover, so much money was poured into agriculture that little was left over for private ventures, even in the sphere of farming.[8]

The Zionist left-wing parties were among the supporters of national capital policy from the start, although they had certain reservations, and this support led to cooperation, especially in the area of agricultural settlement. The head of the Zionist Settlement Department at that time was Arthur Ruppin who was known for his interest in workers' cooperatives even before World War I. From the 1920s, the Settlement and Labor Departments were controlled by the left-wing parties, and the projects of the Jewish National Fund (JNF) were closely coordinated with them. The Zionist Executive thus initiated the establishment of settlements on JNF land with the financial assistance of *Keren Hayesod*, and populated them with young workers who lacked the means to settle on their own. Hence "Labor Settlement" in Palestine evolved as a joint undertaking of the Zionist Executive and the Labor movement.[9]

The German Zionists, among the early proponents of national settlement, gave their blessing to this policy by expressing unflagging support for Weizmann, under whose aegis it was carried out, and maintaining active ties with the institutions involved. Moreover, many of these bodies had German Zionists at their helm. Arthur Hantke was one of the directors of *Keren Hayesod*; Otto Warburg was a JNF board member; Salman Schocken was a member of the *Finanz- und Wirschaftsrat* (Financial and Economic Council) of the Zionist Executive; not to mention Arthur Ruppin who was head of the Zionist Settlement Department.

The German Zionists wholeheartedly endorsed the national capital policy until 1923. From that point, however, cracks began to appear in the formerly solid consensus in the WZO. The empty coffers of the Zionist funds and the onset of an economic recession in Palestine led to doubts over the ability of the Zionist Organization to carry out the projects it had initiated. Critics had already arisen in Palestine, Poland, and the United States, and these voices were growing steadily louder. Even some members of the Zionist Executive called into question the wisdom of investing such a large proportion of the national

---

8   Jacob Metzer, "Economic Structure and National Goals – The Jewish National Home in Interwar Palestine," *Journal of Economic History* 38, no. 1 (March 1978): 101–19; Metzer, *National Capital*, 32–9; Lavsky, *The Foundations*, 81–114.

9   Lavsky, *The Foundations*, 81–114; Alex Bein, *The Return to the Soil* (Jerusalem, 1957), Chapters Four–Six.

capital in agricultural settlement.[10] The outcry quietened somewhat when the Zionist Executive moved to expand the Jewish Agency. This pushed aside many of the question marks that hung over the functioning of the public sector, and gave center stage to the issue of financial consolidation. The debate thus shifted from national capital versus private initiative, to a showdown between those who sought the immediate reinforcement of the public sector and those who feared that financial considerations would mean compromising on matters of principle. The result was a split in the Weizmann camp that pitted groups which supported his economic policy against one another, for example the German Zionists and the Radical Faction led by Gruenbaum, and downplayed their disagreement with the proponents of private investment.

In 1924, the economy of the *Yishuv* in Palestine improved, and this trend continued until the summer of 1925. The Fourth *Aliya*, which began in the spring of 1924, contributed to this growth by bringing in middle-class immigrants from Poland who possessed considerable private capital. It also accelerated the development of the towns, especially Tel Aviv, sparking unprecedented commercial growth and causing real-estate costs to spiral. On the other hand, the public capital sector shrank relative to the scope of immigration, and publicly-funded agricultural settlement came to a virtual halt.[11]

The economic boom triggered by the Fourth *Aliya* refocused Zionist attention on settlement policy. Advocates of public capital feared that the prosperity of the moment might endanger their policy, and articles by Weltsch appeared in the *Jüdische Rundschau* and *Haolam* in the summer and fall of 1924 to draw attention to this phenomenon. Weltsch warned against the anarchy that might erupt if the private pursuits of the immigrants were not balanced by national projects, and argued that rapid urban development made necessary a concerted effort in the agricultural sphere to insure the special character of the economy.[12]

Supporters of private capital in Palestine and Poland were quick to join the fray. They maintained that the time had passed for a policy based on public entrepreneurship and they demanded that the Zionist movement concentrate

---

10 For example, the criticism voiced by Georg Halpern, Financial and Economic Council member, at the 13th Zionist Congress, *Protokoll des XIII. Zionisten-Kongresses*, 1923, 78–83.

11 Dan Giladi, *Jewish Palestine during the Period of the Fourth Aliya (1924–1929) – Economic and Social Aspects* (Tel Aviv, 1973) (Hebrew), Chapter Four.

12 *JR*, July 15, 1924: 402; see also Weltsch's article in *JR*, November 7, 1924: 629–30. From the start, Weizmann had doubts about the solidity of the economic surge. See his letter from Palestine to Vera Weizmann, September 27, 1924, *Weizmann Letters*, vol. XII, 240–2.

on assisting private ventures of all kinds, especially in the towns. Hence, they challenged both the principle of national capital and the centrality of the Labor movement in the agricultural settlement enterprise.[13]

In this way, new struggles overshadowed the old in the Zionist movement and the consensus once enjoyed by Weizmann slowly eroded. As noted earlier, Weizmann had lost considerable support when the radical Zionists opposed him on the expansion of the Jewish Agency, although they still concurred on economic policy. Now he forfeited votes in the private initiative sector which had backed him on the Jewish Agency issue, mainly members of *Et Livnot* in Poland. Moreover, turning the spotlight on the problems of the settlement policy did little to mute the criticism of anti-expansionists. On the contrary, the Radical Faction cited the Fourth *Aliya* as evidence that the expanded Jewish Agency was no longer needed since capital was now flowing into Palestine without it. At the same time, it pointed to the private initiative advocates among the Jewish Agency supporters as proof of their suspicions that the Zionist movement would lose control if the expansion took place.[14]

By now, Jabotinsky and the Revisionists were an additional force to contend with. Jabotinsky had become an opponent of the Zionist Executive since his resignation from that body at the beginning of 1923, and during the Fourth *Aliya* period, he forged an alternative Zionist ideology which also represented middle-class interests. Jabotinsky objected to the very idea that the Zionist Organization was responsible for Jewish settlement in Palestine, either on its own or under the aegis of an expanded Jewish Agency. In his view, this was the task of the Mandatory government, which had undertaken to provide the framework and infrastructure for a Jewish national home. Jabotinsky argued that only a government-sponsored "colonization regime" would pave the way for mass settlement and the creation of a Jewish majority in Palestine. Since most Jews belonged to the middle-class, urban settlement was deemed more suitable than the pursuit of agriculture. Moreover, it was believed that industrialization offered better chances for economic success. Jabotinsky demanded that the Zionist Executive expend its energies not on settlement but on pressuring the British Government to fulfill the duties that came with accepting the Mandate. Experience had shown that without a supportive government framework, settlement efforts were futile in any case, and they were even harmful

---

13 *Protokoll des XIV. Zionisten-Kongresses, 1925*; Giladi, *Jewish Palestine*, Chapter Five.

14 Weltsch's report of the Polish Zionist convention, Grünbaum's descent and the the rise of Gottlieb and Levite, in *JR*, January 16, 1925: 39; Jacob Klatzkin, "Die Agency Unterwegs" *JR*, August 7, 1925: 531, and Weltsch's editorial in the same issue.

because they diverted Zionist attention from the primary objective of expanding the *Yishuv* and exerting pressure on the British Government.[15]

Opposition to Weizmann and the prevailing Zionist leadership thus seeped into the right-wing sector of the General Zionist camp. To compound Weizmann's troubles, in the period prior to the 14th Zionist Congress in the summer of 1925, a tactical pact was formed between the two groups, the Revisionists on the right and the Radical Faction on the left. The antipathy to Jewish Agency expansion that brought the two groups together was apparently more powerful than the chasm between their basic Zionist and socioeconomic beliefs.[16]

Pro-Left Consolidation

After these changes in General Zionism, especially in Poland, which boasted the largest concentration of General Zionists, the German Zionists remained the only unified group supporting all aspects of Weizmann's policy. Thus they decided to organize independently in his defense. A surge of activity followed the 20th ZVfD convention in Wiesbaden, attended by Weizmann at the end of December 1924. At this forum, Alfred Landsberg completed his short tenure as chairman and was replaced by Kurt Blumenfeld, who headed the ZVfD until his move to Palestine in 1933, after the Nazi takeover of Germany. Robert Weltsch had returned to Germany after a year's stay in London and resumed his editorship of the *Jüdische Rundschau*. Landsberg continued to dedicate himself to the Zionist cause and cultivated a personal relationship with Weizmann. He was a key figure in various projects sponsored by the German Zionists, and after settling in Palestine in 1932, became one of the founders of the Rural and Suburban Settlement Company, better known as "RASSCO."

Following this change of guard, the ZVfD began to devise new political stratagems to thwart the right-wing opposition. Blumenfeld, his deputy, Martin Rosenblüth (brother of Felix, director of the Palestine Office in Vienna and the Austrian *Keren Hayesod*), and Robert Weltsch launched a publicity campaign that was directed both inward, toward the German Zionists, and outward,

---

15 Jabotinsky's congress speech, *Protokoll des XIV. Zionisten-Kongresses, 1925*, 236ff; Yaacov Shavit, *Jabotinsky and the Revisionist Movement, 1925–1948* (London, 1988), 190–6, 275–89.

16 Bulletin presenting the platform and list of candidates, CZA, Z4/215/21; see also Ezra Mendelsohn, *Zionism in Poland – The Formative Years, 1915–1926* (New Haven and London, 1981), 316; Nahum Goldmann, *Mein Leben als Deutscher Jude* (Munich, 1980), 189–90.

toward *Jüdische Rundschau* readers all over Europe. They argued that it was the
task of the Zionist movement to concentrate on the development of Palestine
and educational activities that furthered the goals of radical Zionism.
Agriculture and the efforts of the pioneers were perceived as the key to a
Jewish Palestine. Hence the importance of channelling public resources into the
settlement enterprise, without being sidetracked by the narrow interests of
middle-class immigrants and their spokespersons abroad. Jewish Agency expansion, which had previously been promoted as a means of accelerating the
development of Palestine, was now hailed as an instrument for strengthening
the national capital sector and minimizing the anarchy in the private sector.
This argument was addressed to both sources of opposition: the right-wing
bourgeoisie which advocated Jewish Agency expansion, in this case emphasizing the importance of the Jewish Agency for national capital; and the
Radical Faction, which feared harm to its socio-national objectives, emphasizing
the sense of strength that an expanded Jewish Agency would bring to the
Zionist public.[17]

In addition to the publicity offensive, the German Zionists took other steps
to rescue Weizmann's leadership, but this time, they changed their political
tactics. They stopped presenting General Zionism as the antithesis of the
parties, and decided to establish a quasi-political body of radically-inclined
General Zionists in order to create a coalition with the Zionist Left.

To that end, a committee headed by Blumenfeld prepared the platform for
a joint delegation of German General Zionists at the 14th Zionist Congress
which stated the following:

A. Economic development, reinforcement and expansion of the national home
are at the forefront of Zionist activity.

B. Our responsibility for the success of this enterprise requires us to address
economic issues that have no connection with political beliefs.

C. The current Zionist policy was the correct one, namely a national
settlement policy based on national capital, top priority for agriculture,
recognition of the role of the pioneering laborer in the national enterprise,
and the expansion of the Jewish Agency.

---

17 Martin Rosenblüth's circular to the heads of the local Zionist associations, July 2, 1925, CZA,
KH2/180/I; Weltsch's articles in *JR*, July 3, 1925: 451–2, and July 7, 1925: 469; Blumenfeld's article,
JR, July 7, 1925: 464; *JR*, editorial, August 14, 1925.

On a tactical level, the platform called for organizational reforms to facilitate the establishment of a strong Executive empowered by a clear majority.[18]

Tactically, the change in political orientation was three-directional: an intensification of the struggle against the Revisionists and the Radical Faction; liaison with like-minded groups in other countries; and attempts to collaborate with the Zionist Left.

Weltsch and Blumenfeld waged a bitter campaign against the alliance between the Radical Faction and the Revisionists and spoke disparagingly of those behind it – Faction leaders Max Soloveichik, Nahum Goldmann and Jacob Klatzkin, a philosopher and publicist who became active in the Zionist movement after the war. They attacked the political style shared by both groups, and their use of slogans and bombastic declarations that were not accompanied by concrete programs or alternative proposals. Following Max Weber, Blumenfeld called this style *"Gesinnungspolitik,"* policy dictated solely by the image of an ideal that would inevitably collide with reality, as opposed to *"Verantwortungspolitik,"* responsible policy, that was realistic in outlook and translated the ideal into an attainable goal.[19]

Little wonder, then, that the clash with the Radical Faction and Revisionists overshadowed the debate with private initiative advocates such as *Et Livnot* in Poland and other groups in the United States. The latter opposed Weizmann's settlement policy, but saw it as only one facet of a broader program. Thus they called for a change in policy, but not Weizmann's resignation, as was demanded by Gruenbaum and Jabotinsky. Blumenfeld and Weltsch reserved their sharpest barbs for the Gruenbaum faction, which was accused of being so blinded by animosity toward Weizmann that it had abandoned its former radical Zionist approach.

This unrelenting criticism produced the desired effect in General Zionist circles. It created such intense feelings against the opposition that the Radical Faction-Revisionist alliance was ousted from the ZVfD altogether.[20]

18 Blumenfeld's circular of June 16, 1925, and *Landesvorstand* minutes, May 20, 1925, CZA, KH2/180/I; *Zentralkomitee* decisions, May 21, 1925, in *JR*, May 26, 1925: 376.

19 *JR*, July 7, 1925: 464; also see Weltsch's article, *JR*, July 3, 1925: 451–2; Blumenfeld's statement at the Berlin assembly, *JR*, July 31, 1925: 516.

20 Blumenfeld's circular, see note 18 above; Blumenfeld's letter to Soloveichik, May 20, 1925, and the latter's response, May 27, 1925, CZA, KH2/180/I.

In another political effort, the German Zionists attempted to unite with groups in other countries in the hope of strengthening the Zionist Executive. This bid proved unsuccessful.[21]

A third tactic was forming a coalition with the Zionist Left. In this sphere, the heads of the ZVfD expected cooperation from the Labor movement, in light of their argument that it was Weizmann's settlement policy in Palestine that was most in danger. *Hapoel Hatzair*, cognizant of the threat posed by the Fourth *Aliya*, was no longer against the Jewish Agency's expansion. Thus it was easily convinced on this point. In Germany, coalitions with *Hapoel Hatzair* and the Left were almost a tradition. *Hapoel Hatzair* had been a very strong party in Germany and there were ZVfD leaders, among them Blumenfeld, who had risen from its ranks. Formally, Robert Weltsch was still a member. The willingness of this party to join the national list may have been the result of a certain attenuation, since many of its prestigious members, including Chaim and Gerda Arlosoroff, had left for Palestine in the early 1920s. In consequence, the ZVfD was able to establish an alliance with *Hapoel Hatzair* prior to the Zionist Congress.[22]

While a coalition with the moderate Left was successful in Germany, that was not the case in the world arena. The General Zionists in Germany openly professed pro-Left sympathies, but their actions showed ambivalence. Before the Zionist Congress, Weltsch and Blumenfeld had criticized the left-wing parties for trying to further their own interests and demanding that the *Histadrut* (Labor Federation) be granted a monopoly over the Zionist settlement enterprise. This criticism was accompanied by a call for the administration of the settlement enterprise according to general Zionist principles which obviously ruled out an alignment with the Left.

In the platform of the ZVfD, and especially its plan for reforms in the Zionist Executive, a certain displeasure with the labor parties and a weakness of the Executive was evident, but these sentiments were carefully veiled. Indeed, when *Landesvorstand* member Salman Schocken called for

---

21 ZVfD letter to the American Zionist convention, May 28, 1925, CZA, KH2/180/I; Rosenblüth's letter to Lipsky, June 22, 1925, CZA, KH1/121/d1; ZVfD circular to all the Zionist federations and factions, May 1, 1925, CZA, Z4/215/21.

22 The agreement with *Hapoel Hatzair* in Germany, *Landesvorstand* minutes, May 20, 1925, CZA, KH2/180/I; *Zentralkomitee* decisions in *JR*, May 26, 1925: 376; Rosenblüth's letter to the Organization Department in London, May 26, 1925, CZA, Z4/215/21.

depoliticizing the administration of the settlement enterprise, this proposal received no support because of its anti-labor implications.[23]

Be that as it may, the pro-Left stance was accepted in Germany and corresponded with the policies of German Zionism since the end of World War I. The political alignment of the ZVfD thus enjoyed the full support of its electorate with the exception of the *Mizrahi* party. In the elections prior to the 14th Zionist Congress, the General Zionist-*Hapoel Hatzair* list won eight out of nine mandates, whereas the Soloveichik list headed by Nahum Goldmann received only one. (Soloveichik attended the Congress, nonetheless, as a member of the Zionist Actions Committee.) The elections also illustrated that the vast majority of German Zionists supported a national list. The world parties fared poorly: *Mizrahi* won two mandates (Lazarus Barth and Israel Rabin) and *Poalei Zion*, one (Alfred Berger).

The German delegation to the Congress was made up of all the leading personalities: Felix Rosenblüth, one of the founders of the radical Palestinocentric approach, who had returned from Palestine and was about to join the Zionist Executive in London; Alfred Klee, a former head of *Binyan Haaretz*, who represented Zionist politics on a community level; Alfred Landsberg, an initiator of the organizational reform program; Salman Schocken, member of the Zionist Executive's Financial and Economic Council; Siegfried Moses, who was Schocken's friend and business manager, and along with Schocken had been deeply involved in the economic rehabilitation of the WZO; Nahum Goldmann, who held the Radical Faction Mandate; Richard Lichtheim, who despite his Revisionist sympathies had not yet joined the opposition; and Robert Weltsch, who represented *Hapoel Hatzair*. Kurt Blumenfeld and Arthur Hantke were not included in the delegation since they would be participating as members of the Zionist Actions Committee. The diversity of this list illustrates the broad consensus that still existed at this time among German Zionists.[24]

23 Rosenblüth's letter to the executive committee, May 20, 1925; Blumenfeld's circular of June 16, 1925, and *Landesvorstand* minutes, July 25, 1925, CZA, KH2/180/I; Weltsch's articles in *JR*, July 3, 1925: 451–2, and July 14, 1925: 476–7; Weltsch's letter to Weizmann, July 9, 1925, WA.

24 Report of elections in *JR*, July 7, 1925: 466, July 24, 1925: 501, August 7, 1925: 529, and list of delegates in *Protokoll des XIV. Zionisten-Kongresses, 1925*; see also Weltsch's article, *JR*, August 11, 1925: 541.

The 14th Zionist Congress and the Failure of Pro-Left Neutrality

The representation and proceedings of the 14th Zionist Congress reflected the critical state of the Weizmann leadership. As in the past, most of the 261 delegates were "*Stam Zionisten*": 168 had been sent by national federations; 45 by *Mizrahi*; and 46 by the labor parties. The largest labor contingent was the *Hitahdut* with 28 representatives. General Zionism, however, was on the verge of collapse, torn apart by the Radical Faction, which had participated in the pre-Congress elections as a separate faction, and the Revisionists, who organized at the Congress itself. Moreover, the two chief national delegations – the United States with 40 delegates and Poland with 35, were ideologically split and did not have a common platform. The Polish body was composed of two rival groups: *Et Livnot*, under the leadership of Gottlieb and Levite; and *Al Hamishmar*, led by Gruenbaum, the founder of the Radical Faction. The American delegation was also divided into two rival camps – the group under Louis Lipsky, the chairman of the Zionist Organization of America, which was the more powerful of the two, and another group that was ideologically close to *Et Livnot*, headed by Abraham Goldberg. However, unlike the Polish delegation, the Americans kept their differences beneath the surface. They did not formalize the rivalry by drawing up competing lists or establishing separate factions at the Congress. The disarray among the General Zionists served to highlight the unity of the German delegation all the more. It was the only national delegation that arrived with a single list and a platform agreed upon by all.[25]

As anticipated, the Congress turned into an arena for attacks on the Labor movement and the pro-labor policies of the Zionist Executive by the General Zionist right-wing and *Mizrahi*. Leading the assault were Levite and Gottlieb of *Et Livnot*, and Polish *Mizrahi* leader Jehoshua Heschel Farbstein. They were joined by spokesmen of the middle-class in Palestine and American advocates of private enterprise. More specifically, these parties protested against the derogatory attitude toward the Fourth *Aliya*, and demanded a total revamping of the Zionist Executive policy. Rather than limiting investment to agricultural settlement, this "new course" would involve diverting funds to urban development and industry. Instead of utilizing public funding to settle indigent agricultural laborers on national land, assistance would be provided to private initiatives in all branches of the economy through a publicly subsidized credit

---

25 Statistics based on the *Protokoll des XIV. Zionisten-Kongresses, 1925*, 728–33. Also see Jabotinsky's remarks, 236, and the responses, 469–70; Weltsch's pre-congress article in *JR*, August 21, 1925.

system. Only thus, they argued, would it be possible to achieve the primary Zionist objective of swift Jewish settlement throughout Palestine. In their eyes, the Fourth *Aliya* was the perfect opportunity to realize this goal, but the Zionist Executive was standing in the way. They demanded that it free itself from labor party pressure, which had produced the current narrow-minded policy, and face the fact that the new wave of middle-class immigrants had severed the traditional ties between labor and the general good of the Zionist enterprise.

These right-wing accusations were also supported by persons close to the Executive, although they refrained from attacking the labor camp. George Halpern, a member of the Zionist Executive's Financial and Economic Council, spoke in favor of industrialization and private enterprise. Salman Schocken, who sat on the same council, called for a depoliticization of the Executive and the appointment of a professional body to handle settlement affairs (this was the same proposal rejected earlier by the ZVfD).[26]

In response to this situation the heads of the German Zionist list took another step toward political organization. Along with their colleagues on the Zionist Actions Committee, Berthold Feiwel, Victor Jacobson, and Arthur Ruppin, as well as "*Stam Zionisten*" from other countries, they formed the *Freie Zionistische Gruppe* (Free Zionist Group). Membership rose to 17 when Robert Weltsch decided to relinquish his formal affiliation with the *Hitahdut* in favor of this group.

As the spokesman of the *Freie Zionistische Gruppe*, Kurt Blumenfeld adopted a neutral stance, neither Left nor Right, which he deemed the only "responsible" one. His remarks were punctuated with the words "*Verantwortungspolitik*" (a responsible policy), and "*Sachlichkeit*" (a "to-the-point" approach). Blumenfeld called upon all sides to view the Zionist enterprise responsibly, and to refrain from mixing valid criticism with partisan interests. His answer to the right-wing bourgeoisie, which clamored for greater opportunity for the Jewish middle-class, was that the Zionist enterprise was not a "transfer" of the Jewish people from the Diaspora to the Land of Israel, but a social and economic "transformation." As for the Left, which aspired to create an even stronger bond between national capital and the Labor movement, Blumenfeld urged its acceptance of practical reforms in Zionist economic policy. He claimed that the German Zionists had earned the right to make this appeal to both sides because of their particular interest in the

---

26 *Protokoll des XIV. Zionisten-Kongresses, 1925*, remarks of Farbstein, 143–5, Gottlieb, 147–53, Suprasky, 195–8, Levite, 381–4, Halpern, 70–4, and Schocken, 342–52.

economy of Palestine over the years and their loyal support of Weizmann's policy. It was the German Zionists, he said, who had displayed a responsible, practical, non-political approach without turning a blind eye to the problems. All in all, Blumenfeld envisaged a unified Zionist Executive that would continue to be bound by the principles of the Zionist enterprise, while remaining impervious to political pressures.[27]

Blumenfeld and his colleagues were convinced that they were articulating a totally neutral position, and even more importantly, one that could not be construed as anti-Left. There was, after all, a great difference between their generalized appeal for a homogeneous leadership and the explicitness of Schocken, who was not speaking in their name but as a member of the Financial and Economic Council. Schocken wanted control over economic affairs to be wrested from the political parties and handed over to professionals, whereas Blumenfeld, speaking for the German Zionists, called upon the labor representatives to act responsibly and *take it upon themselves* to free economic decision-making from vested interests. He never uttered a word about taking away the share of the workers part in determining the use of the national capital.

These, however, were subtle distinctions that were of no interest to anyone aside from Blumenfeld and his associates. In view of the mood at the Congress and the attentiveness of the Zionist Executive to the criticism of the Right, left-wingers did not distinguish between Blumenfeld and Schocken, or between their demands and those of the Right. As far as they were concerned, they were under attack from all sides. Even those close to the Zionist Executive and declared supporters of the Left among the General Zionists were against them – all of them bent on liberating the Executive from the pressure of the workers' parties. In reaction, the Left took an uncompromising position, turning against the Zionist Executive itself. At the same time, it opposed any program of reform and withheld support for Weizmann in his confrontation with the Right.

A vote of confidence in Weizmann proposed by the Congress standing committee produced a tepid response: 136 votes, or 43 percent of all Congress participants. *Mizrahi* and the workers parties abstained, and the Revisionists and Radical Faction voted against. The 14th Zionist Congress adjourned without reaching any clear decision or electing an Executive. The right-wing

---

27 *Protokoll des XIV. Zionisten-Kongresses, 1925*, 164–171 and appendix; *JR*, August 21, 1925: 562; Weltsch's articles in *JR*, August 25, 1925: 571; and August 24, 1925: 549–50.

opposition did not win approval for its "new course," but it was the Left that prevented Weizmann from gaining the legitimacy he sought.[28]

The German Zionists thus failed in their mission to create a new bloc of support for Weizmann's leadership. They left the Congress feeling that they had suffered a double defeat. On the one hand, they were disappointed in the Left for its refusal to accept a limited program of reform. Robert Weltsch, who was still weighing his continued membership in *Hapoel Hatzair*, was so distressed by the course of events at the Congress that he resigned. However, an even greater disappointment for the leaders of German Zionism was the failure of pro-Weizmann General Zionism to defend itself or put up a fight for its existence. They blamed the American Zionists led by Lipsky, who were not prepared to side with the German Zionists, their natural allies, and had thereby prevented the emergence of a *Linkbürgerlicher Flügel* – a left-leaning middle-class sector that could have established a clear pro-Weizmann majority. At the same time, they criticized Weizmann himself for not taking a clear stand on the program presented by his own supporters.

As the German Zionists mulled over the lessons to be learned, those in favor of political parties concluded that a General Zionist party was preferable to a national organization operating in the framework of the WZO. Arguments along these lines were put forward by Georg Landauer of *Hapoel Hatzair*, Aron Barth of *Mizrahi*, and even Nahum Goldmann of the Radical Faction. Voices from the center, however, including such mainstays of the German Zionist movement as Blumenfeld, Hantke, Weltsch and Rosenblüth as well as Bileski, Schocken and Feuerring, called for the preservation of a national, non-partisan format. The issue at hand was whether such a body could be established and at the same time maintain a pro-Left orientation.[29]

---

28 *Protokoll des XIV. Zionisten-Kongresses, 1925*: remarks of Ben-Gurion, 208, and Kaplansky, 110, and the resolutions. Also see Weltsch's articles in *JR*, August 28, 1925: 579, September 1, 1925: 589; Rosenblüth's article in *JR*, September 11, 1925: 612 (includes a description of the standing committee). Weizmann left the Congress before it was over when he realized that there was no chance of electing an Executive. (This body was chosen by the Zionist Actions Committee at its meeting in October 1925.)

29 Weltsch's articles in *JR*, August 25, 1925: 571, September 1, 1925: 589, September 4, 1925: 595, January 5, 1926: 4; Weltsch's letters to Weizmann, July 9, 1925 and September 14, 1925, and Blumenfeld's letter to Weizmann, September 30, 1925, WA; Weltsch's letter to Bergman, September 4, 1925, NULA, 1502/1334/3; ZVfD Presidency circular, October 14, 1925 and report, November 5, 1925, and Blumenfeld's letter to Hantke, November 9, 1925, CZA, KH2/180/I; minutes of a General Zionist meeting, October 26, 1925, CZA, L9/7; *Landesvorstand* minutes, January 10, 1926, CZA, Z4/2009, and April 26, 1926, CZA, Z4/2141/V. See also Moritz Bileski, "Allgemeiner Zionismus," *JR*, December 30, 1925.

CHAPTER SEVEN

THE LEFTIST CENTER

Establishment of the *Linkes Zentrum*

The first signs that the period of economic prosperity in Palestine was about to end appeared on the horizon in summer 1925. From 1926, the country slid rapidly into a major depression. This turnabout was set off by the gap between the import of private capital, which steadily declined, and the wave of immigration that continued full force until mid–1926. In Palestine, the crisis was clearly felt by the beginning of that year, as companies went bankrupt and unemployment soared, especially in Tel Aviv, where the prosperity had been most evident. However, the overseas Zionist public was alerted to the situation only towards the second half of 1926, when the flow of immigrants began to slow down and when emigration from Palestine rose due to unemployment. By the end of the year, as the extent of the crisis became apparent, the Zionist leadership began to fear for the future of the entire Zionist enterprise.[1]

In describing this crisis, it is important to distinguish between the objective economic processes, which can be fully examined and evaluated only in retrospect, and their subjective effect on those who lived through them and responded, politically and otherwise. Objectively, the crisis reached its lowest point in mid–1926 and affected the urban sector alone, while the agricultural sector continued to flourish. However, such phenomena as unemployment and dwindling immigration, especially emigration, which peaked in 1927, were highly distressing to the Jews of Palestine and even more so, to the Diaspora Zionists. Before that, the emigrants were passed off as transient, and a natural product of the absorption process and mass immigration. The heads of the Zionist institutions and the right-wing thus cooperated in an effort to increase

---

1   Giladi, *Jewish Palestine*, Chapter Six.

public funding and extend more support to private initiatives in the urban and rural sectors that had succeeded in weathering the crisis.[2]

A sense of confidence in Zionist economic policy was especially evident among the German Zionists, who were generally attuned to events in Palestine. In Germany, 1926 was a year devoted to fundraising, expansion of educational and pioneer-training activities among Zionist youth, and general political-ideological debates outside the realm of settlement policy. At the ZVfD convention in Erfurt in August 1926, economics and settlement were absent from the agenda, and the issue of a German Zionist party to exert influence on General Zionist politics was not even raised.[3]

Only at the end of 1926 was attention refocused on the economy, when it became clear that the routine response of stepping up contributions was not enough to solve the financial problems in Palestine, and that the crisis was going from bad to worse. It was no longer possible to turn a blind eye to the Zionist Organization's inability to alleviate unemployment, move its agricultural settlements towards self-sufficiency or solve the serious problems in the *Histadrut*, such as resuscitating the bankrupt *Solel Boneh* contracting firm. As a result, private enterprise advocates, the General Zionist right-wing and the Revisionists renewed their demand for reforms in Zionist settlement policy.

Now, however, it was not only the right-wing opposition that rose up but also the pro-Left General Zionists. The first call came from Weltsch, who recently had left *Hapoel Hatzair*. In his October 1926 article, "Three Demands," Weltsch spoke out in favor of a new immigration policy and more rational economic planning. He also rejected the notion that Palestine was ready to serve as a haven for large numbers of Jewish refugees:

> Palestine is not yet capable of being a country of absorption.... It is a mistake to think that Zionism is in a position today to solve the Jewish problem in a literal sense. Zionism is currently laying the foundations for a great enterprise... and it is guided by the view that *Eretz Israel* will develop *gradually* into a center of power. One day it

---

2   This is the impression which emerges from the newspapers in 1926. In his *JR* article of August 6, 1926, Hugo Herrmann avoided the term *Krise* (crisis), in favor of *"schwierige wirtschaftliche Lage"* (a difficult economic situation). The Urban Settlement Department under Meir Dizengoff was established after the 14th Congress. On increasing the public funding and the founding of a credit or loan fund, see minutes of Zionist Actions Committee, July 1926, CZA, Z4/272/12.

3   *Landesvorstand* report to the Erfurt convention, and the convention minutes in *JR*, August 27, 1926.

will be a natural, living organism that will offer a new and altogether different solution to the Jewish problem.... *However, in order for Zion to fulfill its task as a haven of refuge at some future date it must be allowed to grow and take shape quietly and undisturbed.*[4]

Weltsch doubted that the new fledgling economy of Palestine could absorb masses of immigrants within a short span of time, and believed that restricting the number of immigrants was essential. He also felt that emigration was virtually unavoidable. His main conclusion was that the time for experimentation was over; what was needed now was a rational and productive economy that promoted self-sufficiency and rapid profitability. For the German Zionists, economic reform was viewed as crucial for the advancement of the Zionist enterprise in keeping with its long-standing principles, and for preserving the alliance between Weizmann and the Zionist Left. Hence the renewed attempts at political organization by the German Zionist leadership despite its previous failures.[5]

At the end of February 1927, an advisory conference was held in Berlin attended by Kurt Blumenfeld, Martin Rosenblüth, and his brother Felix, who was a member of the Zionist Executive and head of its Organization Department, Weltsch, Schocken, Bileski, who had left Palestine because of the depression, Berlin lawyer and *Landesvorstand* member Erich Cohn, and lawyer Meinhold Nussbaum, chairman of the Nuremberg Zionist chapter. Also making their debut as Zionist leaders were Werner David Senator of the Joint Distribution Committee, who was involved in Jewish welfare activities in Eastern Europe and emigrated to Palestine in 1930 as a member of the Jewish Agency Executive; Isaak Feuerring, who was already active among the General Zionists and, after moving to Palestine in 1934, promoted agricultural settlement among the middle-class (the village of Beit Yitzhak was established in his name); lawyer Herbert Foerder, a former leader of the KJV student association, who later became a director of RASSCO and *Bank Leumi*; and the physician Alfred Schwarz, also among the heads of the KJV.

The discussions, chaired by Schocken, centered on an economic consolidation program drawn up by Felix Rosenblüth. The outcome was a platform drafted by Martin Rosenblüth that was distributed among ZVfD members and

---

4   The article appeared in two installments: *JR*, October 8, 1926: 559–60, and October 15, 1926: 573–4. See 559 for quotation (emphasis in the original).

5   Executive committee meeting, January 24, 1927; *Landesvorstand* meeting, January 30, 1927, CZA, Z4/3567/I.

sympathizers abroad. For a time, it seemed that, once again, the entire ZVfD would rally around this one program. However, at the *Landesvorstand* in May, it became clear that even if the program represented the majority, a separate faction was emerging. It was here that the name *Linkes Zentrum* (Leftist Center) came into being. After a lengthy debate in the ZVfD and on the pages of the *Jüdische Rundschau*, Blumenfeld and Bileski worked out a detailed proposal for presentation at the 15th Zionist Congress.[6]

The Economic Reform Program

On the surface, the program formulated by the *Linkes Zentrum* appeared to be similar to the German Zionist platform at the 14th Zionist Congress. However, there was a real change. The economic issue, which had been a central concern, was now the exclusive one, and the economy of Palestine was approached as crucial for the future of Zionism. It was argued that the work in the economic sector was the essence of Zionist realization not only because the establishment of a national home was the way to liberate and resuscitate the Jewish people, but because the Zionist enterprise would be judged by its success and achievements. This was not just an internal test of the Zionist movement, but outward proof of Zionism's ability to transform the character of the Jewish people. Economic success would be a fitting response to the skepticism and opposition of the anti-Zionists, who fought against *Keren Hayesod*, and in the international arena, it would demonstrate the Zionists' devotion to their cause, a prerequisite for political achievement and greater bargaining power. This argument was particularly emphasized in light of the Revisionist claim that political gains had to come first.

The program of the *Linkes Zentrum* thus ascribed top priority to pragmatic economic thinking as opposed to dogma. It advocated a balanced and moderate approach that took into account long-term factors, and although the focus here was economic, this type of thought was deemed applicable to all other areas of Zionist policy. In consequence, the *Linkes Zentrum* now adopted the anti-political line that the German Zionists had been wary of endorsing the year before.

---

6   See M. Rosenblüth's circular of March 15, 1927, Schocken Archives, 538/62, and platform proposal; *Landesvorstand* meeting, May 1, 1927, CZA, Z4/3567/I; executive committee meetings, May 22, 1927 and June 13, 1927, detailing Bileski's plan, Schocken Archives, 531/61; Blumenfeld, "Verantwortungspolitik", *JR*, May 25, 1927: 295–6.

The *Linkes Zentrum* supported a comprehensive reform of Zionist economic policy that was aimed at consolidating the existing enterprises and moving them toward self-sufficiency. All expansion was to be frozen, and the future of each enterprise was to be weighed in a pragmatic, business-like manner regardless of any former biases based on corporate patterns and form of ownership, such as whether the venture was public or private. Efforts would be made to rationalize management procedures, and enterprises with no chance of economic success would be closed down.

Linkes Zentrum members held that these reforms and the budget for carrying them out should be in the hands of a neutral committee, and that the Zionist Executive should be restructured. They now adopted Schocken's proposal, rejected at the 14th Congress, to divide this body into political and economic units. The economic unit would thus be apolitical and managed by experts, and settlement policy would be removed from the purview of the Zionist Congress. Regarding immigration policy as part of a comprehensive economic program, the *Linkes Zentrum* came out in favor of restrictions in this sphere, too. At the beginning of 1927, Weltsch even proposed that people be encouraged to leave Palestine in order to reduce unemployment and promote economic rehabilitation.[7]

The *Linkes Zentrum* did not see any inconsistency between its proposals and the traditional German Zionist support for national settlement policy. National capital still took pride of place, as did the role of the Zionist movement in guiding and nurturing the Zionist enterprise. However, national revival, expressed on the economic plane by the productivization of the Jewish people, was bound up with the successful development of the national economy. Without denying the pivotal importance of the agricultural enterprise, which was perceived as a Zionist axiom and theoretically above economic consideration, the *Linkes Zentrum* insisted that unbiased scrutiny and economic efficiency be the determining factors in extending aid to specific agricultural settlements. Since smallholder citrus groves had proven viable even during the

---

7   Weltsch's call for emigration from Palestine appeared on the front page of *JR*, February 1, 1927; on the *Linkes Zentrum* program, see M. Rosenblüth's proposal, Bileski's plan and Blumenfeld's article in note 6 above. Also see Weltsch's articles: "Sorgen des Palästina-Aufbau," *JR*, June 10, 1927: 325–6; editorial, *JR*, June 21, 1927; "Warum Konsolidierung," *JR*, August 12, 1927: 457–8; Bileski's articles: "Die Aufgaben des Kongresses," *JR*, June 24, 1927: 355–6; "Unser Programm," *JR*, July 29, 1927: 425–6, and his Congress speech, *Protokoll des XV. Zionisten-Kongresses, 1927*, 142ff; M. Rosenblüth's article: "Linkes Zentrum," *JR*, August 5, 1927: 441; Blumenfeld's Congress speech, *Protokoll des XV. Zionisten-Kongresses, 1927*, 347–59; *Landesvorstand* minutes, January 30, 1927, CZA, Z4/357/I; Landsberg's letter to M. Rosenblüth, June 21, 1927, Schocken Archives, 538/62; F. Rosenblüth's letter to Blumenfeld, July 26, 1927, Schocken Archives, 531/62.

crisis years, it supported the plan of German agronomist Wilhelm Brünn to establish citrus plantations for middle-class settlers. On the other hand, it opposed the establishment of large-scale *kibbutzim* based on a report by Franz Oppenheimer in 1926 that aroused much controversy in German Zionist circles.[8]

The *Linkes Zentrum* asserted that its program did not dictate the content or social nature of economic enterprises established with the help of national capital. Their idea was to present a system based on rational, apolitical, professional and pragmatic considerations that would enable the *Yishuv* in Palestine to extricate itself from its financial troubles and restore economic growth, whether on private farms or in *Histadrut* enterprises.

The *Linkes Zentrum* regarded itself as a champion rather than a challenger of the prevailing policy. Its aim was to demonstrate how this policy could be enhanced through the introduction of an additional set of considerations apart from the national one. Until now, the Zionist enterprise had been bound up in a period of pioneering sacrifice motivated by ideology, so that experimentation and risk-taking were par for the course. But that period was over, and the time had come for the next stage – economic consolidation and efficient management.[9]

The Crucible of "Leftist" Orientation

One of the motives of the *Linkes Zentrum* was to defuse right-wing criticism of the national settlement policy, and maintain an ideological and pragmatic alliance with the Zionist Left. The founders had stressed from the outset that they wanted to preserve a pro-Left orientation, expecting that the economic crisis in Palestine as well as the known sympathy of the German General Zionists toward the Labor movement would lead to the cooperation of the workers' parties. On the other hand, they feared that their practical recommendations would be interpreted as negative criticism by enterprises of the

---

8 Weltsch, "Durch die Wüste," *JR*, April 13, 1927: 213–4; Wilhelm Brünn, *Prospect über eine zu gründende Orangenpflanzungsgesellschaft in Palästina* (Berlin, 1926). Brünn's program was published in pamphlet form and discussed at the 21st ZVfD convention at Erfurt in August 1926. See convention minutes, *JR*, August 20, and August 27, 1926. Blumenfeld also presented this plan as part of the *Linkes Zentrum* platform at the *Landesvorstand* meeting of May 1, 1927, CZA, Z4/3567/I. On F. Rosenblüth's activities, see correspondence in CZA, Z4/2327.

9 Weltsch, "Warum Konsolidierung," *JR*, August 12, 1927: 457–8; Blumenfeld, "Die Kundgebung der Exekutive," *JR*, May 6, 1927: 255–6.

Histadrut. In consequence, the *Linkes Zentrum* made a point of praising the Labor movement whenever the occasion arose, in public and in private. The movement was cited for its dedication to the settlement enterprise, especially in the early stages of pioneering and heroic idealism, and the "workers of *Eretz Israel*", who combined building the country with the social and economic transformation of the Jewish people, were hailed as the very backbone of Zionism. Among themselves, *Linkes Zentrum* members also emphasized the political reasons for an alliance with the Left. They knew that without the workers' parties, their economic reform program was at risk. Nor did they want to promote these reforms against the workers' will, which would eliminate their *raison d'être* for organizing.[10]

At the same time, because of the difficulties in Palestine and the economic measures they advocated, their program could not totally avoid criticism of the workers. The Labor mnovement had virtually monopolized national capital, and despite its dependence on Zionist funding, the labor settlement sector was battling for autonomy. When the *Linkes Zentrum* urged the introduction of rational economic thinking in Zionist settlement policy, it was therefore targeting not only the Zionist Executive, but also the main beneficiary of national capital, namely the labor economy.[11]

Well aware that the Zionist Left would not view their demands as an expression of support for the workers, the members of the *Linkes Zentrum* went out of their way to explain that their program was actually in the workers' interest. They argued that delaying expansion until the economy was stronger would also benefit the workers' collectives. Moreover, they were still in favor of granting funding to *Histadrut* enterprises capable of training and absorbing the unemployed. Their criticism of the bankrupt *Solel Boneh* had to do with its management, not the principle of a contracting cooperative. In their eyes, the workers had every reason to welcome successful private enterprise in the urban and rural sectors because this meant more jobs and an enhancement of the economy's immigration absorption capacity. In the end, it was the workers who would stand to benefit from the economic reforms, because they

---

10 Ernst Simon, "Ein Praktischer Vorschlag," *JR*, February 8, 1927: 77; Weltsch, "Durch die Wüste," *JR*, April 13, 1927: 213–4; Blumenfeld, "Die Kundgebung der Exekutive," *JR*, May 6, 1927: 255–6; Blumenfeld, "Verantwortungspolitik," *JR*, May 25, 1927: 295–6; *Landesvorstand* minutes, January 30, 1927, and January 5, 1927, CZA, Z4/3567/I; Senator's letter to Schocken, March 7, 1927, and Landsberg's letter to M. Rosenblüth, June 21, 1927, Schocken Archives, 538/62.

11 See note 7 above. For background data see Giladi, *Jewish Palestine*, 98–9, 106–7.

had been affected by the crisis and the unemployment even more than others.[12]

The *Linkes Zentrum* fully believed that it was loosening the grip of the right-wing in the economic policy sphere and that its plan was reconcilable with the leading principles of General Zionism. It was convinced that the road was clear for the cooperation of the Zionist Executive and the leftist parties.

Yet the fears of the *Linkes Zentrum* concerning the reaction of the Zionist Left proved to be well-founded. The Labor movement perceived itself as under attack by its proclaimed sympathizers, and understood all of the *Linkes Zentrum* demands as directed against the workers, who had suffered most from the mistakes of the Zionist Executive. The *Linkes Zentrum* was accused of aligning itself with the right-wing, and thereby relinquishing the last foothold of the Left in the General Zionist camp. The labor leaders charged that Weltsch had done damage to *aliya*, which was so important to the movement, and cited his widely-read articles on the subject as proof of German Zionist enmity. Above all, they were angered by the neutral stance advocated by the *Linkes Zentrum*. In elevating economics above socio-political concerns the *Zentrum* strove for an apolitical Settlement Executive, i.e., devoid of the labor representatives who had staffed the economic departments of the Zionist Executive in Palestine since 1921. This was interpreted as an attempt to detach the development of the country from the socio-ideological guidelines of the Labor movement. The German Zionists were even accused of perpetuating the economic difficulties. Like the American Zionists, they preferred to criticize rather than invest the financial and human resources needed to improve the situation. This argument was predicated on the monopolistic approach that an alliance between the workers and the leadership was essential to the Zionist enterprise, and that its dissolution was a fatal blow. The Zionist Left thus ended up fighting the *Linkes Zentrum* and its reforms tooth and nail.[13]

The response of the Labor movement confirmed the suspicions of *Zentrum* leaders and dashed their high hopes. Felix Rosenblüth, Werner Senator and Alfred Landsberg had warned against this possibility. Now they called for stepping back and refraining from taking the lead in economic reform. In their eyes, the loss of the close bond with the Labor movement was too dear a price

---

12 Weltsch's response to Beilinson, *JR*, March 8, 1927: 137; Weltsch's letter to Bergman, March 30, 1927, NULA, 1502/1334/4.

13 Beilinson, "Die Stunde der Prüfung," *JR*, March 8, 1927: 135; Weltsch–Beilinson correspondence, LBIA, 7185/3/1; F. Rosenblüth's letter to M. Rosenblüth, June 24, 1927, Schocken Archives, 538/62.

to pay. They suggested that the *Linkes Zentrum* either be content with the role of intermediary or introduce modifications in the reform program itself. Felix Rosenblüth, who was close to the Zionist movement nerve center, advocated an executive body that also included representatives of the workers' parties.[14]

Other *Linkes Zentrum* members sent out emphatic calls for neutrality and depoliticizing the settlement enterprise. Weltsch was an outspoken proponent of this view, and earned many Labor movement enemies for his provocative stance on immigration. He charged that the *Histadrut*'s vote against the reforms in 1927 showed lack of maturity and irresponsibility, and smacked of self-interest. Hence Weltsch's support for a strong non-partisan Executive capable of withstanding the influence of pressure groups.[15]

Although there were some in the *Linkes Zentrum* who were hesitant and inclined toward compromise, an overriding sense of political strength tipped the scales in favor of the hardliners. This sense of strength was nourished by the passionate fight put up by the Left, which obviously felt threatened by the *Linkes Zentrum*. It was also stoked by the reaction of the Weizmann camp, which was driven into a position of cautious defense because the German General Zionists, known for their full support of Weizmann and the workers' parties, had joined the reform advocates of the Right. Felix Rosenblüth's report from London was that Weizmann was willing to adopt the consolidation program, apparently in order to please the German Zionists whom he felt had suddenly turned their back on him, seriously strengthening the opposition. Weizmann's visit to Germany in June 1927, and his participation in *Linkes Zentrum* meetings, further convinced German Zionists that they had the power to make or break the Weizmann leadership. The *Linkes Zentrum* thus won endorsement for its economic reform program in return for continued support of Weizmann. At the Zionist Actions Committee meeting in May 1927, it was the German Zionist vote that sent the non-partisan Reorganization Committee

---

14 Senator's letter to Schocken, March 7, 1927; Landsberg's letter to M. Rosenblüth, June 21, 1927, and F. Rosenblüth's letter to M. Rosenblüth, June 24, 1927, Schocken Archives, 538/62; F. Rosenblüth's letter to Schocken, June 26, 1927, Schocken Archives, 551/213/4; F. Rosenblüth's letter to Blumenfeld, July 1, 1927, July 5, 1927, July 26, 1927, and July 31, 1927, Schocken Archives, 531/62.

15 Weltsch, "Ein unvollständiges Programm," *JR*, February 25, 1927: 111–2. See also Weltsch's letter to Beilinson, March 9, 1927, and Weltsch's letter to Bergman, March 30, 1927, NULA, 1501/1334/4.

to Palestine.[16] Henceforth, apolitical neutrality became synonymous with the anti-Leftist approach.

The *Linkes Zentrum* at the 15th Zionist Congress

The idea of organizing nationally on a General Zionist platform was abandoned once the *Linkes Zentrum* came into being. Prior to the 15th Congress, similar groups were formed in other countries, most prominently Czechoslovakia, but Germany's *Linkes Zentrum* was the largest. It ran as the only General Zionist list in the pre-Congress elections, and although this list was not ZVfD-sponsored as at the previous Congress, it featured the names of many *Landesvorstand* members. Nevertheless, the election results were disappointing. Of 6,700 voters, only about 2,400, or 35 percent, voted for the *Linkes Zentrum*. The religious *Mizrahi* party received 32 percent of the vote, and *Poalei Zion*, 22 percent. A small minority voted for the Radical Faction and even fewer for the Revisionists. It can therefore be said that the *Linkes Zentrum* represented almost all non-partisan *Stam Zionisten* in Germany, but *Stam Zionisten* no longer constituted the majority of German Zionists.[17]

The rise of political parties was a reflection of long-term processes affecting German Zionism. The growth of *Mizrahi* and *Poalei Zion* was a measure of the integration of East European immigrants in the ZVfD. During the second half of the 1920s, the Zionist camp was joined by the children of the East European immigrants who had arrived in Germany before World War I and shortly afterwards. From a social and cultural standpoint, these young Zionists were strongly bound to Judaism and Jewish tradition, but at the same time, were acutely aware of the socialist and proletarian trends in the East. The Zionist movement served as an "agent" through which the immigrants achieved social integration in the German Jewish community. A similar role was played by the

16 Weizmann's letters to Schocken, May 15, 1927, June 5, 1927 and July 11, 1927, to Landsberg, May 21, 1927, to Sacher, June 26, 1927, *Weizmann Letters,* vol. XIII, 242, 275, 197–8, 248–9, and 287–8, respectively. Schocken's letters to Weizmann, June 1, 1927, and June 30, 1927, WA; Landsberg's letter to M. Rosenblüth, June 21, 1927; F. Rosenblüth's letter to M. Rosenblüth, June 24, 1927; F. Rosenblüth's letters to Blumenfeld, July 1, 1927, July 5, 1927, and July 26, 1927, *Landesvorstand* minutes, August 13, 1927, Schocken Archives, 538/62; Zionist Actions Commitee minutes, *JR*, May 17, 1927: 279–80, and May 20, 1927: 285.

17 H. Herrmann's letter to F. Rosenblüth, July 7, 1927, CZA, Z4/218/37; Hantke's letter from Palestine (as chairman of the Head Office of *Keren Hayesod* transferred to Jerusalem in 1926), July 27, 1927, Schocken Archives, 531/62; survey of election results, *JR*, August 12, 1927: 457.

socialist movements and orthodox Judaism, attracting many of the newcomers
to the *Mizrahi* party and *Poalei Zion*. Both parties, and especially *Poalei Zion*,
did much of their work through youth movements, creating a cadre of young
immigrants, who later joined their ranks as adults. General Zionism was more
the bailiwick of the veteran Jewish community. Indeed, the election results in
1927 shone a spotlight on General Zionism's neglect of the educational sphere
and activities that might have inculcated General Zionist values among the
children of the middle-class.[18]

It was also clear from these elections that the rise of *Mizrahi* and *Poalei Zion*
was accompanied by the disappearance of *Hapoel Hatzair* and a serious attenuation of the General Zionist camp. This was due not only to the integration of
the East Europeans, but to the end of the German Zionist infatuation with
Hapoel Hatzair that began right after World War I. The movement's attraction
for German Zionists lay in its moderation and its studied avoidance of politics.
Toward the mid–1920s, its membership declined as many of its adherents
settled in Palestine. This, however, was not the only reason. Over the years,
Hapoel Hatzair began to dabble in politics, and was gradually transformed into
a workers' party similar to *Poalei Zion*. Those German Zionists who were not
interested in political commitment beyond their membership in *Hapoel Hatzair*,
withdrew in favor of General Zionism, thereby strengthening its pro-Left
leanings. Many leftist sympathizers, however, were disappointed with the
Linkes Zentrum formed in 1927, and joined what they considered to be an
appropriate alternative – *Poalei Zion*.[19]

The German *Mizrahi* party was another option for pro-Left-wing Zionists
who were moderately religious but had not felt obligated until then to join a
religious party. The social basis of *Mizrahi* in Germany was similar to that of
the Zionist movement in general, and its membership and leaders had been
reared in the same cultural environment. Unlike other chapters of the world
Mizrahi movement, German *Mizrahi* was akin to General Zionism in its

18 On the East European Jews in Germany, see Aschheim, *Brothers and Strangers;* Maurer, *Ostjuden
    in Deutschland;* Shalom Adler-Rudel, *Ostjuden in Deutschland, 1880–1940* (Tübingen, 1959). On the
    youth movements, see Hermann Meier-Cronemeyer, "Jüdische Jugendbewegung," *Germania Judaica*
    12, no. 1/2 and 3/4 (1969); Markel, "Brith Haolim." See also Scholem, *From Berlin to Jerusalem,*
    76–80, 83–94; interviews with Jole Tahler, March 22, 1982, and with Meir and Meta Flanter, May
    9, 1982, OHD; Landsberg, "Das Wahlergebnis in Deutschland und der deutsche Zionismus," *JR,*
    August 19, 1927: 473; Feuerring's memorandum presented to the *Linkes Zentrum,* August 13, 1927,
    Schocken Archives, 538/62.

19 See Samuel, "Reform? Reform!," *JR,* July 26, 1927: 422–3; editorial, "Nach den Wahlen," *JR,* August
    16, 1927; Landsberg, see note 18 above; interview with Weltsch, February 21, 1980, OHD.

political moderation and Labor movement sympathies. *Torah Va'avoda* (Torah and Labor), the sister movement of *Hapoel Hamizrahi* (the *Mizrahi* Worker) in Palestine, was especially strong in Germany and it was here that the idea of communal religious settlement was born. It is not surprising, then, that religious left-leaning Zionists found in *Mizrahi* a substitute for General Zionism.[20]

A significant number of German Zionists thus rejected General Zionism and joined one of the political parties. Many were dismayed that its neutral, apolitical line had been transformed into a definite political program that abandoned traditional support for the Left. These people preferred a clear party affiliation to a General Zionism that disguised a turn from Left to Right.

At the pre-Congress elections *Mizrahi* won four delegates, *Poalei Zion* three and the Radical Faction one. The national delegation, represented by the *Linkes Zentrum*, enjoyed the support of only a third of German Zionists. It sent four delegates to the 15th Zionist Congress: Moritz Bileski, Isaak Feuerring, Martin Rosenblüth, and Hugo Schachtel, a longtime Zionist leader from Breslau. Other German Zionists participated in the Congress in their capacity as WZO office-holders. Felix Rosenblüth was a member of the Zionist Executive and headed its Organization Department; Kurt Blumenfeld, Alfred Landsberg, and Salman Schocken were on the Zionist Actions Committee, and Schocken also represented the JNF. Sammy Gronemann, a writer and lawyer from Berlin, had been chairman of the Congress Court and the Court of Honour since 1921. In effect, the power of the *Linkes Zentrum* derived more from the prestige of the WZO office holders than from its electoral strength in Germany.[21]

The case of the German national delegation reflected a wider phenomenon in the WZO, which involved a reshifting of emphasis from General Zionism to the political parties. At the 15th Zionist Congress, only 54 percent, or 151 of the 281 (both elected delegates and Zionist Actions Committee members) were General Zionists in contrast to 70 percent at the previous Congress. In Germany, the move was in the direction of *Mizrahi* and *Poalei Zion*, whereas elsewhere it was toward the Revisionists and the Radical Faction (with 10 and 11 delegates respectively), both of which hardly had a foothold among German Zionists. The rise in the two leftist parties was not unique to Germany, although their representation at the Congress was almost equal (33 for *Hitahdut* and 30 for *Poalei Zion*). Basically, the same forces were at work: the ascendancy

---

20　See note 19 above. See also: Walk, "The Torah Va-Avodah Movement".

21　*JR*, July 29, 1927: 429, and compare with the list of congress delegates, *Protokoll des XV. Zionisten-Kongresses, 1927.*

of *Ahdut Ha'avoda*, the branch of *Poalei Zion* in Palestine, which influenced political organizing in the Diaspora.[22]

The waning strength of General Zionism posed a tangible threat to Weizmann's power base and enhanced the bargaining power of the *Linkes Zentrum*. This was clear to Weizmann even before the Congress, and prompted efforts to reach an agreement with German Zionists. The situation was abundantly clear to the *Linkes Zentrum* and formed the basis of its policies. At the 15th Zionist Congress, it set up the *Arbeitsgemeinschaft "Linkes Zentrum"* in collaboration with the delegations of Czechoslovakia, Rumania and Bulgaria, and representatives from Austria, Scandinavia and Switzerland. This "working group" was joined by 40 of the 151 *Landsmannschaften* delegates, which lent it considerable weight. Its support of Weizmann was hinged upon the passage of resolutions favoring organizational and economic reform, and it was able to achieve this goal because Weizmann could not risk losing the loyalty of the few remaining General Zionists who had not aligned themselves with the right-wing opposition. Even before the Congress the *Linkes Zentrum* had made conditional demands on Weizmann and was bowed to in a similar fashion.[23]

At the Congress, the power of the *Linkes Zentrum* was demonstrated by the appointment of Kurt Blumenfeld as chairman of the standing committee, the body that compiled the lists of nominees to the Executive and other institutions. Appointments in the same vein were Isaak Feuerring as spokesman of the budget committee; agronomist Wilhelm Brünn, as settlements committee expert; Nathan Grünstein, also of the *Linkes Zentrum*, as urban settlement expert; and Moritz Bileski as a member of the inner resolutions committee.[24]

The outcome of the 15th Zionist Congress was indeed as the *Linkes Zentrum* had hoped. The economic consolidation plan was approved and a non-political Executive was organized under Weizmann, without the workers' parties. Special attention was paid to setting up a non-partisan Executive in Palestine, and the German Zionist favorite, Harry Sacher, was appointed to head it.

---

22 List of Congress delegates, *Protokoll des XV. Zionisten-Kongresses, 1927.* See also: Ben-Naftali's article in *Kunteres* (Hebrew), August 12, 1927: 3–7.

23 M. Rosenblüth's letter to F. Rosenblüth, August 17, 1927, CZA, Z4/218/37; the letters by F. Rosenblüth and Weizmann listed in note 16 above; *Protokoll des XV. Zionisten-Kongresses, 1927; Linkes Zentrum* meeting, August 13, 1927, Schocken Archives, 538/62.

24 15th Congress bulletin, no. 7, CZA, Z4/2947/II; *JR*, September 20, 1927, report on German delegation; Notes on the discussions at Basel before the appointment of the Executive, September 20, 1927 (apparently by Blumenfeld), Schocken Archives, 551/64/1.

In both German Zionist and leftist circles, responsibility for all this was attributed to the policies and activities of the *Linkes Zentrum*.[25]

The End of the Path

The political path trod by the German Zionists in the WZO led them from Left to Right. Through the *Linkes Zentrum*, economic policy was raised from a position of importance to a *sine qua non*. Furthermore, by demanding the separation of settlement policy and politics, General Zionist neutrality became an accepted political principle. In so doing, the German Zionists were asked to choose for the first time between neutrality and support for the Zionist Labor movement. Translating the principles that had guided them since the early 1920s into the language of politics, they decided to abandon the Left. This effectively sealed the fate of their political organizing. From the moment that German General Zionism turned its back on the Left, much of its power was lost, and when it chalked up political gains in the WZO, it also lost what had remained of its prestige – even among former supporters. The political success that followed once the pro-Left orientation had been eliminated, pointed up the awry foundations upon which the *Linkes Zentrum* had been established. Contrary to what its name implied and General Zionist goals until that time – bolstering the Weizmann leadership and maintaining a pact with the Labor movement – the *Linkes Zentrum* turned against and thus isolated the workers' parties.

Indeed, even the leaders of the *Linkes Zentrum* were uneasy about its political moves, and immediately after the Congress, the legitimacy of political activity in the name of a national organization began to be questioned. From then on, there was a process of retreat from involvement in WZO affairs which was tantamount to an admission of failure in the attempt to fashion a General Zionist policy. The German Zionists turned increasingly inward, and immersed themselves in Jewish communal affairs where cooperative efforts

---

25 Rosenblüth's letters, see note 16 above; Weltsch's letter to Bergman, September 7, 1927, NULA, 1502/1334/4; A. P., "From the Congress," *Kunteres*, September 23, 1927: 7–10; M. Neustadt, "The Lessons of the Last Congress," *Kunteres*, November 4, 1927: 10–13; "After the Sixteenth Congress," *Hapoel Hatzair*, September 9, 1927: 1; Bileski, "Die Deutsche Delegation und das Linke Zentrum auf dem Kongress," *JR*, September 23, 1927: 546; Blumenfeld, "Unsere Zionistische Zuversicht," *JR*, October 4, 1927: 563–4 (lead article); Lichtheim, "Mit meinen Augen," *JR*, October 4, 1927, 566–7; Goldmann, "Sinn und Bedeutung des XV. Kongress," *JR*, October 4, 1927: 577. See also *Landesvorstand* minutes, October 30, 1927, CZA, Z4/3567/I.

were possible, especially in the sphere of youth education. In this way, the Palestine-oriented radicalism that had guided German Zionism for almost ten years, began to be replaced by Diaspora *Gegenwartsarbeit*.[26]

26 ZVfD Presidency circular, September 30, 1927; executive committee meeting, October 3, 1927 and October 19, 1927; *Landesvorstand* minutes, October 30, 1927, CZA, Z4/3567/I. On the rift with the Left, see Weltsch's letters to Bergman, August 9, 1928, August 29, 1928, and October 11, 1928, NULA, 1502/1334/4; on the disappointment over Sacher's Executive, see Weltsch's letter to Bergman, October 13, 1927, NULA, 1502/1334/4; Blumenfeld's letter to Weizmann, March 3, 1928, WA. Also see Chapter Ten.

CHAPTER EIGHT

FIRST ENCOUNTER WITH THE ARAB QUESTION

The Roots of Moderation

In the annals of Zionist history, German Zionism after World War I has always been categorized as politically moderate. The roots of that moderacy can be traced to the cultural and political background of Central European Jewry, and especially the liberal humanism embraced by the middle-class. The German Jews had been staunch liberals from the time of the Second Reich, and with good reason, considering that their own cultural, economic and social integration depended on broadmindedness and tolerance. The pattern was even more pronounced among the German Zionists and their university-trained leaders. As middle-class intellectuals, they were characterized by political skepticism, an eagerness for progress, new trends and ideas, social awareness and a rejection of narrow self-interest.

There were, however, other forces which shaped German Zionism and strengthened its moderate political tendencies. The radicalism to which many young German Zionists had subscribed even before World War I, steered them towards the socioeconomic and intellectual-cultural spheres and increased their mistrust of politics. They denied that Zionism could be realized through such means. Their belief in humanist-nationalism, pacifism and moderacy was typical of various radical groups, among them the followers of Ahad Ha'am and the *Bar Kochba* Zionist Students' circle in Prague (Robert Weltsch, Hugo Bergman and Hans Kohn). These tendencies became even stronger after the war, in reaction to political changes in Europe in general, and the Zionist movement, in particular.

Post-war developments not only strengthened German Zionism's radical proclivities, but contributed a new dimension – opposition to the chauvinism in Germany, which intensified after the country's defeat. In the trying period of political disruption that followed the war, Jews gave their support, whether passively or actively, to the social-democratic and democratic forces which had won a victory over the extreme right-wing and established the new republic. In this context, the German Zionists were anxious to shape the moral character of their burgeoning movement and insure that Jewish nationalism had nothing in common with the extreme form taken by German nationalism. This was especially true among younger Zionists who were influenced by the socialist spirit of the new Europe. They merged their social and nationalist aspirations to create a moderate nationalist outlook in which nationalism tempered the class struggle, and national and political programs were tempered by social goals. After the war, *Hapoel Hatzair* was joined by many German Zionists who cultivated this kind of moderate nationalism. But even outside *Hapoel Hatzair*, German Zionism provided fertile ground for the development of conciliatory views and opposition to extreme nationalism.[1]

In the Wake of the May 1921 Disturbances

The initial expression of German Zionism's post-World War I moderation was its relatively low-key response to the political questions which hammered on the door. True, the negotiations between the World Zionist Organization, the British, and representatives of the League of Nations on the content and objectives of the British Mandate were far from complete. Nonetheless, German Zionists rarely addressed politics in their conferences or in public statements. They stressed the need for the settlement and economic development of Palestine, and argued that no political acts, declarations, demands or negotiations could replace this in importance. They were convinced that all political obstacles, including Arab opposition to the Zionist enterprise, could be overcome through socioeconomic achievement.[2]

The same could be said about the World Zionist Organization, which until 1921 was preoccupied with economic matters and the internecine struggles that developed as a result. Foreign policy was generally left to the statesmen, in this case, Chaim Weizmann, whereas the business of the Zionist movement was to

1   Ben-Avram, "The German '*Hapoel Hatzair*'"; Simon, "Martin Buber"; Weltsch, "Deutscher Zionismus"; Landsberg's letter to Weizmann, November 18, 1929, WA; author's interviews with Weltsch, February 21, 1980; and with Ernst Simon, March 16, 1982 and March 23, 1982, OHD.

2   Minutes of 15th ZVfD Convention in *JR*, December 31, 1918 and January 7, 1919; Minutes of the *Palästina Delegiententag*, *JR*, May 27, June 3, 6, 1919; minutes of 16th convention, *JR*, June 23, 29, July 13, 27, August 3, 1920; minutes of 17th convention, *JR*, May 17, 1920.

receive reports and discuss the pertinent issues in the light of Zionist principles. It was widely believed that the main obstacles impeding the fulfillment of the Balfour Declaration had been overcome now that Britain had received the Palestine Mandate and Herbert Samuel was appointed High Commissioner.[3]

However, British policy-makers had become increasingly concerned over Arab opposition since the disturbances in Jerusalem in the spring of 1920, and the situation was no calmer when the High Commissioner took up his post that summer. On the contrary, the Arabs intensified their resistence in an attempt to influence the wording of the Mandate charter before its ratification by the League of Nations. All this had little impact on the Zionist public until the outbreak of rioting on May Day 1921, in the wake of a Jewish workers' demonstration in Jaffa. The violent Arab rampage in that town and nearby Jewish colonies, the hesitancy of the British administration to call the army into action, and the High Commissioner's directive to halt immigration at once were developments that could not be ignored and which set the political question firmly in the center of the Zionist agenda. Now, for the first time, there were demands for a change in policy towards the Mandatory Government.[4]

The demands came from Ze'ev Jabotinsky, who had just been appointed to the Board of Directors of *Keren Hayesod* and the Zionist Executive, and was an active partner in the Weizmann – Brandeis struggle over economic policy. Jabotinsky had spoken out before on relations with the British, and he insisted on acceptance of his proposals as a precondition for taking up these new appointments. Jabotinsky's stand was also well known to the ZVfD. He wanted political pressure to be exerted on the Government to insure that it acted on its obligation to develop the Jewish national home. More specifically he demanded that the Jewish Legion be remobilized and the Zionist Organization be made a partner in the appointment of senior Mandate officials. He also felt that representatives of the Palestine Jewish community should enjoy a preferential status in the institutions of the Zionist Organization.

After the May 1921 outbreaks, Jabotinsky went public. As a member of *Keren Hayesod* he rebuked Jews and Zionists for not participating sufficiently

---

3   The Actions Committee discussions of February/March 1919, August/September 1919, and February 1920, in CZA, Z4/251/2, Z4/251/4, and Z4/252/6 respectively; Minutes of the Annual Conference in London, July 1920, CZA, Z4/241.

4   For a full discussion of the 1920–1922 political processes, see Aaron S. Klieman, *Foundations of British Policy in the Arab World – the Cairo Conference of 1921* (Baltimore, 1970), and Yehoshua Porath, *The Emergence of the Palestinian-Arab National Movement, 1918-1929* (London, 1974), Chapter Three.

in the advancement of Palestine but he also maintained that a Jewish national home required more than financial efforts. In his view, it was imperative to have a supportive political framework, especially a Jewish army under Zionist auspices. He saw economic development as an instrument for creating a Jewish power base in Palestine that would eventually contain and subdue Arab opposition.

The novelty in Jabotinsky's approach was evident when compared to the response of the Zionist establishment as expressed by Arthur Ruppin, head of the Agricultural Settlement Department of the Zionist Commission to Palestine. Both argued that the disturbances would not have occurred if the economy was developing at the proper pace, but Jabotinsky meant building up strength to overpower the Arabs, whereas Ruppin envisaged economic advancement in the Arab sector which could help to mollify their opposition.[5]

Jabotinsky had given the political implications of the economic enterprise a new perspective, but the conflict between his view and the fundamental outlook of the Zionist Organization was as yet far from clear. There was still a basic agreement on the importance of large-scale settlement, directed and carried out by *Keren Hayesod* under the auspices of the national movement. The challenge put forward by Jabotinsky, i.e., establishing political action as equal in importance to economic activity, instituting a more aggressive policy, and demanding the mobilization of a Jewish army, was pushed aside for the time being by his partnership with Weizmann. Nothing better illustrated the order of priorities of the Zionist leadership than the fact that during and after the disturbances in Palestine Weizmann remained in America in order to defeat the Brandeis group and launch a fundraising campaign for *Keren Hayesod.*[6]

The German Zionists too tended to overlook political differences because they felt a consensus on economic policy was more important. At their 17th convention which took place in Hanover, soon after the May riots, the main object was a show of solidarity after having settled serious disagreements in the economic sphere. In the wake of the disturbances, the German Zionists became

---

5   See Chapter Four on Jabotinsky's joining *Keren Hayesod* and the Zionist Executive; Evyatar Friesel, *Zionist Policy after the Balfour Declaration, 1917–1922* (Tel Aviv, 1977) (Hebrew), 165, 219–24; Jabotinsky's letters to Weizmann, October 7, 1920 and March 18, 1921, WA; Jabotinsky's letter to Nordau, October 31, 1920, CZA, A119/60/5/2; Jabotinsky's letter to Hantke, Blumenfeld and J. Berger, November 10, 1920, CZA, KH2/35/1; Jabotinsky's public appeal in the *Jewish Chronicle,* May 20, 1921. Also see Arthur Ruppin, *Tagebücher, Briefe, Erinnerungen,* ed. Schlomo Krolik, (Königstein/Ts, 1985), 322–4, note on May 2, 1921, and letter to Schwartz, May 29, 1921; Ruppin's report to Actions Committee, July 1921, CZA, Z4/257/4.

6   *Weizmann Letters,* vol. X, 179–209; Friesel, *Zionist Policy,* 245–6, 268.

even more resolute in their decision to develop the Jewish national home. They declared full faith in the Mandate administration and the High Commissioner, and expressed the hope that random violence would not affect British policy. While they did protest against this violence, call for adequate protection of the *Yishuv* and demand that immigration be resumed without delay, they stressed that *aliya* and settlement, rather than a political and military struggle, were the prerequisites for success. They also made a point of noting the sincere desire of the Jewish people for the peaceful development of Palestine in cooperation with the Arabs, thereby negating Jabotinsky's position, without openly oposing him. *Hapoel Hatzair*, which was totally opposed to political and military action, also ignored the Jabotinsky program and devoted its convention in Prague in July 1921 to economic development.[7]

The same issues were on the agenda of the Zionist Actions Committee which met in Prague that same month, ostensibly to celebrate Weizmann's return from the United States and victory over Brandeis. The Actions Committee was supposed to approve the appointment of Weizmann's supporters to the Zionist Executive and plan the first phase of the new Zionist economic program. Instead however the deliberations centered on Jabotinsky's demand for a Jewish Legion and his views in general.

Jabotinsky maintained that the disturbances in Palestine were irrefutable proof of the Arab position vis-à-vis the Zionist enterprise, and that it was therefore necessary to create a Jewish majority with all haste which would leave the Arabs with no choice but to accept the situation. Such a majority, which was the essence and primary objective of Zionism, could be established only under the auspices of a forceful government backed up by military might. In Jabotinsky's eyes, an army was the "iron wall" that would enable the national home to develop without hindrance.

Jabotinsky argued that this military force, to be of benefit to the Jews, should be part of the local British army and empowered by the Mandatory Government. This was his response to the advocates of "self defense", most of whom were Labor Zionists. Nevertheless, he contended that command of the force should be given to those who had a direct interest in the country's rapid development, namely the *Yishuv* itself. Jabotinsky charged that if not for the demobilization of the Jewish Legion after World War I, the disturbances in Palestine would never have occurred, or could have been put down from the

---

7 Minutes of the Hanover convention and *JR* editorial of May 15, 1921. Also see Chapter Four. On *Hapoel Hatzair* convention, see *Haolam*, August 4, 1921.

start. The hesitant, fearful response of the British authorities proved that there was no choice but to insist on the reinstatement of the Legion.[8]

A stormy debate ensued over these demands, with many members openly opposed to investing Zionism with strong-arm policies. Nonetheless, only two Zionist leaders took a definite stand against Jabotinsky: Arthur Ruppin, another recent appointee to the Zionist Executive, and Menahem Ussishkin, chairman of the Zionist Commission to Palestine. While the atmosphere at the meeting was volatile because of the recent disturbances in Palestine, and Jabotinsky's charisma was unmistakable, it seems that most of the committee members refrained from voting against him chiefly because of the silence of Chaim Weizmann. One of the items on the agenda was the appointment of Weizmann's supporters, including Jabotinsky, to the Zionist Executive, and this was of crucial importance for both Weizmann and *Keren Hayesod*. It also appears that most of Jabotinsky's opponents thought his ideas would not be acted upon in any case.

Even Jabotinsky's major adversaries, the representatives of *Hapoel Hatzair* and the German Zionists, refrained from taking a clear stance against him. At the *Hapoel Hatzair* convention in Prague, Kurt Blumenfeld delivered an address on the importance of capital investment, and when he spoke before the Actions Committee, he engaged in verbal gymnastics to avoid a direct confrontation. Blumenfeld argued that appointing Jabotinsky to the Zionist Executive was essential, but that declarations of principle were out of place in politics. He also noted that establishing a Jewish Legion was a major financial undertaking, yet expressed no opinion about whether or not it should be done. Arthur Hantke hardly took part in the Legion debate, although he briefly raised the possibility that mobilization of a Jewish army might exacerbate relations with the Arabs.

The Actions Committee meeting concluded with the appointment of members to the Zionist Executive and a statement about *Keren Hayesod* policy, as proposed by Weizmann. In addition, the Executive was authorized to work towards the organization of a Jewish Legion – a resolution that even *Hapoel Hatzair* and Kurt Blumenfeld voted for.[9]

8   Friesel, *Zionist Policy*, 278; Minutes of the Zionist Actions Committee, CZA, Z4/257/4.

9   Minutes of the Zionist Actions Committee, CZA, Z4/257/4; Böhm, *Die Zionistische Bewegung*, vol. II, 154–5; Ruppin, *Tagebücher*, 326, note for July 17, 1921; *Haolam*, July 21, 1921, August 4, 1921; Weltsch's letter to Kaplan and Bergman, August 14, 1921, NULA, 1502/1334/2; Weltsch to Buber, August 2, 1921, in Martin Buber, *Briefwechsel aus sieben Jahrzehnten* ed. Grete Schaeder (Heidelberg, 1972–1975), vol. II, 79–83; H. Kohn's letter to Weltsch, August 25, 1921, LBIA, 7185/4/4.

The Response: Binationalism

The rioting in Palestine and Jabotinsky's proposals, which enjoyed a broad consensus among the Zionist public, called forth a very different kind of response from such figures as Martin Buber, Robert Weltsch, Hans Kohn and Hugo Bergman. Weltsch, Kohn and Bergman had been friends and ideological comrades since their student days in Prague when they belonged to the *Bar Kochba* circle, and all three looked up to Buber, a noted philosopher who had been living in Germany since the beginning of the century. Buber was among the leaders of the Democratic Faction and a founder of the *Jüdischer Verlag*, the Zionist publishing house. In 1916 he inaugurated the prestigious intellectual journal, *Der Jude*. Hugo Bergman, later a well-known thinker and professor at the Hebrew University of Jerusalem moved to London after the war as an employee of the Zionist Organization's Department of Education and Culture and in 1920 immigrated to Palestine as the head of the National and University Library in Jerusalem. Hans Kohn, who was to achieve eminence as a historian of modern nationalism, moved from Prague to Paris and then to London, where he worked for *Keren Hayesod*. In 1925 he was appointed to head *Keren Hayesod*'s Information Department in Palestine and eventually settled in New York. After the war, all four were active in *Hapoel Hatzair,* and in 1920, were among the founders of the *Hitahdut,* a party formed by the *Hapoel Hatzair* and *Tzeirei Zion* in Prague.[10]

From the days of the *Bar Kochba* circle, these personalities were drawn together by the idea of Jewish national renaissance preached by Ahad Ha'am in his "The Revival of the Hearts", and the practical-cultural Zionism upheld by the Democratic Faction, a group organized at the turn of the century by Chaim Weizmann, Leo Motzkin, Martin Buber and Berthold Feiwel in opposition to Herzlian political Zionism.

Inspired by Ahad Ha'am and Martin Buber, who gave a series of lectures in Prague from 1909 to 1911, Weltsch, Kohn and Bergman saw Zionism not as a political solution to the "Jewish problem", but as a means of satisfying the

---

10 Hans Kohn, *Bürger vieler Welten* (Frauenfeld, 1965), 71–81; Hans Kohn, *Martin Buber – Sein Werk und seine Zeit* (Cologne, 1961), 90–1, 147, 314–5; Ruth Gladstein-Kestenberg, "The Beginnings of Bar Kochba," in *Prague and Jerusalem (Leo Herrmann in Memoriam),* ed. Felix Weltsch (Jerusalem [1956]) (Hebrew), 86–110; Reinharz, "Martin Buber's Impact;" Ben-Avram, "The German 'Hapoel Hatzair'". Also see extensive correspondence between Kohn, Weltsch and Bergman in NULA and LBIA, which attests to their close relations.

Jews' yearning for spiritual renewal in their historical homeland. Spiritual renewal meant a return to Jewish cultural sources that contained the key to modern humanist thought and allowed the Jewish people to fulfill their mission as a "light unto the nations", guided by universal values of justice and morality. Their Zionism differed from the narrow materialistic framework which to their minds characterized political Zionism, and from an isolationist form of nationalism that was liable to conflict with universal human justice. Settlement in Palestine was of utmost importance because an independent Jewish community living in its own land and organizing its social life around the principles of morality and justice, would herald a true renaissance of Jewish culture and inspire the entire Jewish people.

Thus settlement in Palestine was seen as a means, rather than an end. Moreover, the ability of the new community to fulfill its assigned task in the realization of Zionism was contingent on the way it was established, its social character and its relations with others. If it did not develop in accordance with the moral imperatives of Judaism and humanism, it would be incapable of serving as the nexus in the revival of the Jewish people. In this respect, the views of the *Bar Kochba* circle and the Democratic Faction coincided with other schools of Zionism which attributed paramount importance to the quintessential nature of the national home and the building process itself, which was envisaged as gradual and selective. Such was the thinking of A.D. Gordon, the ideological mentor of *Hapoel Hatzair*, who viewed the personal transformation of the Jew into a productive being as the cornerstone of Zionist realization. It is not surprising, then, that Buber and his followers found their Zionist niche in *Hapoel Hatzair*.[11]

Jewish-Arab relations thus became a key question in the fulfillment of Zionism. Buber, in particular, saw the revival of Judaism and the mission of the Jewish people in universal terms. It was a message which spoke to the hearts of young Jews in Central Europe, who had seized upon Zionism as a way to return to Judaism and a means of implementing their desire for social reform. As such they were drawn to the ethical side of Ahad Ha'am's teachings, and denounced the fight for material-numerical strength and political

---

11 Jehuda Reinharz, *Chaim Weizmann – The Making of a Zionist Leader* (Oxford, 1985), Chapter Five; Martin Buber, *Drei Reden über das Judentum* (Frankfurt a.M., 1920); Weltsch, "Deutscher Zionismus"; Weltsch to author, July 20, 1979. See also note 10 above.

power, both as values in their own right and as a path that would lead Zionism toward an unavoidable clash with the Arabs of Palestine.[12]

The psychological-political experience of World War I and the test to which the Jews were put by the Balfour Declaration played a crucial role in the approach of this group to the Arab question. The radical, aggressive nationalism then rampant in Central Europe challenged them to show that their brand of nationalism was different and founded on humanism and ethics. After the May 1921 disturbances and Jabotinsky's demand for a Jewish Legion, they felt compelled to find a solution to the dichotomy between the Zionist dream and the spiritual and moral dictates to which they were committed. They sought an acceptable alternative to what they saw as a nationalism of power, extremism and violence. After all, Jewish nationalism was a protest against oppression by other nations, and could not, at this moment of political testing, lose sight of the moral vision upon which it was consecrated. The use of force and the negation of the rights of another people contradicted the very essence of Zionism, and building the national home upon such foundations was totally contradictory to the precepts of Judaism. Thus the Arab problem was a decisive issue in their eyes and the way it was resolved would determine whether it was possible to combine Zionism with their universalist world view.[13]

This group was also realistic. They did not believe that Palestine could be conquered by force, or that the threat of violence would eliminate Arab opposition in the long run. Sooner or later, they argued, the Arabs would gain strength, and resistance would spread over the entire Middle East. Even if Palestine were Jewish, it would be a drop in an ocean of Arabs. They suggested that hostility be prevented from developing in the first place by urging the Jews to integrate into the region in a manner that would appease and win the confidence of their Arab neighbors. This could happen only if the Zionists gave up the demand for Jewish dominion over Palestine. Compromise was well-suited to their national conceptions: They had never perceived Zionism as a solution to the physical threat hanging over the Jews of Europe or as a

---

12 On Ahad Ha'am's influence, especially as transmitted through Buber, see Kohn, *Bürger vieler Welten*, 74–81; Kohn, *Martin Buber*, 40–50; Simon, "Martin Buber". See also Buber's speech at the 12th Zionist Congress, *Protokoll des XII. Zionisten-Kongresses*, 123–9.

13 Buber's speech at the *Hitahdut* convention in Carlsbad, September 1921, see Martin Buber, "Nationalismus," in Paul R. Mendes-Flohr, *A Land of Two Peoples – Martin Buber on Jews and Arabs* (New York, 1983), 47–57; Kohn's articles in the *Freie Zionistische Blätter*, no. 1, 2, and 4, 1921; Weltsch, "Krieg oder Verständigung", *Die Arbeit*, August 1921. See also Buber, *Drei Reden*; Kohn, *Martin Buber*, 167–77.

means of establishing numerical superiority in Palestine, and they were able to find corroboration of their views in the teachings of their mentor, Ahad Ha'am.

Thus the idea of binationalism was born. As Hans Kohn wrote to his colleague, Robert Weltsch, in 1921: "Palestine cannot be a nation-state, not only because it is not a step forward, but because it is a concrete impossibility. Palestine must be binational, not *Eretz Israel*."[14]

The Buber group held that good relations between Jews and Arabs were imperative and that the gradual creation of political equality between the two peoples was both a moral and a practical necessity if the Zionist goal was to be met. They contended that an agreement could be reached within the conceptual political framework of the League of Nations and the British Mandate, and looked forward to a new code of national rights and international relations. Zionism was for them a testing ground for that new order. This was possible because their conception of Zionism did not involve power politics, but the development of an imminent, free nationalism under the auspices of a broad, international political entity.[15]

Until the establishment of the Weimar Republic, there were many points of contact between German Zionism and the *Bar Kochba* circle in Prague. Both were deeply indebted to the Zionist school that preached humanist nationalism and political compromise as the other face of economic, social and cultural radicalism. The Democratic Faction, with its emphasis on practical and cultural Zionism, and close links with Ahad Ha'am, was the spiritual parent of the *Bar Kochba* circle, as well as a magnet for young German Zionists who longed for social change and reacted with horror to the aggressive chauvinism in Germany during and after the war. These affinities proved fertile soil for the development of *Hapoel Hatzair* in Germany and attracted to it members of the *Bar Kochba* circle.

Unsurprisingly, Buber, Weltsch, Bergman and Kohn found an ear for their ideas among the German Zionists. They expounded these views from every accessible platform, publishing not just in the *Jüdische Rundschau* edited by Weltsch, but also in Nahum Goldmann's and Jacob Klatzkin's *Freie Zionistische Blätter*, and especially in *Die Arbeit*, the organ of *Hapoel Hatzair*. Here they reached out to a public that sided with their opposition to Jabotinsky and his Jewish Legion and proved receptive to the alternatives they proposed. At the

---

14 Kohn's letters to Weltsch, August 15, 1921, LBIA, 7185/4/4; and July 30, 1921, LBIA, 7185/14/2. On using Ahad Ha'am as a basis, see Kohn, *Martin Buber*, 339, and epilogue by Weltsch, 434, 439.

15 Weltsch, "Deutscher Zionismus"; Weltsch, "Krieg oder Verständigung".

same time, they worked through *Hapoel Hatzair* to create a concrete political program founded on the idea of binationalism.[16]

Resolution of Compromise

In May 1921, immediately after the rioting in Jaffa and the first reactions of the Zionist public, Robert Weltsch wrote as follows to his fellow *Hapoel Hatzair* members, Eliezer Kaplan and Hugo Bergman:

> All of us bear a certain blame because we did not properly comprehend the Arab question. Official Zionist policy is content with declarations that we want peace and understanding with the Arabs.... We must seek real understanding between nation and nation, not just pretty phrases. Now, when there is much bitterness in the entire Jewish world and among the Jews of Palestine because of the pogrom, we must make clear to ourselves that we will never win Palestine by fighting the Arabs, even if we rely on the military might of the Mandatory power. No power on Earth can help us conquer the country by force. This can be accomplished in one way alone, by reaching an understanding with the Arabs.... Our important mission is to tread this difficult path, which involves a simultaneous battle against the nationalist way of thinking among both our middle-class and our workers and *halutzim* [pioneers].... Now is the time for our party to adopt a clear stand against the Legion, and at the same time present a positive program on the Arab issue....[17]

Weltsch's call to snap out of apathy in the political sphere and to respond head on to the disturbances in Palestine and the challenge posed by Jabotinsky, was not heeded by *Hapoel Hatzair* leaders when they met in July 1921. However, Weltsch and his colleagues continued to hone their political conceptions and present them to the public in the German Zionist press.

In August 1921, as preparations were under way for the 12th Zionist Congress, Weltsch attacked Jabotinsky directly in an article entitled "Krieg

---

16 See note 13 above.

17 Weltsch's letters to Kaplan, May 25, 1921 (with a copy to Bergman) and to Bergman, June 12, 1921, NULA, 1502/1334/2.

oder Verständigung" ("War or Understanding"), published in *Hapoel Hatzair's Die Arbeit*:[18]

> The Congress must decide whether or not we want war with the Arabs.... We have missed the opportune moment to declare loudly and clearly that we do not aspire to rule the Arabs but to live alongside them in Palestine as two nations with equal rights. Enough of the slogan, "a majority in Palestine" which fills all the papers. It gives the impression that our top priority is to bring as many Jews as possible to Palestine not for the purpose of creative labor, which has nothing to do with the number of Arabs living in the country, but to constitute the majority; in other words, to achieve a ruling status and to do what is done by all ethnic majorities in mixed states to their minorities. No nation would sit by and tolerate such a forecast, not even the unorganized Arabs. If this policy continues there will be nothing but war, and indeed, the spokespersons of the clenched fist policy believe there is no other way.

For Weltsch, the prospect of war signalled the end of Zionism:

> This is a question of life or death for Zionism. If we wage war against the Arabs, we are lost – practically speaking, because we are a tiny handful with no real operational base while there are many millions of Arabs; morally, because the moment we set out to take Palestine from its present inhabitants by force, we will not only jeopardize our rights in the eyes of the world, but will be losing our best people in the Jewish world...Jabotinsky does not believe in the possibility of understanding among nations; he believes only in force and the fear of force. In his search to realize Zionism, he sees no other way but the establishment of a Jewish army. For those who really want to incorporate Zionism in this world of ideas, Jabotinsky's plan can be argued with.... For us, Zionism is inseparable from the belief that humane ideas, justice and true cooperation will be victorious. Without such ideals the renaissance of the Jewish people is inconceivable. To build a community in Palestine that lives by the gun barrel, is not the

---

18 Weltsch, "Krieg oder Verständigung", August 1921. Weltsch's emphases. The article was republished in part in Hans Kohn and Robert Weltsch, *Zionistische Politik* (Mährisch-Ostrau, 1927), 247–62.

Zionist goal. That is the reason we are against mobilizing a Jewish army in Palestine.

Weltsch countered each of Jabotinsky's arguments, point by point. He argued that a Jewish army could do no more than the British army, because it would be subject to British orders in any case. Furthermore, the mere existence of a Jewish army, especially when the Jews were a minority, would stir up Arab hostility and create tension that was liable to explode any moment. Weltsch was particularly disturbed by Jabotinsky's implication that "only the revival of the heroic martial spirit would infuse the nation with vitality". He felt that such an attitude constituted spiritual danger to the youth and would spur even further opposition to Zionism. The alternative proposed by Weltsch was clearly articulated:

> *The Congress must* reject the line of thinking which has characterized us thus far, and *declare* that we have no intention of subjugating the Arabs of Palestine; *that our motive is not to establish a Jewish state or a state with special privileges for Jews,* and even if we achieve the famous "Jewish majority", we have no design whatsoever to demand more rights than the Arabs. We desire a Palestinian community of two peoples, each respecting the other's special qualities, who will live and work in close cooperation. Within this community we wish to create a center of Jewish culture and productive Jewish labor, and to accomplish this we will encourage the free immigration of productive workers in line with the economic development of the country. We are aware of the fact that Palestine is situated in the midst of a large, awakening Arab region, and look forward to partnership in pursuing our common interests.

After the publication of this article, Weltsch distributed the draft of a resolution he had prepared for the Congress among his friends. It opened with a statement that the hour was a fateful one not only for the Jewish people, but also for the Arab inhabitants of Palestine who, after their liberation from Turkish rule, were joining the newly awakened Arab national movement. It went on to say that the Jewish people, after long wanderings and suffering, was returning to its ancient homeland in order to become part of the family of Eastern nations and to revive together the cultural heritage of the East. The only aspiration of the Jewish people was to find a resting place and a creative base in its land of origin, and to develop it to the point where many more Jews could be absorbed. There was no intention whatsoever to rule over another nation. Special emphasis was placed on the idea that the country would always belong to two peoples. It was hoped that the government would assure autonomous development for each while enabling Jews and Arabs to work together to build up their shared land, integrated in an Arab Middle East.

The resolution concluded with several items submitted for a Congress decision: a rejection of the conquest of Palestine by force; a rejection of the establishment of a Jewish Legion; a call to the *halutzim* to increase their integration into the world of the East and cultivate fraternity and friendship with Arabs; and an appeal to the Mandatory authorities to safeguard peace and security, prevent acts of violence, and station a mixed Jewish-Arab police force in the cities.[19]

Weltsch and his colleagues discussed these proposals among themselves, but did not present them to the 12th Congress, although copies of Weltsch's article "Krieg oder Verständigung", were distributed among the delegates. Weltsch did not want the resolution to be submitted by an individual, but by an influential party such as *Hapoel Hatzair*. The first step was to persuade *Hapoel Hatzair* to formulate a clear position on the Arab and Jewish Legion issues in contrast to its hesitant approach at the meetings of the Zionist Actions Committee. Martin Buber took this upon himself.

At the *Hitahdut* convention at Karlsbad on the eve of the Congress in September 1921, Buber called for a public appeal to the Arabs from the podium of the 12th Congress, seeking their cooperation in the Jewish settlement movement for the benefit of the entire country. The response was positive and Buber was authorized by *Hapoel Hatzair* to propose such a declaration in its name.[20]

Buber appeared before the plenum on the second day of the Congress, September 2, 1921. After quoting Ahad Ha'am's concept of "The Revival of the Hearts", he expounded his view that diplomatic and political activity was less important for the national renaissance than education and settlement:

19 Draft resolution of August 1921, and an explanatory letter by Weltsch, September 1978, LBIA, 7185/7A/1; Weltsch's letter to Buber, August 2, 1921, in Buber, *Briefwechsel*, vol. II, 79–83.

20 Weltsch's letter to Buber, August 2, 1921, and Buber's letter to Weltsch, August 6, 1921, in Buber, *Briefwechsel*, vol. II, 79–83; Kohn's letter to Weltsch, August 15, 1921, August 25, 1921, LBIA, 7184/4/4/; Weltsch's article, *JR*, August 16, 1921, 464. On the *Hitahdut* convention and Buber's speech, see *Haolam*, September 8, 1921, 6–8, and Buber, "Nationalismus". On the distribution of Weltsch's letter and Weizmann's anger, see author's interview with Weltsch, August 15, 1979, OHD.

It is only right that diplomacy should be secondary to the other objectives, and accompany rather than surpass them in time or importance. First we must work and create a new reality, and only then claim rights and demand what we are entitled to.[21]

In this respect, Buber differed radically from the prevailing notion that "diplomacy was the mistress, and practical work, the handmaiden". He claimed that diplomacy without action was nothing but empty words, and would not succeed. This was the same claim made by the Democratic Faction in its opposition to Herzl, and both Buber and Chaim Weizmann had been active in that group.

Buber maintained that diverting so much attention to diplomacy led to neglect of education and settlement, which were the two areas of greatest importance. According to his thinking, education involved effort that was inward-directed and demanding of each and every individual, whereas diplomacy was outward-directed and demanding of others. Settlement was interpreted as a planned economic and social enterprise initiated by the *halutzim* and workers which was also inward-directed; in this case, the demands were on the Zionist leadership. As for politics and diplomacy, Buber felt they served only one purpose, which was to lay the foundations for productive labor. In his eyes, however, Zionist diplomacy had failed to do even that. Zionism had not provided an authoritative interpretation of the Balfour Declaration, which, as it stood, constituted a general declarative framework and no more. It was this minimal political act that was urgently needed to set the Zionist enterprise on the path of cultural renaissance, justice and morality.

Buber demanded that a manifesto be published which would guide the Zionist enterprise on the one hand, and lay the foundation of trust for an agreement with the Arabs on the other. This, he said, was the only outside agreement necessary for the realization of Zionism:

At this serious hour, we stand before a momentous decision, and we must face it courageously.... Even at this late hour, a new policy can be inaugurated in view of the whole world, but we must clearly announce our intentions and aspirations. Let whomsoever hear who may; we must proclaim them as loudly and clearly as we can.

---

21 See *Protokoll des XII. Zionisten-Kongresses, 1921*, 123–30. Translation of Buber quotations hereafter based on Mendes-Flohr, *A Land of Two Peoples*, 60–3, with certain alterations.

At the same time, he advocated "...large-scale, well-planned settlement which will be visible to the whole world" and "...a clear, realistic economic and political program as the basis for negotiations". For the text of the manifesto, Buber submitted the following:

> We once again declare before the nations of both the West and the East that a strong nucleus of the Jewish people is determined to return to its ancient homeland, there to renew its life, an independent life founded on labor which shall grow and endure as an organic element of a new humanity. No earthly power can shatter this determination, whose strength is found in the lives and deaths of generations of our pioneers. Any act of violence committed against us in our exile sets the seal of blood upon the scroll of our national will.
>
> Our national desire to renew the life of the people of Israel in their ancient homeland, however, is not aimed against any other people. As they enter the sphere of world history and become once more the standard bearer of their own fate, the Jewish people, who have constituted a persecuted minority in all countries of the world for two thousand years, reject with abhorrence the methods of nationalistic domination under which they themselves have long suffered. We do not aspire to return to the Land of Israel with which we have inseparable historical and spiritual ties in order to suppress another people or to dominate them. In this land, whose population is both sparse and scattered, there is room both for us and for its present inhabitants, especially if we adopt intensive and systematic methods of cultivation. Our return to the Land of Israel, which will come about through increasing immigration and constant growth, will not be achieved at the expense of other people's rights. By establishing a just alliance with the Arab peoples, we wish to turn our common dwelling-place into a community that will flourish economically and culturally, and whose progress would bring each of these peoples unhampered independent development. Our settlement, which is exclusively devoted to the rescue of our people and their renewal, is not aimed at the capitalistic exploitation of the region, and does not serve any imperialistic aims whatsoever. Its significance is the productive work of free individuals upon a commonly owned soil. This, the socialist nature of our national ideal, is a powerful warrant for our confidence that between us and the working Arab nation a deep and enduring solidarity of true common interests will develop.

This in the end must overcome all the conflicts to which the present mad hour has given birth. Out of the sense of these links there will arise in the hearts of the two peoples feelings of mutual respect and goodwill, which will operate in the life of both the community and its individual members. Only then will both peoples meet in a new and glorious historical encounter.

Buber's manifesto was very similar in tone to Weltsch's "Krieg oder Verständigung", and faithfully reflected the vision of Zionism as a process of national renewal founded on social justice and universal human ideals. Unlike Weltsch's proposal, however, it contained no specific political references – no proposed form of government, appeal to the Mandatory power, or opposition to Jabotinsky's demands. Buber adopted this approach because he thought it would be more likely to win approval. Instead, he concentrated on the economic and social spheres, advocating wide-scale settlement that was pre-planned and firmly anchored in socialism.[22]

Despite its clear avoidance of politics, Buber's resolution was revised a number of times by the Congress political committee before it was adopted. While no minutes of these meetings are available and the information we have comes from the testimony of the participants at a much later date, we do have the final result as presented to the plenum:[23]

> With sadness and indignation the Jewish people have lived through the recent events in Palestine. The enmity of a part of the Arab inhabitants, incited by unscrupulous elements to commit deeds of violence, can weaken neither our resolve to construct a Jewish national home nor our will to live at peace and in mutual respect with the Arab people, and together with them, to make our home in a flourishing commonwealth whose reconstruction will assure undisturbed national development for each of its peoples. The two great Semitic peoples, who have already been linked before by a bond of common culture, shall again, at this time, comprehend the need for

---

22 On the reason for political restraint, see Kohn's letter to Weltsch, August 25, 1921, LBIA, 7185/4/4.

23 *Protokoll des XII. Zionisten-Kongresses, 1921,* 769. Translation of resolution appears in Mendes-Flohr, *A Land of Two Peoples,* 63. On the discussions of the political committee, see Buber's account in *Der Jude,* October 1921; Buber's letter to Magnes, July 1957, in Buber, *Briefwechsel,* vol. III, 133–5; Ernst Simon, *The Lines of Demarcation* (Givat Haviva, 1973) (Hebrew), 27.

uniting their vital interests in common enterprise. The 12th Zionist Congress calls upon the Zionist Executive to redouble its efforts to secure an honorable Éntente with the Arab people on the basis of this declaration and in strict accordance with the Balfour Declaration. The Congress emphatically declares that the work of Jewish settlement shall not infringe upon the rights and needs of the working Arab nation.

There is no doubt that this final draft differed from the declaration proposed by Buber. Instead of beginning with a positive statement about the aspirations of the Jewish people on returning to its homeland, it opened with a condemnation of Arab violence – despite the fact that the Congress had already passed a separate resolution deploring the May incidents. The appeal for peace was thus accompanied by an expression of anger and disapproval. Moreover, the entire section devoted to ideology was omitted, leaving no trace of Buber's vision of a humanistic and ethical Zionism that rejected nationalism in its dominating form. The final draft was also devoid of any specific reference to the anti-imperialist and anti-capitalist nature of Zionism, and the socioeconomic program meant to win the Arabs' cooperation. Whatever hazy allusions to the binational administration proposed by Weltsch that remained in Buber's manifesto, were revised in such a way as to make them even more vague. Buber wrote:

> By establishing a just alliance with the Arab peoples, we wish to turn our common dwelling-place into a community that will flourish economically and culturally, and whose progress would bring each of these peoples unhampered independent development.

The implication here is that joint economic and cultural collaboration would insure the successful autonomous development of each component, whereas the Congress reworded the statement as follows:

> To live at peace and in mutual respect with the Arab people, and together with them, to make our home in a flourishing commonwealth whose reconstruction will assure undisturbed national development for each of its peoples.

This version eliminates the emphasis on specific areas of cooperation and accentuates the separateness of two peoples operating within the framework of a pact alone. Accordingly, it ends with a reconfirmation of the validity of the Balfour Declaration.[24]

The adoption of this resolution by the 12th Zionist Congress signalled an end to the debate over Jabotinsky and the Jewish Legion. An attempt was made to skirt the issue altogether. When Jabotinsky brought it up at the Congress, he received little, if any, of the same kind of support he had enjoyed at the Actions Committee meeting two months earlier. However, by now Jabotinsky was a full member of the Executive, the policies of *Keren Hayesod* had been finalized, the struggle with Brandeis had been won and Weizmann's path was clear. The need for tactical moves was over. Hence no proposal pertaining to the Jewish Legion was raised at the Congress. The development of Palestine was the major theme, with the only political resolutions being support of Weizmann and optimistic faith in the Mandate Government. On the other hand, the Arab question merited serious attention.[25]

In this respect, Weltsch and his colleagues achieved their goal. They diverted the Zionist debate from the narrow issue of the Jewish Legion to matters of principle, and from internal wrangling to external politics. They succeeded in getting their party, the *Hitahdut*, to take a stand, and to engage Martin Buber, the teacher of Zionist humanism and spiritual guide of *Hapoel Hatzair*, as their spokesman. In this manner, *Hapoel Hatzair* in Germany, then at the height of its power, was able to put its stamp on the Zionist Organization as a whole. Although the approach to the Arab question did not entirely follow the thinking of Weltsch and Buber, it was basically positive, and even Kurt Blumenfeld, who had wavered at the meeting of the Actions Committee, came out strongly against the hard line advocated by Jabotinsky. Without doubt, however, the limelight at this Congress was focused on Buber – not Blumenfeld.[26]

The authors of the resolution adopted by the 12th Congress were divided over its political significance. For Buber, the final draft was an utter failure and a misinterpretation of his intentions. As far as he was concerned, it had lost "the blood and marrow" of the original. Instead of being a compass to direct internal and political affairs, it was merely another set of noncommittal slogans. The deep disappointment this caused him was cited by Buber in later years as

---

24 For some of the main differences see Mendes-Flohr, *A Land of Two Peoples*, 63; Simon, *The Lines of Demarcation*, 24–6.

25 Jabotinsky's speech in *Protokoll des XII. Zionisten-Kongresses, 1921*, 174–82. For the complete wording of the resolutions, see 745–76.

26 *Protokoll des XII. Zionisten-Kongresses, 1921*, 203–10.

the reason for his retirement from Zionist politics. His declarations at the Congress were the cornerstone of his position on the Jewish Arab issue for many years to come, but political activity remained a fleeting episode in his life. He consciously surrendered the opportunity to find a political application for his ideas, and contented himself with his role as thinker and educator.[27]

Not so Weltsch. He saw the Congress resolution as a positive move, albeit insufficient, towards the solution of the Arab problem in the spirit of political compromise that he and his colleagues endorsed. He appreciated the support he had received from the Zionist leadership, the German Zionist community and *Hapoel Hatzair*, and believed that a fundamental agreement existed between Weizmann, the German Zionists and himself which would help him further his ideas in the Zionist Organization. This belief guided his editorship of the *Jüdische Rundschau*, and colored the historical view of events in his writings many years later.[28]

Buber's response and subsequent withdrawal from politics did not have a major impact on the history of German Zionism; it was important for what it said about the man himself and belongs to the realm of biography. Weltsch's appraisal, on the other hand, has definite historical relevance. Whether or not he was correct in his judgment of Weizmann and the German Zionists, there is no doubt that his perceptions shaped the battle he waged on the pages of the *Jüdische Rundschau* and the attitude of the German Zionists towards that battle.

The underpinnings of Weltsch's belief seemed solid. Over the years there had been many points of convergence with Weizmann and the German Zionists. The Democratic Faction, the *Bar Kochba* circle in Prague, and *Hapoel Hatzair* were all associated in some way with the non-political Zionist school inspired by Ahad Ha'am. All emphasized spiritual, moral and social renaissance, and promoted cultural, educational and agricultural activity as opposed to politics and political gain. They all stressed the *process* of social-national development as a goal in and of itself, and tried to further it in light of social and cultural objectives. These groups were influenced by one another, consciously or unconsciously, and in some cases, membership overlapped. Chaim Weizmann was another link in this chain. He belonged to the Ahad Ha'am school, was a leader of the Democratic Faction, and served as a prominent spokesman for

---

27 Quotation from Buber's letter to Magnes, see note 23 above. See also Kohn, *Martin Buber*, 179, and Weltsch's epilogue, 434–9; Simon, *The Lines of Demarcation*, 25–6.

28 Weltsch, "Deutscher Zionismus"; Weltsch's letter to author, July 20, 1979; author's interviews with Weltsch, July 9, 1979, August 15, 1979, February 21, 1980, OHD; Robert Weltsch, "A Tragedy of Leadership – Chaim Weizmann and the Zionist Movement," *Jewish Social Studies,* 13 (1958): 211–6.

"synthetic Zionism", which sought to combine settlement in Palestine with education in the Diaspora and political activity.

These groups had already made their mark on German Zionism before World War I, but their influence grew stronger with the rise of Zionist radicalism that followed it. In the sequence of events described above, the ideas of *Hapoel Hatzair*, Martin Buber and Robert Weltsch converged in a manner which seemed to coincide with the views of the WZO president, Chaim Weizmann. All this prepared the ground in Germany for an extremely moderate position on the Arab question and the emergence of *Brith Shalom*, an organization inspired by the thoughts and actions of the same figures who subscribed to the teachings of Ahad Ha'am.

CHAPTER NINE

BRITH SHALOM

Confronting the Revisionist Challenge: The Binational Plan

The political storm in 1921 which produced the Jewish Legion proposal on the one hand, and the idea of a binational state on the other, eventually subsided. During the coming years, the Zionist movement and the German branch in particular, were mainly preoccupied with the economic development of Palestine and the expansion of the Jewish Agency. Nonetheless, the seeds of political moderation in Germany began to sprout. By 1925, the concept of binationalism among Zionists had achieved a more substantial formulation, culminating in the establishment of the *Brith Shalom* (Covenant of Peace) Association.

In 1925, the peak year of the Fourth *Aliya*, the debate over socioeconomic development intensified. Mass immigration and the emergence of a prosperous middle-class led advocates of private enterprise in Palestine and overseas to attack the settlement policies of the Zionist Executive. Questions also arose about the ultimate political objectives of the Zionist movement and whether the focus of its activity should be diplomacy or economic advancement. It was in the heat of this debate that the Revisionist movement and *Brith Shalom* were formed, both addressing issues that went far beyond the economy. True, they differed in the number of followers and in public and political influence. Moreover, the former was also a party and the latter only an association. Nevertheless, there were broad common grounds for their development. Both were a response to the economic prosperity in Palestine, and their political conceptions were molded in reply to the same challenge. In essence, *Brith Shalom* was established as a counterpoint to the Revisionist opposition in the Zionist movement, and as we shall presently see, it enjoyed strong support in Germany.

When the Revisionist party was founded in Paris in the spring of 1925, Jabotinsky's theories were already circulating; he had resigned from the Zionist Executive and joined the opposition in 1923. However, the changing circumstances in Palestine in 1924–1925 and the rise of groups whose economic interests were compatible with Jabotinsky's political conceptions, enabled him to shape his ideas into a comprehensive world-view that also reflected in a special way the concerns of the middle-class.[1] Both in Poland and among the new immigrants in Palestine, he found the political backbone he needed to establish such a party. The keynote speeches at the founders' meeting of the Revisionist movement focused on the interests of the middle-class, and its delegation to the World Zionist Organization was composed of middle-class representatives of the *Yishuv* and the Zionist movement.[2]

On the whole, the German Zionists were aligned on the other side of the track. Whereas the right-wing bourgeoisie railed against official Zionist settlement policy and favored mass immigration and private enterprise, the Germans, who were among the architects of Zionist economic policy in the early 1920s, believed in socioeconomic reform, a central role for the Zionist institutions, and cooperation with the Labor movement. They contended that the demand for free enterprise threatened to change Zionism from a movement of national renaissance into an ordinary immigration movement in which mass *aliya* and settlement were the "be all and end all".

The German Zionists also opposed the Revisionists' political stance. The latter argued that the realization of Zionist objectives depended on the creation of a Jewish majority through mass settlement, which was impossible without the backing of a supportive government. They called upon the Zionist Executive to pressure the British into providing the necessary conditions for a Jewish national home and inaugurating a "settlement regime", that would allow immigration to flow freely and promote free enterprise in industry and agriculture. The Revisionist attack on the British Government for its inactivity, and on Weizmann for his conciliatory views, was counterproductive as far as the German Zionists were concerned. As proponents of the gradual, planned approach, they felt that efforts should be inner-directed, with the emphasis on national settlement and strengthening the administrative and financial structure

---

1   Jabotinsky's speech at the 14th Zionist Congress, *Protokoll des XIV. Zionisten-Kongresses, 1925*, 236–50. See also Chapter Six.

2   Joseph B. Schechtman and Yehoshua Benari, *History of the Revisionist Movement (I) – 1925–1930* (Tel Aviv, 1970), 33–45; *Protokoll des XIV. Zionisten-Kongresses, 1925*, list of delegates, 7; Jabotinsky's remarks, 236; vote of confidence, 469–76.

of the Zionist Organization. In their eyes, there was no need to ask the government for anything more than a framework that would permit independent Zionist activity.[3]

The Revisionists wanted the focal point shifted to foreign politics. They demanded that the British Government maintain an active pro-Zionist policy that favored the Jewish minority in Palestine and created a protective barrier between the Jews and the Arabs. Jabotinsky's concept of the "iron wall", first publicized in 1921 when he proposed the remobilization of the Jewish Legion, was to become an integral part of the Revisionist platform in 1925.

The Revisionist stand thus required a political response that transcended the current economic and social debate. This response was not long in coming and its spokesmen were two leading Zionists of the day: Arthur Ruppin, head of the Settlement Department and patron of the cooperative labor settlements in Palestine, and Robert Weltsch, disseminator and interpreter of Weizmann's policies in Europe. Under their influence, anti-Revisionism went beyond the acknowledged platform of the Zionist radical school, and with the blessing of their fellow German Zionists, gave rise to a new political entity – *Brith Shalom*.

In the spring and summer of 1925, while Ruppin was organizing discussion groups in Palestine on Jewish-Arab relations, the anti-Revisionists in Germany were putting together a well-defined political program. Working with Weltsch was Felix Rosenblüth, chairman of the ZVfD until 1923, who had drawn up his own list for the 14th Zionist Congress elections in Germany.

In light of the political tranquility in Palestine and the real possibility of achieving a Jewish majority through mass immigration, Weltsch and Rosenblüth pressed for a different kind of political initiative: a "peace offensive" that would allay the Arabs' fear of a large influx of Jews. They believed that the idea of a Jewish nation-state as previously understood, was a mistake, and that a binational solution should be declared the only alternative. Reaching an agreement with the Arabs, they maintained, was crucial not only for the success of the Zionist enterprise, but for insuring that Zionism remained an ideology of freedom, equality and justice. It was thus imperative that the economic, settlement and immigration policies of the Zionist movement consider the needs and rights of the Arab inhabitants, eliminate sources of conflict and avoid an economic crisis which would affect both Jews and Arabs. Hurting the Arabs economically would only increase their

---

3   Weltsch's editorial, *JR*, July 3, 1925: 451–2, and article, July 14, 1925: 476; F. Rosenblüth's remarks at the election conference of Berlin Zionists, *JR*, July 31, 1925: 516. See also Chapter Six.

antagonism and refute the Zionist claims that they also stood to benefit from Jewish settlement.[4]

At this stage, the confrontation with the Revisionists in Germany was sandwiched between the heated polemic with the right-wing bourgeoisie and the debate over the expansion of the Jewish Agency. When Rosenblüth's list won the pre-Congress elections, the victory was interpreted as a broad show of support for Weizmann against the middle-class opposition and opponents of a larger Jewish Agency. The Revisionists, who sided with the opposition on both fronts, failed to win a single delegate. However, the firm anti-Revisionist stand of the German Zionists and their overwhelming support for Rosenblüth paved the way for a new initiative. Weltsch was able to launch a frontal attack against the Revisionists in the knowledge that he had been correct in his assessment all along. The elections clearly showed that there was no tendency towards political activism among the German Zionists, and that they were strongly in favor of reaching an agreement with the Arabs.[5]

Weltsch had not abandoned the ideas formulated by the Buber group in 1921 and he referred to them often, but it was only now that he felt he had the necessary backing to present his binational plan to the public as a viable political alternative. In a programmatic article which combined Weizmann's Zionist policy and response to the Revisionists with a call for binationalism, he wrote:[6]

> We would be mistaken not to recognize that the Zionist opposition has gathered strength. True, the so-called Revisionists constitute but a small group, but their poison is also spreading to the healthy organs of the Zionist body.... They are not suited temperamentally to protracted, arduous and prosaic labor... and they rush to embrace romantic militarism....

---

4   F. Rosenblüth, *JR*, July, 31, 1925: 516; Weltsch's editorial, *JR*, August 7, 1925: 529; on Ruppin's activity, see Aharon Kedar, *"Brith Shalom – The Early Period, 1925–1928,"* in *Studies in the History of Zionism Presented to Israel Goldstein on his Eightieth Birthday by the Institute of Contemporary Jewry*, ed. Yehuda Bauer, Moshe Davis and Israel Kolatt (Jerusalem, 1976) (Hebrew), 224–85.

5   See Chapter Six, on the preparations in Germany for the 14th Zionist Congress. Weltsch on the election results, *JR*, August 11, 1925: 541; report of results, *JR*, August 7, 1925: 529.

6   Weltsch's article "worum es geht", *JR*, August 14, 1925: 449–50, is the source of the quotations which follow (emphases in the original). This article also deals with other problems discussed at the congress. The portion discussed here was reprinted in 1927, in Kohn and Weltsch, *Zionistische Politik*.

Weltsch accused the Revisionists of being obsessed with war, narrow-minded, politically naive and deluded. He maintained that their accusations against the Zionist Executive were a misreading of the political situation, and that they presented a genuine threat:

> Jabotinsky demands the declaration of a Jewish state that includes Transjordan, a repeal of the 1922 White Paper, the establishment of a Jewish Legion. These demands are quoted everywhere, especially in the Arab press.... *In view of all this, the Congress cannot remain silent.* It must be stated in the clearest manner that this is not Zionist policy, neither in goal nor in strategy.

Instead, Weltsch offered a positive alternative that was worked out in detail and based on clear assumptions. He perceived the Balfour Declaration as a basic framework that could be imbued with content as necessary. The task of the Zionist movement at this point was to interpret the Declaration and redefine the goals of Zionism. The fundamental objective, in Herzl's eyes, too, was to solve the Jewish problem through the creation of a political, legal and cultural entity that would allow for an independent Jewish existence. Herzl believed that this could be achieved by the establishment of a Jewish state. "For a people without a land, a land without a people", went the saying (mistakenly attributed to Herzl). However, as Weltsch pointed out Palestine was not a land without a people; it was occupied by a large Arab population deeply attached to its homeland:

> Even if we constitute the majority after 30 or 40 years, it would be a majority of perhaps 51 percent. In other words: *Palestine will always be populated by two peoples, Jews and Arabs.*

Weltsch maintained that the country could never develop properly if one of the two peoples ruled the other. "The future of Palestine", he said, "is dependent on the emergence of a political framework in which both peoples live side by side, enjoying equal rights and bound by the natural ties of transportation, economics and cultural relations". His conclusion was as follows:

> We do not want a Jewish state, but a binational Palestinian community.... Such a regime will assure the attainment of the Zionist

objective, which is to create the complete legal foundations for an independent nation with a healthy socioeconomic structure and national freedom, yet corresponding to the framework delineated in the 1922 White Paper.

Weltsch thus offered an explicit political program with well-defined aims. He also called upon the Zionist Organization to include in its budget an allocation for an information campaign in Palestine and abroad, and for the study of the Arabic language in Jewish schools.

Hence, the binational plan was not just a response to Revisionism but a challenge to Weizmann and the Zionist leadership that predated the 14th Zionist Congress and the presentation of clear ideas on the subject by Ruppin and others in Palestine.

The 14th Zionist Congress and the Establishment of *Brith Shalom*

The 14th Zionist Congress that convened in Vienna in August 1925 was the final incentive for the establishment of *Brith Shalom*. Various factors converged to make this happen: the Revisionist challenge issued from its podium, the response of Weizmann and Ruppin, and the confluence of the Palestinian and German initiatives under the leadership of Ruppin and Weltsch. This combination was sufficient to turn the groping pre-Congress attempts into a cohesive ideological force that produced *Brith Shalom*.

The 14th Congress, where the great economic and social debate took center stage, marked the first appearance of the Revisionist party as a separate faction in the World Zionist Organization and a partner to the right-wing, bourgeoisie attack on Weizmann's settlement policy. In his presentation of the Revisionist alternative, Jabotinsky argued that the Zionist goal could not be achieved without political intervention, not only because of the magnitude of the economic enterprise and the Mandatory obligation to develop the Jewish national home, but because of the presence of another people hostile to the Balfour Declaration and Jewish immigration. The weight of the government, he contended, was needed to safeguard the privileges guaranteed by the Mandate, lest the numerical superiority of the Arabs prevent the Jews from exercising their rights.[7]

---

7   *Protokoll des XIV. Zionisten-Kongresses, 1925*, 236–50.

Both Weizmann and Ruppin were quick to respond to the non-democratic tone of Jabotinsky's words. Their summation was different, but each expressed concern for the rights of the Palestinian Arabs. Weizmann declared:

> Palestine is not Rhodesia. There are 600,000 Arabs living there who in the world's eyes have as much right to live in Palestine as the Jews have to a national home.

His conclusions, however, concerned only the immediate future and lacked clear political intent:

> In true friendship and partnership with the Arabs, we must open the Near East to Jewish enterprise.... Palestine must be built in such a way that the legitimate rights of the Arabs are not impinged upon in the slightest. We must accept Palestine as it is, with its sand and rocks, its Arabs and its Jews.... That is our work. Anything else would be a deception.... We shall rise or fall by our work alone....[8]

Ruppin, who had been preoccupied with the issue of Arab-Jewish relations in the months prior to the Congress, was more outspoken. He maintained that the Arabs would always constitute a large percentage of the country's population, and that Palestine was destined to be a country of two peoples. From these assumptions he drew short and long-term consequences regarding the economic and political future of the country. He looked forward

> ... to creating a community in Palestine of two nations, in which neither one would govern or oppress the other (*Vorherrschaft*) and both would work side by side in absolute equality, for the sake of the economic and cultural development of the country.

For this to occur, "We must take care of our own national needs, but at the same time, respect those of others".

8   Ibid., 328–29.

Ruppin emphasized that all economic projects should be implemented with the anticipated binational framework in mind. It was important not only to avoid financial harm to the Arabs but to help them attain equality with the Jewish population. Economic parity, he said, would provide the basis for political equality and harmony between the two peoples. In consequence, he called for the establishment of a special committee to plan areas of collaboration, especially in the economic sphere.[9]

The frankness with which Jabotinsky, Weizmann and Ruppin confronted the Arab question seems to have been instrumental in the emergence of *Brith Shalom*. There was a distinct feeling that the Weizmann leadership was inclined toward the binational solution, and although Weizmann himself did not present any definite programs he did come out publicly and emphatically on the side of a moderate and conciliatory Zionism that accepted the presence of an Arab entity in Palestine and viewed the realization of Zionism in the context of two peoples living in peaceful coexistence. Ruppin's involvement had begun before the Congress, but he had pursued the matter quietly and had not genuinely formulated his position. Now, for the first time, he appeared in public with an unequivocal stand and a practical scheme. Ruppin was highly regarded as a Zionist leader and a representative of Weizmann's policy despite his resignation from the Settlement Department during the Congress, and together with Weizmann his remarks made a deep impression on the German Zionists, who had closely followed the pre-Congress debate in the *Jüdische Rundschau*. Many equated their leaders' condemnation of the Revisionists with support for the binational idea. The founders of *Brith Shalom*, too, put great stock in winning the approval of the Zionist leadership, as demonstrated by their first moves after the Congress in Palestine and Germany.[10]

The 14th Congress also brought together Palestinian and Diaspora Zionists interested in tackling the Arab problem as a group. Among them were Ruppin and the two long-standing friends, Robert Weltsch and Hans Kohn. Shortly afterwards, Kohn settled in Palestine where he joined Hugo Bergman and others in furthering Ruppin's initiative. It was at Ruppin's Jerusalem home that *Brith Shalom* was founded in November 1925, as "an independent association for fostering Jewish-Arab understanding which aspires to establish the Jewish

---

9 Ibid., 438-39. The quoted passages are on 438.

10 See Weltsch's letter to Bergman, September 4, 1925, NULA, 1502/1334/3; Weltsch's articles during the Congress, *JR*, August 25, 1925: 571, and August 28, 1925: 579.

national home on the basis of full equality for Jews and Arabs in Palestine as a binational state".[11]

Brith Shalom in Germany: The Test

While the idea of binationalism first sprouted in Germany *Brith Shalom* was the joint endeavor of Zionist leaders in Palestine and Europe as a whole. The organization itself was formed in Palestine and most of its meetings took place behind closed doors. There was no branch as yet in Germany, although a widespread and intensive information campaign was in process. From the moment *Brith Shalom* was founded, the *Jüdische Rundschau* gave extensive coverage to binationalism and called for its adoption. The majority of the articles were written by Weltsch, but the paper also served the leaders of *Brith Shalom* in Palestine until the association published its own bulletin, *She'ifoteinu* ("Our Aspirations"), in 1927. The *Jüdische Rundschau*, regarded as the official Zionist publication in the German language, soon became the uncontested mouthpiece of *Brith Shalom* and even Jabotinsky was convinced that the binational idea had been born in Berlin.[12]

From the earliest days, it was obvious that the founders of *Brith Shalom* attributed great importance to the support they believed they enjoyed in the Weizmann camp. The *Jüdische Rundschau* presented the binational solution as fully in line with official Zionist policy, and the idea was touted in countless articles as a new interpretation of Weizmann. In Weltsch's eyes, there was no contradiction between the paper's dual role as Weizmann's commentator and organ of *Brith Shalom*, and he repeatedly argued that the thinking in both cases was essentially the same.

Neither Weizmann nor other members of the Zionist Executive had ever voiced explicit support for the binational plan apart from Ruppin, who had already resigned from the Executive, and Rosenblüth, who had recently joined it. Be that as it may, Weltsch interpreted the Executive's reticence as a tactical

---

11 Weltsch's letter to Bergman (see note 10 above); minutes of the meetings at Ruppin's home, November 15 and 17, 1925; and Kohn's letter to Ruppin, December 6, 1925, LBIA, 7185/3/1.

12 Jabotinsky's statement to that effect appeared in an article in the *Wiener Morgenzeitung*, quoted in *JR*, March 5, 1926: 131. On *Brith Shalom*'s activity in Palestine, see Kedar, "*Brith Shalom*", 232, 257–9, 264–6. For examples of *JR* articles on *Brith Shalom*, see those by Weltsch, December 11, 1925, by Buber, April 16, 1926, by Kohn, June 25, 1926, and by Ruppin, July 6, 1926.

move, to avoid needless political arguments over matters such as a Jewish majority in Palestine that were not of immediate relevance. He insisted that it was his duty as a responsible journalist and political commentator to expose new ideologies and trends, and because Weizmann was a statesman and not at liberty to speak his mind, it was his mission to express these views for him. Weltsch was not alone in the belief that he was representing the true Weizmann. From the very beginning, the founders of *Brith Shalom* in Palestine, especially Ruppin, pointed out the basic affinity between their approach and Weizmann's, which they tried to preserve through low-keyed, non-political work in the intellectual sphere. They saw further proof of Weizmann's tacit agreement with them in an unpublicized grant he extended which enabled the publication of the first issue of *She'ifoteinu*.[13]

Of particular significance was the profound connection between *Brith Shalom* and the broad school of Zionist thought to which Weizmann also subscribed. This school, which stressed the moral, social and cultural renaissance of the Jewish people, was now being challenged by the growing Revisionist camp with its emphasis on political Zionism. As a result the 14th Congress had been turned into a virtual battleground, prompting Weizmann to present a counterproposal that was very similar to binationalism. By so doing, Weizmann strengthened the impression that he supported *Brith Shalom*, and this common denominator, at least the belief in its existence, was the basis for *Brith Shalom*'s special role in Germany.

Shortly after the birth of *Brith Shalom* and the emergence of the *Jüdische Rundschau* as its champion, the paper was put to the test on two accounts: whether it accurately reflected both the public mood and the policies of Weizmann. The response of the German Zionists to two interrelated factors – the rise of the Revisionists and the economic crisis in Palestine – demonstrated that the paper was indeed on the right track.

Due to their ideological background and communal development, the spontaneous reaction of the German Zionists to Revisionism was one of resistance. They fully supported Weizmann, and in light of their post-war experiences, whole-heartedly endorsed his anti-chauvinist stance. Their opposition to Revisionism became even stronger as the economy of Palestine began to decline. Believing in economic development as the key to Zionist

13 On Weizmann's support, see Kedar, "*Brith Shalom*," note 97; Landauer's letter to Weizmann, August 4, 1927, WA. Also see Weltsch's articles, *JR*, July 20, 1926: 409, July 9, 1926: 415, and December 10, 1926: 701, 703; author's interviews with Weltsch, July 9, 1979, August 15, 1979, OHD; Weltsch, "A Tragedy of Leadership".

fulfillment, they were determined to stand by the order of priorities set by the Zionist movement. The German Zionists were so preoccupied with refuting the Revisionist claim that economic issues could be resolved by coercion and political pressure, that the *Jüdische Rundschau* was able to speak out on behalf of *Brith Shalom* for nearly six months without a contrary word.

The deepening economic strain in Palestine compelled the Zionist movement to do some ideological soul-searching. The prospects for Zionist fulfillment, the duration and pace, and even the goals of Zionism were being questioned. Economic policy aside, the very heart of Zionism was under attack. The challenge came from two directions: the opponents of Zionism in general, and the Revisionists. For the anti-Zionists the economic crisis was proof of their contention that Zionism was incapable of solving the Jewish problem. Consequently, they intensified their propaganda in circles which contributed materially to the Zionist enterprise and tried to divert funds to alternative programs, such as the farm colonies project in Crimea.

Revisionism was ostensibly a response to the growing tide of opposition to Zionism, but was, in fact, directed at the Zionist establishment and its leadership. The Revisionists declared that it was not the Zionist idea that was bankrupt, but Zionist policy. The goal of a Jewish majority in Palestine was attainable and the springboard for Jewish national independence, as proven by the Fourth *Aliya*. The economic crisis had occurred because the Mandatory Government had failed in its basic obligation to establish a "settlement regime" conducive to economic advancement and ongoing immigration. The Zionist leadership had been delinquent in not pressing the government on these issues, and even now, in the throes of the crisis, it continued to display political impotence.

The source of the problem in the eyes of the Revisionists was Weizmann's misguided outlook and order of priorities. Weizmann emphasized quality and socioeconomic change, while disdaining the quantitative dimension and the opportunity to create a Jewish majority. No new economic or political moves had been made to encourage mass immigration, and Weizmann continued to insist on policies that had proven deficient. The Revisionists saw the economic difficulties as confirmation that a political offensive and a supportive British framework were indeed prerequisites for Zionist fulfillment, and that the current policy had failed. As far as they were concerned, the crisis was a warning and signalled the need for a change of direction. The time had come, they said, to declare the attainment of a Jewish majority as the main objective and to take the political steps necessary to achieve it.[14]

The despair which began seeping into the Zionist leadership due to the floundering economy, the attacks by anti-Zionists and the antagonism of the Revisionists, took its toll. At the Zionist Actions Committee meeting in July 1926, the Mandatory Government was severely castigated and a stern list of demands was drawn up which even won the approval of the German delegates. The *Jüdische Rundschau*, which usually sided with the conciliatory policy of the Weizmann leadership, also backed the resolutions of the Actions Committee. The editor felt that they were not a contradiction of the accepted order of priorities, but an addendum. There was no call for a Jewish majority, and the demands on others were not at the expense of self-action.[15]

It was impossible, however, to escape the impression that something had changed at the Zionist Executive, despite the reassurances of the *Jüdische Rundschau*. Was Weizmann's anti-Revisionist stand really compatible with the binational idea? To what extent did the paper represent both the German Zionists and Weizmann? These were some of the questions raised at the German Zionist convention at Erfurt in August 1926. Before the convention Weltsch's supporters from the Zionist Association of Frankfurt a.M. initiated a draft resolution to confirm the policies voiced in the paper. The spokesman of the group, Ernst A. Simon, was a disciple of Buber's who was to become one of *Brith Shalom*'s most active members in Palestine.[16]

Some of the delegates at the convention were vehemently opposed to this resolution, among them Richard Lichtheim, a long-time adversary of Weltsch, and Nahum Goldmann, a leader of the Radical Faction. They argued that the *Jüdische Rundschau* no longer articulated the stance of the Zionist Executive. Weizmann and his colleagues had distanced themselves from the British, and had begun to demand active support for the national home, whereas Weltsch was still adhering to the 1922 White Paper which promised Jews and Arabs equal treatment under Mandatory law. Lichtheim went so far as to accuse Weltsch of publishing falsified and misleading reports, and withholding information from his readers. These barbs were aimed less at the one-sidedness

14 The *Revisionist Voice – Election Issue of the Revisionist Zionist Organization* (Tel Aviv, December 3, 1925) (Hebrew); Jabotinsky's speeches, *JR*, November 12, 1926: 635–6, November 30, 1926: 680; Lichtheim's article, *JR*, December 23, 1926: 731–3. See Chapter Six for the anti-Zionist offensive.

15 Minutes of the Actions Committee, CZA, Z4/272/6; articles by Weltsch and Blumenfeld, *JR*, July 20, 1926: 409, July 23, 1926: 413, August 13, 1926: 453, and August 20, 1926: 472.

16 *JR*, August 20, 1926: 472, and report of the convention, August 27, 1926: 480.

of the paper than at the Zionist outlook behind it. Lichtheim and Goldmann charged that the stand of Weltsch and his lofty ideals not only missed the mark as far as truth was concerned, but were guilty of political escapism. In their eyes, the attempt to put forward a Jewish nationalism which professed to be more humane, moderate and tolerant than European nationalism was no more than a stumbling block.

Lichtheim and Goldmann did not even relate to the concept of binationalism or the question of policy vis-à-vis the Arabs. They stood at the podium as supporters of Weizmann whom they claimed was no longer ultra-conciliatory, and in so doing, pulled the rug out from under Weltsch as his only legitimate interpreter and representative. The implication was that unless the *Jüdische Rundschau* changed its line, the leaders of the Zionist Organization in Germany would withdraw their endorsement of the paper.[17]

In his rejoinder, Weltsch elaborated fully on the binational plan and presented it as the basis for his identification with both Mandatory policy and the Zionist Executive. The 1922 White Paper, he said, provided not for a Jewish state but for a political framework where two autonomous national communities would coexist, with Palestinian citizenship for all. Binationalism was indeed the only solution in light of the fact that another people was living in the country, but this did not exclude the possibility of realizing the primary goal of Zionism, namely, a legally-recognized Jewish entity that would serve as the center of world Jewry and expand steadily through immigration.

Weltsch claimed that he was not alone in this view, and that the Zionist Executive's support for the White Paper represented a pragmatic acceptance of binationalism as the only realistic alternative to the outmoded concept of a Jewish state. He did not perceive its recent demands on the Mandatory Government as a deviation from its original outlook. These demands were meant to strengthen the *Yishuv* financially and numerically, but majority status was not foreseeable in the near future, and the government alone did not have the power to make this happen. Thus the Jews had no current basis for demanding rights as a potential majority.

According to Weltsch, the provisions of the Mandate and the Zionist Executive were not at odds at all. Both were anchored in an acceptance of reality, the abandonment of old modes of thinking, and the willingness to sanction a binational state. The *Jüdische Rundschau*, he maintained, was a true

17 Minutes of the convention, *JR*, August 27, 1926.

reflection of the attitude of the Zionist Executive, and one did not cancel out the other. The implication was that German Zionists were not being called upon to choose between Weizmann or the *Jüdische Rundschau* but to opt for binationalism as the sole alternative to Revisionism.

In summing up the meeting, however, Kurt Blumenfeld, the chairman of the ZVfD, ignored these distinctions. He remained silent on the binational issue and made no attempt to draw comparisons. On the contrary, he spoke so vaguely about Weizmann's policies that his expression of support was rendered virtually meaningless. Blumenfeld declared that his organization stood behind Weizmann in general, and had faith in him as a leader and a judge when the need arose. He said that the German Zionists identified with Weizmann's basic approach, which was both realistic and forthright, and abjured political action motivated by empty prestige. Weizmann's order of priorities, with practical labor rather than politics at the top of the scale, was acceptable to them, and they saw no sense in making proclamations about such matters as a Jewish majority. Blumenfeld held that the position of the *Jüdische Rundschau* was within the realm of concencus in this respect, and that its observations were therefore entirely legitimate.

Thus Blumenfeld avoided open support for Weltsch's stance, but he agreed that it was valid within the context of the ZVfD's general backing of Weizmann. In this way he prepared the ground for a resolution which sactioned both lines of thinking and rejected the notion of German Zionist supervision over the paper. This resolution had a double purpose. On the one hand, it confirmed that the *Jüdische Rundschau* was a legitimate organ for Weizmann's policy; on the other, it denied the paper's right to be his sole interpreter, and certainly not the mouthpiece for the German Zionist movement. The *Jüdische Rundschau* thus retained its independence with the approval of the German Zionist leadership, yet without unqualified support for its political stand.

While the convention did not adopt the binational scheme or rule out the relevance of a Jewish majority, it did endorse Weizmann's policy and accept binationalism as a possible, albeit non-binding interpretation. Nonetheless, Weltsch left the premises convinced that the great majority of German Zionists concurred with him. As far as he was concerned, the convention had fully recognized the correspondence between the official view and that of his paper, and affirmed it as the only realistic way to assure the establishment of the Jewish national home.[18]

18 Report on the convention, *JR*, August 27, 1926: 477. In retrospect, Weltsch said that Blumenfeld had actually declined to take a stand. See the author's interviews with Weltsch on July 9, 1979, and August 15, 1979, OHD.

Weltsch was not the only one who drew such conclusions; there were two other parties, both opponents of the *Jüdische Rundschau*. One was Richard Lichtheim, who had long agreed with many of the Revisionist charges against Weizmann but without joining the Jabotinsky camp. In his eyes the convention was the last straw. For years he had tried to maintain an oppositionist stance within the German Zionist movement; he saw his role as that of a gadfly, fighting for the improvement of Zionist policy. The vote in favor of the *Jüdische Rundschau* made it impossible for him to remain any longer. Shortly after the convention at which he had publicly declared "I am not a Revisionist", Lichtheim went over to the Revisionist camp.[19]

The other party that evaluated the outcome of the convention as Weltsch did were the Austrian Zionists. At their national convention at the beginning of November 1926, explicit reference was made to the deliberations of the German Zionists three months earlier. The Austrians were critical of the *Jüdische Rundschau* resolution and drew a distinction between Weizmann, whom they endorsed with certain reservations, and the German Zionists, whose views were equated with those of the *Jüdische Rundschau* and totally rejected. *The Jewish Chronicle*, a British newspaper, known for its pro-Revisionist sympathies, presented the polemic between the Austrian Zionists and the *Jüdische Rundschau* in a similar light.[20]

The Binational Plan and the Zionist Executive

The Austrian convention helped dispel the mist over the meaning and implications of Weizmann's policy and forced both the public and the Zionist Executive to squarely address the political issue and binationalism. The Zionist Executive was represented at the convention by Felix Rosenblüth and it was he who was called upon to clarify the Executive's position with regard to the

---

19 M. Rosenblüth's letter to Weltsch, December 6, 1926, CZA, A167/17; Schechtman and Benari, *History of the Revisionist Movement*, 61.

20 F. Rosenblüth's letter's to Weltsch, November 11, 1926, and to Eder, November 12, 1926, WA; *JR* editorial, November 5, 1926: 620; report on the Austrian convention, *JR*, November 9, 1926: 630, and November 19, 1926: 653; *The Jewish Chronicle*, November 12, 1926.

resolutions of the Erfurt convention. Considerable weight was attributed to
Rosenblüth's views; as the recent chairman of the ZVfD and a newly-elected
member of the Zionist Executive, he was regarded as a link between the two.

Rosenblüth was a firm believer in political moderation, and on the eve of the
14th Zionist Congress, had spoken out in favor of a binational state and against
Revisionism. He was also among those who saw a close resemblance between
Weizmann's ideas and binationalism. After his appointment as head of the
Zionist Executive's Organization Department, he wrote to the Zionist
Committee of Bukovina in this vein, declaring that a major effort should be
made to win the trust of the Arabs and gain their cooperation by guaranteeing
them equal national rights. This was his response to Jabotinsky's demand that
the Mandate Government grant state land exclusively to Jews.[21]

Speaking to the Austrian Zionists, Rosenblüth portrayed the Zionist
Executive to a coalition government that was trying to avoid jargon:

> It is a fact that the bare unadorned and unexpounded term, "Jewish
> state" – I will go further and say: the too primitive conception of a
> "Jewish state" – have [sic] been excluded from the political vocabulary
> of Zionism. And, I think, very properly excluded, because the term
> as such, represents a misleading and provocative slogan.

The resolutions of the 1st Zionist Congress, known as the Basel Program,
stated that: "Zionism aims at the establishment of a national home in Palestine
secured by public right for the Jewish people." Rosenblüth pointed out that
Herzl's friend and successor, David Wolffsohn, had interpreted "national
home" as a "homeland" (*Heimstätte*), not a "Jewish state." An official pamphlet,
The Program of Zionism, handed out at the 10th Zionist Congress in 1911,
maintained that the concept "Jewish state" had no place in a concrete political
context and was meant in the utopian sense. Eliminating this term from the
political lexicon, Rosenblüth argued, was simply an adaptation of policy to
reality. It was not a denial of political Zionism because Herzl had not
necessarily defined the state he foresaw as a nation- state. His vision was of a
territorial concentration of Jews and the transformation of the Jewish people
into an independent nation. This was precisely what the Zionist Executive
wanted: a territorial unit that would embody and facilitate political freedom.

---

21 F. Rosenblüth's letter on behalf of the Zionist Executive to the Zionist Committee of Bukovina,
    December 2, 1925, WA.

At the same time, the Zionist Executive had not disavowed the desire for a Jewish majority. On the contrary, the act of bringing Jews together in a single geographical location implied that they would no longer be a minority as they were in other countries. No responsible Zionist authority had questioned Ahad Ha'am's assertion that "It is in Palestine alone that we shall lead a free national life, because it is there only that we shall form a majority". However, this was not to say that the Arab minority should be denied its own national freedom.[22]

Rosenblüth thus portrayed the official policy of the Zionist Executive, including the Jewish majority component, as supportive of binationalism, thereby deflating the "Jewish state" argument. He worked tirelessly to promote his version of binationalism and dispel the uncertainty surrounding the policies of the Zionist establishment and its backing of the *Jüdische Rundschau* in a concerted effort to keep up the broad united front in support of Weizmann. Much of this was directed toward Weltsch, Blumenfeld and other German Zionist leaders. In a letter to Weltsch he argued that a joint majority was crucial to Zionist realization and posed no conflict with the binational plan:

> So long as we are the minority in Palestine, we will continue to support national autonomy and minority rights, but we will never have the feeling of total freedom. To achieve this sense of liberty and develop our strength to the fullest, we must strive to become the majority and then institute a new set of majority-minority relations.[23]

Rosenblüth wanted Blumenfeld on his side because a cohesive Zionist front in Germany was crucial to hold the Revisionists at bay. In this, Rosenblüth derived help from Jabotinsky himself, who intensified the Zionist polemic all the more in the wake of his countrywide campaign in late 1926. This brought to the fore the basic affinity among the anti-Revisionists and defined the concordance between the *Jüdische Rundschau* and the German pro-Weizmann camp.

---

22 Official English version of F. Rosenblüth's speech, CZA, Z4/2327. See also Rosenblüth's letters to ZVfD, November 1, 1926, to Weltsch, November 2 1926, and to Eder, November 12, 1926, WA. Interview with Rosenblüth, *JR*, November 19, 1926: 650, and report, 653.

23 F. Rosenblüth's letter to Weltsch, December 14, 1926, CZA, Z4/2327. See also Rosenblüth's letters to Weltsch, December 1, and December 6, 1926, CZA, AI67/17.

To counter the Revisionist ideology that Jabotinsky was spreading in Germany, Weltsch continued to downplay the importance of achieving a Jewish majority in Palestine. Aside from the provocative nature of this aspiration, he was concerned about its harmful effect on the economy. To Weltsch's mind, the current crisis was directly related to the short cuts taken in the rush to outnumber the Arabs. To develop a sound economy required patience coupled with slow and solid building – not impulsiveness. Weltsch never went so far as to declare that he was against a majority, and admitted that quantity was not unimportant for a strong Jewish community. Nonetheless, he was reluctant to attach critical significance to numbers and ratios.[24]

Weltsch's arguments failed to win over the German Zionist establishment. Its leaders, with Blumenfeld at the forefront, called themselves anti-Revisionists, but they staunchly supported a Jewish majority and declared that even if the ultimate goal was a binational state, a majority status was no less important. Weizmann's position, supported by the ZVfD, was that the two peoples should be able to share the country in full national freedom, regardless of whether the Jews were now a minority or would one day become the majority.[25]

The debate among the German Zionists was noteworthy in that all its participants saw it as a test of official Zionist policy. Jabotinsky had good reason to address the German Zionist public. The German Zionist establishment, on the other hand, exercised great caution, aware that its statements would be seized upon as representing the Zionist Executive. Blumenfeld felt that as responsible statesmen (*Verantwortungspolitiker*), Weizmann and himself should refrain from making declarations that might not withstand the dictates of reality. He also censured the *Jüdische Rundschau* for assuming an excessively rhetorical line.[26]

To all outward appearances, there was a conflict between the Revisionists and the German Zionists, but the Weizmann camp found it more convenient to remain silent. The only declarative statement in the name of the Zionist Executive came from Felix Rosenblüth, who was never openly acknowledged as its spokesman. No one had authorized Rosenblüth to speak for the German

---

24 Jabotinsky's speeches, *JR*, November 30, 1926: 680; Weltsch's replies, *JR*, November 23, 1926: 663, and December 10, 1926: 701–3. See also Lichtheim's article *JR*, December 23, 1926: 731–2.

25 Blumenfeld's Berlin speech on December 2, 1926, *JR*, December 7, 1926: 697.

26 ZVfD executive meeting, December 15, 1926, Schocken Archives, 531/61.

Zionists, either. Nonetheless, he was more qualified than their elected leaders to articulate official policy.[27]

At this stage, the debate came again to a standstill. The Zionist Organization of Germany as a body made no definite commitment with regard to political objectives and presented no strategies for building up a Jewish majority. Yet the message to the Zionist public was clear: Both the Weizmann leadership and the German Zionists were united on the importance of such a majority. At the same time, they recognized the need for an anti-Revisionist coalition, to which the *Jüdische Rundschau* also belonged despite its different approach to the numerical supremacy and the binational thesis.[28]

---

27 F. Rosenblüth's letter to Weltsch, December 14, 1926, and Weltsch's reply, December 17, 1926, CZA, Z4/2327.

28 ZVfD executive meeting, December 15, 1926, Schocken Archives, 531/61.

CHAPTER TEN

IN THE WAKE OF THE 1929 RIOTS:
A BREAKDOWN OF UNITY

Turning Inward

After the ebbing of the storm aroused by the *Jüdische Rundschau*'s support for *Brith Shalom* in 1925–1926, the German Zionist movement refrained from dealing with matters of Zionist foreign policy. At first, public attention was refocused on the economics of settlement, the serious crisis in Palestine and the political struggles within the Zionist Organization. After the 15th Zionist Congress in 1927, there was a retreat from this activity as well, as the German Zionists turned inward toward the internal problems of their movement – youth education, cultural programming, debating with the anti-Zionists and winning over more Jews to Zionism. The concerted effort on behalf of Palestine came to a halt with a sense of disappointment and self-criticism. From the activity of the *Linkes Zentrum*, it became clear that there were internal weaknesses that demanded attention. If there was any general Zionist issue that still occupied the German Zionists, it was the enlargement of the Jewish Agency. With their experience in cooperating with non- Zionists in *Keren Hayesod*, they had assumed responsibility for setting up the organizational mechanism of the Jewish Agency. But this was also connected in a way to their own national affairs, because it drove them to intensify their struggle against the anti-Zionists who opposed Jewish Agency expansion and their efforts to increase local membership in the Zionist movement.[1]

---

1   On the crisis and subsequent introspection, see Chapter Seven. On the Jewish Agency issue and the struggle with the anti-Zionists, see Chapter Five. See also Blumenfeld's circular to activists, December 12, 1927, executive committee meeting, February 21, 1928, correspondence between Blumenfeld and Zionists outside Berlin that was distributed to *Landesvorstand* on March 13, 1928,

The 22nd convention of German Zionists, held in Breslau at the end of May 1928, was pervaded by this sense of inwardness. The German Zionists were weary of the rifts and controversies, and yearned for positive, fruitful collaboration in the spheres of Zionist education and the strengthening of the German Jewish community. It was decided to form a special committee for *Gemeindepolitik* (communal politics), which was the first time this matter was institutionalized by the ZVfD. The convention also ended with a series of resolutions on the expansion of youth education. This turn inward reinforced the tendency to eschew politics. The convention thus elected an executive committee headed by Kurt Blumenfeld, that incorporated most streams of German Zionism. The General Zionists and Leftists were represented by Moritz Bileski, Martin Rosenblüth and the young doctor Siegfried Kanowitz (later an Israeli Knesset member who promoted environmental issues and had an anti-pollution law named after him). Alfred Berger represented *Poalei Zion*; Georg Landauer, *Hapoel Hatzair*; Nahum Goldmann, the Radical Faction; Richard Lichtheim, the Revisionists; and Max Kollenscher, the right-wing General Zionists and those who gave high priority to communal politics. The only group not participating in the new administration was *Mizrahi*, which withdrew when its demand for religiously-oriented Zionist education was rejected. The shift from world Zionist politics to internal affairs was thus quite obvious.[2]

The preparations in Germany for the 16th Zionist Congress, which was to meet in Zurich at the end of July 1929 to decide on the Enlarged Jewish Agency, were also carried on in this spirit. The Revisionists and the Radical Faction, who fought against the enlargement, failed to win a single mandate in the pre-Congress elections. The votes were divided equally between three factions: the General Zionists, *Poalei Zion*, and *Hapoel Hatzair* and *Mizrahi*, with three mandates each. With the issue of the Jewish Agency already settled, the 16th Congress yielded no political surprises. In the address delivered by

---

CZA, Z4/3567/II; *Landesvorstand* meetings on June 9, 1928, *JR*, June 13, 1928, and on September 9, 1928, CZA, Z4/3567/III; executive committee meeting, July 2, 1928, Schocken Archives, 531/61; Blumenfeld's letter to Weizmann, February 6, 1928, WA; Weltsch's letters to Bergman, March 23, 1928, LBIA, 7185/2/16, and September 9, 1928, NULA, 1502/1334/4.

2 Programmatic articles by Kanowitz, *JR*, April 20, 1928: 221-2 (lead article) and by Hirsch, *JR*, May 1, 1928: 243-4 (lead article); minutes and resolutions of Breslau convention, *JR*, June 1, 1928, and June 5, 1928, and resolutions of the community affairs committee, Schocken Archives, 531/61; executive committee meetings, February 21, 1928, December 17, 1928, December 26, 1928, January 1, 1929, and January 31, 1929, and *Landesvorstand* meeting, February 2, 1929, CZA, Z4/3567/III. On *Mizrahi*, see article by Adler, *JR*, June 22, 1928: 355; *Mizrahi* memorandum, March 21, 1929, Schocken Archives, 531/61.

Blumenfeld, the leader of the German delegation, there was no question about where his country's interests lay. Blumenfeld called for the unification of the Zionist movement and the avoidance of superfluous party politics. This would create a united front in the Jewish Agency and the Jewish community at large as a counterpart to the anti-Zionists. Accordingly, he supported a broad coalitionary Executive, reinstating the labor movement which had been excluded in 1927. He also urged the Zionists to redirect their attention to national endeavors and to step up their local membership and fundraising campaigns.[3]

The concern over Jewish-Arab relations and the position taken by the *Jüdische Rundschau* rose to the fore again in the summer of 1928 when *Brith Shalom* proposed the establishment of a parliament in Palestine. This possibility had already been raised by the Arabs in response to the British endeavors to draft a constitution for Palestine. The second issue of the *Brith Shalom* publication, *She'ifoteinu*, which appeared in August 1928, was entirely devoted to this topic, and the *Jüdische Rundschau*, too, became a sounding board for the new initiative.[4]

The *Brith Shalom* campaign for a Palestine parliament clearly illuminated the conflict between this group and the Zionist leadership. While there may have been a basic consensus on general concepts such as a "Jewish state" or even a "Jewish majority," this was not the case in immediate political matters. The Zionist Executive charged that parliamentary representation would mean giving the Arabs majority status and the right to block the development of the Jewish national home. Moreover, in putting forth this proposal, *Brith Shalom* abandoned the strategy that had kept it aligned with the Weizmann leadership: avoiding political pronouncements and concentrating on social and economic programs as the basis for a national home and good relations with the Arabs. In deviating from this approach, *Brith Shalom* came up against the passivity of the Zionist leadership.

The *Jüdische Rundschau*'s support for the *Brith Shalom* initiative evoked loud criticism from the ZVfD. Blumenfeld publicly took the paper to task and reminded its editor that the *Jüdische Rundschau* was known as the official organ

---

3   *Protokoll des XVI. Zionisten Kongresses, 1929*, 140–5; German General Zionist platform, Schocken Archives, 531/63; programmatic articles by Lichtheim and Goldmann, *JR*, June 18, 1929: 298–9. On the cooperation between Revisionists and the Radical Faction, see also Chapters Five and Nine.

4   Ruppin, *Tagebücher*, 399–409; Neil Caplan, *Futile Diplomacy (I) - Early Arab-Zionist Negotiation Attempts 1913-1931* (London and Totowa), 1983); Porath, *The Emergence*, 253–7; *She'ifoteinu* — Collection of Articles, no. 2 (Jerusalem, 1928) (Hebrew); *JR*, August 31, 1928, editorial and article by Joseph Cowen: 491–2.

of the German Zionist movement. Weltsch was asked to make it clear that these views were personal opinions only, and to avoid political posturing that could be interpreted as official policy. At the same time, the ZVfD executive committee refused to take a stand on the issues at hand. The lesson of the *Linkes Zentrum* was still fresh in its mind, and unity was valued too highly to act otherwise.

The ZVfD executive's chastisement of the *Jüdische Rundschau* showed that the depoliticization process that began after the 15th Congress was now complete:

> The ZVfD Executive calls upon the editors of the *Jüdische Rundschau* to avoid any discussion of unclarified issues of Zionist foreign policy that might create the impression of an official ZVfD position on these matters.[5]

However, the problem of the *Jüdische Rundschau* did not fade. On the Day of Atonement, September 23, 1928, a dispute broke out over arrangements for Jewish prayer at the Western Wall, arousing an outcry around the world. The reports in Weltsch's newspaper were up-to-date and detailed, based on the account of its correspondent in Palestine, Gerda Arlosoroff-Goldberg. Arlosoroff-Goldberg was a member of *Hapoel Hatzair* who had immigrated to Palestine several years before. Her opinions were similar to those of Weltsch, and her tone was often gloomy. Weltsch himself became increasingly outspoken and attacked the Revisionists time and again, prompting their leader Richard Lichtheim to demand his dismissal. Lichtheim's request remained unheeded, but the ZVfD was firm in its decision to steer away from politics. This would change only after the 1929 riots.[6]

---

5   Executive committee meeting, September 27, 1928, Schocken Archives, 531/61. See also the meetings of September 6, 1928, and September 13, 1928, Schocken Archives, 531/61; Weltsch's letter to Bergman, [September] 27, [1928], LBIA, 7185/2/16.

6   Weltsch's editorial, *JR*, November 29, 1928; Gerda Arlosoroff's report, October 18, 1928, LBIA, 7185/3/2; executive committee meeting, November 29, 1928, Schocken Archives, 531/61, and May 23, 1928, CZA, Z4/3567/IV; Lichtheim's letter to executive committee, April 25, 1928, CZA, Z4/3567/IV.

The 1929 Riots and the Public Response

The 16th Zionist Congress, which met in Zurich between July 28–August 11, 1929, voted in favor of the Enlarged Jewish Agency and a founders council convened immediately afterwards. A few days later, when most of the leaders of the Zionist movement and the *Yishuv* were still in Europe, violent rioting broke out in Palestine. On August 15, the Jewish fast day of the Ninth of Av, a group of young people, most of them members of the Revisionist *Bethar* youth movement, held a protest against the restrictions on Jewish prayer at the Western Wall. In the course of an Arab counter-demonstration, a young Jew was killed. His funeral, on August 21, turned into a political rally and resulted in a clash with the police. Two days later, on August 23, the riots erupted. Hordes of Arabs, leaving their mosques after Friday prayers, attacked Jewish neighborhoods in Jerusalem and the vicinity. The violence spread to other parts of the country, reaching a peak in Hebron on August 24, when 66 Jews were murdered, and in Safed, on August 29, where the death toll was 45. The riots lasted a full week, leaving 133 Jews dead and 339 wounded. A total of 116 Arabs were also killed, most of them by the British authorities in a belated attempt to restore order.

These events were greeted with profound shock by members of the *Yishuv*, the Zionist movement and Jewish communities all around the world. Much of the anger was directed at the Mandatory Government, which only shortly before had confiscated the weapons given to the inhabitants of the Jewish settlements for self- defense after the 1921 riots. The British military forces had been reduced to a bare minimum during the days of High Commissioner Lord Herbert O. Plumer (1925–1928), as had the police, most of whom were Arabs. During the riots, close to one-third of the senior officers, including the chief of police, were out of the country. The High Commissioner, Sir John H. Chancellor, was also away, and had left his duties to his deputy, Chief Secretary Harry C. Luke, who was known for his hostility toward the Jewish community.[7]

Chaim Weizmann, hearing of the disturbances while vacationing after the Congress, hurried to London. He demanded that Colonial Secretary Lord Passfield immediately appoint a commission to investigate and determine responsibility for these events. He also called upon the British to halt the disarmament of Jews who had assisted the police during the riots, to dismiss

---

7   *History of the Hagana*, vol. II, ed. Ben-Zion Dinur (Jerusalem and Tel Aviv, 1964) (Hebrew), 312–40.

Harry Luke and the deputy governor of Jerusalem for their failure to intervene, to issue an official statement of policy with regard to Palestine, and to increase the immigration quota.

With the exception of the commission, none of these demands was met. The Colonial Secretary contended that providing the Jews with arms would not only fail to protect them but would provoke a general Arab rebellion that could endanger the entire *Yishuv*. An investigating team known as the Shaw Commission was appointed in early September 1929. Weizmann had hoped that it would conduct a comprehensive survey of the Palestine administration and create the political conditions for accelerated Jewish settlement. He therefore asked that the commission be granted broad powers, enabling it to determine the extent to which the Mandatory Government had carried out its obligations. The Colonial Secretary and his staff, however, saw to it that the commission's authority was limited to investigating the riots; they wished to obviate the slightest doubt about the British ability to fulfill its Mandatory obligations.[8]

Nevertheless, Weizmann remained hopeful that the political situation triggered by the riots would facilitate rapid development. At a Zionist meeting in London, he said:

> After the 1921 riots in Palestine, we were forced to accept the White Paper. Now we will accept nothing but a blue and white paper. No ship will reach Palestine without bringing pioneering settlers. With the subsiding of the disturbances, a new influx of immigrants must inundate the land. The only genuine response the government can offer is to turn the Mandate into a living instrument.[9]

Weizmann thus intensified his pressure on the British Government to carry out the policies to which it had committed itself in a consistent and decisive manner. He did not attack the political conception underlying the Mandate, but rather the haphazard implementation and inimical attitude of the British authorities in Palestine. It was this attitude, he contended, that led the Arabs to believe that violence on their part would bring about a British retreat. If the Arabs were convinced of the government's steadfastness, he was certain they could be brought to the negotiating table. The joint meeting of the Zionist

---

8   Weizmann's letter to Lord Passfield, August 29, 1929, *Weizmann Letters*, vol. XIV, 10–13; Lord Passfield's letter to Lord Melchett, September 2, 1929, WA.

9   *Haolam*, September 6, 1929: 727.

Actions Committee and the Jewish Agency Administrative Committee which met in London on September 6–11, 1929, expressed similar sentiments. The British Government was called upon to uphold the Mandate and the Balfour Declaration by defending the *Yishuv*, actively assisting its development, augmenting Jewish immigration and strengthening the Jewish Agency.[10]

Despite the adoption of a more assertive tone, Weizmann declared that he was not abandoning his traditional approach. He still believed that the Zionist movement and the Jewish Agency should concentrate on the economy and the settlement enterprise as the foundation for any political agreement, but it was up to the British to maintain a supportive policy and guarantee security. Weizmann held that a division of tasks between the authorities and the Zionist movement would demonstrate to the Arabs that there was no turning back from the establishment of the Jewish national home.[11]

Weizmann's avoidance of statements regarding Palestine's political future and the nature of relations with the Arabs was not new. It was based on the contention that economic development and the creation of *faits accomplis* came first, and negotiations with the Arabs second. What had changed now was Weizmann's willingness to approach the British Government, as if he acknowledged the priority of political activity and the accusations of the Zionists' weakness in this sphere. As a result, certain doubts began to be cast on his commitment to the "practical" Zionist school to which his supporters belonged. Weizmann's silence on long-term policies, which had been acceptable in the past, now served to heighten the impression that he was moving toward the opposite camp. Moreover, his actions corresponded with the climate of antagonism toward the Mandatory Government sparked by the riots. When the Revisionists seized upon the new assertiveness of the Zionist Executive as a victory for their side, Weizmann made no effort to challenge this claim. The seeds were thus sown for a confrontation between Weizmann and his longtime supporters.[12]

The bloody riots in Palestine provoked outrage throughout the Jewish world. In Berlin, as in Warsaw, London, and New York, Jews held mass

---

10 Weizmann's letters to Wasserman, September 19, 1929, and Lord Melchett, September 23, 1929, *Weizmann Letters*, vol. XIV, 37–9, 44–6. On the resolutions of the Zionist Actions Committee, see *Report of the Executive of the Zionist Organization, 1931*, 32–5.

11 Weizmann's letter to Warburg, September 24, 1929, *Weizmann Letters*, vol. XIV, 49–52.

12 Weizmann's speech at a public rally in London, *The Jewish Chronicle*, September 6, 1929: 20–4; Harry Sacher's article in *Haolam*, September 13, 1929: 750; articles by Nahum Sokolow such as "Cain," *Haolam*, October 4, 1929: 806–7, and October 11, 1929: 825–6.

protests to express shock and rage. Harsh accusations were flung against the Mandatory authorities, along with vociferous calls for punishing the guilty to the full extent of the law. A number of rallies took place in Berlin. One of the largest was a joint gathering of Zionists and non-Zionist on August 31, in an effort to present a united Jewish front to the Arabs. Other rallies were organized by the ZVfD on September 3, and Jewish Agency leaders on September 5.[13]

In Germany as elsewhere, the public protest was conducted in the spirit of a declaration issued by the Jewish Agency and signed by Weizmann, Lord Melchett, and Felix Warburg which gave their full support to the Zionist Executive and its demands on the British Government. These demands included the dismissal of hostile officials, the reorganization of the police to incorporate a large number of Jews, the assurance of the Jews' right to pray at the Western Wall, the payment of full compensation for damage and injury suffered during the riots, the improvement of conditions for national development and the increase of immigration. The leaders of the Jewish Agency and neutral *Keren Hayesod* in Germany added their own call to step up development and launched a vigorous fundraising campaign under the slogan *"Hilfe durch Aufbau"* ("help through building"). This approach was in total accord with Weizmann's pledge to respond to the riots in a "constructive" manner. At Blumenfeld's suggestion, *Hilfe durch Aufbau* was also adopted as the name of the fund to aid victims of the riots established by the Zionist Actions Committee.[14]

The general support in Germany for the Zionist Executive's new hard line was accompanied by a rise in right-wing nationalism. The Revisionists, who until then were but a small minority among German Zionists, enjoyed a new-found popularity. Local associations began seeking out Revisionists to speak to their members and many Zionists publicly admitted that the Revisionists had

13   Accounts of the rallies in Warsaw, New York, and London, *JR*, September 3, 1929: 447, *The Jewish Chronicle*, September 6, 20, and 27, 1929, *Haolam*, September 6, 1929: 731–2, and September 13, 1929: 753–4; announcements and accounts of rallies in Berlin, *JR*, August 30, 1929, September 3, September 6, and September 10, 1929; Weltsch's letter to Bergman, September 1, 1929, NULA, 1502/1334/5; *Landesvorstand* meeting, September 1, 1929, CZA, Z4/3567/IV.

14   Text of declaration, *The Jewish Chronicle*, September 6, 1929: 25; resolutions of public rally, *JR*, September 3, 1929: 445; report and resolutions of Jewish Agency meeting in Berlin, *JR*, September 6, 1929, and September 9, 1929; declaration of Jewish Agency and neutral *Keren Hayesod*, *JR*, September 13, 1929: 475; also see minutes of Zionist Actions Committee, CZA, Z4/280/8.

apparently been right all along. In Germany, the stronghold of moderate Zionism, this amounted to a virtual revolution.[15]

The German Zionists versus Weizmann

The tension prevailing in Palestine since the Western Wall dispute had concerned the *Jüdische Rundschau* for some time. From the moment the news broke about the rioting, the paper adopted a position that differed radically from that of the Zionist Executive and stood out amidst the anger and growing Jewish extremism. This newspaper's position was expressed in both its editorials and its style of news reporting. In Weltsch's opinion, the Zionist movement had to examine itself on two counts: first, its political tactics, and second, its view of the riots in the context of Arab nationalism.

In the second issue of the *Jüdische Rundschau* devoted to the riots, Weltsch pointed an accusing finger at the British, whose task it was to restore peace, safeguard the Jews of Palestine and investigate the culpability of their officials. However, he also lay part of the blame on the Revisionists. Weltsch maintained that it was their propaganda and arrogant behavior which irritated the Arabs and touched upon their most vulnerable point – their religious sensibilities. Furthermore, the Zionist Executive, in failing to put forth any political initiative which might generate a peace agreement with the Arabs, was a partner to the blunders of the British Government.[16]

These editorial views were reinforced by an article by Ernst Simon, who had immigrated to Palestine in 1928, and quotations from an article by Moshe Beilinson in the Hebrew newspaper, *Davar*. These articles had been written before the riots, against the background of the Western Wall dispute, and were critical of both sides. The Zionist movement and the leadership of the *Yishuv* were admonished for not taking steps to defuse the situation. Simon admitted that the Arab provocation was more serious than that of the Jews, and that the policies of the British were discriminatory. Beilinson, however, deplored the silence of the Zionist bodies which allowed the dispute to become politicized. The religious issue was not so important from a Zionist perspective, but it was

---

15 Wolfsberg's statements at Berlin rally, *JR*, September 3, 1929: 448; Weltsch's letters to Bergman, September 1, 1929, and September 4, 1929, NULA, 1502/1334/5. On the meeting of the *Kartell Jüdischer Verbindungen* in Berlin, see *Der Jüdische Student*, 8 (October 1929): 5.

16 August 30, 1929. The first notice appeared on August 27, 1929.

an effective rallying point for the Arabs. Both articles were introduced by editorial comments that were approving in tone.[17]

Aside from self-accusation, the *Jüdische Rundschau* perpetuated the view that the riots in Palestine constituted the emergence of an Arab national movement. By calling the lead article, "*Die blutigen Kämpfe in Palästina*" ("The bloody battles in Palestine"), and referring to the rioters as *Kämpfer* (fighters) rather than *Mörder* (murderers) or *Raüber* (robbers), Weltsch was making a point that the events in Palestine were not "natural disasters or pogroms," but politically motivated:

> Even at this time of high feeling, we must not forget or hide the truth: that permanent security also *depends on us*. We are now facing a national uprising of the Palestinian Arabs, supported by the Arabs of the neighboring countries...and we all know that such a movement cannot be repressed by force for very long. We who are determined to build our national home in Palestine must live there with awakening Arabs. Our lives cannot be based on continual hostility. Palestine is surrounded by Arab countries. We must find a *modus vivendi* with these neighbors and the [Arab] citizens who live with us. Until now, we have made no serious effort to create conditions for this.... *We want no bloodshed, not of Jewish blood and not of Arab blood either....*

This was quite moderate compared to Weltsch's original intent, which was to place the major blame for the rioting on Jewish shoulders.[18] As the shock and outrage in the Zionist community mounted and the position of the Zionist Executive became clear, Weltsch deliberately toned down reports of the disturbances and carefully chose the items he included in his paper. He avoided detailed descriptions of bloodshed and brutality, shunned terms like "murder" and "robbery," and objected to the calls for revenge that appeared in news items disseminated by the Jewish Telegraphic Agency and were often published by the official Hebrew newspaper of the Zionist movement, *Haolam*. There

---

17 *JR*, August 30, 1929: 438–9, 441. Simon's article, in the form of a letter from Palestine, is dated August 22, [1929]. Beilinson's article originally appeared in the *Histadrut* Organ *Davar*, August 20, 1929.

18 *JR*, August 30, 1929: 438–9, 441. Emphasis are in the original. Compare with Weltsch's letters to Bergman, August 27, 1929, NULA, 1502/1334/5, and August 30, 1929, LBIA, 7185/2/16.

was indeed a marked difference between the reporting of the *Jüdische Rundschau* and that of *Haolam*, which emphasized the horrors.[19]

Weltsch also intensified his castigation of the Zionist leaders. Their past silence, deplorable enough in itself, was now compounded by political actions that seemed to pander to the Revisionists. In Weltsch's eyes, their guidelines to the Zionist public and their demands on the British Government smacked of chauvinism. He accused the leadership of promoting an illusory conception of the possibilities open to the Zionist enterprise, whitewashing the obstacles, and preventing a solution to the Arab problem, upon which the future of the national home depended. The Zionist Executive had thus failed in its basic duty to create a positive atmosphere for cooperation with the Arabs and effectively blocked the path toward political change.

What was this political change which Weltsch regarded as necessary in the aftermath of the riots? Up until then, he could accept, albeit not without criticism, the Zionist leadership's avoidance of political initiative on the assumption that it followed from the priority given to social and economic development. After the terror in Palestine, it was obvious that political action was imperative after all, but the purpose was totally different from that which guided the Zionist Executive:

> Every struggle must be followed by a peace agreement. After this battle, we must sit at the negotiating table, with the knowledge of what we can offer to insure the continuation of our enterprise. On the other hand, we have an obligation to provide the Arabs with guarantees for their continued development. The 12th Zionist Congress set the tone, but took no action. We have neglected the Arab world....

This change was perceived as urgent for two reasons. Firstly, the disturbances had demonstrated that without a political agreement, the daily routine of building a Jewish society could not continue; in other words, the success of the Zionist enterprise depended upon it. Secondly, the state of affairs in Palestine showed the danger of leaving the political field open to the Revisionists.

---

19 Weltsch's letters to Bergman, August 31, 1929, and to F. Rosenblüth, September 2, 1929, NULA 1502/1334/5; Weltsch's letters to Bergman, September 29, 1929, and October 3, 1929, LBIA, 7185/2/16; see also Weltsch's detailed article, "Jüdische Solidarität" *JR*, September 3, 1929: 451, and his editorial, *JR*, October 4, 1929. For horrifying descriptions of the disturbances, see, for example, *Haolam*, September 20, 1929: 765–7, and in Sokolow's articles, "Cain," *Haolam*, October 4, 1929: 806–7, and October 11, 1929: 825–6. See also *The Jewish Chronicle*, August 30, 1929: 9–10.

Advocates of this approach clearly recognized the centrality of the Arab problem, but they drew conclusions that were diametrically opposed to those of Weltsch and wholly unacceptable.[20]

Until the riots, one could say that Weltsch and his followers fought Revisionism because they purported to be the spokesmen of official Zionist policy. They supported Weizmann in the face of Revisionist opposition and worked to expose the differences between them. The rampages in Palestine, and even more so the response of the Zionist leadership, led to a shift in their approach. In blaming the Revisionists for these events, a serious accusation was also being brought against the Zionist Executive for having relied exclusively on *Brith Shalom* and its circle of supporters in Palestine and Germany.[21]

For Weltsch, this reversal meant a reappraisal of his political activity. He regretted that he, himself, had not been more involved in this sphere and thereby shared personal responsibility for the Revisionist ascent. He now demanded that the Zionist leadership map a new course, although he saw its choices as very limited:

> There are only two alternatives: either radical understanding or radical Revisionism. The Zionist Executive seems to tend toward the latter. I thus see it as my duty to raise my voice in protest.[22]

A group of German *Brith Shalom* supporters soon rallied around Weltsch. Other personalities who joined him were Moritz Bileski, Salli Hirsch, Alfred Landsberg, Werner Senator, and Isaak Feuerring, all General Zionists who had been active in the *Linkes Zentrum*; Alfred Berger of *Poalei Zion*; two members of *Hapoel Hatzair* – Etienne Basch, a former employee of the Jewish National Fund in Palestine, and Georg Landauer, who had headed the Labor Department of the Zionist Executive in Palestine and now returned to direct the Palestine Office in Berlin; Dr. Simon Schereschewski of *Tzeirei Hamizrahi* (Young *Mizrahi*), who later became known for his activity on behalf of

---

20 Weltsch's lead article, *JR*, August 30, 1929 (source of quotation), and his articles in note 19 above; Weltsch's letter to F. Rosenblüth, September 1, 1929, LBIA, 7185/2/16; Weltsch's letters to Bergman, August 31, 1929, to F. Rosenblüth, September 2, 1929, and to Kohn, September 2, 1929, NULA 1502/1334/5; Weltsch's letter to Arlosoroff, September 2, 1929, CZA, A44/17.

21 See Weltsch's letters to Bergman and Rosenblüth in note 20 above; Landauer's letter to the executive committee, September 4, 1929, NULA, 1502/1788. Simon's article in note 17 above; Landauer's statements to *Landesvorstand*, November 10, 1929, CZA, Z4/3567/V.

22 Quotation is from Weltsch's letter to F. Rosenblüth, September 1, 1929, LBIA, 7185/2/16; see also Weltsch's letter to Bergman, August 31, 1929, NULA, 1502/1334/5.

Jewish-Arab rapprochement; and Fritz Naphtali (a future minister in the Israeli government), who served as an economic expert for the German Social-Democratic party and had joined the Zionist movement only in 1925. Most members of this group were ZVfD activists, and all leaned leftward to some extent. Hugo Bergman and Hans Kohn, leaders of *Brith Shalom* in Palestine, also participated in its discussions. On September 16, 1929, the group formed an association parallel to *Brith Shalom* called the *Arbeitsgemeinschaft für zionistische Realpolitik* (Working Group for Realistic Zionist Policy).[23]

The *Arbeitsgemeinschaft* had a double purpose: to pressure the world Zionist leadership into changing its operative policies and to halt the drift toward the right within the movement. The founders of the group decided against affiliation with the existing parties and resolved to widen its circle of membership outside of *Brith Shalom*. The idea was to confront both the public and the Zionist leadership with the realities of the situation, to rid them of political illusions, and to replace misleading emotionalism with sound political judgment. At the founders' meeting, a detailed program was formulated for disseminating information and mobilizing support among all the non-Revisionist German Zionist groups. This program was to be implemented through personal contacts, active representation at all Zionist meetings in Berlin, conventions of youth group leaders, local discussion groups and a newsletter. The mimeographed *Korrespondenzblatt* was first issued on September 26, 1929, and continued to appear as late as 1930.[24]

Aside from its general promotional and educational work, the *Arbeitsgemeinschaft* directly addressed the Zionist Executive. Weltsch had already begun to do so before the group was formed, utilizing his editorial status and his personal connections with Executive member Felix Rosenblüth. It was Rosenblüth who had conveyed to him the content of Weizmann's letter to Lord Passfield, and through whom he expressed his serious objections to the alternative plan.[25]

---

23 Minutes of a meeting at Weltsch's home, September 8, 1929; German *Hapoel Hatzair* circular of the same date; minutes of a meeting at the home of Alfred Berger, September 17, 1929, LBIA, 7185/3/2.

24 See note 23 above; editorial, *JR*, October 4, 1929; remarks of Landauer and Weltsch to the *Landesvorstand*, October 10, 1929, CZA, Z4/3567/V; Weltsch's letters to Bergman, September 17, 1929, and September 29, 1929, LBIA, 7185/2/16; a call to Zionist activists, September 18, 1929; issues of *Korrespondenzblatt* (mimeographed), LBIA, 7185/3/2.

25 Weizmann's letter to Lord Passfield, August 29, 1929, *Weizmann Letters*, vol. XIV, 10–3; Weltsch's letters to F. Rosenblüth, September 1, 1929, LBIA, 7185/2/16, to Rosenblüth, September 2, 1929 and to the Central Zionist Office, September 3, 1929, with his articles in *JR*, NULA, 1502/1334/5;

The political course advocated by Weltsch and the *Arbeitsgemeinschaft* was the adoption of binationalism. This meant dropping the idea of a Jewish state from the Zionist agenda and accepting the 1922 White Paper as the basis for Zionist policy. Short-term policy would be the avoidance of any provocation of the Arabs that could lead to war, and moderation of the demands on the British Government because they could not be met and would only heighten militancy on both sides. In the long term, the British authorities would be asked to help negotiate a Jewish-Arab peace agreement, the first stage being the drafting of a constitution for Palestine.

On the domestic front, it would be the responsibility of the Zionist movement to create the optimum climate for political transition and launch leadership training programs that would produce a cadre of politicians capable of negotiating with the Arabs in the spirit of binationalism. Other educational activities would teach the *Yishuv* and the Zionist public about the Arab world and foster their readiness to live together in peace. The economic enterprise would also be run in accordance with the requirements of a binational community, with greater attention paid to the economy of the Arab population and raising living standards to the level of the *Yishuv*.[26]

To convey these ideas, the *Arbeitsgemeinschaft* planned to send the Zionist Executive a joint memorandum signed by its members in Germany and *Brith Shalom* in Palestine. In the end, the signatories were German Zionists only: Bileski, Blumenfeld, Berger, Naphtali, Landsberg, Landauer, Hirsch, Feuerring, and Weltsch. Bearing the signature of ZVfD chairman Kurt Blumenfeld and other prominent German Zionists the memorandum was thus elevated to the status of a German Zionist manifesto.

The text of the memorandum reflected the points outlined above. Without explicitly mentioning a binational state, it stated that "...the potential for a positive policy toward the Arabs lies in the principles expressed in the well-known 12th Congress resolution, and especially the definitions incorporated in the Churchill White Paper of 1922." The memorandum severely criticized the policies of the Zionist Executive over the past decade "...for making no attempt to convince the Arabs that we stand by these

see also "Jüdische Solidarität" *JR*, September 3, 1929: 451.

26 Weltsch's letters to Bergman, August 31, 1929, and to F. Rosenblüth, September 1, 1929, LBIA, 7185/2/16; Landauer's letter to executive committee, September 4, 1929, NULA, 1502/1788; German Zionist memorandum to Zionist Executive, September 16, 1929, CZA, S25/3122; Weltsch's letter to Gerda Arlosoroff, September 3, 1929, NULA, 1502/1334/5; Senator's letter to Bileski, September 25, 1929, LBIA, 7185/3/2; Landauer's statement to *Landesvorstand*, November 10, 1929, CZA, Z4/3567/V.

principles, and that Zionist policy truly has no intention of turning Palestine into a Jewish nation state, thereby depriving the Arabs of their national rights." The signatories totally dissociated themselves from the political tactics of the Zionist leadership:

> By relying on the Mandatory power's unconditional support for Jewish immigration...[the Zionist leaders hoped that] time would work to our advantage, that the prosperity of the Jewish settlements in Palestine would soon tip the scales in our favor, and that the Arab question would be resolved in and of itself by our *faits accomplis.*

The prevailing strategy was placed on a par with the Revisionist alternative; it was presented as equally destructive and incapable of providing the infrastructure for peace. The memorandum explicitly supported a third alternative: improving relations with the Arabs to the point where a Jewish-Arab agreement was possible. To that end, it called for "a total renewal of the spiritual orientation of the Zionist movement, a reassessment of its goals, and a reclarification of Zionist ideology," coupled with immediate efforts in the sphere of Zionist education and insight into the Arab problem. On the foreign policy level it advocated direct contact with Palestinian Arab leaders.[27]

This was a challenge to the Zionist Executive that could not be ignored. The German Zionist supporters of *Brith Shalom*, who had previously stood by the Zionist leadership in the face of the Revisionists, now set themselves up against it, thereby creating a new opposition on the other side of the political map.

Crisis in the ZVfD

Two questions were raised by this new body of opposition: the extent to which *Brith Shalom* and the *Arbeitsgemeinschaft* represented the German Zionist movement, and how far they were willing to go if they failed to win full support from the German Zionists or a response to their demands. These issues were not just academic; in their time they sparked two interrelated crises which threatened both the unity of German Zionism and Weizmann's relations with this movement.

---

27 Quotation from German Zionist memorandum (see note 26, above); Meeting at Weltsch's home, September 8, 1929, LIBA, 7185/3/2; see also Weltsch's letters to Bergman and to Kohn, September 19, 1929, LBIA, 7185/2/16.

Even before Weltsch and his group formed the *Arbeitsgemeinschaft*, they seemed to enjoy considerable support in the German Zionist community. Despite the militant tone of many protest meetings in Berlin, moderate voices were heard as well. In the wake of the Zionist Executive communique published immediately after the riots, the ZVfD issued its own statement urging restraint and emphasizing the importance of a just balance between Jewish and Arab interests. A major Zionist rally in Berlin on August 31, 1929, was characterized by the forceful spirit promulgated by the Zionist Executive, but at the close, there were also some who called for moderation:

> It is our desire to live in peace with the Arabs, with whom we are linked by history and destiny. [We do not seek] mutual hostility but mutual trust.[28]

It seems that it was this militancy emanating from the higher echelons that spurred many of the German Zionists to join Weltsch. In reaction to the calls for revenge at the August rally, particularly by the *Mizrahi* representative Rabbi Emil Levy, most of the speakers at the *Landesvorstand* meeting on September 1, 1929, echoed the moderate tone of the *Jüdische Rundschau*. The warmongering from public platforms alarmed those for whom the memories of August 1914 were still alive, and not a few of those who objected to this belligerency maintained that the cheers greeting the denunciation of the Arabs, and the calls for military mobilization, boycotts and even retaliation recalled the battle cries preceding World War I. There was no denying that nationalist fervor and an atmosphere of aggression were among the forces that led to the outbreak of the war. Many German Zionists thus felt a revulsion against the moral degeneration of their movement and were fearful lest it descend to the level of German chauvinism.[29]

Even ZVfD chairman Kurt Blumenfeld expressed views that coincided with those of the *Jüdische Rundschau*. At the start of the *Landesvorstand* meeting, he tried to preserve a balance by condemning both extremes – the Revisionists and *Brith Shalom*. However, he apologized following protests by Weltsch and Bileski, and his remarks were struck from the protocol. Nevertheless, he was

---

28 See *JR*, September 3, 1929 on the rally; Weltsch's letter to Bergman, September 1, 1929, NULA, 1502/1334/5; ZVfD's statement in *JR*, August 29, 1929.

29 *Landesvorstand* meeting, September 1, 1929, CZA, Z4/3567/V; Weltsch's letter to Rosenblüth, September 1, 1929, LBIA, 7185/2/16; Weltsch's letter to Kohn, September 2, 1929, NULA, 1502/1334/5. Also see Landsberg's letter to Weizmann, November 18, 1929, WA.

willing to concede that part of the blame for the riots lay in the failings of the Zionist leadership. By leaving a vacuum, it had paved the way for the Revisionists, and done nothing to block their mounting provocations. The mood at the *Landesvorstand* meeting was such that Weltsch's opponents were left virtually isolated, and a motion to stand behind the *Jüdische Rundschau* as the authentic voice of the ZVfD was passed by a large majority.[30]

It was the outcome of this vote, as well as the talks with Professor Albert Einstein on the eve of the August rally, that encouraged Weltsch and his supporters to gear up for political activity. The impression created was that this activity was endorsed by the ZVfD – an impression that was strengthened by the opinions and actions of Kurt Blumenfeld. When the Zionist Actions Committee met on September 6–11, prior to the formation of the *Arbeitsgemeinschaft*, Blumenfeld was almost the only participant aside from Ruppin (who belonged to *Brith Shalom*) who took a mollifying position. He maintained that asking the British Government to defend the *Yishuv* was not the solution and that militant slogans were counterproductive. He demanded that the growing anti-Arab stance within the movement be nipped in the bud, that an effort be made to find those Arab groups with whom it was possible to negotiate, and that a comprehensive information campaign be waged to win world public support, especially among the British.[31] As if that were not enough, Blumenfeld signed the September 16 memorandum to the Zionist Executive.

However, the political mobilization of the *Jüdische Rundschau* was not passed over without criticism. While the newspaper had already come under fire in the past for its open espousal of the binational plan, now the circle of detractors was even larger. Heretofore, the debate had been theoretical and moderate in tone, but agitated by the murder and looting perpetrated by the Arabs, many German Zionists began to resent the conciliatory approach of the *Jüdische Rundschau*. It seemed that the discrepancy between the calmness of the paper and the degree of public outrage could no longer be bridged. Moreover, in a break with the past, the *Jüdische Rundschau* and several German Zionist leaders squarely opposed the policies of the Zionist Executive. Many German

---

30 *Landesvorstand* meeting, September 1, 1929, CZA, Z4/3567/V; Weltsch's letter to Bergman, September 1, 1929, NULA, 1502/1334/5.

31 Statements by Blumenfeld and Ruppin, Zionist Actions Committee minutes, September 1929, CZA, Z4/280/8, 42–3, 50–1; Weltsch's letter to Bergman, August 31, 1929, LBIA, 7185/2/16; Einstein's letter read at the rally, *JR*, March 3, 1929: 447; Weltsch's letter to Kohn, September 2, 1929, NULA, 1502/1334/5.

Zionists found themselves in a dilemma, forced to choose between support for their own leaders and traditional loyalty to Weizmann. As a result, German Zionist groups which had never before spoken out or been critical of the *Jüdische Rundschau* voiced a negative view of the paper and the policies of the German Zionist leadership.

A large majority of ZVfD members were subscribers to the *Jüdische Rundschau*, and the paper had been generally respected even by those who did not share its editorial opinions. But now the disaffection was such that many readers decided to cancel their subscriptions, some of them appending a letter of protest. Others took group action against the newspaper, for example, the Jewish students' sports club association which called on its alumni to stop subscribing to this publication.[32]

Protest on the part of rank and file Zionists also came from a different quarter – the German Jews in Palestine. Until then, it had seemed that virtually all of them identified with *Brith Shalom*. Many members and supporters of *Brith Shalom* in Palestine were in fact German Jews: Hebrew University lecturers Gershom Scholem (and his wife Escha), Shmuel Sambursky, Leo Olitzki, and Ernst Simon; the journalist Gerda Arlosoroff, and others. However, over time it became apparent that this was not the entire picture. Among the German Jews who felt otherwise were Julius Berger (his brother Alfred was a *Brith Shalom* supporter), one of the heads of the Jewish National Fund in Palestine, who had been living in Jerusalem since 1924; the doctor and poet Theodor Zlocisti, a member of the Tel Aviv city council who had helped disseminate Palestine-oriented radicalism among the German Zionists before the war and immigrated to Palestine in 1921; and Felix Danziger, brother-in-law of Felix and Martin Rosenblüth, a doctor who immigrated in 1923 and founded a hospital for Jews and Arabs near the Old City of Jerusalem (it was moved to Tel Aviv after the riots). Berger, Zlocisti and Danziger led a group of German Zionists in Palestine who disapproved of the line taken by the *Jüdische Rundschau* and wished to add their voice to those who sought a change in ZVfD policies. Working to their advantage was the fact that they lived in Palestine, knew the Arabs at close hand, and were familiar with the real-life constraints on ethical, humanistic idealism. Their protest made a strong

---

32 Letters to the editor from Alexander Reiter and Hans Werner, *JR*, September 18, 1929; Kurt Nawratzki's letter to the ZVfD, September 21, 1929, Berthold Rosenbaum's letter on behalf of the alumni of the students sports association, September 21, 1929, protest letter of Ernst Hamburger (an active Revisionist) on behalf of the Bar Kochba sports association in Frankfurt a.M., October 3, 1929, LBIA, 7185/3/2. In interviews with over 40 Jews from Germany, the *Jüdische Rundschau* was cited as the main Jewish newspaper and frequently the only one they read.

impression not only in its newness, but because it emanated from people who were practicing and not just preaching Zionism, and because it did away with the popular notion that all German Jewish immigrants were aligned with *Brith Shalom*. *Brith Shalom* members in Palestine countered with a petition of their own in support of the *Jüdische Rundschau*, but this did little to mitigate the effect created by the public appearance of Berger, Zlocisti and Danziger.[33]

The views of the *Jüdische Rundschau* and the political program of the German Zionists also prompted a response among groups that had previously remained low-key. One was the German *Mizrahi* party, whose leader, Aron Barth, took strong exception to the newspaper's policy of withholding information:

> The Jewish world, not to speak of the Zionist world, has the right to know the truth in its entirety.[34]

The September 16th memorandum was followed by two more memoranda to the Zionist Executive – one from the Radical Faction, signed by Nahum Goldmann and Max Soloveichik, and another from the German *Mizrahi* party. Both objected to the September memorandum and declared that it did not represent the majority opinion in the ZVfD.[35]

There was nothing surprising in the Radical Faction memorandum, for Goldmann and his associates had long attempted to undermine the authority of the *Jüdische Rundschau*. It was the *Mizrahi* initiative that was new and merited special attention. In the past, the German *Mizrahi* party had gone along with the General Zionist line that dominated the ZVfD – endorsement of Weizmann's social, economic, and foreign policies; sympathy for the Zionist left; and support for the expansion of the Jewish Agency. In this respect, *Mizrahi* in Germany differed from world *Mizrahi*. When the German *Mizrahi*

---

33 J. Berger's letter to Harry Sacher, October 16, 1929, CZA, A206/72/2; petition of *JR* opponents, signed only by Julius Berger, Theodor Zlocisti and Felix Danziger, October 22, 1929, Gerda Arlosoroff's letter to Weltsch, November 12, 1929, and memorandum of supporters of *Brith Shalom* in Palestine to ZVfD executive committee, October 31, 1929 (with 25 signatories), LBIA, 7185/3/2; Heinrich Margulies' undated memorandum, Schocken Archives, 551/31; executive committee meeting, November 7, 1929, CZA, Z4/3567/IV; *Landesvorstand* meeting, November 10, 1929, Z4/3567/V; see also interview with Mali Danziger, July 11, 1982, OHD.

34 A. Barth's letter to ZVfD Presidency, September 10, 1929, CZA, Z4/3576/IV.

35 Radical Faction memorandum, October 10, 1929, *Mizrahi* memorandum, September 30, 1929 (as cited in F. Rosenblüth's response of October 8, 1929), and Alexander Adler's remarks to the executive committee, September 21, 1929, CZA, Z4/3576/IV.

resigned from the ZVfD executive at the 1928 Breslau convention, the conflict was over educational and cultural policies. Now, however, it was religion and nonconformance with the world Zionist leadership.

Particularly distressing for all the religious groups was the fact that the political tension and the rioting had been ignited by a dispute over the holiest site in Jewish tradition, the Western Wall. The *Jüdische Rundschau* repeatedly argued that turning the Western Wall into a battleground was a distortion of Zionist priorities. This was a religious issue that had nothing to do with politics, and it was advisable, even at this late date, to drop it from the Zionist agenda. Statements of this kind angered the religious Zionists, for whom a separation between religious and political ties to Palestine was out of the question.

Within the German *Mizrahi* party there emerged a division between militant and moderate groups. The militants, led by the party chairman, Oskar Jeschajahu Wolfsberg (Aviad), demanded that the Zionist Executive take a more resolute stance vis-à-vis the British. The moderates, headed by Aron Barth, called for unreserved support of Weizmann. Only a handful, affiliated with *Tzeirei Hamizrahi* under Simon Schereschewski, identified with the *Jüdische Rundschau* and *Brith Shalom*, in their search for an "ethical" Zionism.[36]

It was the moderate group, calling for full support of the Zionist Executive, that prevailed. In a statement of principles formulated after the riots, it was established that there was no contradiction between official Zionist policy and the aspiration for peace based on the recognition of Arab national rights. In the name of these principles, the party dissented from the policies of the ZVfD.

The fact that this position emanated from the moderates indicated that it had much to do with the anti-Weizmann stance of the German Zionist leadership. This factor figured prominently in the decisions of the *Mizrahi* central committee and in the memorandum submitted to the Zionist Executive.[37]

Also clearly opposed to the policies adopted by the ZVfD were the General Zionists under Max Kollenscher. On September 16, 1929, Kollenscher resigned from the ZVfD executive on the grounds that he could not be a partner to

36 Weltsch's view of the Western Wall conflict as a political issue was expressed in many of his articles, especially the *JR* editorial of October 4, 1929. Also see Weltsch's detailed response to Weizmann's demands on Lord Passfield and his letter to F. Rosenblüth, September 2, 1929, NULA, 1502/1334/4/5. On the *Mizrahi*'s stand, see A. Barth, "Innerzionistischer Kampf", *JR*, October 11, 1929: 540. On *Tzeirei Hamizrahi*'s stand, see J. Leibowitz, *JR*, October 18, 1929: 549. As noted earlier Simon Schereschewski was among the founders of the *Arbeitsgemeinschaft*.

37 German *Mizrahi* central committee meeting, *JR*, October 4, 1929: 519; committee resolutions, September 29, 1929, CZA, Z4/3284.

such policies. This step was particularly shocking because he had not been actively involved in the right-wing opposition. Although he had previously been a leading figure in *Binyan Haaretz*, he had spent the last years devoting himself to *Gemeindepolitik* and studiously avoided the conflicts in the WZO known in Germany as *Kongresspolitik*. *Gemeindepolitik* had not enjoyed much prestige during the 1920s, and was low on the ZVfD agenda until the 1928 Breslau convention appointed a special committee to handle this realm. As a result, Max Kollenscher, Alfred Klee and others who played a key role in Jewish communal politics, were not considered part of the mainstream in the ZVfD. They did protest and attempt to change the organization's order of priorities, but they were not outspoken in the area of greatest interest to the German Zionists, namely Palestine-oriented activity. Now, for the first time, Kollenscher adopted an oppositionist stance with regard to Palestine and world Zionist policy.[38]

Kollenscher embarked on his struggle in the name of what he felt was "true" General Zionism. He supported the Zionist Executive in the belief that it was acting as required by the exigencies of the hour. In his view, the Executive was fully justified in standing firmly against the attempts to destroy the national home and insisting that the British Government implement the Mandate and the Balfour Declaration. The *Jüdische Rundschau* and the German Zionist leadership, he charged, were displaying the "defeatist mentality of the ghetto." Calling upon the German Jews to step up their personal involvement, engage in fundraising, and seek a peaceful solution with the Arabs was not sufficient for a national political movement. Kollenscher acknowledged the need for peace, but objected to waving this banner while guns being aimed at the Jews' direction. He did not deny the importance of a sound economy, but felt that a secure political basis came first. This was the essence of the political Zionism preached by the World Zionist Executive, and in deviating from it, Kollenscher claimed that the German Zionist leadership had thrown itself into the path of self-destruction. As far as he was concerned, his position did not constitute an opposition; on the contrary, it was the General Zionists within the ZVfD executive who had lost touch with worldwide General Zionism and become the opposition. The German Zionist movement thus needed a new,

---

38 Letter of resignation, September 16, 1929, and clarifications at the executive committee meeting, September 21, 1929, CZA, Z4/3567/IV; *Landesvorstand* minutes, November 10, 1929, CZA, Z4/3567/V.

representative leadership which would re-establish it on the General Zionist front.[39]

As expected, Kollenscher was joined by his old *Binyan Haaretz* colleagues Arno Blum and Professor Karl Lewin, and by *Gemeindepolitik* activists such as Georg Kareski and Aron Sandler, a doctor and longstanding Zionist. Sandler, unlike most of the others, had been an advocate of "practical" Zionism prior to World War I, and had worked toward the development of public health services in Palestine. Fourteen persons signed their names to an article protesting the conciliatory policies of the ZVfD published in the *Jüdische Rundschau* on October 4, 1929. Kollenscher's new group, *Unabhängige Allgemeine Zionisten* (Independent General Zionists) formed a tactical alliance with the Revisionists and the Radical Faction, and together they embarked on a struggle to halt the growing trend toward party politics among the German Zionist leaders.[40]

Kollenscher's group was clearly right-wing in both political stance and choice of allies, and it was thus perceived by the public. The *Unabhängige Allgemeine Zionisten* was seen as the heir of the opposition factions of the early 1920s, the *Freie Zionistische Gruppe* and its successor, *Binyan Haaretz*, which leaned toward the right on issues of socioeconomic policy and purported to carry on the traditions of Herzlian Zionism. The establishment of the Kollenscher group was thus a step in the direction of a General Zionism split into right and left, leading in the 1930s to the formation of two world Zionist parties.

Opposition to the *Jüdische Rundschau* had prompted the Radical Faction and the Revisionists to join forces before, but now the illfeeling in the Revisionist camp reached a new peak. Their leader Richard Lichtheim, who until that time had objected to the political line of the *Jüdische Rundschau* but remained loyal to the united organization of the ZVfD, now embarked on an all-out war. In a special issue of *Hed Bethar* ("*Bethar* Echo") published in German at the beginning of September 1929, he lashed out bitterly against the ZVfD executive and demanded its resignation. He charged that the attempt to pin the blame for the riots on the Revisionists was ridiculous, and that only the German Zionist leadership could make such foolish statements:

39 Max Kollenscher, "Zur Krisis im deutschen Zionismus," *JR*, October 4, 1929: 521; Kollenscher's statement to *Landesvorstand*, October 11, 1929, CZA, Z4/3567/V. Also see the pamphlet, *Gruppe der unabhängigen Allgemeinen Zionisten (Gruppe Kollenscher), Materialien zum Jenaer Delegiertentag der ZVfD (1929)* (Berlin).

40 Article and signatures, *JR*, October 4, 1929: 521. On the pact between the three groups, see *JR*, November 1, 1929: 577; executive committee meeting, October 3, 1929, CZA, Z4/3567/IV; *Landesvorstand* meeting, November 10, 1929, CZA, Z4/3567/V. Also see Chapter Six.

Let us make it perfectly clear that the Zionist Executive has never made such an idiotic accusation against Jewish groups in Palestine. Nor has this ever happened in Poland, America, or England. Only in Germany and Czechoslovakia, where to our shame and sorrow a well-known group is in charge and exercises control over the press, with hatred for Revisionism and the dubious desire to justify the fantasies of *Brith Shalom* even now – only there have vile attempts been made to lay the "blame" on some of the Jews...and this at a time when England has ordered an inquiry of the riots and politically everything is hanging on the scales.

Lichtheim further declared: "This debasement of Zionism will be remembered as an everlasting abomination." Like Emile Zola, he cried out: "*J'accuse!*," and called for the immediate resignation of the ZVfD executive committee on the grounds that it was "destroying Zionism." A few days later, Lichtheim presented his own resignation from the executive committee.[41]

Lichtheim's article in *Hed Bethar* aroused a tremendous outcry, especially since he was also president of the Zionist students' association, *Kartell Jüdischer Verbindungen*. His opponents accused him of turning the student newspaper, *Der Jüdische Student*, into a platform for his own views, and feared that the *Kartell* would join the opposition. Many called for Lichtheim to step down from office. The indignation was especially great in view of the *völkisch*, chauvinist, and even Nazi associations implicit in his terminology. The Revisionist attempt to monopolize on Jewish nationalism and trivialize the Zionism of the *Jüdische Rundschau* also conjured up negative parallels with German political life.[42]

These associations, the memory of nationalist incitement before and after World War I, and even more so, the growing influence of the Nazi party, explain why Revisionism failed to achieve major inroads into the German

---

41 See Radical Faction memorandum, October 10, 1929, CZA, Z4/3576/IV, and *JR*, November 1, 1929: 577; Richard Lichtheim, "Was tut not," *Hed Bethar*, special issue, September 1929; letter of resignation, September 16, 1929, CZA, Z4/3567/IV.

42 ZVfD executive committee meeting, September 21, 1929, October 3, 1929, CZA, Z4/3567/V; Lichtheim's circular to members of the *Kartell Jüdischer Verbindungen*, October 4, 1929, circular demanding Lichtheim's resignation, and Siegfried Kanowitz's article along the same lines which the society's organ refused to publish, CZA, A339/138; Weltsch's editorial, *JR*, October 4, 1929; Weltsch's letter to Bergman, October 10, 1929, LBIA, 7185/2/16.

Zionist movement, although the 1929 riots and the political agitation that followed did strengthen its foothold.[43]

In the context of the general mood that prevailed after the riots, the German opposition stood out very boldly. During this period, the Zionist Executive enjoyed the backing of both its longtime supporters, aligned with the center and moderate left, and its former opponents in the militant right-wing. Weizmann's veteran supporters continued to stress the tenets of "practical" Zionism and the primacy of economic development, and held to their credo that demographic power would solve the Arab problem. There were some who felt the Zionist Executive was shirking this problem, and agreed with *Brith Shalom* and Weltsch that allowing nationalist incitement free rein was an error. None, however, drew the same conclusions as *Brith Shalom* regarding a shift in priorities in favor of a political solution. On the contrary, they were even more staunch in their conviction that redoubling immigration and development was the only answer. Many spoke of the importance of peaceful relations with the Arabs and curbing the growing tide of hatred, but even these critics of the Zionist leadership supported the demands on the British Government, refused to view the disturbances as a national uprising, and saw no need for a political initiative on the part of the Zionist Executive. The *Hapoel Hatzair* party held opinions which were undoubtedly close to *Brith Shalom*; *Brith Shalom* leaders such as Hugo Bergman, Robert Weltsch and Georg Landauer were in fact members of this party. Nevertheless, *Hapoel Hatzair* did not join *Brith Shalom* in calling for a change in Zionist political orientation.[44]

In addition to its longtime supporters, the Zionist Executive had now won the confidence of the right-wing, but while the backing of the center and left focussed on Weizmann's fidelity to "practical" Zionism, the right-wing endorsed the new militant approach that emerged after the riots. The broad support for the Zionist Executive at this time was thus accompanied by a surge of nationalism. The right-wing General Zionist groups, *Mizrahi* and the Radical

---

43 Blumenfeld's lead article in *JR*, October 1, 1929.

44 See articles by Moshe Beilinson in *Davar*, August 20, 1929, August 22, 1929, September 11, 1929, September 13, 1929, and September 16, 1929 which were also published in Beilinson's book on Jewish-Arab relations, *Zum Jüdisch-Arabischen Problem* (Tel Aviv, 1930). Also see Joseph Sprinzak's letter to Tartakower, October 16, 1929, and to Weltsch, December 10, 1929, in *The Letters of Joseph Sprinzak*, vol. II, ed. Joseph Shapira (Tel Aviv, 1969) (Hebrew), 15–20, 23–5; Chaim Arlosoroff's remarks at a London meeting, *Haolam*, September 13, 1929: 755; Yitzhak Lofban, "For the Sake of Clarification," *Hapoel Hatzair*, November 17, 1929: 3–4; M. Asaf, "On the Polemic with *Brith Shalom*," *Hapoel Hatzair*, November 17, 1929: 6–8; G. Hanoch, "The Vulnerable Point," *Hapoel Hatzair*, December 13, 1929: 5–7.

Faction, which had criticized the Executive for its moderation and compromising tendencies, now created a united pro-Executive front.[45] The Revisionists were the only ones left in the opposition. Against this background, the new challenge posed by the *Brith Shalom* camp stood out in sharp relief.

As a result, *Brith Shalom* and its German Zionist supporters were viciously attacked by the official Zionist newspaper, *Haolam*. The German Zionists were denounced as ivory-tower intellectuals, whose only concern was to appear righteous in their own eyes and those of the world. *Brith Shalom* was presented as a radical alternative that was just as unacceptable as Revisionism. Its supporters were branded traitors who were destroying Zionism or undermining the movement from within.[46] These statements, emanating from the spokesmen and defenders of the Zionist Executive, generated even more opposition to the *Jüdische Rundschau*.

In view of the climate in the WZO after the riots, the path of the German Zionist movement was clearly unique. First of all, Germany was the only country to produce an opposition to the Zionist Executive in the spirit of *Brith Shalom* and to count among its supporters, members of the national Zionist leadership. Secondly, the rise of nationalism and the shift rightward that marked the entire Zionist movement was much more limited. The voice of the Revisionists became louder, but not excessively so. Furthermore, the right-wing support enjoyed by the Zionist Executive in Germany included the Revisionists, whose objection to the German Zionist leadership was grounded in its abandonment of world Zionist policy. In the history of German Zionism, the phenomenon of the Radical Faction and the Revisionists joining forces to defend the official line against the *Jüdische Rundschau* was not new. However, on the world Zionist scene, where the Revisionists fought Weizmann bitterly, this was clearly a reversal. Support for Weizmann in general, and in Germany in particular, could now be found in militant circles. Was this a true turnabout, or just an illusion resulting from the misinterpretation of his policies? Or was it perhaps a response to *Brith Shalom*, the *Jüdische Rundschau*, and the German Zionist leadership as presenting an even less desirable

---

45   Statements issued at mass rallies in Warsaw, New York and London, *JR*, September 3, 1929: 447; *The Jewish Chronicle*, September 6, 20, and 27, 1929; *Haolam*, September 6, 1929: 731–2, and September 13, 1929: 753–4; announcements and reports of rallies in Berlin, *JR*, August 30, 1929, September 3, September 6, and September 10, 1929; Zionist Actions Committee minutes, CZA, Z4/280/8. See also accounts of Zionist rallies in Poland and England, *The Jewish Chronicle*, January 10, 1930: 28, and January 31, 1930: 17–8.

46   Ben-Dvora, *Haolam*, November 1, 1929: 890–1; I. Neiditch, *Haolam*, November 29, 1929: 968; M. Kleinman, lead article, *Haolam*, December 6, 1929; D. Cohen, *Haolam*, December 27, 1929: 1047–8.

alternative? This was soon to be clarified in the course of a confrontation between Weizmann and the German Zionists, but even now, one thing was certain: The consensus that the German Zionist leadership had enjoyed rested chiefly on its support for the policies of the Zionist Executive. By siding with the Weltsch group in opposition to Weizmann, this consensus was lost.

CHAPTER ELEVEN

WEIZMANNISM ON TRIAL

The Confrontation

The relations between Chaim Weizmann and the German Zionist leadership reached a critical point in the summer of 1929. Because the German Zionists had always been steadfast in their support of Weizmann, the opposition of the Weltsch group could not fail to jolt the Zionist Executive. Weizmann himself called Weltsch to London. They met on September 23, 1929, the same day that Weizmann was received by the British Prime Minster and before he had carefully read the German Zionist memorandum sent on September 16th. In all events, Weltsch came out of this meeting with the sense that Weizmann was at one with his views, but that political constraints required him to exercise caution and to work patiently behind the scenes.

Weizmann was then absent from London for a lengthy period of time, and contacts between the Zionist Executive and the German Zionists were mediated by Executive members Felix Rosenblüth and Shelomo Kaplansky. The response of this body to the September 16th memorandum reaffirmed Weltsch's impression that the differences with Weizmann were only tactical. Both Rosenblüth and Kaplansky assured him that Weizmann believed in the importance of Jewish-Arab relations and in the principles laid down by the 12th Zionist Congress concerning cooperation and equality.[1]

---

1   Weltsch's letters to Bergman, September 19, 1929, September 29, 1929, November 26, 1929, and to Hans Kohn, September 9, 1929, LBIA, 7185/2/16; Weltsch's letter to Magnes, September 30, 1929, NULA, 1502/1334/5; Weltsch's letter to Weizmann, November 23, 1928, WA; F. Rosenblüth's letter to Blumenfeld, October 7, 1929, NULA, 1502/1561; Weizmann's letters to Lord Melchett, September 23, 1929, and to Weltsch, November 25, 1929, *Weizmann Letters,* vol. XIV, 44-6, 107-10; Kaplansky's letter on behalf of the Zionist Executive to Bileski, October 8, 1929, Schocken Archives, 551/213/0.

The Executive's reply to the German *Mizrahi* memorandum further strengthened the feeling that Weizmann sided with the Weltsch group. The Zionist Executive flatly rejected the *Mizrahi* party's interpretation of its policies as veering towards Revisionism and displayed an open distaste for the *Mizrahi's* new cadre of right-wing supporters.[2] Hence, it was quite unlikely that the Executive's response to the Weltsch group was merely an attempt to garner its support. After all, the attitude of the Zionist Executive to the *Mizrahi* party could hardly be called welcoming, and certainly did nothing to curry favor from that quarter. In the wake of the petitions that descended on the Zionist London office, some protesting and others praising its militant proclamations after the Palestine riots, the Zionist Executive seems to have had a change of heart. Henceforth it refrained from issuing statements that fanned the flames and sent out press releases that were exceptionally moderate.[3]

The differences of opinion between the Zionist Executive and the German Zionists were serious, but for the time being, they were disguised by a tactical facade. The Executive deliberately avoided a response to the German Zionist demand for reforms in Zionist orientation and the preparation of the public for binationalism; the German Zionist leaders, for their part, respected the need for diplomatic caution and agreed to concentrate on publicity and education on the local level.[4]

There were a number of signs that the opposition of Weltsch and *Arbeitsgemeinschaft* was softening. After the exchange of letters with the London Executive, the *Jüdische Rundschau* was more restrained, and although articles in favor of the binational solution continued to appear, sharp criticism of the Zionist Executive disappeared. Moreover, the writing of Weltsch and his colleagues assumed a didactic tone.[5]

Also notable was the fact that Weltsch backed down from his call for immediate negotiations with the Arabs, the drafting of a constitution and a Palestine parliament. At the same time he became more critical of *Brith Shalom*, which continued to agitate for such action. Apparently, Weltsch had been convinced by the Zionist Executive argument that a public debate could harm future negotiations, and his censure increased when Weizmann renewed his

2   F. Rosenblüth's letter to German *Mizrahi*, October 8, 1929, CZA, Z4/3567/IV.

3   Letters of F. Rosenblüth and Kaplansky, see notes 1 and 2 above. Guidelines issued by the Zionist Executive (undated, most likely late September or early October, 1929), CZA, Z4/3567/IV.

4   Letter of Weltsch and Bileski to the Zionist Executive, October 15, 1929, WA.

5   For example, Bileski's editorial, *JR*, November 1, 1929. See also Weltsch's letter to Bergman, October 10, 1929, LBIA, 7185/2/16.

involvement in Zionist affairs after returning to London in mid-November 1929.[6]

The tension in the ZVfD thus subsided as the consensus that had nearly broken down because of the campaign against Weizmann, was restored. ZVfD leaders felt again that they, and not the right enjoyed Weizmann's full support, and hence made an extra effort to distance themselves from the activities of *Brith Shalom* in Palestine.

This was especially true of Kurt Blumenfeld. Over the years, Blumenfeld had backed Weltsch and the *Jüdische Rundschau* without endorsing *Brith Shalom* or spelling out his own position. This was possible as long as everyone agreed that the Weltsch group was a legitimate part of the Weizmann camp, and that Weizmann did not elaborate his views either. When the *Arbeitsgemeinschaft* came out against Weizmann, Blumenfeld joined in, but not wholeheartedly. At the same time, he was convinced of the need to stop the rightward swing among the German Zionists, and believed that the *Arbeitsgemeinschaft*, despite its dissatisfaction with certain Weizmann policies, was more representative of Weizmannism than the activist right-wing.[7]

However, this stance and the disapproval heaped upon him for daring to challenge Weizmann, led to a situation where Blumenfeld had to fight for the first time for his place in the ZVfD. He was forced to explain why he supported a group of binationalists and show how this was reconcilable with support for Weizmann. It may have been difficult for him to do so before the exchange of letters with the Zionist Executive, but now that the Executive's views were known and the Weltsch group had modified its position, Blumenfeld could denounce the Right without fear and demonstrate that standing by the *Jüdische Rundschau* did not conflict with official policy.

Blumenfeld presented his defense in a *Jüdische Rundschau* editorial at the beginning of October, and more forcefully at the *Landesvorstand* meeting on November 10, 1929.[8] He adopted a stance similar to that of Felix Rosenblüth three years earlier, but added all his weight as ZVfD chairman. He first restated his faith in Weizmann's order of priorities, which was headed by economic

---

6   Weltsch's letters to Bergman, September 29, 1929, and October 10, 1929, LBIA, 7185/2/16; Weltsch's letter to Bergman, November 12, 1929, NULA, 1502/1334/5; Gerda Arlosoroff's letter to Weltsch, November 12, 1929, LBIA, 7185/3/2.

7   On Blumenfeld's hesitancy to sign the memorandum, see Weltsch's letter to Bergman, September 19, 1929, LBIA, 7185/2/16.

8   Blumenfeld's article, *JR*, October 1, 1929: 511-2; Blumenfeld's remarks to the *Landesvorstand*, November 10, 1929, CZA, Z4/3567/V.

development, and then imposed upon it a political explanation. In the immediate future, an increase in population would establish the basis for the political rights extended by the Balfour Declaration and the Mandate, and endow them with true content; in the long run, the Jewish community would grow to become the majority in Palestine. This was a clear break with *Brith Shalom*, but Blumenfeld felt confident that he could say so without being disloyal to Weltsch, in view of Weltsch's own publicly expressed reservations about this group. By the same token, he could advocate the binational solution as presented at the 12th Zionist Congress since Weizmann and the Zionist Executive had raised no objections to it. Blumenfeld thus walked a tightrope, presenting a formula for Zionist policy that somehow managed to stay within the accepted bounds and avoid concrete political conclusions:

> We need a formula today not only for the Arab world, but for all the political authorities with whom we are in contact.... It is also interesting that the rather vague, but to my mind satisfactory concept of a binational state, has gained headway. A large community augmented by a sufficient number of Jews every year will enable us to fulfil all our Zionist hopes. As I have already clarified, there is no justification for limiting *aliya* and I cannot imagine a Zionist opposing the prospect of a Jewish majority in Palestine. Yet even in a binational state with a well-established developing Jewish community, the majority-minority problem cannot be overlooked. Even if we assume that the conditions for national development are such that the majority would be unable to violate the rights of the minority, our goal would still be to reach a position in which we would exercise the prerogative of the majority – in the humane and enlightened manner for which we have struggled and which we ourselves have created.[9]

By presenting a facade of political unanimity between the German Zionists and Weizmann, Blumenfeld was able to repudiate the arguments of the opposition, which claimed that ZVfD unity could only be preserved by dropping fractious politics from the agenda, choosing a new executive committee composed of all factions, and avoiding political declarations in the name of the ZVfD. Unity was also important to Blumenfeld and his colleagues, but not at the price of political neutralization that would drain it of content. Blumenfeld maintained

---

9 *Landesvorstand* meeting, see note 8 above.

that pursuing a clear policy had been the source of German Zionist strength in the past, and would make it possible to influence Weizmann's decision-making in the future. He was adamant that this posed no danger to the consensus.[10] Be that as it may, his faith in the unity of the German Zionist movement was severely shaken when Weizmann returned to Zionist activity in mid-November.

Upon his reappearance in the political arena, Weizmann was shocked to find that Hebrew University Chancellor Judah L. Magnes had joined forces with Sir John Philby, an Englishman who offered to serve as mediator between the Zionists and Mufti Haj Amin Al-Husseini, chairman of the Supreme Muslim Council. These contacts were carried out on Magnes's own cognizance and apparently with the blessing of Hans Kohn and Mania Shochat of *Brith Shalom*. The identification of Magnes with *Brith Shalom* was no secret, but in Weizmann's eyes, his unauthorized activities ran counter to Zionist policy and were akin to treason. Due to his long absence from London, Weizmann was unaware that the Weltsch group had disassociated itself from *Brith Shalom* in Palestine, and therefore linked the "Magnes affair" with the opposition of the German Zionists and the political demands voiced in their correspondence with the Zionist Executive, which he now read for the first time. Weizmann thought that he was being baited by his former supporters in a breach of Zionist discipline.[11] To Kurt Blumenfeld he wrote:

I am exceedingly worried and this time it is our most intimate German friends who are causing me deep concern. I read the Bileski-Weltsch-Executive correspondence very attentively. I have not yet managed to read the *Rundschau*. I know enough about the "activities" of Magnes, who is mainly advised by Hans Kohn and Mania Shochat, and that makes me shudder more than anything.[12]

10 The statements of Blumenfeld, Goldmann, Kollenscher, Landauer, Weltsch, and Wolfsberg to the *Landesvorstand*, see note 8, above. Joint declaration by the Revisionists and the Radical Faction, and the *Mizrahi* platform, *JR*, November 1, 1929: 577; article by M. Nussbaum, *JR*, November 22, 1929: 616; Weltsch's letters to Bergman and Gerda Arlosoroff, November 12, 1929, NULA, 1502/1334/5.

11 Weizmann's letters to Warburg, November 12, 1929, to Blumenfeld, November 13, 1929, to Landsberg, November 13, 1929, to Einstein, November 16, 1929, to Rutenberg, November 28, 1929, *Weizmann Letters*, vol. XIV, 65–70, 84–9, 107–10, 120–1. Also see notes in same volume: note 2, referring to letter no. 70, pages 56–7, and note 3, referring to letter no. 78, page 60.

12 Weizmann's letter to Blumenfeld, November 13, 1929, *Weizmann Letters* (see note 11 above), 67.

On the same day he also wrote to his friend Alfred Landsberg:

> A new kind of Revisionism has developed which in my view is much worse than Jabotinsky's. It seems to originate mainly in Germany, propagated by Weltsch, Bileski and others. I don't know exactly what you and Blumenfeld think of it. This group is undoubtedly in contact with *Brith Shalom*, Hans Kohn, etc.[13]

In Weizmann's mind, the activities of the German group, the "Magnes affair" and the stance of the *Jüdische Rundschau* after the riots were all interrelated and detrimental to the emergence of a constructive approach to the Arab problem. Ironically, he came up with a strategy that, unbeknown to him, had already been accepted by the German Zionists:[14]

> I am not in any way so obstinate as to believe that we will not have to make some concessions, but everything in me rejects superficial, panic-inspired talk; I know the Arabs, the bazaar politicians, and know very well that we will destroy, ruin every possibility of negotiation if we now run around, write that we must and should give in, etc., immediately. I have negotiated in detail with the Prime Minister and the C.O. [Colonial Office] about these matters, and we have agreed that negotiations must be introduced carefully, but only after the *Lord Enquête* [investigating commission] is over and after the country has quietened down.... Any public discussion on these questions, any *démarche* that is made, is a mortal sin against everything we have created so far with so much blood.

Weizmann was afraid that employing the wrong tactics now might harm the possibility of a future agreement:

> Not that I don't believe in a sensible and far-reaching conciliatory policy toward the Arabs, but all this publicity in *our* papers, which is surely known to the Arabs and also to the Colonial Office...makes our attempts to negotiate with the Arabs *impossible* from the outset, makes the Executive a laughing stock and, if it continues, I shall

---

13 Weizmann's letter to Landsberg, November 13, 1929, *Weizmann Letters* (see note 11 above), 68–9.

14 The following quotations are from Weizmann's letters to Blumenfeld and Landsberg, *Weizmann Letters* (see note 11 above), (emphasis in the original).

definitely resign.... To tell the Arabs that we are ready to revise everything is tantamount to delivering ourselves into their hands lock, stock and barrel (they are excellent carpet salesmen). Just another little pogrom and we'll decamp – that's how the Arabs interpret our advances.

As it transpires, Weizmann was more upset by the German Zionist opposition than the pursuits of *Brith Shalom* in Palestine. He regarded the German Zionists as the backbone of his leadership, and confided to Blumenfeld that in the absence of their support, he, too, would be liable to fall:

> I write all this to you and make your life even more burdensome because it pains my soul to look on while our best people themselves destroy what has been built up with so much blood and toil.... I wanted to tell you this, dear friend, and at the same time want to entreat you – if it is still at all possible – to use your influence to maintain discipline. Once the Germans break discipline, we can pack up!
>
> I am better in health but *very deeply* worried. This new Revisionism is much more dangerous than the Jabotinsky kind, because it is voiced by serious people. I merely wanted to utter a cry of pain and to tell you that we find ourselves on dangerous paths and will never be able to justify it before history.

He wrote to Landsberg in the same vein:

> If the organization – and especially the Germans – who have worked so brilliantly and maintained their discipline, have lost their confidence in the Executive, then for Heaven's sake a different one should be appointed; but to make our life and the work impossible in these critical times is a grave sin.... These lines are directed to a friend and Zionist with a plea to maintain true discipline even in these difficult times.

Weizmann's assumptions about the German Zionists may have been mistaken, but his anxiety was genuine and profound. He truly believed that his policies and leadership were in mortal danger. These feelings, however, were mutual. The Weltsch group was stunned by Weizmann's belated and unanticipated attack.

This was evident in the detailed letters of response Weizmann received from Weltsch, Blumenfeld and Landsberg, which stressed the basic affinity between them. Weltsch reminded Weizmann that it was he who had hesitated to endorse the "Jewish state" formula and so eloquently explained the reason for it at the 14th Zionist Congress in 1925.[15] All three pointed out that they had objected to separatism and political activities of the kind pursued by Magnes and *Brith Shalom.* They accepted the Zionist Executive contention that the time was not yet ripe for negotiating with the Arabs and that all efforts should be directed inward for the time being. Weltsch described the forceful impact of his September meeting with Weizmann, and both he and Blumenfeld drew attention to the subsequent policy in the *Jüdische Rundschau.*[16]

At the same time, they expressed astonishment at Weizmann's rejection of their fundamental pacifistic approach and his anger over political actions which they had never taken. They were especially dismayed that Weizmann viewed their position as more harmful than that of the Revisionists. They argued that Weizmann had reason to be pleased with their fight against Revisionism and manifestations of chauvinism in the Zionist movement. In so doing, they showed the world that there was a liberal, enlightened Zionism that could offer acceptable solutions for the realization of national objectives without hurting others. They also called upon Weizmann to strengthen the hand of those who leaned toward the Center and Left in the Zionist political spectrum in order to downplay the right-wing opposition that wrongly set itself up as the true representative of Weizmannism.[17]

Blumenfeld implored Weizmann to issue a public statement that would clarify matters:

> If it were possible for you to deliver a speech outlining your political program it would put an end to the existing confusion.... An elaboration of your position would work wonders. You would have to take a stand – in a broad-based speech or article – on all the questions of development, in Palestine and the Jewish world, and not only on actual political affairs. [You] must be as clear as you can in the political part, to shed light on the situation; express a clear and

---

15 Weltsch's letter to Weizmann, November 18, 1929, WA.

16 Weltsch's letter to Weizmann, November 18, 1929, and Blumenfeld's letter to Weizmann, November 27, 1929, WA.

17 Letters of Weltsch and Blumenfeld (see note 16, above), and Landsberg's letter to Weizmann, November 18, 1929, WA.

unambiguous opinion on the Arab question, possible solutions and
the idea of a "binational" state; and unequivocally demand that a stop
be put to all political infighting.

To Blumenfeld's mind, such a declaration was important on two levels. For
Weizmann, it would immediately clarify who was behind him: "...you would
soon learn that it is the great majority of the organization." For the ZVfD, it
would put to rest the debate over which side represented Weizmann – a
dispute that was undermining the unity of the movement. Blumenfeld saw
restoration of unity and a cohesive "Weizmannist" front as correlated, and
hinged on an authoritative public appearance of Weizmann as leader. Both he
and Weltsch offered to step down if it became clear that their interpretation of
Weizmann's policies was wrong.[18]

An indirect response to Weizmann's diatribe against the Weltsch group was
a change in attitude to *Brith Shalom*, which continued to wage an aggressive
information campaign and stir up controversy. Bergman, the main spokes-
person of the group in Palestine, wrote a series of articles for *Haaretz* that
aroused a public outcry and two issues of *She'ifoteinu* which appeared in 1929
and 1930 were devoted to the political demands of *Brith Shalom*. Members of
the *Arbeitsgemeinschaft* in Germany, and especially Weltsch who was a close
friend of Bergman, tried to exert a restraining influence and encourage the *Brith
Shalom* activists to change their tactics for the sake of the greater common
interests that united them with Weizmann. They urged *Brith Shalom* to stop
the political initiatives advocated by Magnes, adopt a public stand against them,
and refrain from publishing proposals on such issues as a Palestinian
constitution and parliament – "in short, the less written the better."[19]

It soon became apparent, however, that the differences between Weizmann
and the Weltsch group were not limited to Weizmann's mistaken assumption
that the German Zionists were allied with *Brith Shalom*. On November 11,
1929, at a ceremony marking the opening of the academic year of the Hebrew
University on Mount Scopus, Magnes delivered a speech that renewed the
controversy. It contained no real political message and even blamed the British
and the Arabs for the deterioration in security, but it left no doubt about

---

18 Letters of Blumenfeld and Weltsch, see note 16 above.

19 Weltsch's letter to Bergman, [November] 23, 1929, written on behalf of Landsberg, Landauer, and
    others, and Blumenfeld's letter to Bergman, December 19, 1929, NULA, 1502/683; Bergman's
    articles in *Haaretz*, October 4, 1929, November 11, 1929, and November 18, 1929; *She'ifoteinu*,
    no. 3 (1929), and no. 4 (1930).

Magnes's conviction that the Land of Israel was holy to both Jews and Arabs, and to the three major religions – Judaism, Christianity and Islam. In his opinion, the future depended on finding a solution acceptable to all:

> If we cannot succeed in finding a way to peace and understanding, if the Hebrew national home can only rely on the bayonets of some empire, then all our work has not been worthwhile, and it would be better that the eternal people which has existed for so long and has seen mighty empires sink into oblivion, exercise patience, make plans and continue to hope....[20]

This speech set off a whirlwind of protest all over the Jewish world, with particular condemnation from the Zionists. Magnes and *Brith Shalom* were exhorted to stop their political activities, and the students of Bergman reportedly boycotted his classes because of his membership in *Brith Shalom*. In an interview conducted by the Jewish Telegraphic Agency, Bergman voiced full support of Magnes and reiterated the demand for immediate negotiations with the Arabs and a Palestine constitution.[21]

The subsequent exchange between Weizmann and the German Zionists was replete with references to Magnes and displayed a yawning chasm between them. Weltsch spoke approvingly of Magnes and rejected any attempt to deny him the right to speak his mind.[22]

Weizmann, however, felt that Magnes and those who believed as he did should not be allowed to issue political statements *ex cathedra*. In general, he was against public declarations of principle on the essence of the Zionist objective in Palestine, as he clearly stated in a letter to Weltsch on November 25, 1929:

> I was distressed to see that you press us for action, in fact for negotiations with the Arabs, and for declarations now, when, in my opinion, such a step at present would be fatal.... I therefore thought

---

20 The speech was published in *Haolam*, December 13, 1929: 1007–9, which is the source of this quotation.

21 *JR*, November 26, 1929: 622; *Haolam*, November 22, 1929: 959.

22 Weltsch's articles, *JR*, November 26, 1929 (editorial), December 3, 1929: 636, and December 12, 1929: 642; Weltsch's letters to Weizmann, November 29, 1929, and December 1, 1929, WA; Weltsch's letters to Bergman, December 3, 1929, LBIA, 7185/2/16, and to Magnes, December 3, 1929, NULA, 1502/1334/5.

that any premature discussion in public of all these questions could only be interpreted by the Arabs as weakness on our part and as giving away our points before we start bargaining.... Magnes's action, which is no doubt inspired by certain circles of the *Brith Shalom* in Jerusalem, is deplorable, childish, and has put us in a very difficult position. Magnes's and his friends' statements imply that we have been obstructing the idea of cooperation with the Arabs. Just the contrary is true.

The thrust of Weizmann's letter was that the differences between them were tactical rather than fundamental: However, these tactical issues included not only the question of whether to make political demands now or later, but the appropriate timing for a public debate of Zionist plans.

As to the principles of future policy in Palestine and cooperation with the Arabs on binational lines, I have never swerved from it.... Where I differ from you is on the point of time where these ideas have to be propounded.[23]

The implications of this letter were not lost on Weltsch, and he was quick to respond. He was incensed at the silence of the Zionist Executive in the face of the smear campaign against Magnes and the attempt to limit the freedom of speech of university lecturers, and called to mind the swastika demonstrations taking place at the universities of Berlin, Prague and Cracow:

It frightens me that you find a public statement about our goals in Palestine and our understanding of the term "national home," a sign of weakness. This is not a "concession to the pogromists," but an answer to the world, which is waiting to hear from us. The world...is under the impression that the Arabs have no choice but to engage in uprisings and terror, as in the case of Ireland, because without them no one would be aware of their existence. And we have done nothing to dispel this falsehood, although a declaration that we recognize Arab rights in Palestine and that we have *always* sought a compromise (*your*

---

23 Weizmann's letter to Weltsch, November 25, 1929, *Weizmann Letters,* vol. XIV, 107–10, which is the source of these quotations; see also Weizmann's letters to Sacher, November 19, 1929, to Warburg, November 22, 1929, to Kahn, November 28, 1929, and to Weltsch, November 28, 1929, *Weizmann Letters,* 87–9, 95–102, 112–3, 120–1, respectively.

Swiss program!) is neither a concession nor a sign of weakness. This
has nothing to do with tactics, upon which I agree with you. Indeed,
there is no need to enter into details in public. Here, too, the Zionists
could be disciplined into silence if only the Executive made it clear
that such silence was necessary for tactical reasons. However, many
today are under the impression that this is not a matter of tactics, but
that the entire establishment has been swept up in Revisionism. Thus
it is difficult to impose discipline. I also fully agree with you that
compromise is possible only through government mediation and
strong pressure (on both Arabs *and* Jews). Of course it would be
better if we could work out a strategic plan together with the
government. But isn't there a danger that on certain points the
government will reach an understanding with the Arabs more easily
than with us?.... Neither the British Government nor public opinion
would be prepared today to accept a Zionist program defining our
objective as "Jewish predominance." Moreover, this program would
necessarily lead to continued bloodshed in Palestine, and in the long
run, would cast the support of the Jewish world in doubt. It is therefore of the utmost importance that you formulate a declaration on the
state of Zionism and elaborate your program, without expressing
weakness and strongly condemning all acts of violence. You must also
stress that we have never negated the rights of the local Arabs to a
homeland in Palestine, that both peoples must find a place there, and
that we are working toward "cooperation on binational lines" and not
"predominance".[24]

The discrepancies between Weizmann and the Weltsch group were now clear
to both sides. Weizmann, who saw the support of the German Zionists as
crucial for his leadership, realized that it was not unconditional; Weltsch and
his colleagues, who believed that they were strengthening the Weizmann camp,
learned that for Weizmann, the course they followed was a highly questionable
one. In consequence, the alliance between them turned precarious indeed. The
Weltsch group knew that its standing among the German Zionists was contingent on its championship of Weizmann's policy, and sought a declaration
from Weizmann that would elucidate his policy and pinpoint his followers.
The only solution that seemed to offer itself was inviting Weizmann to the

24 The quotation is from Weltsch's letter to Weizmann, November 29, 1929, WA; compare
     Blumenfeld's letter to Weizmann, November 27, 1929, WA.

upcoming German Zionist convention in Jena. Be that as it may, even before the convention, every effort was made to keep the pact between Weizmann and the German Zionists alive in order to prevent a Revisionist "*coup.*"[25]

The Jena Convention and the Restored Pact

The German Zionist convention at Jena was planned for the end of December 1929. The pre-convention elections were held in the traditional format, with each local association choosing its own representatives. In Berlin, however, the elections were clearly party-oriented, and it may be assumed that this was the case in other cities, too. Most of the factions were affiliated with world Zionist parties such as *Mizrahi* and the Revisionists. Other were *ad hoc* groups of General Zionist: The *Unabhängige Allgemeine Zionisten* under Max Kollenscher presented 18 candidates, and the *Allgemeine Zionisten – Linkes Zentrum* led by Kurt Blumenfeld presented 27. In Berlin, Fritz Naphtali put together the *Zionisten Sozialisten* comprised of *Hapoel Hatzair* and *Poalei Zion* members. This was indicative of the splintering and the lack of consensus among the General Zionists.[26]

Weltsch's colleagues from the *Arbeitsgemeinschaft* joined either the *Linkes Zentrum* or the *Zionisten Sozialisten*. As in its early days at the 15th Zionist Congress, *Linkes Zentrum* represented the mainstream who supported Blumenfeld. At that Congress, it focussed on the world Zionist arena in an effort to change economic policy. Its present goal was to address foreign policy and provide a counterpoint to the German Zionist right-wing. Ultimately, however, its basic identity had not changed. The *Linkes Zentrum* remained the choice of General Zionists who were both pro-Weizmann and pro-Left in the broad sense, and felt a close alliance with Labor Zionism and the broader school that emphasized socioeconomic revival, rejected power politics, and favored conciliation with the Arabs even at the price of political concessions. The *Linkes Zentrum* platform did indeed follow these lines, maintaining that an agreement with the Arabs was crucial for the attainment of Zionism's political aims; that a *modus vivendi* could be worked out regardless of the

---

25 Weltsch's letters to Bergman, November 26, 1929, December 3, 1929, December 10, 1929, LBIA, 7185/2/16; Blumenfeld's letter to Weizmann, November 29, 1929, WA.

26 *JR*, December 10, 1929: 655, December 13, 1929: 663.

demographic issue; and that the existence of two free peoples in Palestine was fully reconcilable with Zionist aspirations.[27]

The fact that the *Arbeitsgemeinschaft* had not presented a list of its own reflected its compliance with Weizmann's call for restraint. Hence, its abandonment of an oppositionary stance and acceptance of Zionist norms was evident even before the convention. When the ZVfD convention convened at Jena on December 29, 1929, the opposition could not match the *Linkes Zentrum* in strength. The *Linkes Zentrum* and socialist parties had a total of 106 delegates whereas the opposition mustered only 64. These figures included *Landesvorstand* members participating in the convention, who did have the right to vote.[28]

Weizmann's attendance signified the great importance of the convention not only for the future of German Zionism but for Zionism in general. Another high-ranking participant was Palestine Labor movement leader Berl Katznelson, editor of *Davar* and a member of the Zionist Actions Committee. In the days leading up to the convention, the official WZO newspaper, *Haolam*, ran a series of polemical articles with the German Zionist audience in mind, and the German Zionist leaders, too, were acutely aware of the broader significance of their national forum.[29]

The first day was devoted to a fundamental clarification of Zionist policy. The highlight was Weizmann's opening address, upon which everyone pinned high hopes. In this speech, Weizmann enumerated his priorities, stating that economic development had been at the head of the list for the past ten years in view of the opportunities created by the Mandate. While the disturbances in Palestine had illuminated the severity of the Arab question, nothing changed the importance of this order of priorities. In order to assure Jewish rights there was a need for pressure on the government, but this did not rule out the continuation of peaceful development, which would show the Arabs and the world that the Jews were determined to reach their goal without injury to others.[30]

---

27 The platform was published in *JR*, December 13, 1929: 622.

28 Statistics taken from *JR*, January 7, 1930: 11.

29 *JR*, December 17, 1929, headline; M. Kleinman, "My People will not go with you," *Haolam*, December 6, 1929; G. Hanoch, "A Return to Spiritual Zionism?," and Simon's response, *Haolam*, December 20, 1929; D. Cohen, "More on Giving in to the Compromisers," *Haolam*, December 27, 1929, and Weltsch's response, *Haolam*, January 3, 1929.

30 Jena convention minutes in *JR*, January 3, 1929, and January 7, 1930.

In this way, Weizmann demolished the arguments of the Revisionists and made it clear that he was no closer to them than before. However, at the same time, he toppled all the alternative plans proposed by his German Zionist supporters. This included not only the demand that he commence immediate negotiations with the Arabs, from which German Zionists had already backed down, but also the need to redefine Zionist political goals. Weizmann maintained that until elementary rights to a national home had been guaranteed, such deliberations would only exert undue pressure and keep the leadership from doing its job. He rejected out of hand the contention that people would say the Jews were not interested in compromise. On the contrary, all the upbuilding activities in Palestine showed that the intention was to lay the infrastructure for a common homeland.

For Weizmann, a discussion of the ultimate political objectives of the Zionist movement was out of the question not only in the immediate future but as part of his long-term strategy. He envisaged the establishment of a national home through concerted economic efforts combined with behind-the-scenes diplomatic activity that would gradually break down the barriers. He did not accept the argument that such an approach might lead to a dead end or dictate the outcome in an unintended manner. This was his answer to both the Revisionists, who defined the Zionist goal as a political one and sought to achieve a Jewish state through political means, and to *Brith Shalom*, which upheld binationalism and argued in favor of economic development that was geared to this from the start. These two parties insisted that politics and planning came first, along with a clear delineation of purpose.

The alternative proposed by Weizmann was a formula he had recommended to Palestine Zionist Executive members Arthur Ruppin and Harry Sacher when they appeared before the Shaw Commission:

> If they ask you whether we aspire to be the majority, I would suggest
> the following reply: We want the Mandate to be carried out, and we
> want unrestricted immigration in accordance with the country's
> economic development. The Mandatory power must encourage such
> development and back it up with a set of laws in the spirit of the
> Mandate. Whether this will result in the creation of a majority, one
> cannot say. However, whatever happens, we do not wish to rule over
> anyone or have anyone rule over us.[31]

31 Quotations from Weizmann's speech which was presented in German.

As Weizmann saw it, this was enough of a program, and as far as he was prepared to go to retain the support of the German Zionists. In fact, it was a brilliant solution. It constituted an endorsement of the majority objective, but without drawing in Zionist policy. Aspiring to become a majority was portrayed as legitimate because of its overall strategic implications rather than as the goal itself.

Above all, Weizmann's arguments were a rebuttal of *Brith Shalom*. The Revisionists were long-time adversaries, but *Brith Shalom's* opposition was a new phenomenon, and to Weizmann, no less dangerous. However, he had agreed to appear at the ZVfD convention in the hopes of regaining the confidence of those German Zionists whose support had wavered. In consequence, he took pains to distinguish between *Brith Shalom* in Jerusalem and the German Zionists. He assured his listeners that his fight was not against all the programs presented, but only the "cultural center" expounded by Magnes:

> It is certainly easier for us to say, "For My House shall be called a house of prayer for all peoples," but we will not be swept up in that. Is that what they promised us – a "cultural center" or a national home?

The ensuing discussion was typical of the German Zionists. All the speakers began by voicing their agreement with Weizmann, and only then noted points of dissent.

Moritz Bileski of the *Linkes Zentrum* and Georg Landauer of *Hapoel Hatzair* confirmed that their views were totally distinct from those of Magnes, and Robert Weltsch went even further, saying that Magnes's interpretation of Ahad Ha'am was misleading and conflicted with the basic political Zionist demand for a Jewish national home. On Zionist policy in general and especially the primacy of the economic sector, they aligned themselves squarely behind Weizmann. What they refused to condone, however, was Weizmann's resistance to an explicit political program. In other words, they supported Weizmann as an antithesis to Revisionism, but not his elusiveness on the ultimate goal. In effect, they embraced the formula he recommended to Sacher and Ruppin more for what it omitted than what it contained, i.e., there was no reference to a Jewish state as the ultimate Zionist objective. But they wanted more than that, namely a clear political orientation that would guide the movement internally and externally. Nonetheless, they remained in the Weizmann camp and declared that they would continue to press for a stronger stand on the political front.

Those in opposition also approved of Weizmann's speech. After all, he spoke of material strength, a hard-line foreign policy, no negotiations with the Arabs and no downplaying of the political objective. Both Barth of *Mizrahi* and Kollenscher of the *Unabhängige Allgemeine Zionisten* emphasized that their problem was with the German Zionist leadership – not Weizmann.

Most striking was the endorsement of Weizmann by the leader of the Revisionists. Richard Lichtheim congratulated him for coming out against *Brith Shalom*, although Weizmann's words were directed "...more towards Jerusalem-Mount Scopus than Berlin-Meinecke Strasse," the street where the ZVfD offices were located. Lichtheim maintained that Weizmann had taken only a first step in drawing the line between himself and his *Brith Shalom* supporters, but it was a step in the right direction. Lichtheim thus reserved his barbs for Weltsch and the *Jüdische Rundschau*, whose alternative had also been rejected by Weizmann. Lichtheim was so impressed by what he understood as Weizmann's swing toward Revisionism that he ended his speech on the note that the German Zionists had two alternatives to chose from, not three.

Nahum Goldmann of the Radical Faction, which had always been anti-Weizmann, went even further. He declared that the opposition in Germany was not against Weizmann, but against Weltsch and his paper. Moreover, it was not Weizmann's political principles that were being challenged but his lack of toughness, especially in relation to the British. According to Goldmann, he had corrected this of late, and his current remarks proved that the change was not imaginary. However, most important in Goldmann's eyes was his stance against Weltsch and refusal to succumb to pressure with regard to defining the ultimate Zionist goal, particularly *Brith Shalom*'s interpretation of that goal.

The fact that all sides claimed Weizmann for their own was indicative of the great degree of mutual dependence between Weizmann and the German Zionists as a whole. However, even if the evasiveness of his remarks made this possible, there was an essential difference in approach between the right-wing and the moderate camp. The Right could not conceal its dissatisfaction with Weizmann's emphasis on economic development, whereas the moderate supporters affiliated with the *Jüdische Rundschau* had only his political vagueness to criticize. In other words, the points of agreement were more fundamental, and the differences less glaring.

Under the circumstances, Blumenfeld was able to bring the discussion to a close on a note of full support for both Weizmann and Weltsch. He no longer faced the dilemma of having to choose between them, and there was no question of resigning or losing his German Zionist following. Now, in the presence of Weizmann, Blumenfeld could proclaim his opposition to the "Jewish state" formula and uphold binationalism as the true Zionist goal and the attainment of political freedom for the Jewish people without negating that of others. At the same time, he could wholeheartedly embrace the majority aspiration because if Jews were to become an autonomous community and not dependent on the good will of others, they would have to live in a territorial framework where they constituted the majority.

Henceforth, Blumenfeld could also endorse Weizmann's plea to avoid discussing the ultimate goals in public. After all, Weizmann had complied with their request and specified the direction he thought they should take. Amassing economic strength through immigration and settlement neither precluded the possibility of a binational state nor constituted a commitment to a Jewish one. His speech had also sufficiently clarified the issue of "friend or foe" which so concerned the Zionists who came to hear him. Blumenfeld thus left the intricacies of politics to Weizmann, whom he felt was eminently qualified to handle them.

However, Blumenfeld's support for Weltsch was equally fervent. It was not just out of personal loyalty or appreciation of Weltsch's talents as an editor, which would be lost if he was asked to resign. Blumenfeld saw Weltsch as no less a Zionist and disciple of Weizmann than he himself, and understood as he did that refuting the Revisionist alternative was the call of the hour. The difference between them lay in the fact that Blumenfeld would not play the role of statesman and left the political conclusions to Weizmann. As head of a national Zionist organization, he felt it was his duty to concentrate on activities such as fundraising and publicity, whereas Weltsch and *Brith Shalom* were not afraid to venture into politics, as Weltsch did in theory and *Brith Shalom* in Palestine did in practice. Blumenfeld's championing of Weltsch was thus based on their profound agreement with regard to the general direction of Weizmann's policy, ignoring the differences between them which were largely tactical.[32]

As far as Weizmann was concerned, victory was complete. As he half-jokingly began his concluding remarks:

> Today I am more popular than I have ever been before. Seven cities have been trying to claim me.

---

32 Blumenfeld's letter to Weizmann, November 17, 1929, WA; author's interview with Weltsch, July 9, 1979, OHD; see also Blumenfeld, *Erlebte Judenfrage*, 186–7, and Kurt Blumenfeld, "Auf dem Jenaer Delegierentag," in *Robert Weltsch zum 70. Geburtstag von seinen Freunden*, ed. Hans Tramer and Kurt Loewenstein (Tel Aviv, 1961), 121–3.

Now that he had ironed out his problems with the Weltsch camp and the German Zionist leadership, which had nearly slipped through his fingers, it was easy for him to jest. On this occasion, he spoke of Weltsch and Blumenfeld rather than the rightist opposition as the victors. He maintained that a reevaluation of Zionist policy was no longer needed, and that thanks to Weltsch and his group, the Zionist public had shaken off messianic hopes and illusions. He derided those who accused Weltsch of defeatism and pessimism, praising him instead for his courage, dedication and honest concern for the future of Zionism. His criticism was aimed at the Revisionists, whose demand for a "Jewish state" he deemed "un-Jewish."

With the pact between Weizmann and his German Zionist supporters restored, Blumenfeld was able to achieve his goal, namely an executive committee with clear political guidelines that was fully aligned with Weizmann and prepared to carry out the resolution of the 12th Zionist Congress: "To make our common home in a flourishing Commonwealth whose reconstruction will assure undisturbed national development for each of its peoples." Blumenfeld was now in a position to confront those who disagreed on this point without risking the loss of majority support, and to make his acceptance of the chairmanship contingent on the withdrawal of all motions to censure or fire Robert Weltsch. In this way, many of his supporters were forced to endorse the *Jüdische Rundschau* against their will, and he prevented the formation of an apolitical coalition. The *Mizrahi* party was wooed back to the executive committee, and only three groups were absent – the Revisionists, Kollenscher and the Radical Faction. In addition to Blumenfeld, the executive committee was now composed of two *Linkes Zentrum* members, Siegfried Kanowitz and Siegfried Moses; two leftists, Alfred Berger of *Poalei Zion* and Georg Landauer of *Hapoel Hatzair*; and three *Mizrahi* delegates, Alexander Adler, Edmund Levy and Oskar Wolfsberg.

The process set in motion a year earlier was now complete. Over the past decade, the ZVfD executive combined a wall-to-wall coalition with a political path that largely followed world Zionist policy. At this juncture however, it chose to give up that coalition for the sake of unity in the Weizmann camp, which was tantamount to preserving the unity of the German Zionist movement, albeit in a more restricted sense and not without sending some members into the opposition. This was the price Blumenfeld had to pay for bringing Weizmann's political line into greater definition.

The Jena convention extricated Weizmann and the German Zionists from the crisis set off by the 1929 riots and strengthened the political bond between them which had appeared so critical to all concerned.[33] In fact, the renewed pact was to have little consequence for the future of German Zionism and Weizmann himself as factors beyond their control came into play.

Just a few months after the convention, the Nazi party made impressive gains in the German general elections. Henceforth, the lives of German Jews would never be the same. The Zionists braced themselves for the fight against Nazi antisemitism, immersed themselves in Jewish community work and began to organize for the increasing exodus of Jews from Nazi Germany.

The Jena convention was thus the swan song of German Zionism, ending a political career that kept the German Zionists at the pinnacle of world Zionist affairs for well over a decade.

---

33 See reports and estimates in *Haolam*, January 3, 1930: 16, January 10, 1930: 21-2, 36, and January 31, 1930: 81-2.

CHAPTER TWELVE

CONFRONTING THE NAZI THREAT

The Jena convention marked the German Zionists last leading performance on the world Zionist stage. Their work on behalf of Palestine was a luxury in which they could indulge as long as conditions in Germany were favorable for the Jews. However, when the Great Depression struck Europe, and particularly Germany, the basic flaws of the Weimar Republic were laid bare. The dramatic rise of the Nazi party illustrated more than anything the flimsiness of the democratic foundations. As the Weimar Republic began its march toward doom, the Jewish community and the Zionist movement marched along with it.

The Transition: 1929–1932

As we have seen, the ZVfD modified its Palestinocentric approach and became more involved in local Jewish communal politics in 1928.[1] The focus on Palestine was resumed again in 1929 after the riots, but local problems could no longer be ignored once the Depression and the Nazi menace loomed on the horizon.[2] Before the September 1930 *Reichstag* elections, in which the Nazi party rose to become the second largest political force, the *Centralverein* collaborated with other Jewish organizations to strengthen the country's democratic

---

1 See Chapter Ten, and Brenner, "The *Jüdische Volkspartei*", 231–2.

2 Executive committee meeting, February 19, 1930, CZA, Z4/3567/VI; *Landesvorstand* minutes, May 18, 1930, LBIA, cited in *Dokumente*, 475–9. See also Arnold Paucker, "Der Jüdische Abwehrkampf," in *Entscheidungsjahr 1932 – Zur Judenfrage in der Endphase der Weimarer Republik*, ed. Werner E. Mosse with the collaboration of Arnold Paucker (Tübingen, 1965), 405–99, here: 421.

and liberal parties. This was a first for such cooperation, but the attempt proved to be short-lived and futile.[3]

At the *Landesvorstand* meeting on October 12, 1930, Kurt Blumenfeld reconfirmed his long-standing disapproval of the activities of the *Centralverein*:

> No serious observer can possibly doubt that the developments in German political life are an outgrowth of factors that are very different from those addressed by the *Centralverein*.[4]

Blumenfeld was adamant that all Zionist activity in the Diaspora be concerned with Palestine, and that no cooperation with the *Centralverein* would be sanctioned unless it was willing to accept Palestine as the key to the Jewish problem. On the other hand, he advocated a change in the traditional ZVfD policy of leaving Jewish community affairs in the hands of the *Jüdische Volkspartei*. The *Jüdische Volkspartei* had led the Berlin community since 1926, and Georg Kareski, who had headed this party, became chairman of the community council in 1929–1930. Blumenfeld charged that the *Jüdische Volkspartei*, which had pushed the Palestine issue into a corner, had failed to strengthen the Zionist organization and even harmed the Zionist cause. Now that the Palestine solution had become so relevant, he felt that community politics could no longer be left to this party. It was necessary to redefine Palestinocentrism in such a way that it would include *Gegenwartsarbeit* and become a major priority for the Jews of the Diaspora.[5]

Another conclusion reached by Blumenfeld was the need to bolster WZO efforts to ease the immigration quotas imposed by the British, which he predicted might have especially dire consequences for the Jews of Germany. In the wake of the disturbances in Palestine and the findings of the Shaw Commission, the British Government appointed Sir John Hope-Simpson to report on the economic conditions in Palestine from the point of view of protecting the rights of the Arab population.[6] In October 1930, while the *Landesvorstand* was in session, Britain adopted the recommendation of Hope-Simpson and issued the Passfield White Paper, which severely restricted Jewish immigration and land purchase. As a result, the prestige of Chaim Weizmann, who favored cooperation with the British and rapprochement with the Arabs,

---

3   Craig, *Germany*, 542; Paucker, "Der Jüdische Abwehrkampf," 423.
4   Blumenfeld's remarks to *Landesvorstand*, October 12, 1930, CZA, Z4/3567/VI.
5   See note 4 above.
6   See Chapter Ten.

was dealt a mighty blow. Weizmann's opponents in the WZO lay much of the blame on his alliance with the German Zionists and *Brith Shalom*, and Weizmann himself perceived the turn of events as a personal failure, prompting his resignation. As a result, the British Prime Minister, Ramsey MacDonald, wrote a letter to Weizmann in February 1931 which effectively rescinded the White Paper, but for Weizmann it was already too late.

Blumenfeld's call to support the WZO was acted upon immediately. At the 17th Zionist Congress held in Basel in July 1931, the German Zionists fought long and hard to reinstate Weizmann, but to no avail. Weizmann was forced to realize his resignation from the presidency. Nahum Sokolow was elected in his stead, and the Zionist Executive was henceforth led by *Mapai* (*Eretz Israel Workers* party).[7] Weizmann's descent also signaled the withdrawal of the German Zionists from the forefront of world Zionist affairs. It was not the end of their joint efforts, but their attention would now largely focus on rescuing their own community. The 17th Zionist Congress marked the last time that they could afford to put aside the threats to Jewish life in Germany.

By 1932, the fate of the Weimar Republic – and the German Jews – was sealed. Unemployment steadily increased, and the Nazi SS and SA stepped up their terror. Violent clashes ensued between the Nazis and the Communists. Hitler's gains in the April presidential elections sent the country into a dizzying spiral in which one conservative government fell after another. On January 30, 1933, after the Nazi victories of July and December, Hitler was named prime minister.

During the interval between the 17th Zionist Congress in the summer of 1931 and the demise of German democracy in the spring of 1932, when it still seemed that the conservatives under von Hindenburg could stem the Nazi tide, the rise of the Communists was a growing concern among the Zionists.[8] By the summer, however, the Jews could no longer bury their heads in the sand. Weltsch published a series of articles in the *Jüdische Rundschau* illustrating how the Nazi domination of Germany verified the Zionist thesis:

> We have always held that it is wrong for the Jews to deny or make light of national distinctions and folk traditions in order to make their own assimilation easier. We, because of our Jewish-national sensitivities, are in a position to understand the aspiration of the

---

7 *Protokoll des XVII. Zionisten-Kongresses, 1931.*

8 Blumenfeld's letters to Schocken, September 25, 1931, and to Weizmann, January 5, 1932, in Blumenfeld, *Im Kampf*, 111, 114–7; Fritz Loewnstein's article, *JR*, January 26, 1932: 33.

German people for renewal and self-expression. The recent
developments thus come to us as no great surprise, even though we
are grieved and offended by the form German nationalism has
assumed. From the Jewish viewpoint, the prospect of Hitler's
appointment as chancellor signifies the *total collapse of the idea of
Jewish assimilation.* Judaism in now entering *a new era.*[9]

Weltsch went on to examine how Zionism could deal with German
chauvinism. To his mind, the Zionist movement, more than any other Jewish
organization, was capable of reaching a *modus vivendi* with the *völkisch* ultranationalist groups and even the Nazis. The Zionists, who were well-aware of
the intensity of national feelings, had always contended that integration was
doomed from the start and could thus accept the enforced separation of a
nationalist state, which could be exploited to cultivate Jewish selfhood. On the
other hand, only a firm Jewish national stance could provide the strength to
weather the harsh new reality and the rude awakening from the chimera of
liberal emancipation. In fact, there was no other way because the emigration
of half a million Jews seemed an unrealistic proposition in the near future.[10]

Weltsch was not the only one who viewed Nazism as a foreseeable
consequence of German nationalism. He was joined by the Zionist thinker and
writer Gustav Krojanker, who discerned certain parallels between the Jewish
and German trends but was less sanguine than Weltsch about understandings
with the Nazis. Krojanker argued that emigration was the only solution and
he himself left for Palestine in 1932.[11] Both men were highly influential –
Weltsch, as *Jüdische Rundschau* editor, and Krojanker through behind-the-scenes
activity that proved no less important. Although their apologetic attitude
toward radical German nationalism seemed unusual and even suspicious (see
note 11), it was nonetheless anchored in the Zionist philosophy of Kurt
Blumenfeld as set forth at the 24th ZVfD convention in Frankfurt on
September 11–12, 1932. It was here that Blumenfeld delivered his last speech
as ZVfD chairman. This speech, acknowledged as a brilliant piece of oratory,

---

9 *JR* editorial, August 12, 1932: 305, emphasis in original.

10 Weltsch's articles, *JR*, June 3, 1932: 209, June 17, 1932: 225, July 16, 1932: 311. See also the editorial
    of August 12, 1932: 305.

11 See Gustav Krojanker, *Zum Problem des neuen deutschen Nationalismus – Eine zionistische
    Orientierung gegenüber den nationalistischen Strömungen unserer Zeit* (Berlin, 1932) The pamphlet
    was published by *JR* noting that it did not represent official Zionist policy. See also Daniel
    Fraenkel, *On the Edge of the Abyss – Zionist Policy and the Plight of the German Jews, 1933–1938*
    (Jerusalem, 1994) (Hebrew), 36–7.

was written in collaboration with Gustav Krojanker and then reviewed and edited by members of the ZVfD executive.[12]

Blumenfeld took a bleak view of Germany under the Nazis, and had no doubt whatsoever about their impending victory or about their murderous intentions.

> We are no longer confronting German nationalism that is merely in favor of a totalitarian state. This is a movement...that declares in no uncertain terms that one of its main goals is the annihilation of Jewry.... We have nothing to say to [this movement]; our business is with the other nationalist trends which have evolved outside it. We Zionists know very well how deeply these trends have become entrenched at all levels of German society, and not just there....[13]

Blumenfeld also thought it possible to arrive at an understanding with the German nationalists, although not with the Nazis, by creating a distinction between statehood and nationality. He maintained that the Jews were asked to bind their fate to that of their people not only out of concern for Jewish survival, but to normalize relations between Jews and non-Jews. The German Zionists had always argued against "*Grenzüberschreitung*" – crossing the line and becoming overly involved in German affairs. They had warned assimilating Jews against the tendency to dominate and become the trendsetters of German culture. In Blumenfeld's opinion, the Jews had no business telling the Germans how to be German. On the contrary, he advocated a total separation between citizenship and ethnic identity. We respect the uniqueness of the German people, he said, but we demand that our uniqueness be respected as well. Nevertheless, he clung to the traditional ZVfD rejection of an autonomous Jewish minority:

> We do not demand national minority rights. That possibility was flatly rejected back at our 15th convention in Berlin on December 25, 1918.... The nature of the demand for equal rights and the prospects for putting them into practice are totally dependent on the number of Jews and their class structure in each country. In Germany, the

---

12 Blumenfeld, *Erlebte Judenfrage*, 195.
13 For quotes see *JR*, September 16, 1932: 353–4.

conditions for national minority rights are non-existent; the most we can ask for is a certain measure of cultural autonomy....

Like Weltsch, Blumenfeld envisaged the development of an independent cultural life as a way of turning the inevitable discrimination into something positive. He, too, contended that this could be advantageous from the Zionist standpoint, and harbored the beginnings of a Jewish revolution in which the Jews would recognize their power, rally around a national ideal and nurture their spiritual heritage. In Blumenfeld's view:

> "The struggle for equality will commence only when all Jews demand equal rights for themselves *as Jews.*"

This call for a Jewish revolution did not, however, signal a turn away from Palestinocentrism. For Blumenfeld, Jewish nationalism was meaningless without *Eretz Israel*. Zionism, he argued, was both theory and practice. It had resulted in a body of settlement in Palestine that presented the Jews and the entire world with one viable alternative for a Jewish future. The idea of Jewish nationalism as a means of surviving in Germany had no validity unless it was bound up with the continued development of Palestine as the future homeland of Jews everywhere. Palestine was thus a pivotal issue at the convention, and its presence made tangible by the participation of Palestine Labor movement representatives Berl Katznelson and Enzo Sereni. Also attending were Professor Selig Brodetsky and Arthur Ruppin of the Zionist Executive, Menahem Ussishkin of the JNF Board of Directors, and Hantke of *Keren Hayesod*.[14]

The question that arises is whether Blumenfeld's plans for the ZVfD were realistic now that the Nazis were in power. During and after convention, many criticized him for spreading fear and anxiety, and claimed that aside from astute analysis, his speech offered no strategic outlines. The idea of a struggle for equal rights led to the one practical outcome of the convention, namely the establishment of a 300,000-Mark fund, but prospects for success were non-existent. Zionist pressure could have no influence on the course of events and even the money could not be raised.[15] It was argued that Palestine could not be a panacea for every German Jew, and that Blumenfeld had failed to live up to the expectations of a political leader, which meant devising a plan and

---

14 Blumenfeld, *Erlebte Judenfrage*, 195; *JR*, September 16, 1932: 351.

15 See *JR*, September 16 1932: 351, and October 21, 1932: 407; *Landesvorstand* minutes, August 1, 1932, CZA, Z4/3567/VIII. See also Blumenfeld, *Erlebte Judenfrage*, 195–7.

putting it into practice. Less than a year thereafter, Blumenfeld settled in Palestine and Siegfried Moses assumed the chairmanship in his stead.[16]

On the Brink: 1933–1938

The collapse of the Weimar Republic was now imminent. Shortly after his appointment as chancellor, Hitler dissolved the parliament, but on February 27, 1933, before new elections took place, the *Reichstag* building went up in flames. Hitler declared a state of emergency and all Weimar civil rights were suspended. Nazi terror and government-sponsored street violence reigned. The *Reichstag* soon empowered Hitler as the autocratic ruler of the German people and political parties were outlawed. Large numbers of Communists, Social Democrats and Jews were rounded up and thrown into concentration camps. April 1, 1933 marked the onset of a campaign specifically aimed at the Jews, which began with a one-day boycott of Jewish-owned businesses. Henceforth, Jews were systematically expelled from the civil service, schools and cultural institutions. They were subjected to constant surveillance, persecution, economic discrimination and physical violence. The situation eased somewhat in the summer of 1934, after the economy stabilized and Hitler eliminated his opponents. This *status quo* was maintained for several years, although the Jews' financial state continued to deteriorate and reached a new low with the enactment of the Nuremberg Laws on September 15, 1935. Outwardly, however, there was a semblance of law and order, especially during the 1936 Berlin Olympics. The plight of the Jews worsened again in the summer of 1937, this time irrevocably. Legislation was passed that prohibited Jewish participation in German commercial life; in general the Nazi regime became more radical and harsher, especially in its treatment of the Jews; and responsibility for Jewish affairs was turned over to the SS. After the Austrian *Anschluss* in March 1938, all hell broke loose. Masses of Jews were imprisoned, deported or sent to concentration camps. On November 9–10, 1938, (*the "Kristallnacht"* Pogrom), the Nazis went on a rampage burning synagogues, plundering Jewish homes and businesses and murdering Jews. Only authorized Jewish organizations were allowed to continue their activities, and Jewish

---

16 Fraenkel, *On the Edge of the Abyss*, 39–40, 73, 157; interview with Ernst Simon, March 23, 1982, OHD.

newspapers were closed. From then on, the annihilation of the Jewish community of Germany was a matter of time.[17]

The immediate, spontaneous reaction of the German Zionists was to leave for Palestine *en masse*, turning the trickle which had begun in 1932 into a mighty stream. An entire stratum of old-time Zionists now took the route they had preached for so long. In light of the British restrictions on immigration and the number of certificates issued, first priority was given to veteran Zionists who had been involved in the movement for years. Thousands emigrated to Palestine in the early months of the Nazi regime. By October 1933, the Berlin chapter alone bid farewell to 1,100 of its long-standing activists. Of 10,000 ZVfD members at the end of 1932, only 3,000 were still in Germany at the beginning of 1936. Likewise, only 12 of the 54 *Landesvorstand* members elected in the Frankfurt convention of 1932, remained. The ZVfD executive was in a constant state of flux due to the departure of its trustees,[18] and most of the second generation Zionists who had assumed the mantle of leadership in the 1920s under Blumenfeld had left the political and organizational arena in favor of immigration and absorption work outside Germany. Blumenfeld himself settled in Palestine in August 1933. However, this does not mean they had abandoned the ship. On the contrary, Blumenfeld, Landauer, Lichtheim, Martin Rosenblüth and many others, continued to cooperate closely with German Jewry in the one sphere they deemed appropriate – *aliya*. During this period, the main activity of Zionists in Germany was indeed preparation for *aliya* on the economic, political, organizational and practical levels, and they joined forces with the WZO and the Jewish Agency towards this end.

On the other hand, the German Jewish community was not left totally leaderless. Robert Weltsch became a pillar of moral strength after the Nazi boycott, when he called upon all the Jews to reaffirm their Jewishness in his

---

17 For changes in Nazi policy toward the Jews, see Karl A. Schleunes, *The Twisted Road to Auschwitz – Nazi Policy Toward German Jews, 1933–1939* (Urbana, Chicago and London, 1970); Avraham Barkai, *From Boycott to Annihilation – The Economic Struggle of German Jews, 1933–1943* (Hanover, New England, 1989); Francis R. Nicosia, *The Third Reich and the Palestine Question* (Austin, 1986). Many studies deal with the Jewish perception of Nazi policy, for example, Avraham Margaliot, *Between Rescue and Annihilation – Studies in the History of the Jews in Germany* (Jerusalem, 1990) (Hebrew). It is not our intention to enter that debate, but to examine Zionist activity.

18 *Drei Jahre zionistische Bewegung in Deutschland – Bericht der Zionistischen Vereinigung für Deutschland an den XXV. Delegiertentag in Berlin, 2.–4. Februar 1936* (Berlin, 1936), 46–7, 62; Fraenkel, *On the Edge of the Abyss*, 67–8, 157. Fraenkel cites criticizers who blamed the leaders for emigrating and abandoning the community in Germany.

famous *Jüdische Rundschau* article, "Wear Proudly the Yellow Star."[19] Blumenfeld's successor, Siegfried Moses, helped to establish a national Jewish representative body, and Martin Buber stayed on to lead the community spiritually. Others, such as Ernst Simon and Werner Senator, returned from Palestine for substantial periods of time in order to extend their support. A vivid expression of the unbroken contact between the ZVfD and its former leaders now resident in Palestine was their active participation in the ZVfD *Blätter*, a periodical for Zionist activists which appeared in Berlin from the summer of 1934 until the beginning of 1937.

This was the point at which the burden of leadership fell upon the third-generation Zionists – those trained by the pioneer youth movements, a large percentage of whom were of East European background rather than German-born. Among them were Benno Cohn, who worked to reorganize the ZVfD after the departure of the old leaders and would replace Siegfried Moses when he left for Palestine in 1936; Arthur Rau and Franz Meyer, who ran the Palestine Office; Jacob (Isi) Eisner, head of the religious pioneer organization, *Bahad*; and the leaders of the *Hehalutz* pioneer organization, Georg Josephsthal (Giore Josephtal) and Franz Lichtenstein (Peretz Leshem).[20]

Three challenges now faced the Zionists in Germany: the emergence of Zionism as a mass movement; the dramatically altered status of Zionism in the Jewish community; and the presumption that the Zionists and the Nazis saw eye to eye on the subject of keeping the Jews apart and encouraging emigration to Palestine. The manner in which the Zionist movement responded to these challenges was colored by the Palestinocentrism that had evolved during the Weimar period.

The Challenge of Expansion

In the face of the Nazi threat, the Zionist movement in Germany grew enormously. A total of 10,000 Jews paid membership dues in 1932 compared with 22,500 at the end of 1935, despite the emigration to Palestine of 7,000 long-standing members. From the standpoint of *Shekel* purchases, the increase

19 "Tragt ihn mit Stolz den gelben Fleck," *JR*, April 4, 1933, front page; "Ja-sagen zum Judentum," *JR*, May 16, 1933, front page.

20 Interviews with Benno Cohn, Siegfried Moses and Isi Eisner, OHD; *Drei Jahre*, 216-47; *ZVfD Blätter für die Mitarbeiter der Zionistischen Vereinigung für Deutschland*, Nr. 1-34, Juli 1934 – Januar 1937.

was even more striking. On the eve of the 17th Zionist Congress in 1931, the number of *Shekel*-buyers was 7,500; by the 19th Congress in Lucerne in 1935, the figure had soared to 57,200. By the same token, membership in the *Hehalutz* movement rose from 5,000 in April 1933 to 16,000 by late 1935, most of them "new" Zionists who had never belonged to youth groups. In addition, thousands of young people flocked to *Habonim, Hashomer Hatzair, Werkleute,* Young *Maccabi,* and *Bahad,* bringing membership in the Zionist youth organizations to more than 40,000 by early 1936. The *Maccabi* sports association had 5,000 members in January 1933 compared with 22,000 in December 1935. This growth was also accompanied by a radical change in social composition. These organizations now attracted many working and unemployed youths of East European background.

Another manifestation of the newfound popularity of the Zionist movement was a leap in the circulation of the *Jüdische Rundschau.* The number of subscribers rose from 4,500 to 30,000 after April 1, 1933 and reached 40,000 in 1935. Zionist rallies were a daily occurrence. Over the course of three years, 1933–1935, as many as 974 gatherings were held in Berlin alone – almost one a day. In 1933 and 1934, nearly 40,000 people viewed a *Keren Hayesod* promotional film that was shown in 40 cities, and more than 20,000 visited the Palestine exhibition organized by the ZVfD in Berlin in 1934. Despite the economic setback, there was also a vast increase in contributions to Zionist funds. *Keren Hayesod,* which had suffered a drastic decline in income after the 1929 Depression, marked up 30 percent more donations between 1932 and 1933, 21 percent more in 1934 and a further 30 percent in 1935. Despite the fact that many of its loyal contributors had emigrated, the number of donors grew from 1,121 in 1932 to 4,334 in 1935. In autumn 1933, JNF contributions doubled compared with the previous year, and by 1934, the list of donors reached an unprecedented high of 29,900.[21]

It seems that many of the new supporters were motivated chiefly by the desire for immigration certificates, which were distributed by the Palestine Office. Because the British had imposed a quota and there were not enough to go around, the first to receive them were veteran Zionist activists or those who

---

21 *Drei Jahre; Keren Hayesod, Report 1935,* 488, 497; Fraenkel, *On the Edge of the Abyss,* 65–6; Daniel Fraenkel, "Between Fulfilment and Rescue – *He-Halutz* and the Plight of the Jews in Nazi Germany, 1933–1935," *Yahadut Zemanenu – Contemporary Jewry,* 6 (1990): 215–43 (Hebrew); Hajo Bernett, "Die jüdische Turn- und Sportbewegung als Ausdruck der Selbstfindung und Selbstbehauptung des deutschen Judentums," in *Die Juden im Nationalsozialistischen Deutschland – The Jews in Nazi Germany, 1933–1943,* ed. Arnold Paucker with Sylvia Gilchrist and Barbara Suchy (Tübingen, 1986), 223–37.

had undergone pioneer training. Joining one of the Zionist movement frameworks was thus perceived as a ticket to a place on the waiting list. Toward the middle of 1933, the daily number of callers at the information bureaus of the Palestine Office throughout Germany was estimated at about 1,200, and during the spring and summer, the Berlin bureau was swamped by 600–800 calls a day. In consequence, the staff was increased from 3 to 35, and it became the largest office of its kind anywhere in the world. The inquiries slowed down towards the end of 1933, but after the passage of the Nuremberg Laws, the *Hehalutz* organization and the Palestine Office were again inundated by thousands of applicants. However, the rush to join the Zionist movement abated somewhat as the situation in Germany became calmer, a limited number of alternative emigration routes opened up, and Palestine was beset by economic and political problems.[22]

How did the ZVfD deal with its sudden transformation from a select group of ideologues to a mass immigration movement? Whereas genuine commitment had always been important to the Zionist Organization, it now faced the dilemma of maintaining high standards or opening its gates to all. The solution of the ZVfD was to combine the two. One of the leaders cited Herzl "that Zionism was a return to Judaism prior to returning to the ancestral home-land.... Now the movement confronted the problem of the Jews returning to their land without a prior return to Judaism."[23] The answer of the ZVfD was education. It sought to combine numerical expansion with an intensification of Jewish education that would stress the Hebrew language, Jewish history and Land of Israel studies. The German Zionist leaders now turned into counsellors and teachers, with the *Hehalutz* organization at the forefront. *Hehalutz* was open to all young people, even those who had never belonged to a youth movement before.[24] The Zionist Organization, which had always believed in education as the foundation of national strength, thus took up the gauntlet and allowed itself to become a tool for educating the masses.

Immigration to Palestine was another matter. There were two kinds of limitations: first of all, the quotas imposed by the Mandatory authorities, and

---

22 Fraenkel, *On the Edge of the Abyss*, 103-7; Fraenkel, "Between Fulfilment and Rescue," 241; Ruth Schreiber, *The Palestine Office in Berlin and the "Aliya" of the German Jews*, 1933–1941 (M.A. Thesis, Tel Aviv University, 1988) (Hebrew).

23 Benno Cohn, "Einige Bemerkungen über den deutschen Zionismus nach 1933," in *In Zwei Welten – Siegfried Moses zum fünfundsiebzigsten Geburtstag*, ed. Hans Tramer (Tel Aviv, 1962), 43–54.

24 *Drei Jahre*, 68-72; Jehuda Reinharz, "*Hashomer Hatzair* in Germany (II) – Under the Shadow of the Swastika, 1933–1938," *LBIYB*, 32 (1987): 183–229. Also see report of the ZVfD Berlin convention in *JR*, February 7, 1936.

second, the radical Zionist approach that called for gradual, qualitative building of the national home and rejected a program of mass transfer. In the final analysis the two were interrelated. The "economic absorptive capacity" that dictated British immigration policy also influenced the interpretation of "gradual development." As was abundantly clear from the severe economic crisis at the end of 1935, the country was not capable of absorbing mass immigration at this time. Thus the desire to shape the national home was mingled with concern for its continued survival.[25] Since the demand for immigration certificates far exceeded the number available, certain criteria were laid down which in fact allowed qualitative elements to come into play. While British "labor immigration" (as opposed to "capitalist immigration") certificates issued through the Jewish Agency were granted to candidates between the ages of 17 and 35 who could prove they were in good health, the Palestine Office was much stricter, and required that those leaving for Palestine undergo vocational and "spiritual" training. This training was provided by *Hehalutz*, which was affiliated with the Zionist Labor movement. Preference was given to young people who had agricultural experience or belonged to a pioneer group preparing to settle on a *kibbutz*. For those without private capital, joining such a group was the surest way to reach Palestine.

This was a long-term policy that created a paradoxical situation in the early stages, before there was a ready supply of trained candidates. At the beginning of April 1933, British High Commissioner Sir Arthur Wauchope granted the Jews of Germany 1,200 immigration permits in advance, 1,000 of them to be allocated to "workers" beyond the Jewish Agency quota. *Hehalutz* leaders, among them Georg Josephsthal, Fritz Lichtenstein and Enzo Sereni, refused to allow these permits to be distributed wholesale to those who had not undergone vocational training for fear that this would set a precedent in which both Palestine and the Zionist movement would be the losers. Palestine would be flooded with immigrants who were unprepared for life there, and the Zionist Organization of Germany would forfeit its role as the channel for immigration. This was an extreme approach which was questioned even at the time. In any event, the pool of qualified pioneers soon exceeded the number of permits, and there were not enough training slots for all those who were interested. In July 1935, *Hehalutz* had 13,500 members, 3,500 of them participating in training

---

25 For an opposing view which does not take into account the contemporary economic situation, see Fraenkel, *On the Edge of the Abyss*, 108–20; Fraenkel, "Between Fulfilment and Rescue."

programs; some had been living on training farms for more than two years. By this time, there were 250 graduates awaiting immigration certificates.[26]

Cooperation in a Time of Crisis

The upheavals in Germany also enhanced the status of Zionism in the eyes of those who had not joined the movement. German Jews at large, who had believed in liberalism, felt it slipping away between their fingers, and embarked on a path of rediscovery that brought them back to Judaism. They were now ready to accept, or at least acknowledge the Zionist interpretation of Jewish nationhood. Even the opponents of Zionism had to admit to the indispensability of Palestine even as a partial solution. The Zionist movement demonstrated that it had correctly assessed the situation all along, and that it was the sole party with the tools, however limited, to organize immigration to Palestine. Nonetheless, the non-Zionist leadership was not prepared to relinquish its hopes for continued Jewish existence in Germany. Thus, despite the change in attitude, the non-Zionists remained outside the movement. The Zionists, too, underwent a transformation, recognizing the necessity of "building amongst the ruins." They realized that frameworks to support and guide the new Jewish selfhood developing on German soil was also part of Zionism. However, like the non-Zionists in reverse, they were not willing to give up their Palestinocentrism. The ZVfD, in contrast to the *Jüdische Volkspartei*, had never seen itself as a potential leader of the Jewish community. On the contrary, it had advocated the abandonment of Jewish community life in Germany and never fostered local leadership. At this juncture, the movement had to choose between carrying out its role in the community without being at the political helm, or concentrating on its traditional goal and preparing its members for *aliya*. The ZVfD chose the first path – *Gegenwartsarbeit* – and resolved to promote Jewish education and *hachshara* (training) in Germany until circumstances were ripe for Zionist fulfillment in Palestine.

The ZVfD could adopt this course because of the non-Zionists who were ready to recognize education and pioneer training as an integral part of community work. Their common interests were expressed in the slogan "*Hilfe und Aufbau*" ("Relief and Construction"), and culminated in the establishment

---

26 Statistics based on Fraenkel, "Between Fulfilment and Rescue"; Yoav Gelber, *New Homeland – Immigration and Absorption of Central European Jews, 1933–1948* (Jerusalem, 1990) (Hebrew), Chapter Two.

of the *Zentralausschuß der deutschen Juden für Hilfe und Aufbau* (The Central Committee of the German Jews for Relief and Construction) on April 13, 1933. This was a joint venture of the non-Zionist "Friends of Palestine" under Ludwig Tietz and Zionist welfare experts Werner Senator, head of the Jewish Agency *Aliya* Department; Georg Lubinsky (Giora Lotan), who later headed the Israeli National Insurance Institute; and Max Kreutzberger. Most of the money was raised by the German-Jewish community, but some also came from abroad, from the Joint Distribution Committee in America and funds specifically established for this purpose, such as the Central British Fund for German Jewry.[27]

This committee was a response to the panic-stricken liquidation of assets in the German Jewish community. It aimed to provide constructive assistance and strengthen the standing of the Jews through youth education, cultural programs and attention to social and economic problems. The non-Zionists stressed the aspect of continued Jewish life in Germany, whereas the Zionists saw these activities as preparation for *aliya*. In practice, one did not rule out the other. Moreover, it was the Zionist Organization that provided the ideological and organizational synthesis by promoting Jewish education and culture, pioneer training, vocational retraining and eventually emigration, preferably to Palestine.

In September 1933, the *Reichsvertretung der deutschen Juden* (National Representation of German Jews) was established, with Rabbi Leo Baeck as president. As a liberal rabbi and Zionist sympathizer, Baeck was believed to represent the widest common denominator in the Jewish community. Otto Hirsch, a non-Zionist, was appointed executive director and Siegfried Moses, director. Though the *Reichsvertretung* was meant to be the first overall representative body of German Jewry, there were some groups, such as the *Austrittsorthodoxen* (Independent Orthodox), which remained outside it. Others, like Georg Kareski, head of the *Staatszionistische Organisation* (State Zionist Revisionists), certain leaders of the *Jüdische Volkspartei* in Berlin and community leaders from Frankfurt and Breslau, struggled to gain more control from within. The *Reichsvertretung* also failed to win official recognition. Nevertheless, it represented the largest and most respected Jewish organizations in Germany – the *Centralverein* and the ZVfD, which had managed

---

27 Margaliot, *Between Rescue and Annihilation*, 55–76; David Kramer, "Jewish Welfare Work under the Impact of Pauperisation," in *Die Juden im Nationalsozialistischen Deutschland*, 173–88; Fraenkel, *On the Edge of the Abyss*, 77–9; Yehuda Bauer, *My Brothers' Keeper – A History of the American Jewish Joint Distribution Committee, 1929-1939* (Philadelphia, 1974), 109-19.

to overcome their differences. Funding was derived from internal sources and Jewish organizations around the world, and most of the monies were channelled to *Hilfe und Aufbau*, which became part of the *Reichsvertretung* in May 1935. Only 3 of the 12 board members were from the ZVfD, which was not at all proportional to its true status at the time.[28] Nonetheless, the ZVfD greatly influenced the work of the *Reichsvertretung* in the spheres of education, pioneer training and the organization of *aliya*.

Jewish Education

When the Nazis began expelling Jewish teachers and students from the state schools, an alternative Jewish educational system, including teacher training, was needed. In 1932, there were 140 Jewish elementary schools in Germany with about 12,000 pupils; another 3,000 students attended 10 high schools and teacher's colleges. All told, only about one-seventh of the Jewish student population was enrolled in Jewish schools. By 1935, even before the passage of the Nuremberg Laws, the figures leaped to 70 percent.[29] In the new expanded school system, Jewish culture was fostered as a means of fortifying the students spiritually and bracing them for the future. In the spring of 1933, Martin Buber proposed the establishment of a Jewish board of education with a Jewish nationalist philosophy. However, the focus of this nationalism would remain undefined:

> Do not ask for the sake of which country we plan to educate. For *Eretz Israel*, if we are fortunate enough to get there; for some foreign land to which we may be forced to emigrate; for Germany, if [living here] remains a possibility. [Our] education should be the same

28 The *Reichsvertretung der Deutschen Juden* was renamed in 1935 to *Reichsvertretung der Juden in Deutschland*: Max Gruenewald, "Der Anfang der Reichsvertretung," in *Deutsches Judentum, Aufstieg und Krise - Gestalten, Ideen, Werke*, ed. Robert Weltsch (Stuttgart, 1963), 315–25; *JR*, September 20, 1933: 544; *Drei Jahre*, 43; Margaliot, *Between Rescue and Annihilation*, 1–15, 55–7; Fraenkel, *On the Edge of the Abyss*, 72–9; Kramer, *Jewish Welfare*; Herbert A. Strauss, "Jewish Autonomy within the Limits of National socialist Policy, the Community and the Reichsvertretung," in *Die Juden im Nationalsozialistischen Deutschland*, 125–52.

29 Joseph Walk, "Jüdische Erziehung als geistiger Widerstand," in *Die Juden im Nationalsozialistischen Deutschland*, 230–47; *Drei Jahre*, 73.

for all three, infused with one vision, one goal, one source of enlightenment.[30]

Buber advocated a spiritual revolution in which Jewish youngsters would be taught values that were the opposite of those prevailing in Nazi Germany. In his eyes, the Jewish national dream was an antidote for the ills of this society.

Zionist inspiration also came from another corner. *Hehalutz* had already developed a curriculum of Hebrew language instruction and Jewish knowledge in addition to vocational training. The Jewish welfare organizations also began working with youth, without making participation in their programs contingent on *aliya*. One of these organizations, established in Berlin in 1932 by Recha Freier, was later transformed by her into Youth *Aliya*, a movement for the transfer of Jewish children to Palestine.

In 1933, the *Reichsvertretung* established two educational bodies – *Schulabteilung* (Education Department) and the *Mittelstelle für jüdische Erwachsenenbildung* (Jewish Adult Education Authority). The *Schulabteilung* was run by the non-Zionist orthodox and liberals together with the Zionists, who drew up a uniform curriculum for a student body which reached 24,000 in 1937. The *Mittelstelle* was directed by Buber until his *aliya* in 1938. The ZVfD also established an education department of its own to promote adult education and teacher-training. Indeed many prominent Zionists were active in this realm: Ernst Simon, who had recently returned from Palestine; Hugo Rosenthal (Joseph Yashuvi), the principal of *Mossad Ahava*, a boarding school that was transferred from Germany to Palestine; and Erich Rosenblüth, who would later head the religious division of the *Mikve Israel* agricultural school. On the whole, the Zionists exerted a great influence on the cooperative educational frameworks organized by the German Jewish community.[31]

Agricultural *Hachshara*, Vocational Training and *Aliya*

Productivization, vocational retraining and a change in job stratification were means of rehabilitating the Jewish community and furthering the emancipation process that were generally agreed upon by the Jewish public. For the Zionists,

---

30 Ernst A. Simon, *Aufbau im Untergang: Jüdische Erwachsenenbildung im Nationalsozialistischen Deutschlad als geistiger Widerstand* (Tübingen, 1959), 30.

31 Simon, *Aufbau im Untergang*; Yehoyakim Cochavi, *Jewish Spiritual Survival in Nazi Germany* (Tel Aviv, 1988) (Hebrew), Chapter Two; Margaliot, *Between Rescue and Annihilation*, 55–76; *Drei Jahre*, 73–81.

and especially *Hehalutz*, agricultural training was the way toward Zionist fulfillment and a solid socioeconomic foundation for the national home. After the Nazis seized power Zionists and non-Zionists alike agreed that vocational retraining was necessary for all emigration, not just to Palestine. However, both felt that it should be done thoroughly and had no wish to accelerate the process. The non-Zionists were not anxious to hasten the end of Jewish life in Germany, and hoped that changing the employment structure would help it to continue. The Zionists were in no rush either because slow and steady training was perceived as insurance that the Jewish homeland be soundly built.[32] From the practical standpoint, however, this distinction was meaningless.

In 1933, all the Jewish organizations endorsed the *Hilfe und Aufbau* program, which promoted vocational retraining as a vehicle for Jewish rehabilitation in Germany as well as preparation for emigration. The *Hehalutz* training farms were the primary framework. They helped many of the Jews who had been thrust out of the German workforce, providing an immediate source of livelihood and eventually a new vocation. The discriminatory laws of the Nazis had severely limited such training opportunities, and prohibited payment of wages to trainees on German farms. Many other professions were closed to Jews, too. *Hehalutz* frameworks were virtually the only ones authorized by the Nazis. This posed a serious funding problem for the Zionist institutions. Yet the longer the wait between vocational retraining and *aliya*, the more crucial these frameworks were for Jewish survival in the Diaspora. Thus *Hilfe und Aufbau* channelled much of its resources into *Hehalutz* activities and setting up similar programs outside of Germany. By September 1934, there were 31 training farms in various European countries. Moreover, programs were now developed for 14 to 17 year-olds who had been expelled from school, but were too young to participate in regular *Hehalutz* training. This expansion was possible because *Hehalutz* was considered part of *Hilfe and Aufbau*, and received funding far beyond that which Zionist sources could provide.[33]

The Zionist movement was also invaluable to the *Reichsvertretung* and *Hilfe und Aufbau* in the organization of *aliya*. The Palestine Office operated as a branch of *Hilfe und Aufbau* alongside the *Hilfsverein*, which handled emigration to countries other than Palestine. As such, it enjoyed a regular share of the monies which came in from local contributions and philanthropic institutions

---

32 Margaliot, *Between Rescue and Annihilation*, 55–76.

33 Fraenkel, "Between Fulfilment and Rescue."

in Britain and America. The *aliya* project was given priority not only because of the objective circumstances that placed Palestine at the center of the Jewish emigration map, but because of the readiness of the Zionists to cooperate with non-Zionists in the framework of *Hilfe und Aufbau*. Added factors were the consensus on the need for pioneer training and the establishment of a global *aliya* framework.[34]

The *Gegenwartsarbeit* and Emigration Pendulum, 1935–1938

The Nuremberg Laws led to a change in the positions of both Zionist and non-Zionists. In light of the impediments to *aliya* as a result of the economic and political crisis in Palestine, the Zionists saw in these laws a possibility for continued life in Germany – albeit as a separate and inferior group, but nonetheless protected and allowed to pursue community affairs. At a Zionist meeting in Berlin attended by ZVfD leaders Benno Cohn and Joachim Prinz, agitating for mass emigration was declared inadvisable. Emigration was a major topic at the ZVfD's 25th convention in Berlin in early 1936, but internal matters were in no way passed over.[35] Thus the type of emigration which the German Zionists had in mind was not an immediate panic-stricken departure, but a gradual move at some point in the future, while life in Germany continued on its course. Even the Revisionists, who had previously called for the entire Jewish community to leave Germany, now favored an arrangement that guaranteed minority rights.[36]

On the other hand, the non-Zionists in the *Reichsvertretung*, who had hitherto refrained from endorsing emigration as the only solution, came to see that it was, and followed the major world organizations in granting their blessing to the settlement enterprise in Palestine. As a result, the status of Zionists in the *Reichsvertretung* was greatly enhanced. In the summer of 1936, the *Reichsvertretung* joined forces with *Keren Hayesod*, and according to a parity agreement with the non-Zionists, Zionists received 50 percent of the seats on the board of directors.[37]

---

34 See below.

35 The convention was held on February 2. For complete minutes, see *JR*, February 4, and February 7, 1936.

36 Margaliot, *Between Rescue and Annihilation*, 17–36.

37 Fraenkel, *On the Edge of the Abyss*, 183–5; Margaliot, *Between Rescue and Annihilation*, 17–36; Strauss, "Jewish Autonomy".

As the situation in Germany deteriorated, pan-Jewish cooperation increased. In response to the radicalization of Nazi policy toward the Jews in 1937 and the political developments in Palestine, namely the restrictions on immigration and the Peel Commission partition recommendations, all the Jewish organizations joined forces in a way they had never done before, but they were powerless to effect a change. In March 1938, the Jewish communities lost their status as legal public entities, and the *Reichsvertretung* soon suffered a similar fate.

The Zionist Movement and the Nazis

Even before the Nazi takeover, the ZVfD contemplated reaching some sort of arrangement with the government, citing common interests such as keeping the Jewish community separate and encouraging Jewish emigration. When the persecution of the Jews was stepped up and the international Jewish community declared a boycott on Nazi Germany, the German Zionists were confronted with a moral dilemma: whether to join the protests or work with the authorities to secure the best possible conditions for the Jewish inhabitants and those who desired to emigrate. Jewish organizations abroad were inclined to fight, and many in the WZO, too, opted for an open war on Nazi Germany.

In the ZVfD, feelings were different. The call for battle was perceived as unrealistic, and the victory of German extremism, irreversible. The German Zionists had always believed that radical nationalism would triumph in Germany, although they had never imagined that it would plunge to such depths. Yet here, it seemed, was an unexpected opportunity to further the Zionist dream. For that reason, all segments of Zionism in Germany favored negotiations with the Nazis and efforts were made to persuade the WZO to cooperate.

On March 25, 1933, Minister of the Interior Göring summoned the heads of the Jewish organizations and demanded that a delegation be sent to the United States and Britain to stop the anti-Nazi campaign being waged by the Jewish community. He warned that unless his demands were met, he could not be held responsible for the safety of the Jews in Germany. While the heads of the non-Zionist organizations vacillated, Blumenfeld accepted the mission. On March 29, he sent a memorandum to Hitler and Göring notifying them of the dispatch of Martin Rosenblüth, Richard Lichtheim, and Ludwig Tietz of the *Centralverein*, to London. This memorandum also indicates the motive behind

Blumenfeld's cooperation: the hope of gaining official Nazi support for Zionist activities and the building of Palestine. While the delegation was in London, it did its best to tone down, if not end, the protests, especially the Jewish boycott of German goods.[38]

Did the German Zionists act without choice in the face of Göring's none-too-veiled threat, or wage a calculated attempt to win the Nazi's favor? Neither possi-bility is mutually exclusive. In fact, Zionists stood to gain on two levels: securing Nazi permission for emigration-oriented Zionist activity, and buying time for an organized and gradual exodus from Germany.

In any event, the Nazi boycott of Jewish businesses on April 1, 1933 lasted only one day, as a kind of warning, and Zionist institutions were neither marked nor damaged. On the contrary, the Zionist leadership was allowed to maintain foreign contacts, and despite the strict foreign currency regulations (the Blocked Mark system), wealthy *olim* could buy up to £1,000. Moreover, the Transfer Agreement that was reached shortly afterwards, enabled Jews emigrating to Palestine to take some of their property with them.

The Transfer Agreement[39]

From the beginning of the Depression, and especially after the Brüning government imposed limitations on the transfer of hard currency in 1931–1932, the leaders of German Zionism and newly-established *Hitahdut Olei Germania* (Association of German Jewish Immigrants in Palestine) began to plan ways of rescuing Jewish property by transferring it from Germany to Palestine. When the situation deteriorated in 1933, Felix Rosenblüth, now residing in Palestine, proposed negotiations with the German government on the assumption that it would be interested in an agreement for two reasons, one economic and the other political. First of all, allowing the Jews to buy and take German goods with them because it would help alleviate unemployment. Second, if the goal of the Germans was to encourage Jewish emigration, anything that would facilitate their acceptance by other countries in these times of economic hardship, was to be desired.

---

38 Fraenkel, *On the Edge of the Abyss*, 47–9; Martin Rosenblüth, *Go Forth and Serve* (New York, 1961), 250–64.

39 Werner Feilchenfeld, Dolf Michaelis and Ludwig Pinner, *Haavara-Transfer nach Palästina und Einwanderung deutscher Juden, 1933–1939* (Tübingen, 1972); Nicosia, *The Third Reich*, 29–49; Niederland, *Emigration Patterns*, 125–33; Avraham Barkai, "German Interests in the Haavara-Transfer Agreement, 1933–1939," *LBIYB*, 35 (1990): 245–66; Gelber, *New Homeland*, 7–35, 78–92.

Contacts were initiated at different levels, mainly through *Hitahdut Olei Germania* and the ZVfD. Among those involved were Felix Rosenblüth; his brother Martin, who conducted the dialogue between the ZVfD and the Zionist Executive in London; ZVfD chairman Siegfried Moses, Georg Landauer who returned in 1929 to take charge of the Palestine Office in Berlin; Chaim Arlosoroff, head of the Jewish Agency Political Department; Werner Senator, head of its Immigration Department; Palestine Executive member Arthur Ruppin; and Ludwig Pinner of *Hitahdut Olei Germania*. Their work was encumbered by those in the WZO and Palestine Jewish community who were opposed to any liaison with the Nazis. In consequence, the Jewish Agency remained a passive participant in the negotiations. The Transfer Agreement, known as the *"Haavara"*, was signed on August 17, 1933 between the German Economics Ministry and the Anglo-Palestine Bank.

The Economics Ministry ratified the agreement on August 28, while the 18th Zionist Congress was in session in Prague. The Nazis did not allow a ZVfD delegation to participate, although Martin Rosenblüth and Robert Weltsch attended as observers. The ZVfD position was represented by Ruppin, whose speech was to serve as a guideline for Zionist policy with regard to the Nazis and German Jewry in the years to come. Ruppin argued that there was no point in fighting the Nazis or trying to improve the plight of Germany's Jews. The most effective protest was to help the Jews emigrate in an organized manner, mainly to Palestine. However, because of the considerable controversy over this issue, the Congress declined to discuss it further. When Chaim Arlosoroff was murdered on the Tel Aviv seashore in June 1934, rumor had it that the background was violent opposition to the Transfer Agreement, in which Arlosoroff had played a chief role. In effect, the Agreement was perceived as a ZVfD initiative and was not openly adopted by the World Zionist Organization until the 19th Zionist Congress at Lucerne in the summer of 1935.

The Transfer Agreement called for the establishment of a Jewish trust company, PALTREU, in cooperation with the Warburg Bank of Hamburg and the Wassermann Bank in Berlin. At the same time, the Trust and Transfer Office *Haavara* Ltd. was set up in Palestine in partnership with the Anglo-Palestine Bank. Jews seeking to transfer their capital to Palestine deposited up to 50,000 Reichsmarks per family in one of two PALTREU accounts, one for *olim* and the other for investors. From these accounts, PALTREU paid German exporters for goods sent to Palestine. The Palestinian importers paid *Haavara* Ltd. in Palestine Pounds, and the proceeds were credited to the German *olim* and investors.

The Transfer Agreement gave the wealthy emigrant to Palestine an advantage over those who intended to settle elsewhere, but capital export through these channels was not without loss. Since their goods earned Reichsmarks rather than foreign currency, the German exporters were compensated by PALTREU for the incentives they would have received from the government. The importers in Palestine were granted a subsidy to make up for the uncompetitively high prices they had to pay for the German goods. In addition, there were bank fees, and the costs of operating two companies. All this whittled away at the sum received by the immigrant in Palestine for property sold in Germany. Nevertheless, in view of the losses incurred by German Jews who moved to other countries, this arrangement was clearly preferable, at least for the time being.

By September 1939, 140 million Reichsmarks had been transferred to Palestine (approximately £8 million). However, it became increasingly difficult to exploit this arrangement as the Nazis grew more inflexible as the German economy succeeded in eradicating unemployment. The fluctuating exchange rate also took its toll on the sums that reached the immigrants. As time passed, the Palestinian economy was no longer able to absorb large quantities of foreign goods. In practice, this glut of imports was a major cause of the depression which hit Palestine at the end of 1935. From early 1935 a growing time lapse evolved between money deposits in Germany and actual payment; in some cases, the immigrants waited for more than a year. The situation worsened later that year when the Nuremberg Laws set off a rush of deposits whereas the economic crisis in Palestine had reduced the demand for imports. The difficulties were compounded at the end of 1936, when Göring's four-year armament program limited the export of raw materials and machinery. Thus a bottleneck developed in the transfer of money to Palestine, and by August 1938 the sum had accumulated to 84 million Reichsmarks.

For the Sake of Autonomy

Another area in which the Zionists sought concessions from the government was Jewish community work. In the early years, the Nazis allowed the Jews a modicum of educational and cultural autonomy, which corresponded with their aim of keeping the Jews separate and promoting emigration. The ZVfD looked forward to a continuation of this policy and envisaged the Jewish community as a sort of national enclave in Nazi Germany. On June 29, 1933, Blumenfeld and Weltsch sent a confidential memorandum to Hitler which elaborated on the positive aspects of Jewish autonomy from the Nazi standpoint. Landauer and Senator pursued a similar line in the Jewish arena. In July, Landauer submitted a proposal to the *Reichsvertretung*, and Senator approached the Joint Distribution Committee with the idea of a Jewish-Nazi concordat. Their argument was that autonomy would create a spiritual and social milieu that would strengthen the Jews. Neither plan received support and both were dropped.[40]

Once the *Reichsvertretung* became operative, the ZVfD ceased its attempts to reach an independent agreement with the Nazis. Contact was kept to a minimum, and was limited to matters connected with pioneer training, emigration, the 'Transfer Agreement, etc. The possibility of organizing some kind of autonomous framework was raised in various publications and discussions, especially after the passage of the Nuremberg Laws, but the issue was not taken up with the Nazis.[41] It seems that the ZVfD establishment never crossed the thin line between improving the Jews' lot and collaboration, as opposed to Revisionist leader Georg Kareski, whose activities allegedly did cross that line.[42]

From Germany to Palestine[43]

The responsibility for organizing an institutional and financial mechanism for the exodus of Jews from Germany was largely assumed by the German Zionists.

On March 17, 1933, a number of prominent German Zionist leaders living in Palestine met in Jerusalem to draw up plans for the rescue of their countrymen. Among them were Werner Senator, Arthur Hantke, Abraham Alfred Landsberg, and Felix Rosenblüth, all of *Hitahdut Olei Germania*. Their memorandum served as the basis for the discussions of the Jewish Agency Executive at the beginning of April. The following week, a meeting was held in London attended by members of the Zionist Executive, British Jewish

---

40 Strauss, "Jewish Autonomy"; Fraenkel, *On the Edge of the Abyss*, 81–9.

41 Margaliot, *Between Rescue and Annihilation*, 217–71; Francis R. Nicosia, "The End of Emancipation and the Illusion of Preferential Treatment – German Zionism, 1933–1938," *LBIYB*, 36 (1991): 243–65; Fraenkel, *On the Edge of the Abyss*, 89.

42 Herbert S. Levine, "A Jewish Collaborator in Nazi Germany – The Strange Career of Georg Kareski, 1933–1937," *Central European History*, 8 (1975): 251–81; Francis R. Nicosia, "Revisionist Zionism in Germany (II) – Georg Kareski and the *Staatszionistische Organisation, 1933–1938*," *LBIYB*, 32 (1987), 231–67; Fraenkel, *On the Edge of the Abyss*, 185–93.

43 Gelber, *New Homeland*, 7–23, 40–50; Fraenkel, *On the Edge of the Abyss*, 58–62.

leaders, Chaim Weizmann and Martin Rosenblüth, who was then in London representing the ZVfD. Back in Palestine, Weizmann, Arlosoroff and Senator agreed that preparations for absorbing the new wave of German immigrants would be in the hands of the old-timers. However, *Hitahdut Olei Germania* was adamant that Weizmann take the lead.

In the months that followed, the Jewish Agency Executive, the *Va'ad Leumi* (National Council) and the Zionist Executive in London argued incessantly about Weizmann's role in the rescue effort, fundraising methods, and the allocation of funds. Meanwhile, the Jewish organizational leaders in Britain set up the Central British Fund for German Jewry, and *Hitahdut Olei Germania,* together with the German Zionists in the Jewish Agency Executive, pooled their economic and settlement expertise to plan *aliya* and absorption. In May 1933, Arlosoroff and Senator travelled to Germany to meet with the Zionist organizations and make practical arrangements. Upon his return, Arlosoroff was the driving force behind the establishment of the United Committee for the Settlement of German Jews in Palestine, made up of representatives of the national institutions, municipalities, major organizations and *Hitahdut Olei Germania*. After Arlosoroff's murder, Ruppin took over the operations in Palestine, and Senator handled affairs in Germany.

The foundations for a rescue mission led by Weizmann were laid at the 18th Zionist Congress which convened in Prague in August 1933. Immediately after the Congress, Weizmann met with Ruppin and Senator representing the Jewish Agency, Berl Locker representing the Zionist Executive in London, and Siegfried Moses and Martin Rosenblüth representing the ZVfD. The outcome was a triple-branched operation: the ZVfD-sponsored Palestine Office in Berlin with Landauer and Senator alternating as its liaison in Jerusalem; the Central Bureau for the Settlement of German Jews in Palestine, headed by Weizmann and Martin Rosenblüth in London; and the German Department of the Jewish Agency in Jerusalem, supervised by Ruppin with the assistance of Landauer and Senator.

Funding was the major problem. Despite the Transfer Agreement, absorption could not depend exclusively on transfer capital brought in by the immigrants because many were expected to arrive empty-handed. A serious fundraising campaign was thus necessary, although the global economic crisis did not bode well for its success. Many Jewish philanthropists were not Zionists, and it was by no means certain that all donations would be earmarked for Palestine. On the other hand, due to rampant unemployment in the West, Palestine attracted even non-Zionists. This was recognized by the conference of Jewish organizations that convened in London in October 1933, and paved the way for the cooperation of non-Zionist funds. Foremost in this sphere was the

Central British Fund for German Jewry, founded in April 1933, which was already channelling money to the Jewish Agency in August.

At this point, an agreement was reached whereby funds for immigrant absorption would be routed through the new Central Bureau for the Settlement of German Jews in Palestine, which was established as a body independent of the WZO. Neither was it subordinate to the budgets of the Jewish Agency or the Zionist Executive in London, although there were administrative and personal ties between them. This apparatus was approved by the Jewish Agency Executive in October 1933, and illustrated the centrality of the German Zionists in Germany in setting up the mechanisms, for fundraising and planning in the spheres of *aliya* and absorption.

The German Jewish immigration that reached Palestine during the 1930s, commonly known as the Fifth *Aliya*, was motivated by forces that were not unique to Germany. In the early 1930s, financial distress and fascist persecution were rife throughout Central and Eastern Europe. In their flight from Germany the Jews set their sights on many countries, but their final destination was ultimately determined by which country would admit them. The United States, the major target of Jewish emigrants since the 19th century, had since imposed harsh controls which became stricter during the depression. In Palestine, however, the economy had survived an earlier crisis and was in the midst of a boom that was to last until 1935. Moreover, after the trouble sparked by the 1929 riots, the country was experiencing a political high point under the liberal High Commissioner Sir Arthur Wauchope. Wauchope, who believed that Palestine's absorptive capacity depended on capital import, was quick to see the potential inherent in the German Jewish community and by 1932 had increased the number of immigration certificates accordingly. Thus Palestine became a major destination for Jewish emigrants. Of 380,000 Jews seeking new homes between 1932–1938, a total of 200,000 reached Palestine, with 20 percent hailing from Germany, Austria and Czechoslovakia.

The proportion of German Jews who went to Palestine can be learned from Table IV.

Table IV. Jewish Emigration from Germany in 1933–1938

Destination	1933	1934	1935	1936	1937	1938	Total
All emigration							
To Palestine	7,600	9,800	8,600	8,000	3,700	4,800	43,200
% of total	20.5	42.6	41.0	34.8	16.1	12.0	25.7
To all countries	37,000	23,000	21,000	25,000	23,000	40,00	168,000
Organized emigration							
To Palestine	3,984	4,948	3,982	2,908	1,300	1,140	18,262
% of total	17.7	37.0	38.0	25.2	19.3	10.5	24.6
To all countries	22,501	13,389	10,526	11,539	6,749	10,847	75,551

Percent of organized emigration: 45%
Percent of organized emigration to Palestine: 43.3%

Sources:
General emigration data is based on Niederland, *Emmigration Patterns*, 36, 43–4, tables 5, 6. Data on *aliya* from Germany is based on Feilchenfeld et al., *"Ha'avara – Transfer,"* 89–90.

The problem with these estimates is that: (a) not all the emigrants went through the Jewish emigration offices; (b) the figures for the target countries are not uniform; and (c) the data for Palestine is not entirely clear. There is a considerable discrepancy between government statistics and those of the Jewish Agency due to overland emigration and emigration in stages, especially by non-citizens and Polish Jews. There was also a certain amount of "illegal immigration." Until 1938, many German Jews reached Palestine on tourist visas.

Another drawback is that the calendar years do not accurately reflect the fluctuations in emigration in general, and *aliya*, in particular, caused by political and economic developments. From the German standpoint, the pressure to emigrate subsided in the autumn of 1933, resumed for a time in the spring of 1934, and relaxed again until the summer of 1935 and the enactment of the Nuremberg Laws. There was another period of relief in 1936, when the Berlin Olympics were held, but the pressure mounted once more at the end of that year, and became especially intense from early 1938 when the Jews' economic situation worsened.[44] Conditions in Palestine also affected the emigration. In 1933–1935, there was a consistently high rate of *aliya* because of the flourishing economy and political stability. From 1936 on, due to the depression and the Arab revolt which began in April 1936, the attraction of Palestine lessened. At this point, Britain altered its policies in Palestine (the Peel Commission and the various partition proposals in 1937–1938), and cut back the number of immigration permits it was prepared to issue. Thus when the German Jews needed Palestine more than ever, it became increasingly difficult to gain admittance. This is clearly shown in the table by the *aliya* rates relative to the figures for emigration in general.

Jewish emigration from Germany during this period was motivated by distress. Unlike those who moved to Palestine during Weimar, ideology was no longer a major factor. In this respect the story of Jewish emigration from Nazi Germany was hardly a "Zionist epic." Nonetheless, the German *aliya* in the 1930s was built on foundations laid by German Zionists. To a great extent it relied on their organizational skills and their spirited leadership in the WZO and in Palestine. In sum, German Jewish immigration to Palestine and its impact on the development of the Jewish national home would not have been possible without the German Zionist movement.

44 Niederland, *Emigration Patterns*, 37–8.

CHAPTER THIRTEEN

GERMAN ZIONISM IN RETROSPECT

The Zionist movement was unlike other national movements, in that it was scattered worldwide, just as the Jewish people were. Zionist historiography is thus faced with a double challenge. On the one hand, each branch of the movement must be studied separately, as an integral part of the Jewish community in which it developed. On the other hand, these local branches must not be treated as a sideshow but as an indivisible component of the worldwide organization. Hence the history of the Zionist movement was shaped by different patterns of development dictated by local conditions as well as the interaction between the Jewish communities and the central Zionist leadership.

Centrality and Changing Roles

From the start, German Zionism represented a very unique sector of the German Jewish community, and attracted special attention both in Germany and in the world Zionist movement – much more than might have been expected from a group of several thousand members, comprising at best about three percent of German Jewry and five percent in the WZO. In its early years, before World War I, German Zionism was virtually the backbone of the WZO. German Zionists had supported Herzl in his endeavor to establish the organization, and many of the central functions were filled by German Jews when WZO headquarters moved to Germany after Herzl's death.

During that period, however, and until the end of the first decade of the twentieth century, German Jewry as a whole did not pay much attention to Zionism. It was viewed as a curious phenomenon, something that would soon vanish as the Jews became solidly integrated in German society. To survive and create a modest niche in the community, the Zionists had to invest much of their energies in propaganda.

The centrality of the German Zionists in the WZO began to command the attention of German Jews only in 1911, when Otto Warburg became President and the Central Zionist Office moved to Berlin. By this time the German Zionist leadership was practically identical with that of the WZO. As the German Zionists grew more confident and outspoken, they encountered the antagonism of non-Zionists who feared that the achievements of emancipation might be jeopardized. This pattern – dominance in the WZO leading to greater public attention and also to censure – was evident before World War I, but not overwhelming so. Later on, in the post-war period and throughout the 1920s it would actually dictate the relationship between Zionists and anti-Zionists in Germany.

From the point of view of the WZO, German Zionism reached its peak in the Weimar period. This was a crucial juncture in Zionist history, when the framework for the British Mandate and a Jewish national home in Palestine was established. During this period, Germany ceased to function as the seat of the Zionist movement, but German Zionism continued to play a key role in Zionist politics, accentuating the importance of the national home and trying to mobilize the assistance of all German Jews, supporters and opponents alike.

From the German-Jewish perspective the high point for German Zionism came during the Nazi period. It was then that Zionism became a major movement in Germany and its leaders were accepted as full-fledged members of the local leadership. It was now recognized that Zionism offered the only practical solution, and could provide the spiritual and social support that would keep the Jews afloat until they found refuge in Palestine.

Between East and West

The unique role of German Zionism was also shaped by the special historical circumstances into which this movement was born. As a Central-European phenomenon, German Zionism inherited features of both Western, post-assimilationist Zionism, and of Eastern Zionism, which emerged as a response to antisemitism. The traditional ties with *Eretz Israel* were thus transformed into a modern and pragmatic program that tied in with the political concepts of the time. *Eretz Israel* was to become the destination for Jewish emigration and the focus of a united Jewish national effort. For the German Zionists, however, this did not mean a personal commitment to live in Palestine, nor a radical change in personal life. In that respect, German Zionists of the first generation did not differ much from other Western Zionists and could be described as philanthropic-Platonic Zionists.

Yet, additional factors in the formation of the German Zionist movement linked it more closely to the type of Zionism that characterized Eastern-Europe. German Zionism had come into being against the rising tide of antisemitism in the last decades of the nineteenth century. It was also heavily influenced by the wave of Jewish emigration from the East, that passed through Germany and created a large bloc of Jewish settlement there.

Both the emergence of organized political antisemitism and the influx of East European immigrants had a special impact on the academic world. It was at the universities that Jewish students encountered these two phenomena and were bound as young intellectuals to react to them; it was here that they developed their *weltanschauung*. The universities were thus the cradle of German Zionism, and this fact was to have important implications in the long run.

Due to this early confrontation with antisemitism and the spirit of East-European Jewry, German Zionism was more critical of Jewish life in the Diaspora and adopted a more vigorous Palestine orientation than other Zionist groups in the West. It was absolutely opposed to any participation in German politics, and to fighting antisemitism in the manner of the *Centralverein deutscher Staatsbürger jüdischen Glaubens,* which viewed antisemitism as the last obstacle on the road to full integration. As for preoccupation with Palestine, this was strengthened by the German Zionists' central role in the WZO. Here the German Zionists were exposed to the radicalism of Russian Zionism which was nourished by the various radical-national and socialist Zionist ideologies of the time. On the whole, however, German Zionists still saw themselves and their fellow Jews as loyal citizens of Germany, born and bred in German culture.

National Radicalization

Changing conditions in Germany in the last years leading up to World War I, also sparked a change in German Zionism. A younger generation now pushed itself to center stage, bringing with it the fresh wind of radicalism. These young people were profoundly disturbed by German antisemitism and highly pessimistic about the future of the Jews in Germany. They saw in Zionism the answer to their needs as Jews who had lost their tie to Jewish tradition. The philanthropic-Platonic Zionism of the first generation had proved inadequate in redefining Jewish identity and achieving Zionist goals, and it was the radical Zionist school, whose proponents were mainly East-Europeans, that struck a responsive chord. German Zionism's pivotal position in the WZO magnified its exposure to these ideas. According to this school, Zionism offered not just as a political solution for persecuted Jews, but the opportunity to build a new social framework in the Land of Israel. It also demanded the formulation of a comprehensive program aimed at national revival. At this time, however, this radicalism was more theoretical than pragmatic, it found expression only through a number of formal resolutions which antagonized a few veteran Zionists on the one hand, and fueled a battle with the non-Zionists on the other.

World War I provided the framework and the challenges which brought the radical trends to fruition, solidified the Palestinocentric character of German Zionism and pushed this movement to become a leader in all that concerned the building of the Jewish national home. True, the war and its aftermath provided ample opportunity for old school German Zionism to flourish as well. The Weimar republic offered unprecedented possibilities for Jewish social, political and cultural activity, both within and alongside German society. The peace treaties and the new League of Nations framework enabled the recognition of the Jewish people as a national entity entitled to a national home as well as minority rights within the old and the newly established nation-states. The door was thus opened to full cooperation between Zionists and non-Zionists in a joint effort to build Palestine, eliminating the main reason for contest and rivalry and allowing Jewish life in the Diaspora to continue.

The war, however, strengthened the trend towards radicalism, pushing it to the forefront. The encounter with the Jews of the German-occupied countries to the East, and the manifestation of German antisemitism at home and at the front removed the last vestiges of apprehension in this regard. The new possibilities opened for Zionist fulfillment in Palestine helped to complete the rupture from German society and to lead the Jews single-mindedly in the direction of Palestine. Moreover, the expectations for a better future after the war created an atmosphere in which all sorts of national and social endeavors were accepted as a real possibility, the Jewish national revival included.

The postwar reorganization of German Zionism entailed a confrontation between two generations and two outlooks. However, from the outset, the younger generation and the radical-Palestinocentric approach enjoyed a considerable advantage. The Zionist movement at large now faced the challenge of practical realization, of translating aspirations into a broad-ranging and realistic program and organizing its implementation. The young radicals were much better equipped for this new task but had to fight long and hard with the old respected school, a struggle which came close to destroying Zionist unity in Germany. Eventually the radicals won without causing a real break.

It was during this struggle that German Zionism took on a new transfiguration, both on the community level and in the WZO. The implication of the compromise achieved by the young radicals led by Kurt Blumenfeld was that from then on Zionist activity in Germany would be conducted along two parallel roads. The veterans would run the *Jüdische Volkspartei*, which represented Zionism in the Jewish communities and lent it respectability throughout the Weimar period; the radicals would assume leadership of the ZVfD, transforming it into a Palestinocentric organization, reestablishing its eminence in the WZO, and at the same time engaging in public relations in German and German-Jewish circles.

Palestinocentrism

The heart and soul of the Zionist movement from inception was the Jewish national link with Palestine. The centrality of Palestine to the Zionist program and to Zionist activities varied, however, from country to country and from one period to another. Although the conditions created in the post-war period lent practical efforts on behalf of Palestine an unprecedented significance, not all branches of the Zionist movement responded in the same way to the new challenge. In some countries, persecution of the Jews led to both massive immigration to Palestine, and a program of political action in the Diaspora. The outstanding example of this duality was the Zionist movement in Poland, which constituted the largest national federation in the WZO. There was a duality of a different nature among Zionists in the West, who were apathetic toward the possibility of personal emigration to Palestine. Their lives were not subject to pressure; they lived in freedom and nothing drove them to leave their homelands. Yet perhaps because of that freedom they did not develop a national political agenda for their own Diaspora communities and concentrated exclusively on Palestine's political and economic needs. This Western form of Palestinocentrism was very narrow, and not only in the sense that it omitted the ingredient of personal *aliya*. Western Zionists maintained throughout a positive attitude to Jewish life in their own countries and to Jewish integration in society at large in a manner indistinguishable from the non-Zionists.

In comparison with both Western and Polish Zionism, German Zionism in the 1920s was preeminently Palestinocentric. Its devotion to the cause of building the national home, on the one hand, and its pessimistic attitude toward Diaspora Jewish life, on the other, set its order of priorities and determined the character of its political, organizational and educational programs.

On the subject of emigration to Palestine, German Zionists took a more activist posture than did other Western Zionists. *Aliya* from Germany until the Nazi seizure of power was quite significant; the pioneers were an avant-garde, highly selective and idealistic group. In their public debates, the German Zionists concentrated largely on issues directly connected with the national home – first economic policy and later, questions related to the Arab-Jewish conflict.

In the realm of daily organizational activity, the members of the German Zionist movement were called upon to devote their energies to fund-raising for *Keren Hayesod*. Their achievements in this regard far exceeded the ZVfD's relative size in the WZO, and elevated its standing in the eyes of Jews and non-Jews alike. The *Keren Hayesod* in Germany, directed by the non-Zionist banker, Oskar Wassermann, was an important stepping stone for the *Pro-Palästina Komitee* set up in 1926, and later, in 1929, for the enlarged Jewish Agency.

Work for Palestine succeeded in attracting wide support in Germany, arousing the apprehensions of the anti-Zionists and culminating in a vociferous attack on *Keren Hayesod*. However, the conflict merely strengthened the Palestine orientation and the prestige of the Zionists in the German Jewish community.

Yet another field of Palestine-oriented activity was education and preparation for emigration. These were largely entrusted to the *Kartell Jüdischer Verbindungen* and to the Zionist youth movements. The aim was to wean young people away from their German social and political life, immerse them in Hebrew and Jewish culture, and guide their professional choices in light of the needs of Palestine.

Socioeconomic Policy and Political Moderation

Immediately after World War I, the social and economic development of Palestine became a major priority. The ZVfD devoted itself to this matter more than any other Zionist Federation. Such activity was directly connected with the radical approach, which attributed special significance to restructuring the social and economic fabric of the nation upon its revival. As university graduates, the German Zionists were well trained for dealing with this issue. Furthermore, as members of a national federation which had played a pivotal role in the WZO, they tended to regard it as a personal responsibility.

They brought with them the social outlook of the academic middle-class in Germany, namely a national socioeconomic theory based on *étatisme*. This theory was seen as highly appropriate for the Zionist endeavor in Palestine, interweaving the national aim with the vision of a new, more equitable society. To the radical Zionist mind, deliberate, systematic development of the country in the making was imperative, and it was the duty of the Zionist Organization to shoulder the task.

This thinking was accompanied by moderate socialist leanings, which enjoyed great popularity among young Zionists after the war. The synthesis of Zionist nationalism and moderate reform-socialism linked up with *étatistic* viewpoint was held by most German Zionists. This enabled the German Zionists to adopt a pro-Left platform and to become the standard bearers of the new social and economic order envisioned for the national home. In collaboration with the Labor Zionists, it was the German Zionists who shaped the world Zionist movement's settlement policy in Palestine and stood firmly with Weizmann behind the creation of *Keren Hayesod* as the instrument to carry it out.

Aside from devotion to the economic enterprise in Palestine, German Zionism was marked by its political moderation. In large measure this stemmed from the liberal humanism of the enlightened Central European bourgeoisie. Most German Zionists belonged to the intellectual middle-class and were drawn even more in this direction as Jews. They were characterized by a critical political posture and social sensitivity that eschewed narrow self-interest. This skeptical attitude toward politics was also carried through in their Zionist radicalism, where a lesser significance was attributed to political achievements and the so-called "political" goal of Zionism.

World War I and the chauvinistic upheavals in Germany added a new dimension to this political moderation. In the same way that the war had strengthened the socialistic trends among the German Zionists and resulted in the birth of moderate socialism, it also affected their political outlook. This moderacy was to have a tremendous impact on the German Zionist approach to the problem of Arab-Jewish relations. German Zionism was the cradle of the binational state idea, and Germany was the only country beside Palestine with an active *Brith Shalom* association. This ideology enjoyed a broad consensus among German Zionists for some time and even gained considerable headway among the Zionist leadership there.

Yet, in respect to the Arab conflict German Zionism did not have the same overwhelming influence on the WZO, as it did in the case of socioeconomic planning. At a certain moment, when the 12th Zionist Congress passed a resolution which called for the development of Palestine as a land of two peoples, German Zionism did seem to exert considerable sway; indeed, for several years thereafter, the binational idea appeared to go hand-in-hand with Weizmannist policy. However, this was a mere illusion which was shattered during and after the 1929 riots in Palestine. In this sphere, moderacy remained the prerogative of German Zionism and was not adopted whole heartedly in the world Zionist arena. Even in Germany, agreement on the resolution of the Jewish-Arab conflict was not absolute and never reached the degree of consensus that was achieved in the realm of socioeconomic policy. True, *Brith Shalom* was a marginal phenomenon in terms of world Zionism, but it left an indelible mark nevertheless by virtue of its importance as a rallying point for German Zionism.

The Political Role

German Zionism in the 1920s was characterized by a general consensus on most issues, and could legitimately be labelled Leftist in the social and economic sense, and anti-chauvinist in the political sense. This broad agreement, unique to German Zionism, had a direct effect on the movement's political and organizational structure. Unlike Zionist federations in other countries, Zionism in Germany was basically non-partisan, with a clearly defined and unified program. Insofar as the Zionist parties did secure a foothold, it was their underlying similarity as much as their distinctiveness that mattered. The relatively strong parties – *Hapoel Hatzair* at the beginning of the decade and *Mizrahi* towards the second half – both embraced moderate pro-Left platforms. For *Hapoel Hatzair*, which first developed in Palestine, it was precisely the moderate socialist line that enabled it to make impressive gains in Germany. As for the German *Mizrahi*, it was closer to the labor-oriented *Hapoel Hamizrahi* of Palestine than to world *Mizrahi*, whose main branches in America and Poland leaned more to the Right.

The right-wing Revisionists were completely outside the basic German Zionist consensus and never became firmly rooted in Germany. The only leader to join the German Zionists was Richard Lichtheim, whose affiliation remained an isolated phenomenon. At the peak of their popularity, in the wake of the 1929 Riots, the Revisionists accounted for only 12 of the 149 delegates to the Jena Convention.

This climate of ideological solidarity insulated German Zionism from the factionalism that marked other Zionist federations and helped to avert a threatened split at the beginning of the 1920s. At this time, conflict over *Keren Hayesod* almost led to the resignation of the *Binyan Haaretz* group and the establishment of a rival Zionist organization. At the end of the decade, as well, bitter controversy between supporters and opponents of *Brith Shalom* brought the leaders of German Zionism to the brink, but eventually their sense of unity prevailed. Although partisan recruitment did increase in the late 1920s, the tone set by the General Zionist camp allowed the federation to retain its ability to function as a united nationwide framework. Virtually all ideological trends were represented in the ZVfD's executive committee, steering the federation in a General Zionist direction.

In consequence, German Zionism in the 1920s served as a bastion of "Weizmannism." Like many German Zionist leaders, Chaim Weizmann was a product of the radical Zionist school and a disciple of Ahad Ha'am. He assigned top priority to the economic development of the Jewish home in the spirit of national rebirth and social-cultural renewal, and encouraged strong partnership between the Zionist leadership and the labor movement in Palestine. His political outlook was also markedly moderate, even if not always perfectly clear, and he shared many other ideas espoused by the German Zionists.

The German Zionist movement thus became a sort of laboratory where Weizmann tested his ideas and translated them into policy. As the chief designers of Zionist settlement policy and the main instrument for its implementation – *Keren Hayesod* – the German Zionists also played a central role in driving out Weizmann's rivals and opponents: First Brandeis and his associates, later the various "bourgeois" parties that challenged his pro-labor policy, and above all — the Revisionists. The activities of the movement in this regard reached a peak with the formation of the *Linkes Zentrum* in 1927, as a representative faction of German Zionism in the WZO politics.

However, from here on things began to change. Growing quasi-party activity came to undermine consensus politics and revealed the limits of Weizmann's own accommodation of radical positions. The first crisis hit at the end of 1927 when the emergence of the *Linkes Zentrum* caused the expulsion of the Labor Zionists from the Zionist Executive. The basis for political collaboration was further shaken by the open conflict between Weizmann and *Brith Shalom* in 1929.

There was also the cumulative effect of the economic crisis in Palestine. Palestinocentrism came under attack, and by 1928 German Zionists had begun to devote a considerable part of their time and resources to Diaspora-oriented activity. Apart from a short revival of Palestine-oriented activism in the WZO in 1929, in connection with the establishment of the enlarged Jewish Agency and the riots in Palestine, it appeared that German Zionism's role at the forefront of Jewish national affairs had all but ended. When, in 1931, the Weizmann era came to a close through Chaim Weizmann's resignation from the Zionist presidency, the rupture between the German Zionists and world Zionist politics seemed complete.

Palestinocentrism at the Service of German Jewry

The German Zionist detachment from world Zionist politics virtually coincided with the Nazi seizure of power. By this time, there was no longer any question as to the task of the Zionist movement in Germany. Pushed out from world affairs, it had turned its eyes toward the problems of the Diaspora. Now, the events in Germany began to pull forcibly in the same direction. However, it soon emerged that the unique Palestinocentrism which had guided the ZVfD in the preceding decade was instrumental in readying the movement for its role within the German Jewish community.

For the Zionists, who had been educated to take a skeptic stance toward emancipation and the future of the Jews in the Diaspora, and to prepare themselves for emigration, the rise of the Nazis did not come as a shock. They were no wiser than the anti-Zionists in foreseeing the horrors of the future, but psychologically and spiritually they were better equipped to deal with the Nazi challenge. Unlike other Jews who sank in despair and even contemplated suicide, the Zionists had an ideological, organizational and personal response – immigration to Palestine. Indeed, thousands of Zionists did not hesitate to draw conclusions and act on the ideals they had nurtured for years.

But beyond the power of their basic Zionist beliefs to direct them personally in these difficult times, the German Zionists were also equipped to assist German Jewry as a whole. First of all, many Jews were able to leave Germany by joining the Zionist Organization and receiving certificates for Palestine. Moreover, aside from supervising general Jewish education, the Zionist movement in Germany was instrumental in organizing vocational education and *Hachshara* (pre-*aliya* training); thereby providing a framework for life in Nazi Germany for the time being. This was much more than merely existing. It was a way of strengthening Jewish identity and preparing for emigration not out of necessity but as the proper consequence of being proud Jews.

It was only in one respect that traditional Palestinocentrism proved to be an obstacle. For years, the ZVfD had neglected Jewish communal politics. Now, when it was turned to as a leader, it was neither willing nor able to take full responsibility for German Jewry. It is no wonder that most German Zionist leaders did not act in the manner expected of leaders, which was to remain with their flock in times of trouble. There were those who did so, but they were a minority. The German Zionists had never felt a commitment toward those who rejected Zionism, and now that many former non- or anti-Zionists had jumped on the bandwagon, they felt no need to change.

Yet, in a paradoxical way, the huge task of rescuing German Jewry pushed German Zionism again to forefront of the WZO, this time in the field of immigration and absorption in Palestine. Once more, the German Zionists took center stage in the spheres of settlement and economic leadership, and devotedly applied themselves in the relevant WZO departments. Arthur Ruppin and Georg Landauer, Chaim Arlosoroff and Ludwig Pinner, Alfred Landsberg and Martin Rosenblüth, Selig Soskin and Wilhelm Brünn and many others were the architects of a network of financing and settlement plans for German Jews in Palestine. It was a turning point in the history of immigration absorption in Palestine, and yet another stage of German Zionists involvement in world Zionism and the upbuilding of the national home.

Epilogue

German Zionism constituted the bridgehead to Palestine for many German Jews. *Aliya* from Germany was by no means an immigration of Zionists. It was German Zionist tradition, however, which determined the future of German Jews in Palestine for better or for worse. On the one hand, the German Zionists designed new patterns of rural and urban development which paved the road for German-Jewish influence on the economy of the *Yishuv* and the future State of Israel. On the other hand, their political traditions delimited German-Jewish influence in the public sphere. The fact that German Zionists shied away from party politics, adopted unity as their strategy, adhered to a policy of political moderation and were consistent in their pursuit of economic goals all affected the character of the German Jewish community in *Eretz Israel*.

German Jews never became political leaders and their impact in politics and political culture remained marginal. Be that as it may, German Zionist Palestinocentrism set Palestine on a pedestal as the destination of all Jews and the only option for a Jewish future, creating a significant link between German-Jewish tradition and Zionist realization.

ABBREVIATIONS

BLBI	*Bulletin des Leo Baeck Instituts*
Centralverein	*Centralverein deutscher Staatsbürger Jüdischen Glaubens*
CZA	Central Zionist Archives (Jerusalem)
CZO	Central Zionist Office
JR	*Jüdische Rundschau*
Hilfsverein	*Hilfsverein der deutschen Juden*
LBIA	Leo Baeck Institute Archives (New York)
LBIYB	*Leo Baeck Institute Year Book*
NULA	National and University Library Archives (Jerusalem)
OHD	Oral History Division at The Institute of Contemporary Jewry, The Hebrew University (Jerusalem)
WA	Weizmann Archives (Rehovot)
WZO	World Zionist Organisation
ZVfD	*Zionistische Vereinigung für Deutschland*

BIBLIOGRAPHY
Archives

Central Zionist Archives (Jerusalem) (CZA)
Official Archives
The Central Zionist Office in London (Z4)
Keren Hayesod - Central Office in London (KH1)
Keren Hayesod Office for central Europe in Berlin (KH2)
The Presidency of the Zionist Actions Committee (L9)
The Zionist Executive, Political Department (S25)
The Zionist Executive, Settlement Department (S15)
The *Zionistische Vereinigung für Deutschland* (F4)

Personal Archives
Arlosoroff, Chaim (A44); Berger, Julius (A206); Blumenfeld, Kurt (A222); Bodenheimer, Max (A15); Böhm, Adolf (A141); Calvari, Moses (A329); Goldmann, Nahum (A172); Gronemann, Sammy (A135); Hantke, Arthur (A11); Hirsch, Salli (A158); Kalmus, Ernst (A67); Klatzkin, Jacob (A40); Klee, Alfred (A142); Landauer, Georg (K11/233); Lichtheim, Richard (A56); Moses, Siegfried (K11/309); Rosen, Pinhas (Rosenblüth, Felix) (A339); Ruppin, Arthur (A107); Sandler, Aron (A69); Schachtel, Hugo Hillel (A102); Smoira, Moshe (A215); Trietsch, Davis (A104); Weltsch, Robert (A168); Zlocisti, Theodor (A48).

Leo Baeck Institute Archives (New York) (LBIA)
Rabbi Fuchs' Collection
Robert Weltsch's Archives (7185)

The National and University Library Archives (Jerusalem) (NULA)
Shmuel Hugo Bergman's Archives (1502)

Schocken Archives (Jerusalem)

Weizmann Archives (Rehovot) (WA)

Oral History

The Oral History Division of the Institute of Contemporary Jewry, The Hebrew University (Jerusalem) (OHD)

Interviews conducted by the author
Danziger, Mali (Tel Aviv, July 11,1982)
Flanter, Meir and Meta (Jerusalem, May 5, 1982)
Jacoby, Paul (Jerusalem January 11, 1981)
Latte, Chaim (Pardes Hana, March 24,1982)
Michaelis, Dolf (Jerusalem, March 9, 1980; January 4,1981)
Olitzki Arieh Leo (Jerusalem, June 1, 1982)
Pelz, Hava (Ramat Hasharon, November 6, 1981)
Sambursky, Shmuel (Jerusalem, May 27, 1982)
Shiloni, Israel (Nahariya, November 16, 1981)
Simon, Ernst Akiva (Jerusalem, March 16, 1982; March 23,1982)
Simon, Ernst Emmanuel (Givataim, July 11, 1982)
Tahler, Jacob (Jole) (Tel Aviv, March 22, 1982)
Robert Weltsch (Jerusalem, July 7, 1979; August 15, 1979; February 21, 1980)

Other interviews in the OHD colletions
Blumenfeld, Kurt; Cohn, Benno; Eisner, Jacob (Isi); Lotan, Giora (Georg Lubinski); Michaelis, Dolf; Pomeranz, Hans; Rosen, Pinhas (Felix Rosenblüth); Ex-*Blau-Weiss* members (Interviewd by Hana Weiner)

Questionaires distributed by the author, and filled up by German Jews in Israel (about 40).

Newspapers and Periodicals

Die Arbeit (Organ der zionistischen volkssozialistischen Partei Hapöel Hazair (Berlin, fortnightly, then monthly, 1919–1925).

Aufbau – Blätter des Keren Kajemeth Lejisrael (Jüdischer Nationalfonds) (Berlin, monthly, 1924–1928).

Freie Zionistische Blätter, (Heidelberg, 1921).

Erez Israel, Mitteilungen des Hauptbüreaus des jüdischen Nationalfonds (The Hague, annual, 1916–1923).

Haaretz (Tel Aviv, daily, 1919–) (Hebrew).

Hapoel Hatzair (Tel Aviv, weekly, 1907–1977) (Hebrew).

Haolam (London, weekly, 1919–1936) (Hebrew).

Hed Bethar (Berlin, monthly, 1929).

Informationen der Zionistischen Vereinigung für Deutschland (Berlin, 1921).

Jewish Chronicle (London, weekly, 1841–).

Der Jude (Berlin, Monthly, 1916–1924, 1925–1928).

Jüdische Rundschau (Berlin, biweekly, 1919–1938).

Der Jüdische Student (Berlin, monthly, 1902–1933).

Kunteres (Tel Aviv, weekly, 1919–1929) (Hebrew).

Mitteilungsblatt des Binjan Haarez (Berlin, 1921–1922).

Palästina Wirtschaft – Berichte über Handel, Industrie und Aufbau in Pälastina, (Berlin, quarterly, 1922–1925).

The *Revisionist Voice – Election Issue of the Revisionist Zionist Organization* (Tel Aviv, December 3, 1925) (Hebrew).

She'ifoteinu – Collections of Articles (Jerusalem, annual, 1927–1930) (Hebrew).

Volk und Land, jüdische Wochenschrift für Politik, Wirtschaft und Palästina-Arbeit (Berlin, weekly, 1919–20).

ZVfD Blätter für die Mitarbeiter der Zionistischen Vereinigung für Deutschland (Berlin, monthly, 1934–1937).

Publications Cited

Adler-Rudel, Shalom. *Ostjuden in Deutschland, 1880–1940* (Tübingen, 1959).

Aschheim, Steven E. *Brothers and Strangers – The East European Jew in German and German-Jewish Consciousness, 1800–1923* (Madison, 1982).

Barkai, Avraham. "German Interests in the Haavara-Transfer Agreement, 1933–1939," *LBIYB*, 35 (1990): 245–66.

———. *From Boycott to Annihilation – The Economic Struggle of German Jews, 1933-1943* (Hanover, New England, 1989).

———. "Die Juden als sozio-ökonomische Minderheitsgruppe in der Weimarer Republik," in *Juden in der Weimarer Republik*, ed. Walter Grab and Joachim Schoeps (Stuttgart and Bonn, 1986), 330-46.

Bauer, Yehuda. *My Brothers' Keeper – A History of the American Jewish Joint Distribution Committee, 1929-1939* (Philadelphia, 1974).

Beilinson, Moshe. *Zum Jüdisch-Arabischen Problem* (Tel Aviv, 1930).

Bein, Alex. *The Return to the Soil* (Jerusalem, 1957).

Ben-Avram, Baruch. "The German 'Hapoel Hatzair' – The History of an Intellectual Group (1917-1920)," *Zionism*, 6 (1981): 49-95 (Hebrew).

Bericht über die Tätigkeit der Zionistischen Vereinigung für Deutschland an den XX. Delegiertentag in Wiesbaden (Berlin, 1924); *an den XXI. Delegiertentag in Erfurt* (Berlin, 1926); *an den XXII. Delegiertentag in Breslau* (Berlin, 1928); *an den XXV. Delegiertentag in Berlin* (Berlin, 1936).

Berkowitz, Michael. *Zionist Culture and West European Jewry before the First World War* (Cambridge, 1993).

Bernett, Hajo. "Die jüdische Turn- und Sportbewegung als Ausdruck der Selbstfindung und Selbstbehauptung des deutschen Judentums," in *Die Juden im Nationalsozialistischen Deutschland – The Jews in Nazi Germany, 1933-1943*, ed. Arnold Paucker with Sylvia Gilchrist and Barbara Suchy (Tübingen, 1986), 223-37.

Bieber, Hans Joachim. "Anti-Semitism as a Reflection of Social, Economic and Political Tension in Germany, 1880-1933," in *Jews and Germans from 1860 to 1933 – The Problematic Symbiosis*, ed. David Bronsen (Heidelberg, 1979), 33-77.

Birnbaum, Max P. *Staat und Synagoge – Eine Geschichte des Preußischen Landes-Verbandes Jüdischer Gemeinden (1918-1938)* (Tübingen, 1981).

Blumenfeld, Kurt. "Auf dem Jenaer Delegiertentag," in *Robert Weltsch zum 70. Geburtstag von seinen Freunden*, ed. Hans Tramer and Kurt Loewenstein (Tel Aviv, 1961), 121-3.

———. *Erlebte Judenfrage* (Stuttgart, 1962).

———. *Im Kampf um den Zionismus – Briefe aus fünf Jahrzehnten*, ed. Miriam Sambursky and Johanan Ginat (Stuttgart, 1976).

———. "Ursprünge und Art einer Zionistischen Bewegung," *BLBI*, 4 (1958): 129-40.

Bodenheimer, Max I. *Prelude to Israel – The Memoirs of M. I. Bodenheimer* (New York, 1963).

Böhm, Adolf. *Die Zionistische Bewegung*, vol. II (Tel Aviv, 1937).

Brenner, Michael. "The *Jüdische Volkspartei* – National Jewish Communal Politics during the Weimar Republic," *LBIYB*, 35 (1990): 219–43.

Breslauer, Walter. "Vergleichende Bemerkungen zur Gestaltung des jüdischen Organisationslebens in Deutschland und England," in *In zwei Welten – Siegfried Moses zum fünfundsiebzigsten Geburtstag*, ed. Hans Tramer (Tel Aviv, 1962), 87–96.

Brünn, Wilhelm. *Prospekt über eine zu gründende Orangenpflanzungsgesellschaft in Palästina* (Berlin, 1926).

Buber, Martin. *Drei Reden über das Judentum* (Frankfurt a.M., 1920).

––––. *Briefwechsel aus sieben Jahrzehnten vol. I–III*, ed. Grete Schaeder (Heidelberg, 1972–1975).

––––. "Nationalismas," in Paul R. Mendes-Flohr, *A Land of Two People – Martin Buber on Jews and Arabs* (New York, 1983), 47–57.

Caplan, Neil. *Futile Diplomacy (I)* – Early Arab-Zionist Negotiation Attempts 1913–1931 (London and Totowa, 1983).

Cochavi, Yehoyakim. *Jewish Spiritual Survival in Nazi Germany* (Tel Aviv, 1988) (Hebrew).

Cohn, Benno. "Einige Bemerkungen über den deutschen Zionismus nach 1933," in *In Zwei Welten – Siegfried Moses zum fünfundsiebzigsten Geburtstag*, ed. Hans Tramer (Tel Aviv, 1962), 43–54.

Craig, Gordon A. *Germany, 1866–1945* (New York and Oxford, 1980).

Dokumente zur Geschichte des deutschen Zionismus, 1820–1933, ed. Jehuda Reinharz (Tübingen, 1981).

Doron, Joachim. "Social Concepts Prevailing in German Zionism, 1883–1914," *Studies in Zionism*, 5 (Spring 1982): 1–31.

Drei Jahre zionistische Bewegung in Deutschland – Bericht der Zionistischen Vereinigung für Deutschland an den XXV. Delegiertentag in Berlin, 2–4. Februar 1936 (Berlin, 1936).

Elam, Yigal. *The Jewish Agency – Formative Years, 1919–1931* (Jerusalem, 1990) (Hebrew).

Eloni, Yehuda. *Zionismus in Deutschland von den Anfängen bis 1914* (Gerlingen, 1987).

Engel, David. "The Relations between Liberals and Zionists in Germany During the First World War," *Zion*, 47 (1982): 435–62 (Hebrew).

Feilchenfeld, Werner; Michaelis, Dolf; and Pinner, Ludwig. *Haavara-Transfer nach Palästina und Einwanderung deutscher Juden, 1933–1939* (Tübingen, 1972).

Fraenkel, Daniel. *On the Edge of the Abyss – Zionist Policy and the Plight of the German Jews, 1933–1938* (Jerusalem, 1994) (Hebrew).

———. "Between Fulfilment and Rescue – *He-Halutz* and the Plight of the Jews in Nazi Germany, 1933–1935," *Yahadut Zemanenu – Contemporary Jewry*, 6 (1990): 215–43 (Hebrew).

Friedman, Isaiah. *Germany, Turkey and Zionism, 1897–1918* (Oxford, 1977).

———. "The *Hilfsverein der deutschen Juden*, the German Foreign Ministry and the Controversy with the Zionists, 1901–1918," *LBIYB*, 24 (1979): 291–320.

Friesel, Evyatar. "Jewish-Zionist Relations in Germany During the Weimar Republic," in *Proceedings of the Seventh World Congress of Jewish Studies – The History of the Jews in Europe* (Jerusalem, 1981), 179–84 (Hebrew).

———. "The Political and Ideological Development of the *Centralverein* before 1914," *LBIYB*, 31 (1986): 121–46.

———. *Zionist Policy after the Balfour Declaration, 1917–1922* (Tel Aviv, 1977) (Hebrew).

Gay, Peter. *Weimar Culture – The Outsider as Insider* (New York, 1968).

Gelber, Yoav. *New Homeland – Immigration and Absorption of Central European Jews, 1933–1948* (Jerusalem, 1990) (Hebrew).

Giladi, Dan. *Jewish Palestine during the Period of the Fourth Aliya (1924–1929) – Economic and Social Aspects* (Tel Aviv, 1973) (Hebrew).

Gladstein-Kestenberg, Ruth. "The Beginnings of Bar Kochba," in *Prague and Jerusalem (Leo Herrmann in Memoriam)* ed. Felix Weltsch (Jerusalem [1956]), 86–110 (Hebrew).

Goldmann, Nahum. *Mein Leben als Deutscher Jude* (Munich, 1980).

Greive, Hermann. *Geschichte des modernen Antisemitismus in Deutschland* (Darmstadt, 1983).

Gruenewald, Max. "Der Anfang der Reichsvertretung," in *Deutsches Judentum, Aufstieg und Krise – Gestalten, Ideen, Werke*, ed. Robert Weltsch (Stuttgart, 1963), 315–25.

Gruppe der unabhängigen Allgemeinen Zionisten (Gruppe Kollenscher), Materialien zum Jenaer Delegiertentag der ZVfD (1929) (Berlin).

Halpern, Ben. *A Clash of Heroes – Brandeis, Weizmann and American Zionism* (New York and Oxford, 1987).

History of the Hagana, vol. II, ed. Ben-Zion Dinur (Jerusalem and Tel Aviv, 1964) (Hebrew).

Jochmann, Werner. "Die Ausbreitung des Antisemitismus," in *Deutsches Judentum in Krieg und Revolution, 1916–1923*, ed. Werner E. Mosse and Arnold Paucker (Tübingen, 1971), 409–510.

Die Juden im Nationalsozialistischen Deutschland –The Jews in Nazi Germany, 1933-1943, ed. Arnold Paucker with Sylvia Gilchrist and Barbara Suchy (Tübingen, 1986).

Jungmann, Max. *Erinnerungen eines Zionisten* (Jerusalem, 1959).

Katz, Jacob. *From Prejudice to Destruction – Anti-Semitism, 1700-1933* (Cambridge, Mass., 1980).

Kedar, Aharon. "*Brith Shalom* – The Early Period, 1925-1928," in *Studies in the History of Zionism Presented to Israel Goldstein on his Eightieth Birthday by the Institute of Contemporary Jewry,* ed. Yehuda Bauer, Moshe Davis and Israel Kolatt (Jerusalem, 1976), 224–85 (Hebrew).

Keren Hajessod (jüdisches Palästinawerk E.V.) Das Palästinawerk – Eine Kundgebung deutscher Juden im ehemaligen Herrenhaus zu Berlin am 4. März 1926 (Berlin, 1926).

Keren Hayesod, Reports of the Head office to the 12th–21st Zionist Congresses, 1921–1939, and to the Annual Conference, 1922.

Klieman, Aaron S. *Foundations of British Policy in the Arab World – the Cairo Conference of 1921* (Baltimore, 1970).

Knütter, Hans H. *Die Juden und die Deutsche Linke in der Weimarer Republik* (Düsseldorf, 1971).

Kohn, Hans. *Bürger vieler Welten* (Frauenfeld, 1965).

———. *Martin Buber – Sein Werk und seine Zeit* (Cologne, 1961).

Kohn, Hans and Weltsch, Robert. *Zionistische Politik* (Mährisch-Ostrau, 1927).

Kollenscher, Max. *Ein Wort an den 12. Zionisten-Kongress* (Berlin, 1921).

Kramer, David. "Jewish Welfare Work under the Impact of Pauperisation," in *Die Juden im Nationalsozialistischen Deutschland – The Jews in Nazi Germany, 1933-1943,* ed. Arnold Paucker with Sylvia Gilchrist and Barbara Suchy (Tübingen, 1986), 173–88.

Krojanker, Gustav. *Zum Problem des neuen deutschen Nationalismus – Eine zionistische Orientierung gegenüber den nationalistischen Strömungen unserer Zeit* (Berlin, 1932).

Lamberti, Marjorie. "The *Centralverein* and the Anti-Zionists – Setting the Historical Record Straight," *LBIYB,* 33 (1988): 123-8.

———. "From Coexistence to Conflict – Zionism and the Jewish Community in Germany, 1897–1914," *LBIYB,* 27 (1982): 53–82.

Lavsky, Hagit. *The Foundations of Zionist Financial Policy – The Zionist Commission, 1918–1921* (Jerusalem, 1980) (Hebrew).

———. "German Zionist Leadership," in *Zionist Leadership,* ed. Jehuda Reinharz and Anita Shapira (forthcoming).

Levine, Herbert S. "A Jewish Collaborator in Nazi Germany – The Strange Career of Georg Kareski, 1933-1937," *Central European History*, 8 (1975): 251–81.

Levy, Richard S. *The Downfall of the Antisemitic Political Parties in Imperial Germany* (New Haven and London, 1975).

Lewis, William A. *Economic Survey, 1919–1939* (London, 1949).

Lichtheim, Richard. *Der Aufbau des Jüdischen Palästinas* (Berlin, 1919).

———. *The History of Zionism in Germany* (Jerusalem [1951]) (Hebrew).

———. *Rückkehr* (Stuttgart, 1970).

Margaliot, Avraham. *Between Rescue and Annihilation – Studies in the History of the Jews in Germany* (Jerusalem, 1990) (Hebrew).

Markel, Richard. "*Brith Haolim* – Der Weg der Alija des Jung-Jüdischen Wanderbundes (JJWB)," *BLBI*, 9 (1966): 119–88.

Matthäus, Jürgen. "*Deutschtum und Judentum* Under Fire – The Impact of the First World War on the Strategies of the *Centralverein* and the *Zionistische Vereinigung*," *LBIYB*, 33 (1988): 129–48.

Maurer, Trude. *Ostjuden in Deutschland, 1918–1933* (Hamburg, 1986).

Meier-Cronemeyer, Hermann. "Jüdische Jugendbewegung," *Germania Judaica*, 12, 1/2 and 3/4 (1969).

Meilensteine – Vom Wege des Kartell Jüdischer Verbindungen (KJV) in der Zionistischen Bewegung (*eine Sammelschrift*), ed. Eli Rothschild (Tel Aviv, 1972).

Mendelsohn, Ezra. *Zionism in Poland – The Formative Years, 1915–1926* (New Haven and London, 1981).

Mendes-Flohr, Paul R. *A Land of Two Peoples – Martin Buber on Jews and Arabs* (New York, 1983).

Metzer, Jacob. *National Capital for a National Home, 1919–1921* (Jerusalem, 1979) (Hebrew).

———. "Economic Structure and National Goals – The Jewish National Home in Interwar Palestine," *Journal of Economic History*, 38 (March 1978): 101–19.

Nicosia, Francis R. "The End of Emancipation and the Illusion of Preferential Treatment – German Zionism, 1933–1938," *LBIYB*, 36 (1951): 243–65.

———. "Revisionist Zionism in Germany (II) – Georg Kareski and the *Staatszionistische Organisation*, 1933–1938," *LBIYB*, 32 (1987): 231–67.

———. *The Third Reich and the Palestine Question* (Austin, 1986).

Niederland, Doron. *Emigration Patterns of German Jews, 1918–1938* (Ph.D. Thesis, The Hebrew University of Jerusalem, 1988) (Hebrew).

Niewyk, Donald L. "The German Jews in Revolution and Revolt, 1918–1919," *Studies in Contemporary Jewry*, 4 (1988): 41–66.

——. *The Jews in Weimar Germany* (Louisiana and London, 1980).

Oser, Jacob and Blanchfield, William C. *The Evolution of Economic Thought* (New York, 1975).

Paucker, Arnold. "Der Jüdische Abwehrkampf," in *Entscheidungsjahr 1932 – Zur Judenfrage in der Endphase der Weimarer Republik*, ed. Werner E. Mosse with the collaboration of Arnold Paucker (Tübingen, 1965), 405–99.

Penslar, Derek J. *Zionism and Technology – The Engineering of Jewish Settlement in Palestine, 1870–1914* (Bloomington and Indianapolis, 1991).

Pinner, Felix. *Das Neue Palästina* (Berlin, 1928).

Poppel, Stephen M. *Zionism in Germany, 1897–1933 – The Shaping of a Jewish Identity* (Philadelphia, 1977).

Porath, Yehoshua. *The Emergence of the Palestinian-Arab National Movement, 1918–1929* (London, 1974).

Prinz, Arthur. *Juden im deutschen Wirtschaftsleben – Soziale und wirtschaftliche Struktur im Wandel, 1850–1914*, ed. Avraham Barkai (Tübingen, 1984).

Protokoll der Verhandlungen der XII.–XVII. Zionisten-Kongresses (1921–1931, titles and places of issue vary).

Protokoll des XV. Delegiertentages der Zionistischen Vereinigung für Deutschland (Berlin, 1919).

Ragins, Sanford. *Jewish Responses to Antisemitism in Germany, 1870–1914* (Cincinnati, 1980).

Reinharz, Jehuda. "Advocacy and History – The Case of the *Centralverein* and the Zionists," *LBIYB*, 33 (1988): 113–22.

——. "Ahad Ha'am und der deutsche Zionismus," *BLBI*, 61 (1982): 3–73.

——. *Chaim Weizmann – The Making of a Zionist Leader* (Oxford, 1985).

——. "The *Esra Verein* and Jewish Colonisation in Palestine," *LBIYB*, 24 (1979): 261–89.

——. *Fatherland or Promised Land – The Dilemma of the German Jew, 1893–1914* (Ann Arbor, 1975).

——. *The German Zionist Challenge to the Faith in Emancipation, 1897–1914* (Spiegel Lectures in European Jewish History, no. 2, ed. Lloyd P. Gartner, Tel Aviv, 1982).

——. "*Hashomer Hatzair* in Germany (II) – Under the Shadow of the Swastika, 1933-1938" *LBIYB*, 32 (1987): 183–229.

——. "Martin Buber's Impact on German Zionism before World War I," *Studies in Zionism*, 6 (Autumn, 1982): 171–83.

———. "Three Generations of German Zionism, *The Jerusalem Quarterly*, 9 (Fall, 1978): 95–110.

———. "The Zionist Response to Antisemitism in Germany," *LBIYB*, 30 (1985): 105–40.

Report of the Executive of the Zionist Organization Submitted to the XVIIth Zionist Congress at Basle June 30th July–July 10th, 1931 (London, 1931).

Rosebluth, Martin. *Go Forth and Serve* (New York, 1961).

Ruppin, Arthur. *Der Aufbau des Landes Israel* (Berlin 1919).

———. *Tagebücher, Briefe, Erinnerungen*, ed. Schlomo Krolik (Königstein/Ts, 1985).

Rürup, Reinhard. "Emancipation and Crisis – The 'Jewish Question' in Germany, 1850–1890," *LBIYB*, 20 (1975): 13–25.

Schechtman, Joseph B. and Benari, Yehoshua. *History of the Revisionist Movement (I) – 1925–1930* (Tel Aviv, 1970).

Schleunes, Karl A. *The Twisted Road to Auschwitz – Nazi Policy Toward German Jews, 1933–1939* (Urbana, Chicago and London, 1970).

von Schoenaich, Freiherr. *Palästina – Eine Fahrt ins gelobte Land* (Halberstadt, 1926).

Scholem, Gershom. *From Berlin to Jerusalem – Memories of My Youth* (New York, 1980).

Schorsch, Ismar. *Jewish Reactions to German Antisemitism, 1870–1914* (New York and London, 1972).

Schreiber, Ruth. *The Palestine Office in Berlin and the "Aliya" of the German Jews*, 1933–1941 (M.A. Thesis, Tel Aviv University, 1988) (Hebrew).

Schumpeter, Joseph. *History of Economic Analysis* (Oxford, 1954).

Shapiro, Yonathan. *Leadership of the American Zionist Organization, 1897–1930* (Urbana, Chicago and London, 1971).

Shavit, Yaacov. *Jabotinsky and the Revisionist Movement, 1925–1948* (London, 1988).

Simon, Ernst A. *Aufbau im Untergang – Jüdische Erwachsenenbildung im nationalsozialistischen Deutschlad als geistiger Widerstand* (Tübingen, 1959).

———. *The Lines of Demarcation* (Givat Haviva, 1973) (Hebrew).

———. "Martin Buber and German Jewry," *LBIYB*, 3 (1958): 3–39.

———. "Unser Kriegserlebnis (1919)," in *Brücken – Gesammelte Aufsätze* (Heidelberg, 1965), 17–23.

Sprinzak, Joseph. *The Letters of Joseph Sprinzak*, vol. II, ed. Joseph Shapira (Tel Aviv, 1969) (Hebrew).

Strauss, Herbert A. "Jewish Autonomy within the Limits of National Socialist Policy, the Community and the Reichsvertretung," in *Die Juden im Nationalsozialistischen Deutschland – The Jews in Nazi Germany, 1933-1943*, ed. Arnold Paucker with Sylvia Gilchrist and Barbara Suchy (Tübingen, 1986), 125-52.

Toury, Jacob. "Organizational Problems of German Jewry – Steps Towards the Establishment of a Central Organization (1893-1920)," *LBIYB*, 13 (1968): 57-90.

Turnowsky, Walter. *Die Arbeit des Keren Hayesod in Deutschland* (Berlin, 1924).

Urofsky, Melvin I. *American Zionism from Herzl to the Holocaust* (New York, 1975).

Volkov, Shulamit. "Antisemitism as a Cultural Code – Reflections on the History and Historiography of Antisemitism in Imperial Germany," *LBIYB*, 23 (1978): 2-46.

———. "The Dynamics of Dissimilation – *Ostjuden* and German Jews," in *The Jewish Response to German Culture*, ed. Jehuda Reinharz and Walter Schatzberg (Hanover and London, 1985), 195-211.

Walk, Joseph. "Das 'Deutsche Komitee Pro Palästina', 1926-1923," *BLBI*, 52 (1976): 162-93.

———. "Jüdische Erziehung als geistiger Widerstand," in *Die Juden im Nationalsozialistischen Deutschland – The Jews in Nazi Germany, 1933-1943*, ed. Arnold Paucker with Sylvia Gilchrist and Barbara Suchy (Tübingen, 1986), 230-47.

———. "The Torah Va-Avodah Movement", *LBIYB*, 6 (1961): 236-56.

Weinberg, Jehuda L. *Aus der Frühzeit des Zionismus – Heinrich Loewe* (Jerusalem, 1946).

Weizmann, Chaim. *The Letters and Papers of Chaim Weizmann*, vol. X-XIII, ed. Barnet Litvinoff et al. (Jerusalem, 1977-1978).

Weltsch, Robert. "Deutscher Zionismus in der Rückschau" (1962), in *An der Wende des Modernen Judentums* (Tübingen, 1972), 51-64.

———. "A Tragedy of Leadership – Chaim Weizmann and the Zionist Movement," *Jewish Social Studies*, 13 (1958): 211-6.

Wertheimer, Jack. *Unwelcome Strangers – East European Jews in Imperial Germany* (New York and Oxford, 1987).

Wiener, Alfred. *Kritische Reise durch Palästina* (Berlin, 1927).

Wistrich, Robert S. *Socialism and the Jews – The Dilemma of Assimilation in Germany and Austria-Hungary* (London and Toronto, 1982).

Witkowski, Gustav. *Die Krise im Zionismus* (Bonn, 1921).

The World Zionist Organization and the Keren Hayesod Controversy in America (London, 1921).

Zechlin, Egmont. (with the collaboration of Hans J. Bieber), *Die deutsche Politik und die Juden im ersten Weltkrieg* (Göttingen, 1969).

Zimmermann, Moshe. "The Impact of German Nationalism on Jewish Nationalism – The German Jewish Students' Organizations in Germany at the Beginning of the Twentieth Century," *Zion*, 45 (1980): 299–326 (Hebrew).

———. "Social Structure and Social Expectations in German Zionism before World War One," in *Nation and History – Studies in the History of the Jewish People*, vol. II, ed. Shmuel Ettinger (Jerusalem, 1984), 117–99 (Hebrew).

———. *Wilhelm Marr, "The Patriarch of Anti-Semitism"* (New York, 1986).

INDEX

Adler, Alexander 225

Agricultural settlements, see Settlement in Palestine

Agricultural training, see *Hachshara*

Agudat Israel 96

Ahad Ha'am (Asher Zvi Ginzberg) 28 29 141 147 148 154 160 178 222 262

Ahavat Zion, 19 161, see also *Hovevei Zion*

Ahdut Ha'avoda faction 138

Ahlem, gardening school in 103

Al-Hamishmar faction 107

Al-Husseini, Mufti Haj Amin 211

Alexander II, Czar 14

Alexander III, Czar 14

Aliya 69 78 103–105 133 145 210 234 239–245 250 251 253 258 259 261; First Aliya 19; Second *Aliya* 28; Third *Aliya* 112; Fourth *Aliya* 113 115 116 120 122 123 162 172; Fifth *Aliya* 251, see also Immigration to Patestine, Jewish Emigration from Germany, Youth *Aliya*

Allenby, Edmund H. 32

Allgemeiner Rabbiner-Verband in Deutschland 91 96

Allgemeine Zionisten – Linkes Zentrum 219, see also *Linkes Zentrum, Arbeitsgemeinschaft "Linkes Zentrum"*

America, see United States

American Jews 32 85

American Zionism/Zionists 33 42 84 85 106 125 133

Anglo-Palestine Bank 247

Anschluss (of Austria by the Nazis) 233

Anti-Zionism/Anti-Zionists 30 31 37 45 99 100 101 129 172 181 183 255 259 263 264

Antisemiten-Liga 13

Antisemitism 11–21 25 26 28 30 35 37 42 44 68 72 109 226 256 257

Apfel, Alfred (1882–1941) 93

Arabs 143–146 149–154 156 164–169 173 174 177 179 183 185–191 194–198 201 204 208 212–221 223 228; Arab National Movement 153 190; "The Arab Question" 141–161 169 195 204 215 220; Jewish-Arab relations 183 207; Negotiations with Jews 187 208 212 221 223; Opposition 142 143 144 149 153 190; Palestinian Arab Leaders 195; Peace Agreement with Jews 189 191 194 190; Rights 152 153 158 164 166 167 168 177 195 200 217 218 228; Riots of Arabs in Palestine, in 1921 142–147 151 185 186; 1929 181–198 200 202–205 225 251 261 262 263, in 1936–1939 253; Supreme Muslim Council 211

* Index prepared by Daniela Ashur

Die Arbeit (journal of *Hapoel Hatzair*)
46 49 149 151

Arbeitsgemeinschaft für Zionistische Realpolitik 193–197 208 209 215 219 220

Arbeitsgemeinschaft "Linkes Zentrum" 138, see also *Linkes Zentrum*

Argentina 94

Arlosoroff, Chaim (1899–1933) 44 52 73 247 250 264

Arlosoroff-Goldberg (Luft), Gerda 103 120 184 198

Assimilation 11 12 15 16 18 28 44 45 72 97 229

Association of Rabbis in Germany, see *Allgemeiner Rabbiner-Verband in Deutschland*

Auerbach, Elias (1882–1971) 48 52 55 69

Aufbau (journal of JNF in Germany) 95

Auhagen, Hubert 100

Austria 138 251; Austro-Hungarian Empire 14; Austrian Zionists 110 138 176 177, see also *Anschluss*

Austrittsorthodoxen, see Orthodox Jews

'Avoda' group 103

Badt, Herrmann (1887–1946) 41 52

Baeck, Leo 91 93 100 240

Baer, Albert (1888–1975) 52 56

Baerwald, Alexander (1887–1930) 48

Bahad movement, see *Brith Halutzim Datiim*

Balfour Declaration 32 36 38 45 46 61 62 66 71 72 75 84–86 143 149 155 158 159 167 187 201 210

Bambus, Willy (1863–1904) 19–22

Bank Leumi 128

Bar Kochba (Zionist Students' Circle) 141 147 148 150 160

Barth, Arnold Aron (1890–1957) 93 109 125 199 200 223

Barth, Lazarus Eliezer (1880–1949) 108 121

Basch, Etienne (1898–1972) 192

Basel 21 68 229; Program 75 78 177

Baumgardt, David (1890–1963) 50

Bavaria 39 40 42

Becker, Karl Heinrich 100

Beer Hall *Putsch* in Munich 40

Beilinson, Moshe 189

Beit Alpha 94

Beit Yitzhak 127

Beit Zera 94 102

Berger, Alfred (1891–1940) 44 47 94 121 182 192 198 225

Berger, Julius (1863–1948) 24 28 44 70 83 88 198 199

Bergman, Shmuel Hugo 141 147 150 151 169 193 204 215 216

Berlin 12–14 19–21 23–25 27 29 30 32 33 39 40 44 46 48 51 52 66 67 72–75 88 93 96 98 111 112 128 137 170 187 188 192 193 196 217 219 223 228 231 233–237 240 242 244 247 250 253 255; Olympics 253

Berliner Bewegung 13, see also Antisemitism

Berliner Tageblatt 99 100

Bethar youth movement 185, see also Revisionism/Revionist Party

Bileski, Moritz Moshe (1889–1946) 88 103 111 125 128 129 137 138 182 192 194 196 211 212 222

Binationalism 147–151 162–168 170–181 194 208 221 223, see also *Brith Shalom*

Bingen on the Rhine 21

Binyan Haaretz faction 73–87 92 121 201 202 262

Bismarck, Otto von 13

Blau-Weiss youth movement 29 80 95 103

Blum, Arno 202

Blumenfeld, Kurt (1884–1963) 24 28–30 35 43 47 48 73 77 79 82 83 86 118– 121 123–125 128 129 137 138 146 159 175 179 182 183 188 194 196 197 209–215 219 223–225 228–235 245 246 248 258

B'nai B'rith 96 98

Bodenheimer, Max Isidor (1865–1940) 21 22 23 24 27 48 74

Bolshevik Revolution 33

Brandeis, Louis D. + group 63 64 65 73 74 75 77 80 84 85 86 92 144 262; Brandeis-Weizmann controversy 64 65 73 74 75 84 143 145

Breslau 12 14 17 51 83 94 137 182 200 201 240

Britain 22 38 53 63 64 75 94 143 228 244 245 250 253; British Army 145 153; British Colonial Office 206; British Government 32 64 116 117 163 186–189 191 194 197 198 201 204 218 228; Mandate, see British Mandate; British Prime Minister 207 229; British Zionists 32

Brith Halutzim Datiim (*Bahad* movement) 102 235, see also *Hapoel Hamizrahi*, *Mizrahi*

Brith Shalom Association 83 161 162–200 203–205 208–217 221–224 239 260–263, see also Binationalism

British Mandate 36 57 64 75 142 143 153 163 172 173 183 185–187 189 194 200 215 223 228 234 236 238 255

Brodetsky, Selig 232

Brüning government 246

Brünn, Wilhelm Ze'ev (1884–1949) 48 53 131 138 164

Buber, Mordechai Martin (1878–1965) 28 29 49 83 147 148 150 154–162 173 235 241 242

Bukovina 177

Bulgaria 94 138

Bund Jüdischer Corporationen (1901), see under Jewish Students' Associations in Germany

Bündnispolitik 79 107

Carlsbad 86 109

Central British Fund for German Jewry 240 250 251

Central Europe 26 28 35 36 61 70 88 93 148 149 251; Central European Jewry 148

Centralverein deutscher Staatsbürger jüdischen Glaubens 17 26 30 37 38 42 43 44 91 92 96–100 227 228 240 245 256

Chancellor, Sir John H. 181

Chauvinism/Anti-Chauvinism 36 49 141 150 191 196 203 214 230 260 261

Churchill, Winston 194

Cohn, Benno (1894–1975) 235 244

Cohn, Erich (1887–1962) 128

Cohn, Lotte 103

Cohn, Oskar 41

Cologne 12 21 22 24 94

Colonization Company (plan) 59 64

Committee of Jewish Delegations 62, see also Versailles Treaty/Peace Conference

Communists 229 233, see also Socialism, *Spartacus*

Constantinople 24 32

Copenhagen 32

Cracow 217

Crimea (Jewish settlement in) 99 172

Czechoslovakia 94 135 138 203 251

Danziger, Felix 199

Davar (Histadrut's newspaper) 198 220

De-Lieme, Nehamia 92

Democratic Faction 28 29 147 148 150 155 160

Deutsche Bank 91
Deutscher-Israelitischer Gemeindebund 93
Dizengoff, Meir 57
Dresden 109
Dubek cigarette factory 69
Dyk, Solomon 48

Eastern Europe 14–16 18 19 21 25 26
   32 38 42 44 49 61 114 128 251;
   East-European Jews (*Ostjuden*) 19 20
   21 25 27 36 37 43 235 236 256 257,
   see also *Verband der Ostjuden*
Ebert, Friedrich 39 41
Ein Harod 103
Einstein, Albert 98 100 197
Eisner, Jacob (Isi) 235
Eisner, Kurt 40 41
Emancipation 11 12 18 15 25 28 45 230
   242 255 263
England, see Britain
Erez Israel (JNF's Annual publication)
   47
Erfurt 127 177
Esra association 19, see also *Hovevei
   Zion*
Et Livnot faction 107 110 111 16 119
   121
Étatisme/Étatists 49–51 56 260

Farbstein, Jehoshua Heschel 126
Federation of American Zionists (FAZ),
   see American Zionism/Zionists
Feiwel, Berthold 123 147
Feuerring, Isaak (1889–1937) 111 125
   128 138 192 194
Financial and Economic Council, see
   under World Zionist Organization
Foerder, Yeshayahu Herbert
   (1901–1970) 128
France 32
Frankfurt a. M. 12 21 94 173 230 234
   240

Frankfurter Zeitung 99 100
Freiburg 51
Freie Zionistische Blätter (journal) 150
Freie Zionistische Gruppe, faction 1920
   67 68 70–76 202; faction 1925 123
Freier, Recha 242
Freikorps 39 40
Friedemann, Adolf (1871–1933) 20 30
   37 74
Fuchs, Hugo 100

Galicia 14
Gegenwartsarbeit 48 65–73 140 228 239
   244
Gemeindepolitik 201 202
General Zionists 87 106–111 117 118
   120 122–124 127 134 135 137 138 182
   192 200–202 219 223, see also *"stam
   Zionisten"*, *Unabhängige Allgemeine
   Zionisten* faction
German Jewish Congress 42 98
German Jews, background 11-17 20 35
   36 38 49 97 141 201 226 229 239 240
   248, see also Assimilation
German Jews in Palestine 103 104 198
   250–255 264 265, see also *Hitahdut
   Olei Germania*, Immigration to
   Palestine
German Zionist Federation, see
   *Zionistische Vereiniguny für
   Deutschland*
German Zionist Leadership 23 30 47 49
   87 88 111 128 175 198 200–202 205–
   207 223 225 255 261 264
Germany, Christian-Social Workers'
   Party 13; Depression, in 1873 12,
   in 1929 50 89 96 227 246; Inflation
   (1922) 40 89 93 94 104 105; German
   Army 37 48; German Democratic
   Party 39–41; German Economics
   Ministry 247; German Foreign

Office 90 97; German Newspapers 98–99; German Social-Democratic Party 39 41 193 233; German Universities 16; German War Ministry 34; Legislation of 1869 16; Reichstag 11 13 41 227 233; Revolution of 1848–1849 15; Second Reich 141; Social Revolution in Russia & Germany 36 41; Wars of 1860s & 1870–71 15, see also Weimar Republic, Nazism

Goldberg, Abraham 122

Goldmann, Nahum (1894–1982) 43 108 119 121 125 150 173 174 182 199 223

Gordon, Aharon David 148

Göring, Hermann 245 246 248

Goslar, Hans (1889–1945) 41 52

Gottlieb, Jehoshua 107 122

Gronemann, Sammy (1875–1952) 83 137

Gruenbaum, Yitzhak 62 107 115 119 122

Grünstein, Nathan 138

Haaretz (newspaper) 215

Haavara – Transfer, Transfer Agreement 246–248; Trust and Transfer Office Haavara Ltd. 247; PALTREU 247 248

Habonim youth movement 236

Hachshara (agricultural training) 103–105 239 242–244 264, see also Vocational Training

Haifa 48 69

Haifa Technion 48

The Hague 32 47

Halpern, George 123

Hamburg 12 19 83 91 94

Hanover 44 82 83 103 144

Hantke, Arthur (1874–1955) 20–22 24 29 43 46 47 52 58 59 67 77 82 83 86 88 91 93 111 114 121 125 146 232 249

Haolam (weekly of WZO) 115 190 191 205 214

Hapoel Hamizrahi faction 136 260, see also Mizrahi Party, *Brith Halutzim Datiim*

Hapoel Hatzair faction 46 48 49 51 53 55 66–68 71 76 79 81 82 107 109 119 120 124 126 135 141 144–147 149 150 153 158–160 181 183 191 203 218 221 224 260; convention in Prague (1921) 146, see also *Hitahdut,* Zionist Labor Movement

Hashomer Hatzair youth movement 236

Hasmonaea, see under Jewish Students' Associations in Germany

Hebrew educational system 69 102 113 259, se also Jewish education

Hebrew language 61 68 102 237 242

Hebrew University of Jerusalem 103 104 198 211 215

Hebron 185

Hed Bethar (bulletin of German Revisionists) 202 203

Heftziba 95 103

Heidelberg 19 51

Hehalutz movement 95 102 235–238 242 243

Herzl, Theodor 21–25 27 43 83 155 166 177 237 254; Herzlian Zionists/Zionism 21 23 28 30 67 75 83 147 202

Herzl Bund 111

Hilfsverein der Deutschen Juden 38 42 92 243

Hindenburg, Paul Von 30 229

Hindes, Mathias 111

Hirsch, Otto 240

Hirsch, Salli (1885–1950) 77 80 192 194

Hirsch, Siegmund 92 100

Histadrut Labor Federation 120 127 131 132 134

The Historical School 50

Hitahdut (Hapoel Hatzair & Tzeirei
Zion) 110 111 122 123 137 147 154
159; convention in Carlsbad (1921)
154, see also Zionist Labor movement
Hitahdut Olei Germania 246 247 249
Hitler, Adolf 229 230 233 245 248
Hochschule für die Wissenschaft des
Judentums 20
Holland 39 43
Hope-Simpson, Sir John 222
Hovevei Zion groups 19 20 21 26 68

Immigration from Eastern-Europe to
Germany 14 15 18 44 256
Immigration to Palestine 19 30 44 52
53 59 91 102–105 126 127 130 132
133 142 144 152 155 161 162 163 166
171 173 185–187 194 203 220 223 227
233 235 236 238 244 251 252 256 257
262 263, see also *Aliya,* Jewish
Emigration from Germany
Informationsstelle für die gemeinsamen
Interessen der zionistischen
Landsmannschaften 111
"Iron wall" (Jabotinsky's theory) 145
164
Israeli National Insurance Institute 240
Israeli Supreme Court 102
Israelitische Rundschau (newspaper) 22

Jabotinsky, Vladimir Ze'ev 107 108 110
116 119 143–147 149–153 157 159
163–170 176–179 212 213
Jacobson, Victor 111 123
Jaffa 143 151
Jena 219–227 262
Jerusalem 33 48 143 185 198 217 222
223 249 250; Old City 198
Jewish Agency for Palestine 64 110 116
118 178 188 234 238 240 247 249 250
251 252; Adminitrative Committee
187; Executive, see under World

Zionist Organization;
Expanded/Enlarged 101 106–110
115–118 120 162 165 181 182 185 199
259 263
Jewish-Arabs relations, see Arabs
The Jewish Chronicle 172
Jewish Colonial Trust 24 59
Jewish Council 63 64
Jewish education 66 237 239 240–242;
Mittelstelle für jüdische
Erwachsenenbildung 236;
Schulabteilung 242, see also *Hachshara,*
Hebrew educational system,
Vocational Training
Jewish Emigration from Germany 103
104 246 253 255 256, see also *Aliya,*
Immigration to Palestine
Jewish Legion 143 145 146 149 150 154
159 162 164 166
Jewish Majority issue 145 153 163 164
171–174 178–180 183 210
Jewish National Fund (JNF – Hebrew
KKL) 24 32 47 55 58 59 61 70 73 88
114 137 232 236, see also Settlement
in Palestine
Jewish National Home in Palestine 32
36 45 46 49 53 55 60–63 66 67 70 79
80 87 99 116 127 128 143–145 157
163 167 170 175 183 187 222 253 255
257
"Jewish Problem"/Jewish Question 36
78 147 166 172 214 221–225 228
Jewish State issue 166 174 177 178 183
194 223
Jewish Students 14 16–20 26 198 241
256
Jewish Students' Associations in
Germany 16 17 20 21 24 48; *Bund*
Jüdischer Corporationen (1901) 21
29; *Hasmonaea* (Berlin 1903) 77;
Jüdische Humanitätsgesellschaft (Berlin
1893) 20; *Jung Israel* (Berlin 1892)

20; *Kartell Convent der Verbindungen deutscher Studenten Jüdischen Glaubens* (1914) 17 20 21; *Kartell Jüdischer Verbindungen* (KJV) 21 77 80 102 128 203 259; *Kartell Zionistischer Verbindungen* (KZV 1906) 21; *Russischer-Jüdischer wissenschaftlicher Verein* (1889) 20; *Vereinigung jüdischer Studierender an der Universität Berlin* (1895) 20; *Viadrina* (Breslau 1886) 16 20
Jewish Telegraphic Agency 190 216
Jewish Youth Associations 95; Youth Movements 44 45 102 136 259; Zionist Youth Organizations 236
Jezreel Valley 48 95
Joint Distribution Committee 128 240 249
Josephsthal, Georg (Giora Josephtal) (1912–1962) 235 238
Der Jude (journal) 147
Judenzählung (Jews count) 35 109
Jüdische Humanitätsgesellaschaft (Berlin 1893), see under Jewish Students' Associations in Germany
Jüdische Rundschau (German Zionist organ) 22 24 47 49 103 112 115 117 118 129 150 160 169 170–176 178–181 183 184 189 190 191 196–203 205 208 209 212 214 223 225 229 230 235 236
Der Jüdische Student (journal of Zionist Student Association) 203
Jüdische Volkspartei 43 44 67 75 98 101 228 239 240 258
The Jüdischer Verlag 29 147
Jüdisches Volksheim 44
Jung Israel, see under Jewish Students' Associations in Germany
Jungmann, Max (1895–1970) 20
Jungzionistische Gruppe faction 69

Kalischer, Solomon 93

Kalischer, Zvi Hirsch 93
Kalmus, Ernst (1869–1959) 83
Kanowitz, Siegfried (1900–1961) 182 225
Kaplan, Eliezer 151
Kaplansky, Shelomo 207
Kapp, Wolfgang (Kapp Putsch) 40
Kareski, Georg (1879–1947) 43 74 202 228 240 249
Kartell Convent der Verbindungen deutscher Studenten Jüdischen Glaubens, see under Jewish Students' Associations in Germany
Kartell Jüdischer Verbindungen (KJV), see under Jewish Students' Association in Germany
Kartell Zionistischer Verbindungen (KZV), see under Jewish Students' Association in Germany
Kassel 84
Kathedersozialisten 51
Katznelson, Berl 220 232
Kaufmann, Leo 94
Kaufmann, Richard 103
Keren Hayesod 44 57–61 65 66 70 71 73–77 79 80 82–103 106–108 114 129 143 144 146 147 159 181 226 230 232 236 244 259 260 262; American 96; Austrian 117; German 88 89 93–96 99 107 112; Ma'aser (Tithe) 89–90 93; Neutral *Keren Hayesod* 94 96 98 107 188; *Verein Palästina Grundfonds, Keren Hajessod E.V.* 93; World *Keren Hayesod* 91 95
Keren Kayemet (KKL), see Jewish National Fund
Kibbutzim 95 103 131
Kiel, sailor's mutiny in 39
Klatzkin, Jacob (1882–1948) 119 150
Klee, Alfred (1875–1943) 43 62 67 68 73 74 121 201
Kohn, Hans 141 147 150 169 193 211

212

Kollenscher, Max (1875–1937) 43 62 74
    83 85 86 182 200–202 219 223 225
Kölnische Zeitung 99
Komitee für den Osten 37
Königsberg 14
Kornberg, Fritz 103
Kreutzberger, Max 240
"Kristallnacht" 233, see also Nazism
Krojanker, Gustav (1891–1945) 230 231

Landau, Eugen 92 93 98
Landauer, George (1885–1954) 80 83
    125 182 192 194 204 222 225 234 247
    249 260 264
Landauer, Gustav 40 41
Landsberg, Alfred Avraham
    (1887–1964) 35 109 114 121 132 137
    192 194 212–214 249 264
Lazarus, Paul Pinhas 100
League of Nations 40 63 142 143 150
    257
Leftist Center, see *Linkes Zentrum*
Leipzig 14 30
Leszynsky, Eduard (1884–1967) 21 74
Levin, Shmaryahu 20
Levite, Leon 107 122
Levy, Edmund 225
Levy, Emil (1879–1953) 196
Lewin, Karl (1876–1930) 74 202
Lichtenstein, Franz (Peretz Leshem)
    235 238
Lichtheim, Richard (1885–1963) 20 24
    28 29 47 52 72 73 77 81 82 108 110
    121 173 174 176 182 184 202 203 223
    234 245 261
Liebknecht, Karl 38
Linkes Zentrum 126–135 137 139 181
    184 192 219 220 222 225 262, see also
    *Allgemeine Zionisten - Linkes
    Zentrum,* Arbeitsgemeinschaft *"Linkes
    Zentrum"*

Lipsky, Louis 110 122 125
Lisser, Alfred 91 94 100
Lithuania 62 108
Locarno treaties 40
Locker, Berl 250
Loewe, Heinrich (1869–1951) 20–22 52
    69 83
Loewenstein, Fritz (1892–1964) 77 80
London 32 33 57 59 63 65–67 73 90–94
    103 112 117 121 134 147 185 187 207
    208 209 211 245–247 249–251
Löwengart, Stefan 103
Lubinsky, Georg (Giora Lotan) (1902–)
    241
Lucerne 236 247
Luke, Harry C. 186
Luxemburg, Rosa 39

Ma'aser, see under *Keren Hayesod*
Maccabi, see Young *Maccabi*
MacDonald, James Ramsey 229
Magnes, Judah L. 211 212 214–217 222
Mandate, see British Mandate
Mann, Thomas 100
Mapai, Eretz Israel Workers' Party 229
Markenhof group/training farm 95 103
Marr, Wilhelm 13
Marxism, see Socialism
Mayer, Edward 100
Melchett, Lord (Alfred Mond) 188
Merhavya 48
Meyer, Franz 235
Mikve Israel (agricultural school) 242
Mitteilungsblatt des Binjan Haaretz
    (bulletin) 83
Mizrahi Party 81 83 107–111 121 122
    124 125 135–137 182 192 196 199 200
    204 208 209 223 225 261, see also
    *Hapoel Hamizrahi, Brith Halutzim
    Datiim*
Moscow 14
Moses, Siegfried (1887–1974) 77 83 121

225 233 235 240 247 250
Moses, Walter (1892–1955) 69 73
Mossad Ahava children's home 242
Motzkin, Leo 20 28 62 147
Mount Scopus 103 215 223
Munich 14 21 40 51 94

Naphtali, Fritz (1888–1961) 193 194
  219
Nathan, Paul 92
National Capital 59 60 61 64 110
  113–116 118 123 130–132, see also
  Settlement in Palestine
National Home, see Jewish National
  Home
Nationaler Einheitsblock faction 77–83
Nationalism, European Nationalism 26;
  German Nationalism 12 35 36 39
  142 230 231 245; Jewish Nationalism
  18 22 23 36 39 43 44 46 49 67–69 71
  75 78 85 141 142 149 203–205 232
  241 260
Nazism, Nazi Party 40 203 230; Nazi
  Period 226–253 255, see also
  Kristallnacht, Nuremberg Laws, SA,
  SS
New York 32 33 96 147 187
Non-Zionists 31 37–39 43 63 75 79 82
  88 90–94 101 106–108 113 239 240
  243 244 250 255 257 258
Nuremberg Laws 223 237 241 244 248
  249 253
Nussbaum, Meinhold (1888–1953) 128

Olitzki, Arieh Leo 198
Oppenheimer, Franz (1864–1943) 26 30
  37 48 131
Orthodox Jews/Judaism 19 81 136 200
  240, see also *Agudat Israel,*
  Allgemeiner Rabbiner-Verband in
  Deutschland, Hapoel Hamizrahi,
  Mizrahi

Ostjuden, see under Eastern Europe
Ottoman Empire 38

Palästina Delegiertentag (Berlin 1919),
  see ZVfD – Conventions
Palästina Wirtschaft (journal) 95
Palästinaarbeit 65–73 76 88
Palestine Arabs, see Arabs
Palestine, depression in 126
Palestine Jewish Community, see
  Yishuv
Palestine Land Development Company
  103
The Palestine Office, see under World
  Zionist Organization
Palestinocentric Approach 31 37 44 62
  66 68 70 72 73 227 228 232 235 239
  257 258 279 263 264 265
Palestinocentric Radicalism 42–45 68 85
  97 112 121 140 198 257, see also
  Zionist Radicalism
PALTREU, see under *Haavara-Transfer*
Paris 33 147 163
Passfield, Lord (Sidney Webb) 185, see
  White Paper of 1930 228
Peel Commission 245 253
Philanthropic Zionism 27 28
Philby, Sir John 211
Pinner, Felix 100
Pinner, Ludwig 247 264
Pioneer Training, see Hachshara
Pioneer Youth Movement, see Hehalutz
Plumer, Lord Herbert O. 185
Poalei Zion Party 41 94 121 135–138
  182 192 219 225, see also Zionist
  Labor Movement
Pogroms of 1881 14
Poland 14 33 48 61 62 94 107 108 110
  114–117 119 122 163 203 258 261;
  Polish Jews 11 33 252; Polish
  Zionists 33 259
Polytechnikum in Berlin 93

Posen   30 74 75
Prague   49 86 141 145–147 150 160 217
    247 250
Preuss, Hugo   41
Preußische Jahrbücher (journal)   13
Preußischer Landesverband jüdischer
    Gemeinden   99
Prinz, Joachim   244
Private Capital/Enterprise   51 53 54 56
    76 81 86 92 115 122 123 126 127 132
    162 163 238, see also Settlement in
    Palestine, see also Settlement in
    Palestine
Pro Palästina; Deutsches Komitee zur
    Förderung der jüdischen
    Palästinasiedlung (1918)   63; Deutsches
    Komitee Pro Palästina (1926)   100 259
Productivization   130 242

Rabin, Israel Avraham (1882–1951)   121
Radical Faction   110 111 115–119 121
    122 124 125 135 137 173 182 199 202
    205 223 225
Radicalization, see Palestinocentric
    Radicalism, Zionist Radicalism
RASSCO, Rural & Suburban
    Settlement Company   117 128
Rathenau, Walther   40 41
Rau, Arthur   235
Reichert, Israel   49
Reichsbank   91
Reichsvertretung der deutschen Juden
    240–245 249
Reorganization Commission to
    Palestine (1920)   92
Reorganization Committee (1927)   134
Revisionism/Revisionist Party   75 107
    108 110 116 117 119 121 122 127 129
    135 137 162–167 169 171–173
    175–180 182 184 185 187–189
    191–193 195–197 202 203 205 208
    212–214 218 221–225 240 244 249 261

263, see also Staatszionistische
    Organisation
Rhine region   95
Riots of Arabs in Palestine, see under
    Arabs
Rodges (a Bahad farm)   102
Rosenberg, Egon (1881–1946)   77 83
Rosenblüth, Erich   242
Rosenblüth, Felix (Pinhas Rosen)
    (1887–1978)   20 28 29 47 73 77 80 82
    83 88 93 103 107 109 111 117 121 125
    128 133 134 137 164 165 170 176–179
    193 207 209 246 247 249
Rosenblüth, Martin (1886–1963)   24 47
    117 128 137 182 198 234 245 247 250
    264
Rosenthal, Hugo (Joseph Yashuvi)   242
Ruhr Valley   40
Rülf, Isaak   19
Rumania   14 138
Ruppin, Arthur (1876–1943)   25 48 59
    64 114 123 144 146 163 164 167–171
    221 222 232 247 250 264
Russia   14 36 49; Russian Jews   11 14
    19 20 32 33; Russian
    Zionism/Zionists   33 256
Russischer-Jüdischer wissenschaftlicher
    Verein, see under Jewish Students'
    Associations in Germany

SA (Sturmabteilung)   40 229, see also
    Nazism
Sacher, Harry   138 222
Safed   185
Sambursky, Shmuel   198
Samuel, Sir Herbert   143
Samuel, Rudolf (?–1949)   52 108
San Remo Conference (1920)   75 85
Sandler, Aron (1879–1954)   202
Scandinavia   138
Schachtel, Hugo Hillel (1876–1949)   83
    137

Schapira, Zvi Hermann (1898–1940) 19
27
Schereschewski, Simon (1900–1987) 192
200
Schocken, Salman (1877–1959) 83 114
120 121 123–125 128 130 137
Schoenaich, Count Paul von 100
Scholem, Escha 198
Scholem, Gershom Gerhard 198
Schwarz, Alfred (1886–1977) 128
Senator, Werner David (1876–1953) 128
133 187 192 235 240 247 249 250
Sereni, Enzo 232 238
Serubabel (organ of Hovevei Zion) 19
Settlement in Palestine 19 26 27 44 60
63–66 68 73 78 91 94 95 114 116 123
132 142 148 154 156–158 161 164 195
232 250 251 264; Agricultural
Settlements 19 26 52 94 101 113–116
122 123 127 130; "Labour Settlement"
144 132; "Settlement Regime" 163
172; Zionist Policy of 55 57 113–115
118–120 123 127 130–132 134 139 144
162–164 167 262, see also JNF,
National Capital, Private
Capital/Private Enterprise
Shaw Commission 221 228
She'ifoteinu (*Brith Shalom* organ) 170
171 183 215
The Shekel (Zionist Fee) 22 29 235 326
Shochat, Mania 211
Simon, Ernst Akiva (1894–1988) 35 173
189 198 235 242
Simon, Julius 59 64 92
Simonsohn, Emil (?–1938) 21
Smoira, Moshe (1888–1961) 102
Sobernheim, Moritz 91
Socialism 36 49–52 56 76 77 157 260;
Marxism 36 50 56, see also
Communists, *Spartacus*, Zionist
Labour Movement, *Zionisten
Sozialisten faction*

Sokolov, Nahum 229
Solel Boneh (construction company) 95
127 132
Soloveichik, Max (Mordechai Solieli)
(1883–1957) 62 108 111 119 121 199
Sombart, Werner 51
Sondheimer, Fritz 94
Soskin, Selig 264
South Africa 94 96
Spartacus (Communist group in
Germany) 39, see also Communists,
Socialism
SS (*Schutzstaffel*) 40 229 233, see also
Nazism
St. Petersburg 14
Staatszionistische Organisation 240, see
also Revisionism/Revisionist Party
"stam Zionisten" 122 123 139, see
also General Zionists
Sternberg, Fritz (1895 – ?) 50 52 55
Stöcker, Adolf 13
Strauss, Georg (1897–1975) 69
Straus' Health Station 48
Straus, Nathan 48
Stresemann, Gustav 40
Stuttgart 21
Supreme Muslim Council, see Arabs
Switzerland 138
Syria 21

Tel Aviv 115 126 198 247
Tietz, Ludwig 240 245
Toller, Ernst 41
Torah Va'avoda movement 137, see
also *Hapoel Hamizrahi*
Transfer, see *Haavara*-Transfer
Transjordan 166
Trietsch, Davis (1870–1935) 47 53
Turkey 32; Turkish Law 153
Turnowsky, Walter (1898–1959) 94
Tzeirei Hamizrahi group 192 200, see
also *Hapoel Hamizrahi*, *Mizrahi*

Tzeirei Zion faction 49 110 147, see also *Hitahdut*

Ukraine 61
Unabhängige Allgemeine Zionisten faction 202 219 223, see also General Zionists
United Committee for the Settlement of German Jews in Palestine 250
United States 14 33 38 50 75 84 85 92 94 96 103 104 106 109 114 119 122 144 145 240 244 245 251 261
Ussishkin, Menahem 62 119 146 232

Va'ad Leumi 250
Verband der Ostjuden 108, see also East European Jews
Verband jüdischer Jugendvereine Deutschlands 96
Verein für Sozialpolitik 50 51
Verein zur Förderung der jüdischen Ackerbaukolonien in Syrien und Palästina 21
Vereinigte Landsmannschaften 110
Vereinigung für das liberale Judentum in Deutschland 96
Vereinigung jüdischer Studierender an der Universität Berlin, see under Jewish Students' Associations in Germany
Versailles, Peace Treaty/Conference 40 62, see also Committee of Jewish Delegations
Viadrina, see under Jewish Students' Associations in Germany
Vienna 23 24 117 167
Vocational Training 238 240 242–244 263 264, see also *Hachshara,* Jewish Education
Volk und Land (journal) 46
Vossische Zeitung 98 99

Wagner, Arno 73

Waldman, Moses 107
Warburg Bank of Hamburg 247
Warburg, Felix 188
Warburg, Max 91
Warburg, Otto (1859–938) 24–26 47 48 53 54 58 114 255
Warsaw 187
Wassermann, Oskar (1859–1934) 91 93 98 100 259; Wassermann Bank 247
Wauchope, Sir Arthur 238 251
Weber, Max 51 107 119
Weil, Gotthold (1882–960) 67 74
Weimar Republic/Period 39–42 44 45 97 103 150 227 233 253 255 257 258, see also Germany
Weizmann, Chaim + camp 20 28 32 38 61–87 96 98 99 106 107 109–112 114–117 119 120 122 124 125 128 134 138 139 142–147 155 159–161 163– 165 167–179 183 185–195 198–200 204–226 228 229 250 260 262 263; Weizmannism 207–226 261 262, see also Brandeis-Weizmann controversy
Die Welt (Zionist organ) 22 24
Weltsch, Robert (1891–1982) 49 82 96 107 111 112 115 117 119–121 123 125 127 128 130 133 134 141 147 150–154 157–161 164–168 170 171 173–179 184 189–194 196 197 204 206–219 222–225 229 230 232 234 247 248
Werkleute (youth movement) 236
Western Europe 11 19 106
Western Wall 188 189 200
White Paper of 1922 166 167 173 174 186 194
White Paper of 1930 228 229
Wiesbaden 103 198 117
Witkowski, Gustav 43 75
Wolffsohn, David (1856–1914) 21 23–25 177
Wolfsberg, Oskar (Yeshayahu Aviad) (1893–1957) 200 225

World Jewish Congress 42

World War I 14 19 22 24 27 28 30–33 35 36 38 39 41–43 46 49 50 55 61 62 98 108 198 114 121 135 136 141 142 145 149 161 196 202 203 254 255 256 257 259 260

World Zionist Organization (WZO) 21–27 29 30 32–34 44 46–48 52 56 57 59 64 76 77 80 87 90 92 98–100 107 111 112 114 121 125 137 161 201 205 220 228 229 234 245 247 251 253–264; Annual Conferences, London (1920) 59 65 66 73 90, Carlsbad (1922) 109; Central Zionist Office (CZO) 24 25, in Berlin 255; *Finanz- und Wirtschaftsrat* (Financial & Economic Council) 114 121 123 124; The Palestine Office, in Palestine 25 235 236 238, in Berlin 192 237 243 247 250, in Vienna 117; The Political Committee (The Hague) 32; Provisional Executive Committee for General Zionist Affairs (New York) 32; Zionist Executive 82 83 89–92 95 103 107–110 113–116 120–124 128 130 132 136 142 144 145 157 161 162 165 169 172–178 182 186–196 198–200 202–210 213 216 220 228 231 246 248–250 261, Department of Education and Culture 146, Immigration Department 246, Labor Department 114 192, Organization, Department 103, Political Department 241 247, Settlement Department 114; Zionist Actions Committee 24 48 57 59 63 83 86 89 91 121 123 134 137 145 154 173 187 188 197 220; The Zionist Bureau in Copenhagen 32; The Zionist Office in Constantinople 32, see also Jewish Agency, Zionist Commission to Palestine

Yishuv (Jewish Community) in Palestine 32 33 37 38 44 55 115 117 131 145 163 174 185–187 189 194 197 264

Young *Maccabi* 236

Youth *Aliya* 242

Youth movements, see Jewish Youth Organizations

Yugoslavia 94

Zentralausschuß der deutschen Juden für Hilfe und Aufbau 240 241 243 244

Zentralwohlfahrtsstelle der deutschen Juden 38 42

Zion (*Jung Israel* journal) 22

Zionei Zion faction 67–72 83

Zionism, "Conservative Zionism" 42; "Platonic, philanthropic Zionism" 28; "Political Zionism" 25 107 146 148 170 176 259; "Post-assimilatory Zionism" 25; "Practical Zionism" 25 27 149 201 203; "synthetic" Zionism 28 160, see also General Zionism, Labor Zionist Movement, Revisionism/ Revisionist Party

Zionist Commission to Palestine 146; Agricultural Settlement Department 144

Zionist Congresses: 24 34 83 89; First (Basel 1897) 21 68; Eighth (The Hague 1907) 27; Tenth (Basel 1911) 177; Twelfth (Carlsbad 1921) 82 86 92 108 151 158 159 191 207 210 255 261; Thirteenth (Carlsbad 1923) 109–113; Fourteenth (Vienna 1925) 117 118 120 122–125 129 164 167–170 177 214; Fifteenth (Basel 1927) 129 135–138 181 219; Sixteenth (Zurich 1929) 182 185; Seventeenth (Basel 1931) 229 236; Eighteenth (Prague 1933) 247 250; Nineteenth (Lucerne 1935) 236

Zionist Labor Movement 48 49 75 76 113 115 119 121 122 130–132 135 137–139 161 181 218 230 236 238 260, see also *Hapoel Hatzair, Hitahdut, Poalei Zion*

Zionist Leadership 23 30 47 49 59 61 62 64 87 88 111 117 126 128 144 155 160 167 169 172 173 175 183 191–193 195 197 198 200–202 204–207 223 225 246 254 255 261 262

Zionist Organization, see World Zionist Organization

Zionist Organization of America (ZOA), see American Zionists/ Zionism

Zionist Radicalism 25–31 37 68 71 97 112 137 140 141 150 238 256 258 260 262, see also Palestinocentric Radicalism

Zionist Settlement Policy, see Settlement in Palestine

Zionist Student Associations, see Jewish Student Associations

Zionist Youth Organizations, see Jewish Youth Organizations

Zionisten Sozialisten faction 219, see also Zionist Labor Movement

Zionistensteuer (Zionist tax) 58 89

Zionistische Vereinigung für Deutschland (ZVfD) 21 22 24 29 42–47 52 56 58 60 67–69 73–75 77 78 80 82 84 88 89 92 93 98 101–103 109 111 117 119 120 121 123 128 129 135 143 164 175 177 179 182–184 188 193–206 209 210 215 220 222 223 225 227–237 239–245 247–250 258 259 262–264; Blätter 235 Conventions, 1st (Bingen 1897) 21, 2nd (Basel 1897) 21, 3rd (Frankfurt 1897) 21, 13th (Posen 1912) 30, 14th (Leipzig 1914) 29, 15th (Berlin 1918) 43 46 47 52 213 16th (Berlin 1920) 67 69 70 72 73, 17th (Hanover 1921) 44 82 83 144, 18th (Kassel 1922) 84, 19th (Dresden 1923) 109, 20th (Wiesbaden 1924) 103 112 117, 21st (Erfurt 1926) 127 173 175–177, 22nd (Breslau 1928) 182 200 201, 23rd (Jena 1929) 219–226 227 262, 24th (Frankfurt 1932) 230 234, 25th (Berlin 1936) 231 244, *Palästina Delegiertentag* (Berlin 1919) 46 50 52 56–58; *Landesvorstand* 82 120 128 129 135 196 197 209 228 234

Zionists Revisionists, see, Revisionism/Revisionist Party

Zitron, Julius 74

Zlocisti, Theodor (1874–1943) 20 198 199

Zola, Emil 203

Zurich 182 185

"Zvi" group 103

Zwirn, Isaak (1880–1960) 20 74